THE LITERARY BACKGROUND OF THE GOTHIC
REVIVAL IN GERMANY

1. *Cologne Cathedral as it appeared in 1809, from Boisserée's* Ansichten, Risse und einzelne Theile des Doms von Köln.

THE LITERARY BACKGROUND OF THE GOTHIC REVIVAL IN GERMANY

A Chapter in the History of Taste

BY

W. D. ROBSON-SCOTT

Reader in German, Birkbeck College, University of London

CLARENDON PRESS · OXFORD
1965

Oxford University Press, Amen House, London E.C.4

GLASGOW NEW YORK TORONTO MELBOURNE WELLINGTON
BOMBAY CALCUTTA MADRAS KARACHI LAHORE DACCA
CAPE TOWN SALISBURY NAIROBI IBADAN ACCRA
KUALA LUMPUR HONG KONG

Made in Great Britain at the Pitman Press, Bath

TO

MY WIFE

TO

MY WIFE

FOREWORD

In these days of ever more detailed specialization there is something to be said perhaps for a broader type of literary history—especially in the study of a foreign literature—which shall take account of the total artistic achievement of a particular epoch. The tendency to study the various aspects of a nation's cultural life in watertight compartments can easily lead to distortion. The student of German literature in the first half of the eighteenth century, for instance, will form a very lopsided view of the creative genius of the German people during this period, if he confines himself to the literary sphere. The true, or at least truly significant representatives of the German spirit in these years were not König, Brockes, Hagedorn *et hoc genus omne*, but Bach and Handel, Fischer von Erlach and Johann Balthasar Neumann, Johann Michael Fischer, and the brothers Asam, Dientzenhofer, and Zimmermann. The pioneer studies of Richard Benz, which treat the German Classical and Romantic periods in all their aesthetic manifestations as cultural units, show how fruitful this approach can be.[1] It is my hope that this study of the relationship between the arts of literature and architecture in one particular period and context may be accepted as a modest contribution to this wider concept of literary history.

The Gothic Revival, whatever one may think of its architectural consequences, will always remain one of the most remarkable chapters in the history of taste. As far as England is concerned, this chapter has been admirably written by Sir Kenneth Clark[2] and from a more exclusively architectural point of view by his predecessor in the field, Sir Charles Eastlake.[3] Strangely enough no book exists, either in Germany or in any other language, on the Gothic Revival in Germany.[4] The Germans do not even have a word for it. *Neugotik*

[1] Cp. *Deutsches Barock* (Stuttgart, 1949); *Die Zeit der deutschen Klassik* (Stuttgart, 1953); *Die deutsche Romantik* (Leipzig, 1937); *Goethe und die romantische Kunst* (Munich, 1940).

[2] *The Gothic Revival* (London, 1928; revised and enlarged edition, 1950).

[3] *A History of the Gothic Revival* (London, 1872).

[4] There are of course innumerable articles and papers devoted to particular aspects of the Gothic Revival in Germany, the more relevant of which are listed in the Bibliography. There are also two books which deal partly with the subject: Hermann Schmitz, *Die Gotik im deutschen Kunst- und Geistesleben* (Berlin, 1921), which is a history of German Gothic in the widest sense, including chapters on Gothic Survival and Gothic Revival;

is not the same thing. *Die Wiedererweckung der Gotik* is perhaps the nearest equivalent, but that is a paraphrase rather than a translation. And yet there was no country after England and France in which the Gothic Revival played a more important part.

The term 'Gothic Revival' is of course ambiguous, meaning as it does two very different things. On the one hand it signifies the re-awakening of interest in medieval architecture in the eighteenth and early nineteenth centuries. On the other hand it is used to describe the neo-Gothic architecture which arose as a direct result of this reawakened interest. This book—it should be explained at once—deals only with the former. It is intended as a contribution to the history of taste, not to the history of architecture. What it is concerned with is the literary background, the development of the intellectual climate, which made the architectural revival possible.

This needs no apology, for it is safe to say that no movement in the history of architecture has been so deeply influenced by literary factors as the Gothic Revival. And this is certainly as true of Germany as of any country. It is an aspect of Romanticism—one of the most important aspects indeed of that Romantic medievalism which, in Heine's view at least, forms the essence of the German Romantic movement. The Romantics themselves realized this. Friedrich Schlegel, for instance, declared that 'the spirit of the Middle Ages in general, and of the German Middle Ages in particular, finds more complete expression in the monuments of so-called Gothic architecture than anywhere else'.[1] And for Hegel 'the Gothic architecture of the Middle Ages forms the characteristic centre of the essentially Romantic'.[2]

As the *termius ad quem* of this study I have chosen the inauguration of the completion of Cologne Cathedral by King Frederick William IV in 1842. That symbolic act may be regarded as the final triumph of the Gothic Revival in Germany. From then on the movement loses its interest for the historian of taste and becomes a branch of the history of architecture.

My thanks are due to the editors of *The Modern Language Review*

and Paul Frankl, *The Gothic* (Princeton, 1960). This latter volume, which appeared, un-fortunately, after my researches for this study were virtually completed, embodies a wealth of information on what has been thought and written on the subject of Gothic from the Abbot Suger down to the present day. The book is a history of Gothic theory through the ages, and only deals incidentally with the literary background, but it never-theless contains much material which is relevant to the purpose of this study and I am deeply indebted to it.

[1] *Kritische Friedrich-Schlegel-Ausgabe* (Munich, 1959 etc.), Abteilung I, Band vi, 202.
[2] *Vorlesungen über die Ästhetik* (Berlin, 1837), ii, 332.

and the *Publications of the English Goethe Society* for permission to reprint material from articles published in those journals, and to Professor Wolfgang Schadewaltd and the *Arbeitsstellen* of the *Goethe-Wörterbuch* for references to Goethe's use of the word 'Gothisch', &c. I also wish to thank my friends and colleagues Mr. F. W. Bateson, Mr. F. J. B. Watson, Dr. G. A. Wells, and Professor E. M. Wilkinson for their kindness in reading through parts of my manuscript and making many valuable suggestions. Above all I should like to express my gratitude to my colleague Professor Nikolaus Pevsner, whose interest in the book from its inception and whose assistance and advice, at all times generously given, have been invaluable to me. Finally, I wish to thank my wife for the patience, helpfulness, and encouragement with which she has accompanied me on this Gothic journey.

The translations in the text, unless otherwise indicated, are by the author.

ABBREVIATIONS:

SB: M. Boisserée, *Sulpiz Boisserée* (2 vols., Stuttgart, 1862).
WA: *Goethes Werke: Weimarer Ausgabe* (143 vols., Weimar, 1887–1919).

CONTENTS

LIST OF PLATES

Plates 1 and 6 are from photographs by the British Museum and the remainder by Bildarchiv Foto, Warburg

PART ONE

INTRODUCTORY

1. THE ECLIPSE OF GOTHIC

It would be hard to find a parallel for the fluctuations of taste to which the architecture of the Middle Ages has been subject. At the moment we pride ourselves on a certain detachment in this matter. Having survived both the Classical and Gothic Revivals and emerged into the epoch of functional architecture, which owes little to either, we are perhaps in a better position to assess these phenomena objectively.

The bare chronicle of these fluctuations affords strange reading. With startling suddenness the Gothic style makes its appearance about the middle of the twelfth century in the Île de France and remains the dominating, indeed the exclusive architectural style of western Europe north of the Alps until roughly speaking the beginning of the sixteenth century. Then for some two hundred years and more it is almost as though it had never been. Despite a kind of clandestine existence in some countries—Gothic Survival as opposed to Gothic Revival—the Gothic style is almost totally supplanted by the architecture of the Renaissance and the Baroque. Gothic is forgotten; in so far as it is remembered, it is a subject of contumely and abuse.

How can this strange phenomenon be explained? After all, the monuments of Gothic architecture still stood in, and for the most part still dominated, the towns and villages of northern and western Europe. What did the inhabitants of Chartres, Cologne, or Lincoln really think of their Gothic cathedrals in the seventeenth and eighteenth centuries? It is hard to say how they struck the inarticulate masses, but we do know how they struck the articulate aestheticians of these centuries, who, if they mention the Gothic buildings at all, mention them only to pour contempt upon them. The exceptions to this, as we shall see, are few.

The anti-Gothic attitude goes back, of course, to the art critics and historians of the Italian Renaissance.[1] It is an offshoot of the historical scheme of the Three Ages of Art which underlay all Renaissance art history. According to this scheme the history of art was

---

[1] For the origins and development of the Renaissance attitude towards Gothic see Julius Schlosser, *Präludien* (Berlin, 1927), pp. 270–95; E. Panofsky, 'Das erste Blatt aus dem "Libro" Giorgio Vasaris. Eine Studie über die Beuteilung der Gotik in der italienischen Renaissance' (*Städel-Jahrbuch*, vi, 1930); Paul Frankl, *The Gothic* (Princeton, 1960), pp. 237–315.

2

divided into the golden age of classical art, the decay of art in the
Middle Ages, and the rebirth of art in the Italian Renaissance. This
concept is already adumbrated as early as the middle of the fourteenth
century in Boccaccio's *Decameron* (in the tale of Messer Forese) and at
the turn of the fourteenth and fifteenth centuries in Filippo Villani's
life of Giotto. It is fully worked out by the middle of the fifteenth
century in the introductory chapter of Ghiberti's history of the Tre-
cento and by Alberti in the dedicatory epistle of his work on painting.
The latter, for instance, passes over the Romanesque and Gothic
architecture of his Tuscan homeland as if it had never existed, and
dismisses the pointed arch because it was unknown to the ancients
and was in any case of little practical value.

   The anti-Gothic trend is carried a step farther by Ghiberti's contemporary Filarete in his *Trattato dell' architettura* (1460–4). In this
treatise Filarete espouses wholeheartedly the cause of the *usanza
antica* as opposed to the *usanza moderna* (i.e. Gothic). With him we
meet for the first time that downright abuse of the Gothic style
which was to become the prevailing tone of most utterances on the
subject for the next three hundred years: 'I beg everyone to give up
using this modern style; and do not let yourselves be advised by
those masters who employ this botchery. Cursed be he who invented
it! I believe it was none other than barbarians who introduced it
to Italy.'[1] This latter point is elaborated in the anonymous life of
Brunelleschi attributed to Antonio Manetti, which must have been
more or less contemporary with Filarete's treatise and which contains
a succinct and for its time remarkable history of architecture in miniature. After tracing the rise of classical architecture in Greece and
Rome the author goes on to describe its decay and destruction as a
result of the barbarian invasions of the Vandals, *Goths*, Lombards,
Huns and others. It is at this point that the connection between the
Germans and medieval architecture is established for the first time.
For—says the author—when the barbarians overran Italy they brought
with them craftsmen from the peoples they had conquered, and especially from Germany, to help out their own incapacity. And these
craftsmen filled all Italy with buildings constructed in their manner.
After Charlemagne had temporarily introduced a better style (he is
referring to the Tuscan proto-Renaissance) the architects reverted to
the German manner of building ('vigore e modi Tedeschi'), which
then prevailed until the time of Brunelleschi.

   [1] Cp. Frankl, op. cit. p. 257, where this passage is quoted from a manuscript letter by
Filarete.

The concatenation of ideas—medieval, barbarian, German—as applied to Gothic architecture is further elaborated in the dedicatory epistle to Pope Leo X on the condition of the monuments of Rome, which was formerly attributed to Raphael and which dates from about 1518–19. This, like the *Vita di Brunelleschi*, contains a miniature account of the development of architecture from the beginnings to the author's own day, but his historical sense is more acute than that of the author of the *Vita*. For he draws a clear distinction between the buildings 'del tempo de' Gotti', which were 'senza misura e senza grazia alcuna', and the later medieval buildings of the *Tedeschi*, which showed an improvement on their Gothic predecessors, though they suffered from grotesque and tasteless ornamentation and were far removed from the 'bella maniera de' Romani'. Specially interesting, in view of later theories on the subject, is his contention that the origin of the 'maniera Tedesca' is to be found in the bent branches of trees tied together, which gave the form of the pointed arch. This seems to be the first occasion on which this botanical analogy finds expression in literature.

Here we already have the complex of associated ideas: medieval architecture—Goths—Germans—lack of proportion—tasteless ornamentation—and the arboreal origin of the style. The way was well prepared, then, for Vasari, who assembled and codified these views in his *Lives of the Painters* (1550).[1] Since Vasari's work attained European fame (neither Filarete's *Trattato*, nor the life of Brunelleschi, nor the epistle to Leo X was printed till long after 1600), it had an enormous influence on the European attitude towards Gothic architecture in the succeeding centuries. It may be said to have crystallized the anti-Gothic point of view, and in face of its lasting effect it is important to be clear as to what Vasari did actually say on the matter.

Vasari's remarks on medieval architecture are mainly concentrated in the third chapter of his *Introduction to the Three Arts of Design*, prefixed to the *Lives*:

We come at last to another sort of work called German, which both in ornament and in proportion is very different from the ancient and the modern [i.e. Renaissance]. Nor is it adopted now by the best architects, but is avoided by them as monstrous and barbarous, and lacking anything that can be called order. Nay, it should rather be called confusion and disorder. In their buildings, which are so numerous that they have contaminated the whole world, doorways are ornamented with columns which are slender and twisted like a screw and which cannot have the strength to sustain a weight, however light it may be. And so on all the façades and wherever else there is decoration, they

---

[1] *Le Vite de' piu eccelenti Architetti, Pittori, ed Scultori Italiani* (Florence, 1550).

built an abomination of little niches one above the other, with so many pinnacles and points and leaves that they do not look as if they would be able to
keep themselves from toppling over. Indeed they have more the appearance
of being made of paper than of stone or marble. On these buildings they made
so many projections, openings, corbellings and scrolls that they threw them
all out of proportion; and often, with one thing being put above another,
they reach such a height that the top of a door touches the roof. This manner
was invented by the Goths, for after they had destroyed the ancient buildings
and killed the architects in the wars, those who were left constructed the buildings in this style. They fashioned the vaults with pointed arches of quarter
circles, and filled all Italy with these abominable structures, so in order not to
have any more of them their style has been totally abandoned. May God
protect every country from such ideas and style of buildings! They are so
far removed from the beauty of our buildings that they are not worth any
further discussion.[1]

Here in a nutshell we have the main lines of the anti-Gothic position,
as it was to be repeated with slight variations in every civilized country
of Europe for the next two hundred years and more. The essential
points of Vasari's indictment of medieval architecture are that it
lacks order and proportion, that its ornament is overladen and fussy,
and that it appears flimsy and insecure. No one before him had written
with such sardonic asperity of medieval architecture, and in this respect, too, he set the tone for the ensuing centuries.

And finally, the Goths. It is frequently said that Vasari was the
first to use the epithet 'Gothic' to describe the pointed architecture
of the later Middle Ages. But this is not so. On the contrary, he
almost always refers to what we should call Gothic architecture as
'German' ('maniera tedesca'), though on one or two occasions he uses
the expression 'maniera de' Gothi'.[2] On the other hand Vasari was the
first to make the definite assertion that medieval architecture (and
it is clear from his description of it that he was thinking of Gothic
and not Romanesque architecture) was the invention of the Goths
('questa maniera fu trovata da i Gothi'). Since the Gothic style was not
in fact evolved until the middle of the twelfth century, Vasari is
some six hundred years out in his reckoning. Nevertheless, this passage
is without doubt the source from which subsequent writers were to
derive the term 'Gothic' as applied to later medieval architecture.

It is not easy to determine when this use of the term first appeared.
As far as is known, it was not used in this sense by any Italian art
historian before the end of the sixteenth century. It has been said

---

[1] Cp. *Vasari on Technique*, translated by Louisa S. Maclehose (London, 1907), pp. 83–84,
from which with a few alterations this translation is taken.
[2] Cp. Frankl, op. cit. p. 294.

that Palladio employed it,[1] but in fact he makes no reference whatever to medieval architecture in his famous treatise—a silence which is more damning than pages of abuse; and in his correspondence on the subject of S. Petronio in Bologna he uses 'tedesca' for Gothic throughout.[2] The term 'tedesca' (which had superseded 'moderna') was evidently accepted as a tolerably accurate description of Italian Gothic, and no need was felt to invent a new word for it. But it was a different matter north of the Alps, where entirely different conditions prevailed.

Dr. E. S. de Beer has argued convincingly that the origin of the epithet 'Gothic' as an architectural term is to be traced to the Jesuit 'renaissance' of Gothic architecture in the Spanish Netherlands and Northern France at the beginning of the seventeenth century.[3] Since this was in the nature of a revival of a once universal but now more or less discarded local style, the need was felt for a suitable term to describe it. There seems no doubt that the term chosen—ludicrously inappropriate as it was—derives from the passage in Vasari quoted above, in which he ascribes the invention of the pointed style to the Goths. The earliest instances of the use of the term noted by de Beer all have some connection with the Netherlands or Northern France. The first two both date from 1610. One occurs in a description of the Antwerp Bourse in a guide to Antwerp by the Jesuit writer C. Scribanius.[4] The other is from an account of King's College Chapel, Cambridge, in the diary of Hans Jakob Wurmsser von Vendenheym, secretary to Prince Ludwig Friedrich of Württemberg, who accompanied his master on a visit to this country in 1610.[5] The diarist describes the chapel as one of the most beautiful in Europe 'tant pour la nettete de loeuvre Gotique que pour la haulteur de la voulte'.[6] The interesting point in favour of de Beer's argument is that the guide who showed the visitors round the Cambridge colleges and to whom the term is presumably due was a certain 'Magister Richardus Tomson natif Danvers'. Again, in his Palazzi di Genova, published at Antwerp in 1622, Rubens employs the expression in the epistle to the reader.

[1] Cp. J. Britton, The Architectural Antiquities of Great Britain (London, 1826), v. 33.

[2] Cp. Panofsky, op. cit. pp. 50–51.

[3] Cp. his two invaluable papers on the subject: 'Gothic: origin and diffusion of the term; the idea of style in architecture' (Journal of the Warburg and Courtauld Institutes, xi. 143 ff. 1948); and 'Gothic and some other architectural terms'. (The Diary of John Evelyn, ed. E. S. de Beer, vi. 1–7, Oxford, 1955).

[4] Antverpia (Antwerp, 1610), p. 51.

[5] Cp. my German Travellers in England, 1400–1800 (Oxford ,1953), pp. 83–84.

[6] British Museum, ADD. MS. 20,001, f. 11.

All these occurrences have some connection with the Low Countries. By the late twenties of the seventeenth century the term began
to spread beyond this orbit. De Beer lists examples from Italy in 1627,
from France in 1639, from England (Evelyn's Diary) in 1641. By the
sixties its use is becoming fairly common.

As we have seen, one of the first instances of the word occurs in
the diary of a German, but the language of the diary is French.
Another use of the term by a German—in Latin this time—is to be
found in the guide-book of J. H. von Pflaumern, *Mercurius Italicus*,
published at Augsburg in 1625, in his description of Siena.[1] Other
early instances of the use of the term by Germans are to be found in
the *Ulysses Belgico-Gallicus* (1631) of Abraham Göllnitz, who reproduces
the passage on the Antwerp Bourse from Scribanius, and in the Jesuit
Hermann Crombach's history of Cologne, in a chapter describing the
cathedral.[2]

To sum up the results of de Beer's enquiries, it would appear
that the term 'Gothic' as applied to an architectural style originated
in Jesuit circles in Flanders in the early years of the seventeenth century, but that it did not become at all widespread until at least the
third or fourth decades of the century. Its use in these early references
is ambiguous: firstly in scope, in that it sometimes connotes medieval
architecture in general, both Romanesque and Gothic, sometimes
Gothic only; secondly in tone, in that sometimes it is employed purely
descriptively as a stylistic term, while at other times it carries with it
the implication of barbarous. Rubens, for instance, writes in 1622 of
'la maniera d'Architettura, che si chiama Barbara, ò Gothica'.[3]

This conception of Gothic as something barbarous is, as we have
seen, a direct legacy of Vasari and other Italian humanists. In the course
of the seventeenth century it was to become an accepted commonplace in all European countries. Sir Henry Wotton, for instance, in
his *Elements of Architecture* (1624) writes that pointed arches "both
for the naturall imbecility of the sharpe *Angle* it selfe, and likewise
for their very *Uncomelinesse*, ought to bee exiled from judicious
eyes, and left to their first inventors, the *Gothes* or *Lumbards*, amongst
other *Reliques* of that barbarous *Age*".[4]

In Germany the tale begins with Joachim von Sandrart's *Teutsche
Academie der Edlen Bau- Bild- und Mahlerey-Künste* (1675). Sandrart's

---

[1] Pflaumern, op. cit. p. 129.
[2] *Primitiae Gentium seu Historia SS. Trium Regum Magorum* (Cologne, 1654) iii, 799.
[3] Rubens, *Palazzi di Genova* (Antwerp, 1622), epistle to the reader.
[4] Wotton, op. cit. p. 51.

Academie is the first German history of art, and it was to remain without a serious rival for the next hundred years at least. Sandrart's ambition was no doubt to be the German Vasari, but in fact his book is considerably wider in scope than its illustrious predecessor, embracing as it does the lives of the artists—painters, architects, sculptors, and engravers—not only of his native land, but of all nations and ages. The emphasis, of course, is on the artists of his own fatherland (for whom it remains a valuable source to this day), and in this respect it takes a high place—along with the *Sprachgesellschaften*, Opitz, Lohenstein, etc.—among the signs of the awakening national consciousness of Germany in the seventeenth century.

The splendidly produced baroque volume of 1675 proved so popular that the author added a second volume in 1679 and a Latin translation for the benefit of foreign readers in 1683. A much enlarged and revised edition by the travel writer J. J. Volkmann appeared in 1768–75, and it was still used as a source book by the Romantics— Wackenroder, Tieck, Boisserée—in their pursuit of the German past. In view of all this, Sandrart's remarks on Gothic architecture, few though they are, must be considered a factor of some importance in determining the German attitude on the matter throughout the eighteenth century.

Following the example of Vasari, Sandrart placed his animadversions on the Gothic style in the introductory section of his work on the theory and practice of the plastic arts, at the end of the chapter dealing with the Five Orders:

There is still another sixth order, called Gothic, which has departed very far from the ancient orders both in skill and propriety, because it observes neither right order, proportion, nor measure. It is equally capable of supporting the main portal, which bears the greatest weight, with small slender columns, as on the other hand of affixing ponderous props to the doorways of a garden pavilion. Moreover the columns are wreathed with grapes and vine leaves, sometimes so thickly and profusely that one might think a whole vineyard had been planted upon them, sometimes again with such delicacy, subtlety and minuteness that they look like little leaves cut out of paper. In this labyrinth our German forbears pilgrimaged long and lavishly, holding such devices to be embellishments. For almost all our old buildings are full of this sort of disorder. This base style was brought into Italy by the Goths. For after they had pillaged and destroyed Rome, and almost all the Roman architects had perished in the wars, they subsequently introduced this vile manner of building, whereby they brought down upon their heads more than a thousand million curses throughout all Italy.[1]

---

[1] *L'Academia Todesca della Architectura, Scultura e Pittura: oder Teutsche Academie der Edlen Bau- Bild- und Mahlerey-Künste* (Nürnberg, 1675), p. 17.

Sandrart, then, is primarily responsible for introducing into German art criticism the negative view of medieval architecture evolved by the Italian humanists of the fifteenth and sixteenth centuries. This negative view was to continue with certain fluctuations of tone throughout the course of the eighteenth century. Its development can be traced in the dictionaries and encyclopedias of the time. On the whole the entries under the word 'Gothisch' imply either ignorance, indifference, or hostility. The word does not occur at all in Kramer's German-Italian dictionary (1702), nor in Christian Ludwig's English-German-French dictionary (1706), nor in his German-English dictionary (1716), nor for that matter in the first edition of Adelung (1774). Johann Leonhard Frisch's German-Latin dictionary (1741) merely states that 'Gothic architecture is no longer in use'. Zedler's *Universal-Lexicon* (Vol. xxv, 1741), scarcely less laconic, informs us that the Gothic order 'differs in proportion and decoration from the Greek, is full of absurdity, and so can never be approved by rational architects.' Jakob von Eggers's *Neues Kriegs-Lexicon* (1757) is one of the first German works to introduce the bogey of Taste: 'Gothic is the name given to everything in architecture which is constructed without taste, rules, proper disposition of the mouldings, and proportion.' Similarly Volkmann's version of Sandrart (1768): 'Gothic is that kind of architecture which became general after the decline of Good Taste, in which neither correct proportions, proper *ordonnance*, nor appropriate decoration are to be met. The Goths introduced this style into Italy after all the good architects had been driven out. This Bad Taste prevailed for long indeed in our German fatherland. Many church spires, such as that of St. Stephen's in Vienna, the Minster in Strasbourg, and many cathedral churches in France bear witness to this.'[1]

Instances of this negative attitude to medieval architecture could be multiplied indefinitely, and would make very tedious reading, for they vary but little. Two or three, however, may be selected as of special interest. The first comes from a treatise on good taste in poetry and rhetoric by Johann Ulrich König, which was appended to his edition of Canitz's poems (1727). König was one of the exponents of neo-classical ideals in literature at the beginning of the eighteenth century in Germany, and his treatise is primarily directed against what remained of baroque taste in the literature of his day. He begins by tracing the origin and rise of Good Taste among the Greeks and Romans down to its decline and disappearance with the collapse of the Roman Empire, and proceeds: 'The so-called Nordic peoples then

[1] Sandrart, *Teutsche Academie*, ed. J. J. Volkmann (Nürnberg, 1768) i. 21.

THE ECLIPSE OF GOTHIC 11

flooded the whole of Europe with their ignorance and with that Bad Taste which clung permanently to their descendants; this can still be recognized today from the remains, among other things, of their badly composed writings, rambling romances, immoderate passion for rhyming, clumsy monkish script, coarse-sounding speech, barbarous music, graceless costumes, badly-drawn paintings, and above all from their Gothic architecture.'[1]

The passage is particularly interesting as showing, from one of its earliest apostles in Germany, how the new doctrine of Good Taste derived from Boileau reinforced the anti-Gothic attitude derived from the Italian humanists. Gothic architecture is now condemned root and branch as the major example of that universal Bad Taste which disfigured all the cultural products of the Middle Ages.

König stands at the outset of the German *Aufklärung*. One of the latest and greatest products of that movement, Immanuel Kant, was to give expression some forty years later to very much the same attitude to Gothic architecture and the Middle Ages in his *Beobachtungen über das Gefühl des Schönen und Erhabenen* (1764). Kant ends his observations on the Sublime and Beautiful with a brief historical review of the progress of taste, which might almost have been written by an Italian humanist of the fifteenth or sixteenth century, so completely does it reflect the Renaissance scheme of the Three Ages of Art. Thus, the ancients showed a clear sense of the Sublime and Beautiful, which degenerated during the later Roman Empire and disappeared entirely with the advent of the barbarians, who introduced 'a certain perverted and grotesque taste which is called Gothic'.[2] This depraved taste manifested itself not only in architecture, but in scholarship and other walks of life. It disdained the ancient simplicity of nature and resorted either to exaggeration or triviality. Examples of this Gothic taste were the Crusades, the trappings of chivalry and romance, and medieval scholasticism. Now that the human spirit has, by a kind of palingenesis, risen again from almost total ruin, we are witnessing in our own days a revival of the true taste for the Beautiful and Noble, both in the arts and sciences and in the moral sphere. For Kant, then, the Gothic taste in architecture, as in everything else, is eccentric and debased, in that it offends against Reason, Nature, and Propriety.

The anti-Gothic attitude of the eighteenth century was summed up

---

[1] *Untersuchung von dem Guten Geschmack in der Dicht- und Rede-Kunst* appended to Freiherr von Canitz's *Gedichte* (Leipzig/Berlin, 1727), p. 234.

[2] Kant, *Beobachtungen über das Gefühl des Schönen und Erhabenen* (Königsberg, 1766), p. 108.

in Johann Georg Sulzer's encyclopedia of the arts, the *Allgemeine Theorie der schönen Künste* (1771–4). The onslaught of the *Sturm und Drang* on this repository of neo-classicism has obscured for subsequent generations the not inconsiderable merits of Sulzer's conscientious, knowledgeable, and on the whole well-written work. To us at least it is valuable for the completeness with which it represents the prevailing aesthetic of the later eighteenth century in Germany. The *Allgemeine Theorie* was enormously popular in its day. Edition followed edition in rapid succession. It became indeed the Bible of the German art-lover, and its influence on the taste of its period was very considerable.

Sulzer's aesthetic attitude is firmly based on the eighteenth-century notion of Good Taste, and he judges everything from this angle. Thus for him the word 'Gothisch' is synonymous with Bad Taste pure and simple. He begins his article on the subject with the unequivocal declaration: 'The epithet "Gothic" is frequently applied to the fine arts to designate a barbarous taste; although the meaning of the expression is seldom defined exactly. It seems to be used principally to indicate clumsiness and lack of beauty and good proportions, and originated in the clumsy imitations of ancient architecture perpetrated by the Goths who settled in Italy.'[1]

Sulzer then goes on to apply the term to all nations which engage in cultural pursuits before their taste has been adequately formed. Thus Gothic comes to mean something very like *parvenu*, and one can talk of Gothic behaviour as well as of Gothic art: 'If a man who has been brought up in humble circumstances suddenly attains to power and riches, then his attempts to imitate the fashionable world will deserve to be called Gothic.'[2]

He tries to define the term more precisely as applied to the fine arts: 'Gothic is a tasteless excess in works of art, which are lacking not in essential qualities, nor even always in greatness and splendour, but in beauty, charm, and delicacy.' Then turning specifically to architecture: 'Thus it is not only the clumsy buildings erected by the Goths which are called Gothic, but also the bizarre structures, overladen with a thousand useless ornaments, of which presumably the Saracens who had settled in Europe gave the first examples. One also finds buildings where both these kinds of Bad Taste are combined.'[2] Sulzer, then, like the author of the epistle to Leo X before

---

[1] Sulzer, op. cit. i. 489.
[2] Loc. cit.

him, shows a dim apprehension of the distinction between Romanesque and Gothic.

Sulzer ends his article on 'Gothisch' by deducing from what has gone before that the Gothic taste arises when an artist is not sufficiently clear in his mind as to the nature and purpose of the subject in hand. Hence a tree cut in the form of an animal, a column twisted like a snail, a beaker standing on high and very thin legs can all be described as Gothic, because they all offend in some respects our sense of what is just and appropriate.

Sulzer develops his views on Gothic still further in his article 'Baukunst'. He lists the qualities which go to make good architecture: order, propriety, beauty of form, regularity, good taste in the external and internal ornamentation. Now these are the very qualities, it appears, in which Gothic architecture is almost completely lacking.

For Sulzer Good Taste is more than an aesthetic, it is a moral quality. He has a firm belief that a nation's architecture is an index of its spiritual health, and, conversely, that a nation's spiritual health is influenced by its architecture. Now since he equates good architecture with classical architecture and bad architecture with Gothic architecture, it follows that Gothic architecture must have a deleterious effect on a nation's morale. This strange doctrine is stated by Sulzer in so many words: 'Bad buildings which have been planned or constructed without order or intelligence or which are overladen with foolish, grotesque, or exuberant decoration necessarily have a bad effect on the mentality of the people.'[1] It is clear from all he has said on the subject that Sulzer is here thinking of Gothic buildings. Here we have a new element in the anti-Gothic movement. Gothic architecture is not only bad aesthetically, it is positively immoral. This represents the furthest point to which the negative attitude of the eighteenth century towards Gothic architecture was to go.

Sulzer then proceeds to a brief history of architectural development very much in the manner of, and no doubt influenced by, Vasari; certainly it is dominated by the humanist concept of the Three Ages of Art. Thus the barbarian invasions put an end to what traces of Good Taste still remained in the vulgarized architecture of the later Empire:

Almost all the rules of beauty were lost sight of, and instead what was laboured, finicky, strange and uncouth became the fashion. Most of the cities of Germany and most of the churches in the entire western world were built during these ages of barbarous architectural taste; we can still observe in them

[1] Ibid., i. 129.

the stamp of an architectural style which wantonly deviates from all the rules. These buildings astound the beholder through their size, excess of ornament and total neglect of proportion . . . Despite their incredibly elaborate workmanship there is something unwholesome about almost all these amazing structures. This must be said even of the minster in Strasbourg, which was built in the thirteenth century and is reckoned among the most astonishing buildings in the world.[1]

This is the most uncompromising statement of the neo-classical position that we shall meet in Germany; it amounts to a total rejection of Gothic as a serious architectural style. So extreme an attitude was bound to provoke a reaction, and, as we shall see, the reaction was not long in coming.

It is interesting to observe how little the indictment has changed during the centuries between Vasari and Sulzer. We are, it is true, no longer told that the Gothic buildings are flimsy and insecure, and Sulzer's moral attitude is new, but otherwise his objections to Gothic are fundamentally identical with Vasari's. That is to say, Gothic is barbarous, it lacks order and proportion, and its decoration is overladen, finicky and arbitrary.

The contempt and dislike with which Gothic architecture was for the most part regarded in the eighteenth century is reflected in the pejorative uses to which the epithet was put throughout this period. In their turn, of course, these connotations—mainly borrowed from English and French sources—no doubt influenced the contemporary attitude towards Gothic architecture by literally giving it a bad name. Barbarous, tasteless, uncouth, ignorant, superstitious, old-fashioned, clumsy, formless, irregular, unharmonious, asymmetrical, overladen, arbitrary, eccentric, unnatural, grotesque—even baroque: such were some of the main usages to which the much-abused word 'Gothic' was subjected in the course of the century.[2]

What then, we must ask, is the real explanation of this blind hostility of the eighteenth century to Gothic architecture? The reasons are various, and are rooted in the intellectual climate of the time.[3] It is based in the first place on the humanist construction of the Three Ages of Art, which underlies the attitude of Vasari and his successors right down to the end of the eighteenth century.

[1] Ibid., i. 130–1.
[2] Cp. Grimm's *Deutsches Wörterbuch*, article 'Gotisch'.
[3] I am greatly indebted in what follows to Arndt Schreiber's valuable dissertation, *Frühklassizistische Kritik an der Gotik* (Leipzig, 1938).

Secondly, it is an aspect of the faith of the *Aufklärung* that there are certain universally applicable norms of beauty, valid at all times and in all places. In the sphere of architecture, no less than in that of drama, these norms were supplied by the Greeks. In the view of the *Aufklärung* classical forms in architecture constitute architectural beauty, and they alone are worthy of imitation, if architectural excellence is to be preserved. It was this belief which accounted more than anything else for the asperity of the neo-classical attitude towards the Gothic style, for it was felt to undermine the very basis of architectural taste. The constituent qualities of classical beauty in the architectural sphere, according to the neo-classical aesthetic, were above all simplicity, regularity, just proportions, propriety. The Gothic style offended against all these. Therefore it must be condemned.

Thirdly, the eighteenth-century disapproval of Gothic, as far as Germany is concerned, was closely connected with the neo-classical attitude towards the baroque-rococo tradition. Neo-classicism began, of course, as a reaction against the extravagances of this tradition. Now the neo-classicist aestheticians found much in common between the baroque-rococo tradition and the Gothic style, and they objected to both on very much the same grounds. In their eyes both were distinguished—or rather disgraced—by the love of the bizarre, the arbitrary and the excessive. Both offended against Nature, as the neo-classicists understood the term. The aim of both was to astonish, rather than to please. Hence the emphasis by many of the eighteenth-century critics on the boldness (Kühnheit) of Gothic buildings, a boldness expressed, for instance, in their excessive height and apparent instability—which was by no means necessarily a matter for admiration. We have seen how Sulzer writes of there being 'something unwholesome about almost all these astonishing structures'.

The chief point of resemblance between the two styles in the view of the neo-classicists was their excess of detail, their overladen ornamentation, which forms perhaps the most persistent ground of complaint against Gothic architecture. In this respect above all others the example of the Gothic style served as an invaluable ally to the neo-classicists in their campaign against the baroque-rococo. Thus an anonymous contributor to Gottsched's *Neuer Büchersaal der schönen Wissenschaften und freyen Künste* (1746) inveighs against 'new-fangled' (i.e. rococo) ornaments, the inventors of which 'will lapse if they are not careful into the Gothic frippery from which our recent artists have been so happily delivered'.[1]

[1] *Neuer Büchersaal der schönen Wissenschaften und freyen Künste*, (Leipzig, 1746), ii. 410.

An interesting indication of the affinity sensed by the later eighteenth-century critics between the two styles is to be found in the use
of the term 'Gothic' to include what we should call baroque or rococo.
Sulzer, for instance, in the passage quoted above lists barley-sugar
columns among other examples of what he means by Gothic taste.
Lessing's brother, Carl, refers to the title vignette of *Emilia Galotti*,
which represents a Thalia enthroned on clouds surrounded by cupids,
as 'etwas gothisch',[1] and Herder describes a similar rococo vignette
affixed to a collection of *Neue Lieder zum Singen* (Hamburg und Leipzig,
1764) as 'Gothischdeutsch'.[2] It is not too much to say that a great
deal of the later eighteenth-century anti-Gothicism can be interpreted
as a veiled form of attack on the baroque-rococo tradition. This
situation has no parallel in England, where the hostility to Gothic had
nothing to do with a reaction against the baroque-rococo tradition.
On the contrary, in its early stages the Gothic Revival in England was
itself an offshoot of that tradition.

The eighteenth-century hostility to Gothic was also based on
what one can only call a physical distaste for the angular and the pointed.
Sulzer expresses this unequivocally in his article on 'Falten' (folds):
'The eye loves above all what is curved . . . on the other hand, the
angular, *and especially the pointed*, is highly disagreeable to it.'[3] The
spikiness of Gothic—the infinite repetition of the pointed form in
spires, turrets, pinnacles, arches, doors, and windows—made the
eighteenth-century observer feel positively uncomfortable. Winckelmann, for instance, is reported to have likened the effect on him of the
spire of St. Stephen's Cathedral in Vienna to the pain of 'a great
needle sticking into his eye'.[4] And Goethe in *Von Deutscher Baukunst*
speaks of the impression which he expected Strasbourg Minster to make
on him as that of a 'malformed bristly monster'.

Much of the eighteenth-century criticism of Gothic is due to the
failure to understand its functional purpose. This explains the reiterated
emphasis on its finickiness and flimsiness, on the decorative detail,
and the concern with the parts rather than the whole. For the eighteenth-century critics did not really see that there was a whole.
What struck them was the infinite multiplicity of the parts. As Goethe
put it in the essay on architecture he wrote on his return from Italy
(*Baukunst*, 1788): 'Unfortunately all Northern church decorators

[1] *Briefe von und an Lessing*, ed. F. Muncker, iv. 491.
[2] Herder, *Sämmtliche Werke*, ed. B. Suphan, i. 106.
[3] Sulzer, op. cit. i. 367.
[4] Cp. Carl Julius Weber, *Deutschland oder Briefe eines in Deutschland reisenden Deutschen*
(Stuttgart, 1827), ii. 561.

sought to obtain an impression of greatness solely through the multiplication of detail.'[1] Hence the recurrent talk of the 'petty taste' (kleiner Geschmack) of the Gothic style. Lessing, for instance, refers to Gothic buildings as 'enormous piles of stone, heaped up without taste or in a very petty taste'.[2] The decorative detail was felt to be something superficial and superadded, without functional meaning and in no organic relationship to the whole.

Strange as it must seem to us, the great Gothic cathedrals appeared to their neo-classicist critics as a kind of architectural freak, a species of filigree work on a monumental scale. A characteristic illustration of this attitude is Goethe's suggestion in his *Baukunst* essay of 1788 that the origin of Gothic architecture is to be found in miniature wooden shrines which were later imitated in stone and on a grand scale. Perhaps the main difference between our attitude to Gothic and that of the eighteenth century lies precisely in our recognition of the functional purpose underlying the multiplicity of Gothic detail.

[1] WA I. 47, 64.
[2] Lessing, *Sämtliche Schriften*, ed. Lachmann–Muncker (Leipzig, 1900), xv. 508.

2. THE SURVIVAL OF GOTHIC

THE reader may well ask at this point how the formidable edifice of misconception and prejudice which we have just been discussing came to be shaken, so thoroughly shaken indeed that within some six decades of the first appearance of Sulzer's encyclopedia it had been shattered to its foundations. It is the object of this book to trace this process.

In the first place, it should be emphasized that the condemnation of Gothic had never been complete. Even the Italian humanists had occasionally referred to Gothic buildings in laudatory terms. Petrarch, who was in Cologne in 1333, wrote of the cathedral as 'an uncommonly beautiful church, which, though still incomplete, can with good reason be called most magnificent'.[1] Aeneus Sylvius Piccolomoni, later Pope Pius II, spoke enthusiastically in his Germania (1457) of Strasbourg Minster and of St. Stephen's in Vienna. The epistle to Leo X had drawn a distinction between the crude buildings of the 'Gothic' age and the improved style of the later 'German' medieval architecture. In Vasari and Sandrart, it is true, the blackness of the Gothic night is unrelieved. But J. T. Jablonski, the first of the eighteenth-century encyclopedists to notice the term 'Gothisch', gives an un-expectedly positive account of the style, describing it as solid and splendid and possessing its own criteria of decoration and proportion, which differ widely from those of classical architecture.[2] Even Sulzer, the arch-classicist, has unwillingly to admit that Gothic does not always lack impressive qualities.

Perhaps the most convincing testimony to a continued feeling for Gothic in this period is to be seen in the sphere of painting, namely in the church interiors of such Dutch artists of the seventeenth century as Saenredam, de Witte, or Houckgeest, which show a surprisingly sensitive appreciation of the qualities of the style.[3]

As far as the written word is concerned, it is among the topographers and antiquaries of the sixteenth and seventeenth centuries that we find the clearest evidence of a persisting interest in medieval architecture. And though this interest is certainly antiquarian rather than

[1] Quoted from Paul Clemen, Der Dom zu Köln (Düsseldorf, 1937), pp. 59–60.
[2] Allegemeines Lexicon der Künste und Wissenschaften (Leipzig, 1721).
[3] Cp. Hans Jantzen, Das niederländische Architekturbild (Leipzig, 1910).

aesthetic in flavour, it does at least show that the Gothic buildings were not forgotten. For the most part these writers seem to have accepted the Gothic style as a matter of course and even in some cases to have evinced a definite liking for it.

In Germany this interest in medieval architecture was from the first centred in the two great cathedrals of Strasbourg and Cologne, as the outstanding examples of the Gothic style in the German-speaking lands. This concentration on these two buildings was to remain a feature of the Gothic Revival in Germany throughout the succeeding centuries, and is one of the factors which differentiate it sharply from the parent movement in England, where there was no such preoccupation with any particular monument. The main reason for this no doubt is the simple fact that in Britain there are no Gothic edifices which stand out so markedly from their fellows as to take on the almost symbolic significance with which the Gothic enthusiasts in Germany invested Cologne and Strasbourg.

The tale begins with a fanfare from the Alsatian humanist Jakob Wimpheling, who devotes the sixty-sixth chapter of his *Rerum Germanicarum Epitome* (1505) to the architecture of the Germans. He starts by quoting Aeneus Sylvius's famous eulogy of the unsurpassed excellence of the German architects, a testimony which, he says, is amply borne out by the example of Strasbourg Minister and its tower:

> I would maintain that there is nothing in the whole world more rare and excellent than this one building. Who can sufficiently admire or praise the tower of Strasbourg, which in its carved work and variety of sculptures easily surpasses all other buildings in Europe . . . The miracle is how it was possible to raise such a pile to such a height. What? If Scopas, Ctesiphon or Archimedes . . . were to rise from the dead, assuredly they would publicly confess that in the science of architecture they had been vanquished by us. And they would far prefer this structure to the temple of Diana at Ephesus or the pyramids of Egypt or the other seven wonders of the world.[1]

Wimpheling's *Epitome* is inspired throughout by a strong German, and more especially German-Alsatian patriotism, but even allowing for this his paean on Strasbourg Minster is a remarkable testimony to a Gothic building from German humanist circles. Certainly in this passage there is no hint of the anti-Gothicism of contemporary Italian humanists. No more enthusiastic tribute to the German achievement of Strasbourg Minster was to appear until Goethe's *Von Deutscher Baukunst* some 270 years later.

[1] *Rerum Germanicarum Epitome* (Hanoviae, 1594), pp. 198-9.

3

Similar sentiments to those of Wimpheling are expressed by Sebastian Münster. In his *Cosmographia* (1544), the fountain head and invaluable source-book of so much topographical writing in the sixteenth century, he says of the tower of Strasbourg Minster that its like is not to be found in the whole of Germany, France, or Italy, and that it may well be accounted the eighth wonder of the world. This passage is repeated word for word in the German translation of Braun and Hogenberg's famous topographical work, *Civitates Orbis Terrarum* (1572).[1] Münster, a native of Basle, has nothing to say of Cologne Cathedral, but Georg Braun, who lived and worked in the city, writes of it as a vast building which, *if completed*, would easily surpass all other churches in Germany for size and beauty and would take its place among the most remarkable objects to be seen in all Europe.

These words, with their hint of an appeal for the completion of the cathedral torso, were to find many an echo in subsequent writers— such as Eberhard Winheim in his *Sacrarium Agrippinae* (1607), a detailed account in Latin of the churches of Cologne, who remarks that even in its unfinished state the cathedral is an object of astonishment to all who behold it, which, if completed, would be overwhelming in its majesty. Braun's description is repeated verbally by the popular topographer and native of Cologne, Matthias Quad von Kinckelbach, in his *Teutscher Nation Herligkeit* (Cologne, 1609), who also takes his account of Strasbourg from the same source, repeating Braun's and Münster's assertion that the cathedral tower should be reckoned among the wonders of the world. Osaeus Schadaeus's guide to Strasbourg Minster, *Summum Argentoratensium Templum* (1617), written despite its title in German and a work which enjoyed considerable popularity in its day, says much the same thing.[2] This volume, with its detailed description of the minister and its copperplate engravings, is a remarkable testimony to the survival of interest in a great Gothic building. It can lay claim indeed to be the first illustrated guide-book devoted exclusively to a single example of medieval architecture.[3] There is a refreshingly personal note, rare at this date, about Schadaeus's attitude. He asserts roundly in the preface that he has been moved to write his book by 'the pre-eminence, dignity, and splendour of the minster, which has often moved me to astonishment and still does so

---

[1] *Beschreibung und Contrafactur der vornembster Stätt der Welt* (Cologne, 1574).

[2] *Summum Argentoratensium Templum: Das ist: Auszführliche und Eigendtliche Beschreibung dess viel Künstlichen, sehr Kostbaren und in aller Welt berühmten Münsters zu Strassburg* (Strasbourg, 1617).

[3] Cp. P. Frankl. op. cit., p. 330.

whenever I set eyes upon it'. Like his fellow-Alsatian Wimpheling, he is inspired by a strongly patriotic spirit, saluting the minster 'not only on account of its size and height, but also and indeed much more for the ingenuity of the craftsmanship expended on it . . . All right-thinking people will either prefer it to most of the Seven Wonders of the world, or at least will allow it to be the eighth'.[1]

By now, then, Sebastian Münster's 'eighth wonder of the world' has become a commonplace reiterated by everyone who undertook to put pen to paper on the subject of the minster tower. A neat variant of the theme occurs in Julius Wilhelm Zincgref's epigram 'Vom Thurn zu Strassburg, warumb der andere darneben nit auffgebawet worden', in which the poet rebukes the spectator for lamenting that this splendid tower lacks its fellow, for Nature in this way has seen to it that it shall have no rival:

> Natur hats eingestelt
> Dass neben diesem Thurn noch einer solt gefallen,
> Dann so ist er allein der schönst und höchst vor allen,
> Und hat seins gleichen nicht in dieser weiten Welt.[2]

It is clear that this enthusiasm for the Strasbourg spire, as for the lofty choir of Cologne, was evoked by the sheer technical skill and ingenuity of the Gothic builders rather than by an appreciation of the Gothic style as such. The same is largely true, no doubt, of the many other topographical works of the seventeenth and early eighteenth centuries which show a persisting interest in German medieval antiquities. Examples in question are Matthäus Merian's multifarious guidebooks dating from the middle decades of the seventeenth century, which repeat with slight variations what Münster, Braun, and Quad had said before them; also Ferdinand von Fürstenberg's *Monumenta Paderbornensia* (Amsterdam, 1672); Regher's *Monumenta Landgraviorum Thuringiae* (Gotha, 1692); Bartel Ranisch's *Beschreibung aller Kirchen-Gebäude der Stadt Dantzig* (Danzig, 1695); and Elias Frick's description of Ulm Minster, *Templum Parochiale Ulmensium* (Ulm, 1718). It is worth noting that many of these tomes went into several editions in the course of the eighteenth century. Though they cannot be said to manifest any real understanding of Gothic architecture, they do at least bear witness to the lively interest shown by the Germans of the seventeenth and early eighteenth centuries in their great medieval

---

[1] Schadaeus, op. cit., *Vorrede*.
[2] From the appendix to Zincgref's edition of Opitz's *Teutsche Poemata* (Strassburg, 1624), p. 189.

buildings. This holds good especially for Schadaeus's work on Strasbourg, Ranisch's on the Danzig churches, and Frick's on Ulm.

Of interest in this connection is the little illustrated guide to Strasbourg Minster by Georg Heinrich Behr, *Strassburger Münster-und
Thurn-Büchlein* (1st ed. Strasbourg, 1732; new and enlarged ed.
1744), which appeared in both German and French and ran into several
editions.[1] It thus provides a striking proof of the minster's popularity
in the eighteenth century, and has an added appeal for us in that it
was the guide used by Goethe during his stay in Strasbourg. Behr,
like his predecessors, lavished unstinted praise upon the world-
famed spire, 'which can verily be called one of the most excellent
marvels of architecture, since, as is well known, no other is to be found
in all Europe which can bear the slightest comparison with it for height,
just proportions, ornamentation or cunning craftsmanship'.[2] Here
too it is the technical skill of the Gothic builders which lies at the root
of the author's admiration: 'It is highly astonishing that so delicate a
structure, reaching almost to the clouds, should remain so firmly
stablished.'[3]

There is one work of the mid seventeenth century which stands
out from all these topographical writings for its understanding of
Gothic architecture. This is Hermann Crombach's history of the Three
Kings of Cologne (*Primitiae Gentium seu Historia SS. Trium Regum
Magorum*, Cologne, 1654). The author of this stately Latin volume was
professor of moral theology in the Jesuit college in Cologne, but his
leisure hours were spent in the pursuit of local archaeology, and especially in studying the old churches of his native city. Crombach was
the first writer since work on the edifice had ceased in the middle of
the sixteenth century to advocate in unequivocal terms the continuation and completion of the cathedral, though many before him had
expressed a passing regret at its incomplete state. He appeals to the
Archbishop of Cologne to resume the good work which has rested
so long, and thus erect a worthy sepulchre for the Three Kings and a
noble monument to his own piety. He also calls upon the City Fathers
to recall the sacrifices their forbears had made in the service of the
building and to keep in mind the advantages which would accrue to
the city as a whole from the completion of the great church. As a
practical aid to this end he includes in his history reproductions of two

---

[1] Paul Frankl is mistaken in his assertion (op. cit., p. 330 n.) that Behr is merely a new
edition of Schadaeus. It is in fact an independent work, though naturally it draws upon its
predecessor for some of its information.

[2] Behr, ed. 1744, *Vorrede*, p. 8.

[3] Ibid. p. 27.

of the medieval plans: a ground plan of the whole, and an elevation of the west front with the twin western towers. Copies of these plans were sent to each member of the City Council.

In the third part of his book Crombach includes a description of the cathedral which is so remarkable for its date that it deserves quotation:

> In this chapter I shall make use of architectural terms borrowed from Vitruvius which I shall try to adapt to a Gothic building . . . The proportions of whole and parts obey no fixed rules of Ionic, Corinthian, or Composite style, but rather Gothic practice. Thus the builder's art has succeeded in expressing all his ideas with the greatest technical skill, so that the whole seems to rival Nature herself, while yet observing an absolutely just proportion between all its parts. Neither in bases, columns, and capitals, nor in the style of the whole does it show the proportions of the old Italian school, but actually surpasses it in solidity, strength, and, where appropriate, in decoration. Especially is this so in the whole exterior aspect of the cathedral, the beauty of which is everywhere more clearly revealed to the eyes than in the interior. For from base to summit, in the vast belfry as in the fourteen twin buttresses which support and strengthen the entire wall of the exterior of the choir, every part has its appropriate decoration—mouldings, blind windows, statues, pinnacles, pillars with their capitals of back-curving leaves and stalks, all carved with the same elegance, care, finish, splendour, lavishness, and artistic skill, even though most of the high wall decoration could scarcely come within one's range of vision unless it was examined close at hand from the triforium.[1]

There are several notable points about this passage: first, the deliberate attempt to adapt Vitruvian terms to a Gothic building; secondly, the realization that Gothic obeys different principles from the classical style; thirdly, the concept of a Gothic building rivalling nature; fourthly, the recognition of a just proportion between all the parts; fifthly, the acknowledgement of the superiority of Gothic to classical architecture in solidity, strength and decorative skill. All this constitutes what must surely be the most remarkable tribute to a Gothic building in Germany before Goethe, a tribute which the description of the leaf capitals, for instance, shows to have been based on close observation of Gothic detail. Crombach, as we have already indicated, was a Jesuit, a member therefore of an order which had as one of its aims the carrying over of medieval ideas into the baroque age. We have already seen in the previous chapter that the origin of the term 'Gothic' is closely connected with the Jesuit renaissance of Gothic architecture in Flanders. The case of Crombach suggests that an understanding of Gothic architecture in the seventeenth century is most

---

[1] Crombach, *Primitiae Gentium*, vol. iii. book iii. chap. 49, p. 799. I am indebted for this translation to the kindness of my former colleague, Professor A. M. Webster.

readily to be found in Jesuit circles. This argument could be reinforced easily enough from a study of the Jesuit churches of the first half of the seventeenth century in Germany.[1]

In Jesuit circles, it would seem, the Gothic tradition had never quite died, and it is legitimate, perhaps, to regard Crombach as one of the last exponents of this Gothic Survival rather than as a true herald of the Gothic Revival of the eighteenth century. Indeed all the testimonies to an interest in Gothic architecture in the seventeenth century which we have adduced in this chapter run parallel to the Gothic Survival rather than to the Gothic Revival proper—to what the Germans so conveniently call *Nachgotik* as opposed to *Neugotik*.[2]

[1] Cp. Joseph Braun, S. J., *Die Kirchenbauten der deutschen Jesuiten* (Freiburg im Breisgau, 1908, 10).

[2] Cp. E. Kirschbaum, *Deutsche Nachgotik. Ein Beitrag zur Geschichte der Kirchlichen Architekur von 1550–1800* (Diss: Maastricht, 1929).

3. ENGLISH INFLUENCES

(a) *Rococo Gothic*

If the manifestations we have been discussing in the last chapter belong to the Survival rather than to the Revival of Gothic taste, when and where can the Gothic Revival proper be said to begin? This is a complex question and none too easy to answer, but one at least of the essential differences between Survival and Revival in Germany lies in the fact that the former carried on a native tradition which had never quite died, whereas the latter was essentially foreign, and in the first place English, in its inspiration. This is what we should expect, for in England, earlier than elsewhere, began the revolt against the neo-classical aesthetic which was the essential prerequisite to the Gothic Revival.

In his essays on the Chinese and Gothic fashions of the eighteenth-century[1] Professor A. O. Lovejoy has convincingly argued that the first impulse toward this revolt came from Sir William Temple's essay *Upon the Gardens of Epicurus* (first published in 1692, but written in 1685), which discusses the *irregular* beauty of the Chinese taste in gardens:

> Among us, the Beauty of Building and Planting is placed chiefly in some certain Proportions, Symmetries, or Uniformities; our Walks and our Trees ranged so, as to answer one another, and at exact Distances. The *Chineses* scorn this way of Planting . . . their greatest Reach of Imagination is employed in contriving Figures, where the Beauty shall be great, and strike the Eye, but without any Order or Disposition of Parts, that shall be commonly or easily observ'd. And though we have hardly any Notion of this sort of Beauty, yet they have a particular word to express it; and where they find it hit their Eye at first Sight, they say the *Sharawadgi* is fine or is admirable, or any such Expression of Esteem. And whoever observes the Work upon the best Indian Gowns, or the Painting upon their best Skreens or Purcellans, will find their Beauty is all of this Kind, (that is) without Order.[2]

This ideal of a beauty without order (or at least manifest order)

---

[1] 'The Chinese origin of a Romanticism' and 'The first Gothic Revival and the Return to Nature', both included in *Essays in the History of Ideas* (Baltimore, 1948).

[2] *The Works of Sir William Temple, Bart.* (London, 1720), i. 186.

was taken over and propagated in turn by Shaftesbury,[1] Addison,[2] and Pope,[3] and then received practical application in the art of the landscape gardeners themselves. In the hands of Bridgeman, Kent, and 'Capability' Brown the qualities of wildness, irregularity, variety came to be regarded as merits, and conversely 'regularity, symmetry, proportion, passed for violations of the first and great commandment, to "follow nature" '.[4]

It was, then, a small step to transfer the taste for such 'romantic' qualities from the sphere of landscape gardening to that of architecture. Gothic architecture, in the view of the early eighteenth century, was characterized by irregularity, variety, lack of symmetry, boldness, and freedom from the rules—the very attributes, that is to say, which it had now become fashionable to admire in the new art of landscape gardening. This change of attitude with regard to Gothic architecture is well illustrated in a letter to Sanderson Miller, the Gothic improver, from a friend who wrote in 1753 requesting a design for a new house: 'I would by no means have my Front regular . . . since the beauty of Gothick Architecture (in my opinion) consists, like that of a Pindarick Ode, in the Boldness and Irregularity of its Members.'[5] Or still more unequivocally in William Mason's poem The English Garden (1779), in which, speaking of his hero's Gothic dwelling, he comments:

> No modern art
> Had marred with misplaced symmetry the pile.[6]

The result of this change of taste was a complete revolution in the connotation of the word 'nature'—that most Protean as well as most pervasive of eighteenth-century aesthetic terms. Both the Classicists and the Gothicists were united in their exaltation of nature as the great norm and criterion of art. Both were agreed that the aim of art was the imitation of nature; where they differed was in their interpretation of the term. To the Neo-classicist nature stood for regularity and simplicity; to the Gothicist it stood for irregularity and variety. Gothic architecture, then, regained aesthetic respectability

---

[1] Cp. The Moralists, first published 1709, republished in Characteristicks of Men, Manners, Opinions, Times (London, 1711), ii. 393–4.

[2] Cp. The Tatler, Nos. 161, 218 (1710), and The Spectator, Nos. 412, 414, 477 (1712).

[3] Cp. The Guardian, No. 173 (1713), and Epistle to the Earl of Burlington (1731).

[4] Lovejoy, op. cit. p. 157; cp. also B. Sprague Allen, Tides in English Taste (1619–1800) (Cambridge, Mass., 1937) ii. 122 ff, and N. Pevsner, 'The Genesis of the Picturesque', (Architectural Review, xcvi. Nov. 1944).

[5] An Eighteenth-Century Correspondence, ed. Lilian Dickins and Mary Stanton (London, 1910), p. 303.

[6] Quoted from Lovejoy, op. cit. p. 158.

under the mantle of nature, but of a nature which had reversed its meaning owing to the impact of the new ideals of landscape gardening.

There was, however, another and more literal sense in which Gothic was held to imitate nature, namely in its employment of plant and arboreal forms. We have seen that this notion goes back at least as far as the epistle to Leo X at the beginning of the sixteenth century, but it was not till the eighteenth century that it became a commonplace of architectural criticism. In his *Itinerarium Curiosum* of 1724 the antiquary William Stukeley commends the fan vaulting in the cloisters of Gloucester Cathedral 'because the idea of it is taken from a walk of trees, whose branching heads are curiously imitated by the roof'.[1] But it was Bishop Warburton's note on Pope's *Epistle to the Earl of Burlington* which first gave a more general currency to the theory:

When the *Goths* had conquered Spain . . . they struck out a new species of Architecture unknown to Greece and Rome; upon original principles, and ideas much nobler than what had given birth even to classical magnificence. For having been accustomed, during the gloom of paganism, to worship the Deity in GROVES (a practice common to all nations) when their new Religion required covered edifices, they ingeniously projected to make them resemble *Groves*, as nearly as the distance of Architecture would permit; at once indulging their old prejudices, and providing for their present convenience, by a cool receptacle in a sultry climate. And with what art and success they executed the project appears from hence, That no attentive observer ever viewed a regular Avenue of well grown trees intermixing their branches over head, but it presently put him in mind of the long Visto thro' a Gothic Cathedral; or ever entered one of the larger and more elegant Edifices of this kind, but it represented to his imagination an Avenue of trees. And this alone is that which can be truly called the GOTHIC style of Building.

Under this idea of so extraordinary a species of Architecture, all the irregular transgressions against art, all the monstrous offences against nature, disappear; every thing has its reason, every thing is in order, and an harmonius Whole arises from the studious application of means proper and proportioned to the end. For could the *Arches* be otherwise than *pointed* when the Workman was to imitate that curve which branches make by their intersection with one another? Or could the *Columns* be otherwise than split into distinct shafts, when they were to represent the Stems of a group of Trees? On the same principle was formed the spreading ramification of the stone-work in the windows, and the stained glass in the interstices; the one being to represent the branches, and the other the leaves of an opening Grove; and both concurring to preserve that gloomy light inspiring religious horror. Lastly, we see the reason of their studied aversion to *apparent* solidity in these stupendous masses, deemed so absurd by men accustomed to the *apparent* as well as *real* strength of Grecian Architecture . . . When one considers, that this surprising lightness was

---

[1] Stukeley, op. cit. p. 64.

necessary to complete the excution of his idea of a rural place of worship, one cannot sufficiently admire the ingenuity of the contrivance.[1]

It will be seen that Warburton's theory not only seeks to explain the origin of Gothic architecture, but also—and more important— provides a complete justification for all those ingredients of the style which were most offensive to eighteenth-century taste. The passage thus remains a particularly important document in the rehabilitation of Gothic. It was quoted, pilfered, and paraphrased over and again by Gothic apologists in the later eighteenth and early nineteenth centuries, not least in Germany.

What Warburton (and Stukeley before him) is here assuming is a *deliberate* imitation of the forms of nature. Many more eighteenth-century critics were content to note the analogy between the two, without asserting that the resemblance was intentional.

There is a more concrete link between the art of landscape gardening and the taste for Gothic architecture than the aesthetic ideal of irregularity and variety common to both. It is well established that the art of landscape gardening in England was strongly influenced by the seventeenth-century Italian landscape painters, more especially by Claude and Salvator Rosa.[2] Now one of the most conspicuous ingredients of their landscapes was the Ruin, and this feature was eagerly adopted by the landscape gardeners. The artificial landscape was soon felt to be incomplete without its artificial (or occasionally genuine) ruin. At first, in imitation of the Italians, these were classical— Batty Langley in his *New Principles of Gardening* (1728) suggests only classical models—but gradually fashionable taste came to prefer Gothic ruins for landscape purposes; partly because genuine ruins in this country are almost invariably Gothic (or at least medieval) and partly, as we shall see, for literary reasons.

Nor was the sham ruin the only Gothic ingredient of the eighteenth-century landscape garden. The temples, pavilions, arbours, which were introduced to add variety to the scene, were, like the ruins, classical in the first instance, but later they were frequently Gothic or even Chinese. Largely owing to Batty and Thomas Langley's egregious volumes, *Ancient Architecture Restored and Improved* (1742) and the revised version, *Gothic Architecture Improved by Rules and Proportions* (1747), a fashion for what might be called Garden Gothic grew and flourished in the middle decades of the eighteenth century

[1] *The Works of Alexander Pope*, ed. Warburton (London, 1751), iii. 267–8 n.

[2] Cp. Elizabeth Manwaring, *Italian Landscape in Eighteenth Century England* (New York, 1925), pp. 121 ff. and Christopher Hussey, *The Picturesque* (London, 1927), pp. 128 ff.

in England. Gothic temples and Gothic summer-houses, Gothic hermitages, Gothic gazebos, and Gothic umbrellos became all the rage. Langley had obligingly supplied designs for many of these curiosities, and other even more fantastic volumes followed suit.[1] The common characteristic of these examples of Garden Gothic—as of the closely allied Gothic furniture—is their fripperishness. They are marked by a lightness and frivolity which unite them in spirit clearly enough to the Rococo. This mid-century Rococo Gothicism was never more than a mode, a means of tickling the jaded palate of the 'enlightened' connoisseur or amateur of taste with an exotic flavour—on a level precisely with the rage for *chinoiserie*, which often accompanied and sometimes even mingled with it.[2] Thus the taste for Rococo Gothic had very little to do with a serious appreciation of Gothic architecture, but it did at least accustom people to Gothic forms—pointed arches, pinnacles, crockets, and so forth—in however debased a shape, as an alternative to the accepted classical orthodoxy. Moreover through its main exponent in England it played a part of some significance in the Gothic Revival in this country. For despite elements of genuine antiquarianism Horace Walpole's Strawberry Hill was essentially rococo in spirit.[3] It has just that air of flimsy prettiness which is characteristic of the Garden Gothic we have been considering.

In England, then, it is not difficult to establish a connection between the art of landscape gardening and the awakening taste for Gothic architecture, even if in rococo form. A similar development is observable in Germany, though it occurred many decades later than in England, and for reasons which will be explained did not play so direct or important a part in the Revival.

In the park of the Nymphenburg Palace in Munich there is a strange building which has some claim to be considered the first example of Rococo Gothic in Europe, antedating by several years similar erections in this country. This is the Magdalenenkapelle, which was built for the Elector Max Emanuel of Bavaria by his court

---

[1] e.g. Charles Over's *Ornamental Architecture in the Gothic, Chinese and Modern Taste* (London, 1758), and P. Decker's *Gothic Architecture Decorated* (London, 1759).

[2] Cp. Thomas Chippendale, *The Gentleman and Cabinet-Maker's Director* (London, 1754) and William and John Halfpenny, *Chinese and Gothic Architecture properly ornamented* (London, 1752).

[3] Cp. Sir Kenneth Clark, op. cit. p. 75 ff. and *Architectural Review* (July 1945), xcviii. 151–2.

gardener, Effner, in 1725-8. The exterior has something of the artificial ruin about it, and though the general effect is baroque the tracery of the choir windows is definitely Gothic in character.[1] We have to wait some thirty years for the next example—namely, the Nauener Tor in Potsdam, which was erected in 1755 to the design of Frederick the Great, and which is clearly influenced by British models (e.g. Inverary Castle). It may seem strange that the first genuine example of neo-Gothic architecture in Germany should owe its existence to one of the most uncompromising anti-Goths of the eighteenth century, but under the aegis of his friend Marshal Keith, Frederick had been interested for some time in English architectural developments, including evidently experiments in neo-Gothic.[2] But the Magdalenenkapelle was a freak, and the Nauener Tor was classicistic rather than rococo in character. The true beginnings of Rococo Gothic in Germany are to be found in the park of Prince Franz of Anhalt-Dessau at Wörlitz, which dates from 1768. The palace and grounds of Wörlitz constitute the most famous and the most complete monument we possess to the penetration of English taste into Germany in the eighteenth century, though the park was by no means the first example of English landscape gardening in the country.[3]

The creator of Wörlitz, Prince, later Duke, Leopold Friedrich Franz of Anhalt-Dessau (1758-1817), was one of the many notable Germans of the eighteenth century who saw in England the land of their dreams. For them this country was the home of Enlightenment and of the Liberal Arts *par excellence*. Like his collateral ancestor Prince Ludwig of Anhalt-Cöthen, founder of the *Fruchtbringende Gesellschaft*, he journeyed thither to find inspiration for the cultural and political administration of his own diminutive territory. He was accompanied on his visits—in 1763 and 1766—by Friedrich Wilhelm von Erdmannsdorf, a young Saxon nobleman of artistic tastes, who was later to become his court architect, and much of their attention was directed to the architecture and landscape gardening of this country. The Prince was evidently impressed both by the Anglo-Palladian country houses which he visited and also by the early manifestations of the Gothic Revival which met his eye.

[1] Cp. H. Schmitz, op. cit., p. 259.
[2] Cp. A. Neumeyer, 'Die Erweckung der Gotik in der deutschen Kunst des späten 18. Jahrhunderts' *Repetorium für Kunstwissenschaft* (Berlin/Leipzig, 1928), xlix. 86.
[3] Cp. E. Bachmann, 'Anfänge des Landschaftgartens in Deutschland', *Zeitschrift für Kunstwissenschaft* (Berlin, 1951), v. Heft 3/4.

These, he decided, should be the models for his own projected residence at Wörlitz. It is said that the Prince wished to erect the Schloss itself in the neo-Gothic manner,[1] but the classically-minded Erdmannsdorf fortunately managed to dissuade him and built instead an admirably proportioned mansion in the purest Anglo-Palladian style (1769–1773), which would look perfectly at home in the depths of the English countryside. Prince Franz, however, found opportunity enough to gratify his neo-Gothic enthusiasm among the architectural features—temples, grottoes, hermitages, etc.,—with which his park was so liberally sprinkled. At first this Garden Gothic was on a modest scale—a summer-house and a hermitage or two. Then he conceived the idea of building a Gothic House, a kind of Strawberry Hill, in the middle of the park, where he could retire and indulge to the full his medieval propensities.

With the assistance of his valet-turned-architect, Georg Christoph Hesekiel, who was apparently more complaisant towards the Gothic style than Erdmannsdorf, he set about this task in 1773. It was a long time building, and the strange erection was not finally completed until 1809. Strange indeed it is to English eyes, no doubt because its inspiration is by no means purely English. For Prince Franz had travelled in Italy as well as in England, and had observed Italian, and especially Venetian, Gothic with no less attention than he had accorded to Strawberry Hill. This is obvious on the front facing the canal, which was the first part to be built; the back and sides, on the other hand, are clearly reminiscent of English models. This applies even more strongly to the interior with its flimsily delicate Rococo Gothic patternings on walls and ceilings. To enhance the medieval atmosphere the Prince installed a collection of old pictures, armour, tapestries and pewter jugs, and the neo-Gothic windows were filled with genuine old glass from Switzerland. One room, significantly, was decorated with paintings of English Gothic cathedrals. Bizarre and overladen, the Gothisches Haus at Wörlitz is anything but a success aesthetically. But its very imperfections have a certain pathetic charm, and historically it is important as the first major example of Rococo Gothic in Germany.[2]

[1] Cp. F. Reil, *Leopold Friedrich Franz, Herzog und Fürst von Anhalt-Dessau* (Dessau, 1845), p. 26.
[2] For a contemporary description of Wörlitz see August Rode, *Beschreibung des Fürstlichen Anhalt-Dessauischen Landhauses und Englischen Gartens zu Wörlitz* (Dessau, 1788). See also Paul Clemen, 'Strawberry-Hill und Wörlitz', *Neue Beiträge deutscher Forschung, Zum 60. Geburtstag Wilhelm Worringers* (Königsberg, 1943), pp. 37–60; A. Neumeyer, loc. cit.; and Marie Luise Gothein, *Geschichte der Gartenkunst* (Jena, 1914), ii. 392–4.

It was, however, not so much the architecture as the park of Wörlitz that awoke the admiration of contemporaries and posterity. Though not actually the first, it was certainly the most successful example of the English taste in landscape gardening that had yet appeared in Germany. Its serpentining walks and artfully but unsymmetrically contrived groups of trees, its lakes and cascades and grottoes, soon became famous and drew a steady stream of admirers. In May 1778 Goethe and Carl August of Weimar paid one of several visits on their way to Berlin. Goethe records his impression in a letter to Frau von Stein:

> It is infinitely beautiful here now. Yesterday evening as we made our way by the lakes, canals and plantations I was very touched to see how the gods have allowed the prince to create a dream around him. As one wanders round, it is like being told a fairy tale and has all the character of the Elysian fields. One thing merges into the other in the gentlest variety; the eye is not drawn to one particular point by rising ground; you roam about without asking where you have come from or where you are going to. The shrubs are in their youthful beauty and the whole place has the purest charm.[1]

Shortly after this Goethe began to supervise the new layout of the park at Weimar, which was to remain one of his favourite preoccupations for many years. He himself confesses that it was largely the Wörlitz park which awakened his interest in landscape gardening, and which served as a model for the transformation of the old formal garden at Weimar into a 'succession of aesthetic pictures' in the English style.[2] Tribute was paid to the neo-Gothic taste in the shape of a hermitage and artificial ruin, and Goethe even designed a garden table which was 'a bit Gothic' in appearance.[3] Decades later he was to apply what he had learnt in the practical activity of laying out the Weimar park to the landscape garden background of Die Wahlverwandtschaften. That too, it is expressly stated, was carried out on the model of 'englische Parkbeschreibungen'.

A landscape garden in South Germany—Hohenheim near Stuttgart—which was famous for the fantastic number of its architectural embellishments is perhaps deserving of mention here, since it drew the attention of both Goethe and Schiller. The latter approved of this 'englische Anlage' on the whole, describing it as an example of

---

[1] 14 May 1778.
[2] Schema zu einem Aufsatze die Pflanzencultur im Grossherzogthum Weimar darzustellen (WA II. 6, 229). Cp. Das Luisenfest (WA I. 36 (ii), 233–4); and also, for the Weimar park, Gothein, op. cit. ii. 395–8.
[3] Cp. letter to A. F. Oeser of 15 June 1778.

'nature animated by intelligence and exalted by art',[1] whereas
Goethe, who visited it on his way to Switzerland in 1797, was put
off by the plethora of curious objects. Strangely enough, the only
one of these architectural fantasies which he exempts from his censure
is 'an old-Gothic chapel now being constructed with a great deal of
taste.'[2]

A good example of the English landscape garden with 'Gothic'
trappings is the Neuer Garten in Potsdam, laid out for Frederick
William II by his court architect, Carl Gotthard Langhans, who had
visited this country in 1775. Like Prince Franz of Anhalt, Frederick
William was an enthusiastic admirer of the English taste in gardening
and architecture, and he was inspired to his creation by the example of
Wörlitz. The park contained, among other extravagances, a Gothic
library, a kitchen disguised as a temple, and a hermitage housing a
luxuriously appointed bath. In the park of Charlottenburg there
was an elegant Gothic fishing house. Gothic dairies were to be found
in the Neuer Garten and on the Pfaueninsel near Wannsee. All these
curiosities were erected by Langhans in the late eighties and early
nineties.[3]

If one wants to see German Garden Gothic at its craziest one must
turn to the fantasies of the Landgrave William IX of Hesse, who found
satisfaction for his Gothic romanticism by erecting a ruined Ritterburg
(1793–8), supposedly modelled on an English fourteenth-century
castle, in a corner of his park at Wilhelmshöhe. The ruin had all the
appurtenances of the medieval burg of romantic fiction—drawbridge,
moat, ramparts, chapel, &c. To complete the illusion, the Löwenburg
as it was called, was staffed with a seneschal and guard in medieval
costume. It might, in fact, have come straight out of one of the fashionable Gothic Romances of the time, to which it is closely allied in
spirit.[4]

The absurdities of Garden Gothic inevitably called forth a reaction.
Already in Der Triumph der Empfindsamkeit (1786), which was directed
against all forms of sentimentality, including the sentimental garden,
Goethe had attacked the more foolish aspects of the genre, such as
'chinesisch-gotische Grotten'.[5] Even earlier Justus Möser had written
Das englische Gärtchen (1773). Möser, lover and student of the German

[1] In a review of Cotta's Gartenkalender auf das Jahr 1795 (Säkular-Ausgabe, xvi. 271–9).
[2] WA I. 34 (i), 296.
[3] Cp. Schmitz, op. cit., p. 195, and Neumeyer, op. cit., p. 114.
[4] Cp. Paul Heidelbach, Die Geschichte der Wilhelmshöhe (Leipzig, 1909) and Karl
Paetow, Klassizismus und Romantik auf Wilhelmshöhe (Cassel, 1929).
[5] WA I. 17, 38.

past and admirer of England, was nevertheless irritated by the pseudo-romanticism and snobbery inherent in the craze for the English land-scape garden. In this little squib a girl writes to her grandmother to tell her how her orchard and kitchen garden have been transformed in her absence into an 'English' garden, complete with hills and valleys and serpentining paths, shrubbery, and Chinese bridge, 'for which my husband has procured the latest model from England . . . Beyond the bridge there is going to be a darling little Gothic cathedral, not much bigger than Uncle Toby's sentry box in *Tristram Shandy* . . . In short, dear Grandmama, your dear little garden now resembles an enchanted island, on which everything is to be found which you would not expect, and nothing is to be found which you would expect.'[1]

In Germany the contribution of Rococo Gothic to the main stream of the Gothic Revival was more peripheral than in England. This was partly due to the fact that in Germany, despite Wörlitz, there was no personality or building of the calibre of Horace Walpole and his Rococo Gothic castle, and partly because the English taste in Garden Gothic arrived on the scene so late in the day that it was soon superseded by other and more significant Gothicizing factors. The summer-houses and hermitages of Wörlitz or Potsdam were in the nature of a blind alley. Like their English prototypes they may be said to have accustomed the spectator to Gothic forms, but they contributed little to the serious appreciation of medieval architecture. For that we must look elsewhere—to the sphere of literature and the beginnings of the Romantic Movement.

(b) *The Gothic Mood*

We have seen that the fashion for Rococo Gothic in Germany was borrowed straight from England, and that the Gothisches Haus in Wörlitz cannot be understood without reference to Strawberry Hill. In another and cognate sphere the influence of England was equally strong: in the contribution of literature to the evocation of a Gothic Mood.

In his study of the Gothic Revival in England Sir Kenneth Clark observes: 'From the first the new taste for Gothic architecture was no more than a symptom of a great change of ideas which we call the Romantic Movement . . . The taste for Gothic is therefore an essential expression of Romanticism, so closely related to every other expression of the same impulse that it is difficult to write on the Gothic

[1] *Patriotische Phantasien* (Berlin, 1778), ii. 335–6.

Revival without plunging into the history of the Romantic Movement.'[1]

This difficulty is at its greatest in writing of the Gothic Mood,
for this mood is compounded of almost all the varied ingredients of
eighteenth-century Romanticism or pre-Romanticism—graveyard
poetry, the school of melancholy and night, Ossian, bardic verse,
ballads and folksong.[2] All these contributed to an intellectual and emotional climate which, though containing few specifically Gothic
elements, was yet calculated to stimulate a taste for medieval architecture.

Of these the most germane to our purpose is the curious fashion of
graveyard or sepulchral poetry, which is sometimes referred to simply
as Gothic poetry. It is closely related to the taste for sham ruins, which
it certainly influenced, and is characterized by the same meretricious
and theatrical air. An excellent example is provided by a passage from
David Mallet's *The Excursion*, which was written in 1726:

> Behind me rises huge an awful *Pile*,
> Sole on this blasted Heath, a Place of Tombs,
> Waste, desolate, where *Ruin* dreary dwells,
> Brooding o'er sightless Sculls, and crumbling Bones.
> Ghastful *He* sits, and eyes with Stedfast Glare
> The Column grey with Moss, the falling Bust,
> The Time-shook Arch, the monumental Stone,
> Impaired, effac'd, and hastening into Dust,
> Unfaithful to their Charge of flattering Fame.
> All is dread Silence here, and undisturb'd,
> Save what the Wind sighs, and the wailing Owl
> Screams solitary to the mournful Moon,
> Glimmering her western Ray through yonder *Isle*,
> Where the sad *Spirit* walks with shadowy Foot
> His wonted Round, or lingers o'er his Grave.[3]

Here already at this comparatively early date we have all the ingredients of Gothic Poetry presented with a most satisfying completeness:
blasted heaths, moss-grown ruins, desolate tombs, crumbling skeletons,
melancholy moonlight, wailing owls, and lingering ghosts. It is the

[1] Clark, op. cit. (revised and enlarged ed., London, 1950), p. 87.
[2] The history of German pre-Romanticism has still to be written. Paul van Tieghem's
Le Préromantisme covers certain aspects of the subject, but no one has yet done for German
literature what H. A. Beers so admirably accomplished in the English field as long ago
as 1899 in his *History of English Romanticism in the Eighteenth Century*.
[3] *The Excursion. A Poem in Two Books* (London, 1728), p. 23. For other examples of
Gothic poetry and a full discussion of the subject see R. Haferkorn, *Gotik und Ruine in der
englischen Dichtung des achtzehnten Jahrhunderts* (Leipzig, 1924).

4

same sham Gothicism which was later in the century to find expression in the Gothic Romances of Walpole and his many imitators. Germany, too, had its sepulchral poetry. Indeed the baroque poets of the seventeenth century positively wallowed in images of dissolution and decay and all the paraphernalia of mortality. Gryphius's *Gedanken über den Kirchhof und Ruhestätte der Verstorbenen*, for example, with its appalling picture of the various stages of decomposition in the grave far surpasses in morbid horror anything produced by the eighteenth-century graveyard school either in England or Germany. But this sepulchral poetry of the seventeenth century, which assuredly deserves the name of Gothic, cannot in fact have had any influence on the Gothic Revival in Germany for the simple reason that it had been completely forgotten by the middle of the eighteenth century. The graveyard fashion in Germany came not from its own past literature, so rich in this respect, but like most literary fashions of the eighteenth century—from England.

Traces of the mode are to be found in most of the German poets and poetasters of the mid-eighteenth century—Klopstock, Zachariä, Schubart, Löwen, Heydenreich, and many others.[1] Echoes still persist in poets as late in the century as Hölty and Matthison. A good example of the popularity of the genre, and also of its English provenance, is Zachariä's version of Thomas Warton's *The Pleasure of Melancholy* (*Die Vergnügungen der Melancholey*, 1760), with its quintessentially 'Gothic' lines:

> Unter jener verfallnen Abtey bemoosten Gewölben,
> Will ich oft sitzen, allein, in jenen dämmernden Stunden,
> Wenn der traurige Mond in den fürchterlicheinsamen Kreuzgang
> Einen flimmernden Stral von strömenden Lichte hineinwirft,
> Und ein tiefes heiliges Schweigen auf allem umher herrscht,
> Ausser der Eule klagendem Lied, die, unter dem Schutte
> Dumpfigter Hölen verscheucht, ihr ödes Wohnhaus erbauet;
> Oder der ruhig säuselnden Luft, die zwischen dem Laube
> Des breitblättrichten Epheu rauscht, der an den Gemäuern
> Eines hangenden Thurms sich an den Wänden hinaufschlingt.[2]

[1] Cp. van Tieghem, op. cit. ii. 128–9; and Lotte Kander, *Die deutsche Ruinenpoesie des 18. Jahrhunderts bis in die Anfänge des 19. Jahrhunderts* (Diss: Heidelberg, 1933).

[2] F. W. Zachariä, *Poetische Schriften* (Brunswick, 1763–4), v. 144. This translation of Warton was printed in Zachariä's *Poetische Schriften* without any indication that it was not an original poem, which has misled Paul van Tieghem in his *Préromantisme* (ii. 128) into asserting that 'c'est du Young traduit presque littéralement de la première Nuit.' It was first printed in *Die Schöpfung der Hölle nebst einigen andern Gedichten* (Altenburg, 1760), where the true authorship is acknowledged in the preface. For the original poem, see p. 308.

Closely allied to this Gothic poetry of ruins and mouldering tombs, but by no means identical with it, is what one might call the poetry of Melancholy and Night. Of this the great exemplar is of course Edward Young's *Night Thoughts* (1742-5). Though it is not always realized by those who have not read it, this poem is in fact singularly devoid of Gothic trappings. It consists for the greater part of moralizing reflections on the human condition in face of death and eternity. The background to these melancholy musings is solitude and night, but not the graveyard or the ivy-mantled tower. As Van Tieghem puts it: 'Young reste le plus classique de tous les poètes de la Mort; et justement son influence a été d'autant plus grande qu'elle était pure de détails rebutants et parfois ridicules.'[1]

In Germany at any rate his impact far surpassed that of the grave-yard poets proper. The story of Young's influence on German litera-ture in the eighteenth century has been often and thoroughly investi-gated, so there is no need to recapitulate it here.[2] It is sufficient to say that between 1751—the date of J. A. Ebert's prose translation of the first seven 'Nights'—and 1759 no less than ten versions by various hands of the whole or part of the *Night Thoughts* appeared in Germany. Its vogue was extraordinary. Bodmer, Klopstock, Gellert, the young Wieland, Gerstenberg, Hamann, and Herder were all enthusiastic admirers of the work. The climax was reached in an article by J. A Cramer published in *Der Nordische Aufseher* in 1758, which claimed not only that Young's genius was far superior to that of Milton, but also that of all men who had ever lived he came nearest to the spirit of David and the Prophets.[3] This astonishing statement evoked a protest—though a surprisingly mild one—from Lessing in the forty-eighth *Litteraturbrief*.

Young was imitated as well as translated—most blatantly perhaps by Freiherr von Creuz in his long poem in six books, *Die Gräber* (1752-69), which is a typical example of the poetry of Melancholy and Night in German dress. The *Night Thoughts* also stood sponsor to Zachariä's *Die Nacht*, from *Die Tageszeiten* (1755), to J. F. V. Cronegk's *Einsamkeiten* (1757), and to many other very minor works.[4]

[1] van Tieghem, op. cit. ii. 32.
[2] Cp. J. Barnstorff, *Youngs Nachtgedanken und ihr Einfluss auf die deutsche Literatur* (Bamberg, 1895); J. L. Kind, *Edward Young in Germany* (*Columbia University Germanic Studies*, Vol. ii. No. 3. New York, 1906); P. van Tieghem, op. cit. ii; L. M. Price, *English Literature in Germany* (*University of California Publications in Modern Philology*, Berkeley and Los Angeles, 1953) pp. 113 ff.
[3] Vol. i. Stück 13, pp. 158-182.
[4] Cp. van Tieghem, op. cit. ii. 126 ff.

An interesting testimony to the connection between Young and
Creuz and their relation to the Gothic Mood is provided by a note of
Herder's in the section on the imitation of Latin elegies in his *Fragmente* (dritte Sammlung). He describes how he has found the most
favourable setting for the enjoyment of Young's *Night Thoughts*
or Creuz's *Gräber* to be a starlit summer night in a garden bordering a
churchyard 'where ancient lime trees, stirred by the breath of night,
rustled shudders into the soul, and the philosophic owl emitted from
time to time its hollow accents from the ruins of a medieval castle
or from its abode in the old Gothic church tower'.[1]
The most distinguished of those German writers who were influenced by Young was of course Klopstock. His importance for our
enquiry is that he united in his single person almost all the varied
ingredients of pre-Romanticism, and owing to the prestige of his
poetry gave them a general currency which they would otherwise
have lacked. Klopstock was in fact the most formidable opponent of
the neo-classical tradition who had yet appeared in Germany.
He first became acquainted with Young's work through his friend
J. A. Ebert. He promptly fell under its spell, attracted no doubt by
the mixture of moralizing and melancholy, which was akin to his
own bent of mind. He even wrote an ode to Young (1752), commencing,
not perhaps very tactfully:

Stirb, prophetischer Greis, stirb! denn dein Palmenzweig
Sprosste lang schon empor.[2]

He confessed to Ebert that he read the *Night Thoughts* for inspiration
while working on *Der Messias*, and many passages bear witness
to the truth of this statement.[3]
If Young was a kindred spirit to Klopstock, then Ossian in Macpherson's dress, who took Germany by storm in the sixties, was even
more so, and his impact was correspondingly more intoxicating.[4]
What was common to both Young and Ossian was the elegiac mood,
and this appealed strongly to Klopstock's own elegiac propensities.
But Ossian also appealed to Klopstock's penchant for the vague and
nebulous, a tendency which is amply illustrated in *Der Messias*.

---

[1] Herder, *Sämmtliche Werke*, ed. B. Suphan, i. 484 n.
[2] Die, prophetic old man, die! For your palm branch sprouted forth long ago.
[3] Cp. Barnstorff, op. cit. 34 ff.
[4] Cp. R. Tombo, *Ossian in Germany* (*Columbia University Germanic Studies*, Vol. i.
No. 2, New York, 1901).

As Tombo discreetly puts it: 'There is a certain mistiness in Klopstock's great epic that reminds one of the shadowy atmosphere in which the heroes of the Ossianic epics are enveloped.'[1] The most striking features of Macpherson's Ossian are at the same time salient ingredients of the Gothic Mood. First, the melancholy of the landscape: the mist-clad hills, the wild deserted heaths, the stormy skies, the lonely foam-tossed seas and moonlit wastes of the Scottish Highlands. And secondly, the elegiac note: the frequent laments for the dead, the invocation of their ghosts, the shadowy figures of the noble warriors of the past, the atmosphere of old, unhappy, far-off things, and battles long ago. Now all this was meat and drink to Klopstock, and his poems soon began to show the new influence.

But Ossian's greatest service to Klopstock was that he helped to provide him with a new mythology. He first came under the spell of Ossian in 1764 (the earliest German translations had appeared in 1762), at which date he was already engaged in trying to recreate a picture of the Teutonic past, centred round the figure of Arminius and constructed mainly from Tacitus's *Germania*. In this endeavour Macpherson's poems with their vision of a primitive heroic world peopled by bards and shadowy warriors were more than welcome to him. For Klopstock shared a common fallacy of the time, which was given wide currency by P. H. Mallet's history of Denmark, that the Celts too were a Teutonic race. As he put it in a letter to the poet Gleim (30 June, 1769): "Ossian was of German origin, because he was a Caledonian."[2] Or, more aggressively, in an epigram published in the *Hamburgische Neue Zeitung*, 1771, (No. 183), entitled *Gerechter Anspruch* (Just Claim):

> Sie, deren Enkel jetzt auf Schottlands Bergen wohnen,
> Die von den Römern nicht provinzten Kaledonen,
> Sind deutschen Stamms. Daher gehört auch uns mit an
> Der Bard und Krieger Ossian,
> Und mehr noch als den Engelländern an.[3]

Klopstock, then, simply annexed Ossian, and now conceived of the German past as a conglomeration of Tacitus and the Celtic bard. Thus in his odes and *Bardiete* (dramas dealing with the life and death of Arminius) we have ancient British druids and Ossianic bards

[1] Ibid. p. 83.
[2] Ibid. p. 85.
[3] For translation, see p. 308

serenading Teutonic warriors to the accompaniment of their Celtic lyres.

To make confusion worse confounded Klopstock then introduced a new element into this hotch-potch in the shape of Norse mythology. The world of Old Norse poetry and legend had recently been revealed to Europe through Paul Henri Mallet's *Introduction à l'historie de Danemark* (1755) with its accompanying volume of specimens of Old Norse poetry, *Monuments de la mythologie et de la poésie des Celtes, et particulièrement des anciens Scandinaviens* (1756).

The first German writer to exploit this new world of legend for poetic purposes was Heinrich Wilhelm von Gerstenberg in his *Gedicht eines Skalden* (1766). This poem, which made ample use of Nordic mythology and is preceded by a brief explanatory list of the Nordic names and terms mentioned, had a great success and led to a host of imitations among the so-called Bardic poets. From this time, too, Klopstock, who was a close friend of Gerstenberg, began to introduce the Nordic mythology into his own poetry. For Klopstock, indeed, the Germanic pantheon presented to him by Mallet and Gerstenberg was, literally, a godsend. One of the difficulties with which he was confronted in his attempt to construct a picture of the remote German past was precisely the lack of a specifically Germanic mythology. Caesar and Tacitus were distressingly vague on the point; nor had Ossian much to offer in the way of gods and goddesses. Klopstock now had at hand a complete system of Teutonic divinities, and he lost no time in introducing them into his poems and plays. Indeed he even went so far as to rewrite his old poems, substituting Nordic deities for the original classical ones, wherever they occurred.

Though there is nothing specifically Gothic or even medieval—if anything it is pre-medieval—about the world of Klopstock's imagination, it is of importance from our point of view in that it represents the first significant breakaway from the hegemony of the neo-classical tradition. Above all it offered an alternative mythology to the so firmly established classical pantheon, and a heroic age which was for once not that of the Greek and Roman heroes.

A fitting postscript to this chapter is provided by an elegy written by Herder in 1763, when he was nineteen, in reference to the death of his father:

> Wo bin ich? — in Einsiedeleyen
> find ich, fühl ich mich!
> Gespenster schatteten weg — Gedankentiefen
> brausen herab und ruhn! —

Da wo im Mitternachtshain auf Scheidewegen
Feen wandelten —
Und Cypressen den Thau herunterrauschten
auf mein entblösstes Haupt

Um mich Gräber der Brüder; Geisterstimmen
aus der Urne schoos
hörs; sie dumpfen herauf, — St! jener Moder
lispelt Antwort und schweigt —

und auf sterbenden Gipfeln ewger Ulmen
wandelt, hörts! der Sturm
der von sinkenden Ritterlichen Trümmern
meinen Tempel heran

Steigt, in dem Gespenster den neuen Todten
vor dem Altar weihn.
Kaum sieht Hekate selbst durch alte Fenster
ihren Gelübden zu

und vom Gothisch gehörnten Thurme seufzen
Eulen halbes Ach! —
und mein Vater vor mir — ich schaudre, schaudrend
wach ich und um mich Nacht! —[1]

This is one of the most thorough going examples of Gothic poetry
we have in German—a kind of German counterpart to the passage from
Mallet's *Excursion* quoted above. Hermitages, ghosts, midnight
groves, cypresses, funeral urns, feudal ruins, Gothic towers, mouldering graves and sighing owls—all the stock in trade of the genre is
there. Not only Ossian, but Mallet, Young, Warton, Gray, and the
whole tribe of the Gothic poets, English and German, have stood
sponsor to these verses.

It is of course impossible to assess accurately the influence of the
Gothic Mood on the Gothic Revival proper. Its effect was even
more indirect and intangible than that of Rococo Gothic. The most
one can say is that the ivy-mantled towers, moonlight melancholy
and gibbering ghosts of the Gothic poets were closely allied in spirit
to the sham ruins, hermitages and Gothic burgs of Rococo Gothic.
They were indeed their literary equivalent, and like them were calculated to stimulate an interest in the past, and especially the medieval
past. And this in its turn provided a suitable atmosphere for a genuine
revival of interest in and understanding of Gothic architecture.

[1] Herder, ed. cit. xxix, 230–1. Translation on p. 308–9 below.

4. FRENCH INFLUENCES

As we have seen, the initial inspiration of the Gothic Revival in Germany was English. Both Rococo Gothic and Gothic Poetry were English inventions. Both contributed in some, even if small, measure to the revolution in architectural taste with which we are concerned. But a more direct contribution to this revolution came, not from England, but from France.

Despite the dominance of the classical tradition in the seventeenth and eighteenth centuries, the French aestheticians seem in general to have shown a more enlightened attitude towards medieval architecture than their colleagues in other countries.[1] This may have been due partly to the simple fact that it is harder to ignore the presence of medieval architecture in France than in any other land. But it may also have been due to an instinctive apprehension of the logical qualities of Gothic construction, and its affinities, in this respect at least, with the natural bent of the French mind.

Of course the approval of the French critics is a qualified one. Never is it suggested that the Gothic style could be considered a serious rival to 'good' architecture. The classical tradition remains the norm; the Gothic style, whatever its qualities, is always an aberration.

The orthodox French attitude towards the style is well summed up by Molière in *La Gloire du Val-de-Grâce* (1669), where he speaks of the

> fade goust des ornemens gothiques;
> Ces monstres odieux des siècles ignorants,
> Que de la barbarie ont produits les torrens,
> Quand leur cours inondant presque toute la terre,
> Fit à la politesse une mortelle guerre,
> Et, de la grande Rome abbatant les remparts,
> Vint, avec son empire, étouffer les beaux arts.[2]

[1] Cp. J. Corblet, 'L'Architecture du moyen-âge jugée par les écrivains des deux derniers siècles' (*Revue de l'art chrétien*, 1859), iii. 398–405; R. Lanson, *Le goût du moyen âge en France au xviii siècle* (Paris/Brussels, 1926), pp. 31–41; P. Frankl, op. cit., pp. 336–48; W. Herrmann, *Laugier and eighteenth-century French theory* (London, 1962) pp. 68–90; R. D. Middleton, 'The Abbé de Cordemoy and the Graeco-Gothic Ideal: a prelude to romantic classicism', *Journal of the Warburg and Courtauld Institutes*, 1962, xxv. 278–320.

[2] *Œuvres complètes de Molière* (*Collection nationale des classique français*, ed. G. Michaut) x. 206.

Even here though, it is worth noting, it is Gothic ornament rather than Gothic architecture which is attacked.

In any case there is ample evidence from the number and tone of the guide-books to the medieval cathedrals published in the seventeenth and eighteenth centuries that the people of France had never ceased to love their Gothic churches. As early as 1609 the historian André Duchesne refers to Notre Dame in Paris in terms of the highest praise as 'a church that far surpasses all other churches of Christendom, both in style and size'.[1] In the same year Sébastien Rouillard writes of the sculptures of Chartres as 'so exquisite and remarkable that at the mere sight of them all the Polyclituses of old would throw away their chisels', and of the cathedral as a whole he says 'all the Vitruviuses of the past would want to take this masterpiece as a model of their architecture'—a warm tribute despite the conventional rhetoric in which it is couched.[2] In 1627 Adrien de la Morlière writes of Amiens in even more enthusiastic terms: the proportions are so excellent that no description can do them justice. 'They are entirely admirable, both in the body of the church as a whole and in all the details. It is a wonder to behold!'[3]

But the most remarkable tribute to an individual Gothic building in seventeenth-century France comes from Vincent Sablon, curé of Chartres, who wrote a little guide to the cathedral (1671) 'pour plusieurs Habitans de cette ville, et pour un grand nombre de Pelerins, et de gens de la Campagne *qui la demandent tous les jours*', and whose enthusiasm for the exterior of the cathedral is such that he is moved to write the whole of the chapter which is devoted to it in verse. Here is a specimen:

> Ce Temple est merveilleux en son Architecture,
> Merveilleux en son art, non moins qu'en sa structure,
> Merveilleux au dedans, merveilleux au dehors,
> Et merveilleux enfin en tout son vaste corps.[4]

Even that pillar of classicism, François Blondel the elder (1618–86), the influential director of the Academy of Architecture, whose *Cours d'architecture* (1675) remained the chief authority on the subject for the greater part of the ensuing century, applauds in a passage later quoted with approval by Goethe (*Von Deutscher Baukunst 1823*) the symmetry

[1] *Les Antiquitez et recherches des villes, chasteaux, et places plus remarquables de toute la France* (Paris, 1609), Pt. I. p. 73.
[2] Corblet, op. cit. pp. 403–4; Frankl, op. cit. p. 337.
[3] *Antiquitez, histoires et choses les plus remarquables de la ville d'Amiens* (Paris, 1627), p. 9.
[4] *Histoire de l'auguste et vénérable église de Chartres* (Chartres, 1671), p. 23.

and proportions of some Gothic buildings 'which make themselves felt despite the ugly ornaments which accompany them'. He adds significantly, 'and if we examine these proportions carefully we shall find that they are on the whole the same proportions as in buildings constructed according to the rules of good architecture.'[1] In another passage he writes with positive enthusiasm of the façade of Milan Cathedral 'which is considered the most beautiful work of Gothic architecture in the world and which I have never contemplated without being touched by a feeling of veneration and pleasure'.[2]

But such utterances are the exception. In general Blondel is the declared enemy of 'cette façon énorme et insupportable', as he calls it. A much more positive and remarkable tribute to the Gothic style comes from the writings of Jean-François Félibien des Avaux (1658–1733). Son of a more famous father, André Félibien des Avaux (1619–95), historiographer royal and first secretary of the Académie royale d'architecture, Jean-François also became secretary of the Académie and was the author of several well-known architectural works. Since his views had much influence on writers on architecture throughout the first half of the eighteenth century, not only in France but also in Germany, it is worth considering them in some detail.

Félibien's remarks on Gothic are to be found in his *Recueil historique de la vie et des ouvrages des plus célèbres architectes* (Paris, 1687) and in his *Dissertation touchant l'architecture antique et l'architecture gothique*, appended to his book *Les plans et les descriptions de deux des plus belles maisons de campagne de Pline le Consul* (Paris, 1699).

Among the architects mentioned in the *Recueil* are several of the medieval masters, such as Jean de Chelles, Pierre de Montreuil, Robert de Luzarches, Thomas de Cormont, Robert de Coucy, Erwin von Steinbach. Both they and their buildings are treated in a surprisingly positive manner considering the date of the book. The Sainte-Chapelle is commended for its great delicacy and the beauty of its general proportions. Chartres, unsurpassed in its day for beauty, size, and stability, can still take its place among the most magnificent buildings to be seen in Europe. Amiens is no less famed for the beauty and excellence of its workmanship than for its great size; few Gothic buildings are more perfect, its only defect being the excessive height of the nave in relation to its width. Strasbourg is more to be admired for its façade and spire, the height and delicacy of which are nothing short of marvellous. Félibien, moreover, pays a passing tribute to

---

[1] *Cours d'architecture*, (2nd ed. Paris 1698), Pt. V, Bk. 5, Ch. 16, p. 774.
[2] Ibid., Ch. 17, p. 774.

the 'art and magnificence' of the Gothic architecture of Germany and England as well as of his own land.[1]

But it is his remarks on medieval architecture in his *Dissertation* that give Félibien his place in the history of the Gothic Revival. These are notable in several respects. In the first place, his attitude, as in the *Recueil*, is surprisingly positive for his time. The Gothic buildings, he says, appear light, delicate, and of an astonishing boldness. Among a considerable number of great churches constructed in this manner in diverse parts of Europe there are some which lack neither beauty nor stability, as is proved by their subsisting to this day as complete as if they had just been built. These churches are remarkable not only for their good construction, but also for their proportions.

Félibien is the first writer to discriminate clearly between the main phases of French medieval architecture: Romanesque, Gothic, Flamboyant. 'Ancient' Gothic (i.e. Romanesque) is massive and coarse and has nothing to recommend it but its solidity and bulk, whereas 'modern' Gothic is light and delicate and is characterized by simplicity, *ordonnance* and durability. In the third and decadent phase of medieval architecture Gothic degenerated into an inordinate boldness of construction and a confused mass of intricate ornamentation which resembled filigree work. Félibien, then, was not only the first writer on architecture to distinguish clearly and unequivocally between Romanesque and Gothic, but he was also the first to differentiate between Gothic of the great period with its classical virtues and Late Gothic with its excess of decoration and 'filigree' delicacy. It is worth noting that the greater part of eighteenth-century criticism of Gothic was really directed against this latter, in which context it makes some sense; whereas the endlessly reiterated complaints about the fussiness and frivolity of the style seem to bear no relation whatever to the great churches of the thirteenth century. Félibien's unusual understanding of the nature of medieval architecture is further illustrated by his recognition of the function of the pointed arch in diminishing the lateral thrust of the vaults—a piece of insight surely far in advance of his day.

Much of Félibien's disquisition on Gothic is occupied with tracing the natural origin of the various phases of the style, and it is this aspect of his work above all others which gives it its importance in the evolution of eighteenth-century taste. Half a century before Warburton he finds the true justification of Gothic to lie in its literal imitation of nature: 'If one considers attentively those churches which have been

[1] *Recueil* (2nd ed. Paris, 1696), p. 234.

constructed in the purest Gothic taste, one will recognize that what at
first seems most extraordinary about them, and strongly opposed
to nature, is in fact founded on the examples of nature herself, from
which each manner of building has drawn its first origin.' Thus in its
coarse massiveness Romanesque 'retains something of the uncouth-
ness of the dens and caverns which the northern peoples formerly
inhabited', whereas Gothic 'partakes of the lightness of those natural
arbours which one meets in the woods or which the inhabitants of
temperate climes make for themselves to provide shade in open
country'.[1] So Gothic is natural in two respects: first, in its imitation
of, and origin in, the forms of nature herself; and secondly—a motif
which also plays a considerable part in eighteenth-century discussions
of the subject—in its imitation of, and origin in, the dwellings of primitive man.

Félibien enters with some particularity into the resemblance between
the Gothic style and natural forms, comparing the slender columns
of a Gothic church to a forest of stems and the ribbed vaulting to the
bent branches of trees. This arboreal analogy was to play an enormous
part in the discussion of Gothic architecture throughout the eighteenth
century, and even later. Nowadays it seems an obvious, indeed a
trite analogy, but at that time it still had a visionary novelty and is
repeated with imaginative fervour by one Gothic enthusiast after the
other.

Félibien, however, despite his surprisingly positive attitude towards
the style, cannot by any means be described as a Gothic enthusiast.
In his comparison of ancient and Gothic architecture he leaves the
reader in no doubt as to where his preference lies. Gothic, whatever
its qualities, lacks the fundamental virtues of Reason and Propriety.
Even the arboreal analogy works out to its disadvantage. For classical
columns, too, were imitated from trees, but from the trunks of trees,
and not from those flexible branches to which the Gothic columns
are compared and which at the most are suitable for sustaining garden
arbours or pavilions. If Gothic columns are too flimsy, then Romanesque piers are too coarse; true proportion is only to be found with the
ancients. He ends: 'Thus Gothic buildings would be little regarded
today, were it not for the size of some of these structures and for a
certain happy choice of general proportions which is to be met with
in some churches, though even then the choice seems arbitrary and the
proportions are rarely sufficiently correct'.[2]

---

[1] *Dissertation*, pp. 172–3.
[2] Ibid. pp. 188–9.

Up to the middle of the eighteenth century most French writers, when they came to deal with medieval buildings, simply borrowed, without acknowledgement, from Félibien des Avaux.[1] Thence his remarks on Gothic made their way into German works on architecture, and so indirectly affected the German attitude towards the style. A good example of this is the German version (1751) of Chomel's popular *Dictionnaire œconomique*, where the article on Gothic is compounded from a mixture of Jablonski and Félibien.

Another passage which had considerable resonance in Germany owing to the fame of the author is to be found in Fénelon's *Lettre sur l'éloquence* (1716). Fénelon is comparing the elegance and ingenuity of modern writers unfavourably with the ancients, 'qui n'ont que la simple nature'. To underline his meaning he takes an analogy from architecture, contrasting the simplicity and propriety of Greek architecture with the over-ornamentation and impropriety of Gothic:

The inventors of the architecture called Gothic, which is, they say, of Arabic origin, believed no doubt that they had surpassed the Greeks. A Greek edifice has nothing about it which is purely decorative. The parts necessary to support or protect it, such as the columns and cornice, derive their beauty solely from their proportions: all is simple, restrained, confined to its function. Neither audacity nor caprice impose upon the sight. The proportions are so perfect that, however great the scale, nothing appears too large. Everything is designed to satisfy true Reason.

The Gothic architect, on the other hand, raises on very slender pillars an immense vault which reaches to the clouds. One would expect the whole structure to collapse, but in fact it lasts for centuries. It abounds in windows and pinnacles, and the stone looks as though it had been cut out of cardboard; everything is perforated and as if hanging in air.[2]

This passage was reproduced by the author of the article 'Gothique' in Diderot's *Encyclopédie* and so obtained the widest possible currency. It penetrated into Germany through the agency of Jakob von Egger's *Neues Kriegslexicon* (1757). Eggers incorporates the passage in his article on Gothic, but distorts its import by suggesting that Fénelon is an apologist for the style.

The main points of Fénelon's remarks are echoed and re-echoed by writers on architecture throughout the century. Again and again we hear of the extravagant boldness of the Gothic builders, which led them to undertake feats of breath-taking architectural gymnastics;

---

[1] Cp. Lanson, op. cit. p. 33.

[2] *Dialogues sur l'éloquence*, to which is appended the *Lettre sur l'éloquence* (Paris, 1718), pp. 416–17.

of the apparent instability, but actual durability of the buildings; of
the excess of fussy and over-refined decoration.

Only through a misunderstanding could Fénelon be considered
an apologist for Gothic architecture, but there are other utterances
on the subject, from the middle years of the century, which show a
surprising degree of feeling for the style.[1] The most notable instance
of the open-mindedness of the French towards medieval architecture
at a time when the rest of Europe was still more or less ignorant and
contemptuous of the matter is the case of Jacques-Germain Soufflot
(1713–80), the architect of the Panthéon. For the central ambition of
Soufflot's life was to produce an architecture which should combine the
good qualities of the classical and medieval modes, which, as one of
his pupils put it, 'should unite the lightness of construction of the Gothic
buildings with the purity and magnificence of Greek architecture'.[2]

To this end Soufflot made a prolonged and thorough study of
the monuments of Gothic architecture both at home and in Italy.
On 12 April 1741, as a young man of twenty-eight, he read a paper
embodying the results of his investigations to the Académie des
Beaux-Arts in Lyons. One may safely assert that this paper is the
first serious study of Gothic architecture which had appeared in
Europe. It is all the more impressive because of its sober and judicious
tone. Soufflot is careful not to claim too much. He admits that Gothic
decoration is frequently bizarre and tasteless, and that the comparatively simple façades of churches built in the classical style are superior
to the Gothic. The pointed arch is stronger than, but not so graceful
as, the classical. The excessive height of Gothic churches in relation to
their width makes them appear larger than they are, whereas the just
proportions of Renaissance churches produce the opposite effect.
'In the former a closer investigation destroys one's pleasure, whereas in
the latter it increases it.'[3]

Nevertheless Soufflot's considered opinion is that there is much
which the modern architect can learn from the Goths, especially in
their methods of construction, which are 'more ingenious, bolder
and more difficult than ours',[4] and which produce an admirable
combination of lightness and firmness. Moreover in the planning
of our churches we have followed the Goths without acknowledg-
ment: 'It is from these churches, built long before the renaissance of
ancient architecture, that we have taken the idea of our own; in doing

[1] For fuller details cp. Herrmann, op. cit.
[2] Cp. J. Monval, *Soufflot* (Paris, 1918), p. 423.
[3] Ibid. p. 430.   [4] Ibid. p. 428.

so we have shown approval for the work of those very people whom we treat as crude and barbarous; we have indeed imitated them at all points. We should then regard them as our masters in this respect, and despite the contempt in which we hold them, we cannot refuse them this pre-eminence . . . in this they are creators, for they cannot be taxed with having themselves imitated the temples of the ancients.'[1]

The importance of Soufflot's paper is that he was the first writer on medieval architecture to take Gothic seriously, to recognize the originality of the Gothic builders, and to realize how much the modern architect could learn from them. Unlike the Rococo Gothicists he is concerned with essentials—construction and planning—and not with trivialities of detail. And this despite the fact that he is no Gothic enthusiast, but a convinced supporter of the classical tradition and its ideals of simplicity, regularity, and propriety.

The same can be said of the Abbé Laugier,[2] whose *Essai sur l'architecture* appeared in 1753, twelve years after Soufflot had read his *Mémoire sur l'architecture gothique* to the academy at Lyons. Marc-Antoine Laugier (1713-69) was, it is worth noting, a Jesuit, and, after retiring from active clerical life, a diplomat and man of letters. He was thus an amateur, where Soufflot had been a professional, but the conclusions he reached on the subject of Gothic architecture were essentially the same as his. He is as firmly anchored in the classical tradition as the creator of the Panthéon, but like him he recognizes the merits of Gothic and the lessons that can be learnt from it. He too envisages a type of ecclesiastical architecture which shall combine the lightness of Gothic with the purity and magnificence of the classical style.

Nevertheless his remarks on Gothic are highly ambivalent. On the one hand he writes of the new system of architecture introduced by the barbarians, 'where the false proportions and masses of bizarre ornaments have nothing to offer but fretwork stones and what is misshapen, grotesque, and excessive. Too long this modern architecture constituted the delight of all Europe. Unfortunately the majority of our great churches are destined to preserve its traces to remotest posterity.'

Having thus made his bow to neo-classical orthodoxy, Laugier proceeds: 'But let us be frank; with its numberless defects this architecture has its beauties. Although there prevails in its most magnificent productions an altogether shocking heaviness of spirit and grossness

<hr>

[1] Ibid. p. 427.
[2] For a full account of Laugier's life and work see W. Herrmann, op. cit.

of sentiment, one cannot help admiring the boldness of the outlines, the delicacy of the carving, the air of majesty and spaciousness to be found in certain examples of the style.'[1]

It is clear from the tone of these remarks that the Abbé—like most writers of the seventeenth and eighteenth centuries—has failed to distinguish between Romanesque and Gothic. Otherwise it is hard to understand how one and the same style can be both heavy and gross and delicate and finicky at one and the same time.

But Laugier makes full amends for these contradictions by the remarks on Gothic in the fourth chapter of his book, which deals specifically with ecclesiastical architecture. Like Soufflot, he is far from satisfied with the neo-classical churches of his time, such as Saint-Sulpice or Saint-Roch, with their heaviness and lack of true delicacy and majesty. The truth is, he says, that a really satisfactory style of ecclesiastical architecture has not yet been evolved, but the best that we have is the Gothic: 'Despite the mass of grotesque ornaments by which our Gothic churches are disfigured, they convey an inexplicable impression of grandeur and majesty. They exhibit both ease and delicacy; it is only simplicity and naturalness which is lacking.'[2]

Laugier then goes on to describe the effect produced on him by the interior of Notre-Dame: 'At the first glance my eyes are arrested and my imagination is struck by the length, height, and spaciousness of this vast nave; I am forced to yield for some moments to the surprise excited in me by the majesty of the whole. If, having recovered from this first admiration, I turn to the details, I find innumerable absurdities, for which however I blame the spirit of the age. With the result that having carped and cavilled to my heart's content I return to the middle of the nave and am still filled with an admiration which moves me to exclaim: Voilà bien des défauts, mais voilà qui est grand!'[3]

Above all it was in the construction of towers that the Gothic architects excelled, and in this genre the tower of Strasbourg Minster has no equal. 'This superb pyramid is a masterpiece which enchants one by virtue of its prodigious height, its exquisite tapering, its pleasing form, by the accuracy of its proportions and the singular delicacy of its workmanship. I do not believe that any architect has ever produced anything so boldly conceived, so happily thought out, or so satisfactorily executed.'[4]

Laugier followed up his *Essai sur l'architecture* twelve years later with a sequel entitled *Observations sur l'architecture* (The Hague, 1765).

[1] Laugier, *Essai sur l'architecture*, pp. 4–5.
[2] Ibid. p. 200.   [3] Ibid. pp. 201–2.   [4] Ibid. p. 233.

PLATE 2

Gothisches Haus in Wörlitz

PLATE 3

St. Nikolaikirche in Leipzig

Most of the book is concerned with a somewhat technical discussion of classical proportions and orders, but the third section, *De la difficulté de décorer les églises gothiques*, amplifies in several respects what Laugier had to say on the subject of Gothic architecture in his *Essai*, and shows if anything an even warmer appreciation of the style.

Laugier's main principle in the decoration of Gothic churches is that there should be no mixing of styles. 'If you want to reconstruct the façade of a Gothic church, it is absolutely essential to reconstruct it gothically (gothiquement).'[1] The habit of affixing classical fronts to Gothic churches, as at Saint-Gervais, is to be deplored. The decoration should be adapted to the spirit of the particular type of architecture you are dealing with. As far as Gothic churches are concerned, this means primarily the removal of all superfluous ornament, so that their purely architectural qualities shall be revealed to full advantage:

> Place yourself beneath the crossing of one of our beautiful Gothic churches, such as the cathedral of Amiens, Rheims, or Paris. Remove in imagination everything which blocks the view. What do we see? A charming disposition, where the eye wanders deliciously across several rows of columns to the side chapels, whose stained glass windows diffuse the light profusely but unevenly; a polygonal apse, where these features are multiplied and diversified still more; a blending, a sense of movement, a riot of apertures and wall-space, which play and contrast, and of which the total effect is ravishing.[2]

This must surely be the most eloquent and discerning account of a Gothic interior to be found before Georg Forster's description of Cologne Cathedral some twenty-five years later. Altogether Laugier, despite his neo-classical reservations, shows more feeling for the aesthetic qualities of Gothic architecture than any writer of his day. His criticisms, it will be found, relate almost entirely to details, and not to the architecture as such. Characteristically, it is the subject of Gothic vaulting that calls forth his most unstinted tribute to the genius of the medieval builders: 'It is here that Gothic architecture displays its most brilliant powers. The vaults, bold, light, with their singular decoration, are astonishing in their effect ... one must agree that if we have surpassed our ancestors in many other things, we are still far behind them in the art of vaulting.'[3]

Laugier shares the views of Félibien on the 'natural' origin of the style. He compares the uninterruptedly perpendicular effect of the pillared interior of a Gothic church, of which he highly approves,

[1] *Observations sur l'architecture*, p. 149.
[2] Ibid. p. 130.   [3] Ibid. pp. 283-4.

to the *grande allée* of the Tuileries gardens, and assumes that this is no chance resemblance, but represents a deliberate attempt on the part of the Gothic builders to imitate nature. He goes so far as to suggest that the modern French architects might well follow the Goths in the interior of their churches, leaving the Greek orders for the exterior.

Laugier is of significance for our purpose owing to the esteem in which his works on architecture were held in Germany. A translation of the *Essai* appeared in 1756, and another in 1758. The *Observations* likewise appeared in two translations, the first by the Dresden architect, F. A. Krubsacius, in 1768, and the second by J. J. Volkmann in 1771. The number of translations within so short a period of the publication of the original is sufficient evidence of the popularity of Laugier's works. If you had some interest in architecture and wished to acquaint yourself with the latest views on the subject from the cultural centre of Europe, then you read Laugier. Among those who did so was Goethe's father, who possessed both the *Essai* in translation and the *Observations* in the original.[1] This, as we shall see, was not without consequences for the development of the Gothic Revival in Germany.

But Laugier's writings and the relatively enlightened attitude of some French academic and architectural circles towards medieval architecture were to have a more direct effect upon German practising architects in the latter half of the eighteenth century. At the time of which we are speaking, the middle years of the century, Paris was still regarded as the architectural centre of the world, and the more enterprising young German architects went there to study. Among these was the Dresden architect Christian Traugott Weinlig (1739–99), who worked under Le Roy and the younger Blondel and who must certainly have come in contact with Laugier's writings.[2] He went to Paris in 1766, one year after the publication of Laugier's *Observations*. From there he proceeded to Rome, where he stayed nearly three years and from where he wrote a series of letters on architectural matters, which he afterwards published under the title *Briefe über Rom* (3 vols. Dresden, 1782–7). Weinlig's most admired master was Palladio, but in one of his letters (dated 28 January 1769) he gives what he calls 'a quasi-apology for Gothic architecture in Rome', which betrays clearly enough the influence of Laugier.

Laugier had understood that it was no use trying to measure Gothic

[1] Cp. Ernst Beutler, *Von Deutscher Baukunst* (*Reihe der Vorträge und Schriften des Freien Deutschen Hochstifts*, iv. 31).

[2] For Weinlig see Paul Klopfer, *Christian Traugott Weinlig und die Anfänge des Klassizismus in Sachsen* (*Dresdner Baumeister. Beiträge zur Bauwissenschaft*, ed. C. Gurlitt, Vol. v) Berlin, 1905.

architecture with a classical yardstick and that the Gothic style was based on principles which were entirely different from those of classical architecture. Weinlig takes up and amplifies this point: 'The Gothic rules of proportion and beauty rested on totally different principles from those of the Greeks, but to judge from the great and sublime effect which many Gothic churches produce, their principles of architectural beauty were not so badly conceived . . . Taken by and large the Gothic system was certainly very well thought out, and allowed the architect enough liberty to give his work interest and movement, which in modern buildings are not infrequently completely lacking.'[1] Weinlig's attitude to Gothic is even more positive than Laugier's. 'The Gothic masters understood the laws of gravity and stability in the highest degree. Bramante tried to emulate them without knowing these rules; had he known them he would have been one of the greatest of architects.'[2] He protests against the tendency to equate 'Gothic' with 'tasteless', and disapproves the contempt with which many modern architects cloak their ignorance of the style. He for his part would feel very chary of submitting a great many modern buildings to the critical judgement of the Gothic masters. 'Would they not with justice find reprehensible our ungainly piers and arches, which we sometimes embellish with partly embedded columns, and would they not find inexplicable and irresponsible the extravagant waste of building material in our churches? Would they not indeed come to the conclusion that our architects are not very experienced in the practical side of their art and necessarily deviate into absurdity through sheer ignorance . . . How often has the heretical thought occurred to me that the Goths produced great effects with moderate resources, whereas we moderns produce very meagre effects with abundant resources.'[3]

Weinlig laments the lack of a Gothic Vitruvius, who would have provided us with information which can now be obtained only by the study and comparison of the many still extant Gothic buildings. 'But in view of the rooted prejudice on the subject, where is one to find an architect who would dare to risk his reputation and his fortune by a study of this sort?'[4]

Weinlig's Roman letter is the most outspoken plea for a more serious attitude towards Gothic architecture—and incidentally for a history of the subject—which had yet appeared in Germany. But his advocacy remained purely theoretical; his own architectural practice was strictly classical. There were contemporaries of his, however, who were

Briefe über Rom, iii. 78–9. [2] Loc. cit. [3] Loc. cit. [4] Loc. cit.

influenced by Laugier and the school of Paris actually to employ Gothic forms in their work. Such a one was Franz Ignaz Neumann, son of the great baroque master Balthasar Neumann, who built the central tower of Mainz Cathedral in 1767 in what has been called a *Louis seize* Gothic, with late Gothic windows, but with balustrades and pyramidal finials in neo-classic style.[1]

The most direct instance of Laugier's influence on German architectural practice is to be seen in Johann Friedrich Carl Dauthe's adaptation of the Nikolaikirche in Leipzig. This was begun in 1784, and follows closely Laugier's recommendations for the renovation of Gothic churches in his *Observations*. First, Laugier advises, remove all obstacles which block the view. Then try if possible to round off the pillars, so making them more like classical columns; you can then cover them with marble or else flute the stone, and give them more correct bases and capitals. Similarly you can substitute mouldings in good taste for those in a barbarous taste, and apply mosaics or other decorations to the pendentives of the vaults. He also envisages the interior of a church in which the columns take the form of palm trees with spreading branches to support the vaults. Now this is exactly what Dauthe has done in the Nikolaikirche. He has transformed the original Late Gothic pillars into fluted columns, from whose capitals spring palm branches, which in their turn support a Gothic vault with classical coffering.

Laugier would no doubt have approved strongly of Dauthe's creation, and indeed from any point of view it is a striking architectural interior. But it was not from this source that the serious revival of interest in medieval architecture was to come. Although their contribution to the early stages of the Gothic Revival in Germany is more acceptable than that of the Rococo Gothicists, Neumann, Dauthe, and their like were strict classicists at heart, as were their French masters. There was no conviction behind their Gothic experiments. To bring about the revolution of taste which is the subject of this book, passion and enthusiasm were necessary, and these were supplied in full measure through the literary movement of the *Sturm und Drang*, to which we must now turn.

[1] Cp. Hermann Schmitz, *Die Gotik im deutschen Kunst- und Geistesleben* (Berlin, 1921), p. 178.

PART TWO

STURM UND DRANG

STURM UND DRANG

1. HERDER

Up to the early seventies the Gothic Revival had followed roughly the same course in Germany as in England. Its main manifestations in both countries were Rococo Gothic on the one hand and the Gothic Mood in poetry on the other. Common to these various expressions of Gothicism was what one can only call their triviality. Gothic was either something whimsical and entertaining or else something deliciously melancholy.

But now with the seventies a new element of seriousness enters in, which totally revolutionized the German attitude towards medieval architecture. And this new element was intimately bound up with the movement known to historians of German literature as the *Sturm und Drang*. It is the *Sturm und Drang* which most notably differentiates the course of German literature from that of English in the second half of the eighteenth century, and it is the close connection between the *Sturm und Drang* and the new attitude to Gothic architecture which primarily accounts for the differing course taken by the Gothic Revival in Germany and England in this period.

The *Sturm und Drang* is no exception to the rule that all the main literary or intellectual movements of eighteenth-century Germany owe their primary inspiration to England. But whereas the *Aufklärung* and the *Empfindsamkeit* are simply the German counterparts of the Enlightenment and the Sentimental Movement, the *Sturm und Drang* has no equivalent in English literature. What it did was to take up certain ideas which had been adumbrated by various English writers in the first half of the century, and to pursue them with ruthless consequence to their logical conclusion.

These ideas were concerned above all with the nature of the original genius and the nature of inspiration. In his *Soliloquy or Advice to an Author* (1710) Anthony Ashley Cooper, third Earl of Shaftesbury, had written:

> I must confess there is hardly any where to be found a more insipid Race of Mortals, than those who we Moderns are contented to call *Poets*, for having attain'd the chiming Faculty of a Language, with an injudicious random use of Wit and Fancy. But for the Man, who truly and in a just sense deserves the Name of *Poet*, and who as a real Master, or Architect in the kind, can describe both *Men* and *Manners*, and give to an *Action* its just Body and

Proportions; he will be found, if I mistake not, a very different Creature. Such a *Poet* is indeed a second *Maker:* a just PROMETHEUS, under JOVE. Like that Sovereign Artist or universal Plastick Nature, he forms *a Whole,* coherent and proportion'd in it-self, with due Subjection and Subordinacy of constituent Parts.[1]

Now there were two points in particular about this passage which appealed to German writers in the second half of the eighteenth century, and especially to the writers of the *Sturm und Drang:* first, the comparison between the poet and the Promethean Creator;[2] and secondly, the idea that the work of art partakes of the character of nature herself, in so far as it, like nature, forms an organic self-sufficient whole. These ideas, as we shall see, informed much of the thinking of the young Herder and the young Goethe. Sulzer, incidentally, included the entire passage in his *Allgemeine Theorie der schönen Künste* (article 'Dichter'), thus ensuring for it the widest currency.

A further reinforcement, if slightly different emphasis, was given to Shaftesbury's concept of the poet as godlike creator by Edward Young's *Conjectures on Original Composition* (1759). The aim of this essay is to exalt originality over imitation, the original genius over the learned imitator. Young never defines very clearly what he means by genius, beyond the fact that it is divinely inspired. 'Learning we thank, genius we revere . . . this inspires, and is itself inspired; for genius is from heaven, learning from man.'[3] It is mysterious in its workings and may be compared to a magician who 'raises his structure by means invisible'.[4] Genius is spontaneous: 'An *Original* . . . rises spontaneously from the vital root of genius; it *grows,* it is not *made*'.[5] Genius, like conscience is the 'god within.'[6]

The great exemplar of such a genius—and this was the main significance of Young's essay for the *Sturm und Drang*—is of course Shakespeare, who is the brother, not the son, of the ancients,—'that giant, that much more than common man, at which we now gaze with amazement, and delight'.[7] And this, despite his lack of learning, for he was master of the two books that matter: the book of nature and the book of man. To the genius rules and learning are unnecessary obstacles. 'Who knows whether Shakespeare might not have thought less, if he had read more?'[8] 'Rules, like crutches, are a needful aid

---

[1] *Characteristicks of Men, Manners, Opinions, Times,* 3 vols. (London, 1711), I. 207.
[2] Cp. Oskar Walzel, *Das Prometheussymbol von Shaftesbury zu Goethe,* 2nd ed. (Munich, 1932).
[3] Young, *Conjectures on Original Composition,* ed. E. J. Morley (Manchester, 1918), p. 17.
[4] Ibid. p. 13.   [5] Ibid. p. 7.   [6] Ibid. p. 15.   [7] Ibid. pp. 35–36.   [8] Ibid. p. 35.

to the lame, tho' an impediment to the strong.'[1] Though Shaftesbury's Prometheus symbol occurs in the course of the essay, the stress is on the divine inspiration of the poet rather than on the more active concept of the poet as creator—*Originalgenie* rather than *Schöpfergenie*. Both concepts were to play a large part in the *Sturm und Drang*. The contrast between the reception of Young's essay in England and in Germany is extraordinary. In its own country it evoked little interest, and to this day it is comparatively neglected by English scholars. In Germany, on the other hand, it was greeted with enthusiasm and had a profound and lasting influence. Two reasons for this immediately suggest themselves: first, Young's ideas would certainly appear less original to English readers than to German, for he had many forerunners in his own land in this particular aspect of the battle of the ancients and moderns;[2] and secondly, the Germans are notoriously more susceptible to general ideas than the English.

The first German writer to be influenced by the ideas of the creative and original genius, as promulgated by Shaftesbury and Young respectively, was Johann Georg Hamann. It is true that Hamann was much too original a genius himself to have needed any help from outside sources in the evolution of such a concept. But he was well acquainted with Shaftesbury's works, and the Englishman's formulations on the subject of genius must have been highly congenial to his bent of mind.

Already a year before Young published his *Conjectures* Hamann had given expression in his *Biblische Betrachtungen* to the concept of the Holy Ghost as the author of the Bible and the divine prototype of the creative genius. In his next important work, the *Sokratische Denkwürdigkeiten* (1759) he develops and so to speak secularizes his concept of genius. In words very reminiscent of Young he writes: 'What makes up for Homer's ignorance of the rules which Aristotle contrived from his example, and what Shakespeare's ignorance or neglect of those critical precepts? "Genius" is the unanimous reply.'[3] Hamann, like Young, believes in the divine afflatus of genius. Original works of art are like nature herself, emanations of the divine spirit. The prerequisites of genius are originality, passion and enthusiasm: 'Passion alone gives hands, feet and wings to abstractions and hypotheses; gives spirit, life and voice to images and symbols.'[4] Hamann was the most formidable opponent the *Aufklärung* had yet

[1] Ibid. p. 14. [2] Ibid. pp. xii–xvi.
[3] J. G. Hamann, *Sämtliche Werke*, ed. J. Nadler, 6 vols. (Vienna, 1949–57), ii. 75.
[4] *Kreuzzüge des Philologen*, ibid., ii. 208.

encountered. In his advocacy of passion versus reason, of imagination versus the rules, of original genius versus imitation, he struck at the roots of the Enlightenment. But for us he is of importance, not so much for what he wrote himself, as for the impact he made on Herder and the young Goethe and on the whole development of the *Sturm und Drang*.

It was Herder above all others who spread abroad Hamann's gospel of the original genius and the artist as creator. Both Shaftesbury and Young were favourite authors from Herder's early years. He was already a student of Shaftesbury while he was listening to Kant's lectures in Koenigsberg.[1] Early in his writings there appears the concept of the creative genius, of the poet as a semi-divine being who can body forth the creatures of his imagination like a god, a 'second Prometheus' in fact.[2] Creative power, creative genius, the poet as creator—such phrases recur again and again in Herder's early writings.[3] Conversely, God himself is seen as the supreme genius and the supreme artist.[4]

From an early age, too, Herder was acquainted with Young's *Conjectures*. He copied excerpts from them into his oldest notebook, and in a review in the *Königsberger Gelehrten und Politischen Zeitungen* in 1766 dealing with the problem of imitation he quotes and defends Young's views.[5] The *Fragmente* (1767), especially the second and third, abound in echoes, sometimes verbal, of the *Conjectures*.[6]

To Herder, as to Young, the great exemplar of the original genius was Shakespeare, and it is in his Shakespeare essay (1773) that he has given expression most eloquently and most unequivocally to his views on the subject. Shakespeare for him was above all the poet of nature, whose works were virtually a part of nature: 'Single leaves, wafted by the storm of the ages, from the book of circumstance, of Providence, of the world!' 'Approach his stage,' he cries, 'as a sea of events where wave succeeds wave. The scenes of nature ebb and flow; interweave, however disparate they seem; appear and disappear, in order that the aim of their creator, who would seem to have combined them all in an ecstatically disordered scheme, should be fulfilled—to draw by means of such symbols the outline of God's plan.'[7]

---

[1] Cp. R. Haym, *Herder nach seinem Leben und seinen Werken*, 2 vols. (Berlin, 1877–85), i. 37.

[2] Walzel, op. cit. pp. 26–29.

[3] e.g. *Fragmente* (i. 256); *Kritische Wälder* (iii, 103). All references are to Herder's *Sämmtliche Werke*, ed. B. Suphan, 33 vols. (Berlin, 1877–1913).

[4] *Älteste Urkunde des Menschengeschlechts* (vi. 321 f.).

[5] i. 121–3.   [6] Cp. Haym, op. cit. i. 150.   [7] v. 219–20.

Shakespeare is the creative genius *par excellence*, himself part of the divine process of creation. Herder exalts him almost into a god, referring to him in such phrases as 'mortal endowed with divine power', 'happy son of the gods' and 'dramatic God'. Despite the teeming profusion and variety of his stage, it, like nature herself, is inspired by a fundamental organic unity, a unity which gives a characteristic and unique colour and atmosphere to each of his so disparate dramas. 'In this', exclaims Herder, echoing Young's words, 'Shakespeare is Sophocles' brother'.[1]

This exaltation of Shakespeare, which was characteristic not only of Herder, but of the *Sturm und Drang* generally, was not without its significance for the Gothic Revival. For from the point of view of the eighteenth century Shakespeare and Gothic architecture had many points in common. They had indeed the same merits and the same defects. It was Pope in the Preface to his edition of Shakespeare (1725) who first gave clear expression to this analogy:

I will conclude by saying of *Shakespear*, that with all his faults, and with all the irregularity of his *Drama*, one may look upon his works, in comparison of those that are more finish'd and regular, as upon an ancient majestick piece of *Gothick* Architecture, compar'd with a neat Modern building: The latter is more elegant and glaring, but the former is more strong and more solemn. It must be allow'd, that in one of these there are materials enough to make many of the other. It has much the greater variety, and much the nobler apartments; tho' we are often conducted to them by dark, odd, and uncouth passages. Nor does the Whole fail to strike us with greater reverence, tho' many of the parts are childish, ill-plac'd, and unequal to its grandeur.[2]

Now if the qualities of irregularity, variety, and a certain wildness were to be condoned in Shakespeare for the sake of his more sublime qualities, then it was only logical that the same considerations should apply to Gothic. And indeed it was not for long a question of condoning. As we have seen in the sphere of landscape gardening, the qualities which had most offended neo-classical taste had come to be regarded as positive virtues. And so with Shakespeare. His greatness was now felt to be dependent upon those factors for which his classical critics had felt bound to apologize. It was precisely his lawlessness, his defiance of the rules, his lack of scholarship, his contempt for the niceties of classical balance and proportion that opened the way for the splendours of his original and creative genius. Herder had now

[1] v. 225.
[2] Quoted from *Eighteenth Century Essays on Shakespeare*, ed. D. Nichol Smith (Glasgow, 1903), p. 62.

completed the process by his vision of Shakespeare as the divine Maker endowed with the superabundant energy, the wild profusion, the infinite variety and sublime majesty of Nature herself—the very qualities, be it noted, which Goethe was to admire in Strasbourg Minster.

The analogy between Shakespeare and Gothic in the eyes of the *Sturm und Drang* was exact. The same contempt for the classical rules, the same creative energy, the same original genius had produced the Gothic cathedrals and the masterpieces of Shakespeare. The properties of sublimity, variety, organic unity were common to both. It was the appreciation of these qualities which was to transform the taste for medieval architecture from a trivial titillation for jaded palates into a serious preoccupation with one of the noblest manifestations of the human spirit.

Herder's concept of the original genius was closely related to another favourite subject of his, the folk-song. For in his view the folk-song was the product of the original genius of the folk, before it had been corrupted by civilization and artificiality. Such a view is already hinted at in the passage from Shaftesbury quoted above; but it was not Shaftesbury, but the native folk-songs of his own Baltic provinces that had first turned Herder's attention to popular poetry, and this interest was to remain with him throughout his life. What drew Herder so strongly to the folk-song and to all forms of what he considered to be popular poetry was the belief, imparted by Hamann, that "poetry is the mother tongue of the human race", and that therefore the more primitive the people, the more genuine its poetry will be. The qualities Herder looked for in popular or folk poetry were lyricism, vivid imagery, bold transitions and juxtapositions (Sprünge und Würfe, as he calls them), passion and spontaneity, and above all energy (Kraft). It is these qualities that give folk poetry that genuine 'ærugo' or patina which distinguishes it from the polished artificialities and insipidities of 'modern' verse.

With these views on Shakespeare and the folk-song one would naturally expect Herder to have been an enthusiastic admirer of Gothic architecture. After all it is pre-eminent in those very qualities of creative energy, imaginative boldness, genuine 'ærugo', which he admired so much in the literary sphere. It would be difficult indeed to find an art which was in his sense of the words more primitive and popular and at the same time less vitiated by artificiality and polish. But no. Taken by and large Herder seems to have had a blind spot for medieval architecture. It is as though in this instance he failed to apply the key provided by his own insight into the nature of original genius and of popular art.

Part of the reason for this no doubt is the fact that Herder was not very interested in architecture of any kind. In all his æsthetic writings he only deals with it in detail in one passage—in the posthumously published fourth *Kritisches Wäldchen*, where he tries to establish a kind of hierarchy of the arts. In this hierarchy architecture is allotted the lowest place. It is only an 'embellished mechanical art' and 'a foster child of the other arts'. Nevertheless its qualities of stability and simplicity render it a good starting point for the amateur of beauty: 'Its sublime dignity, its exact regularity, its noble proportions should be a kind of plastic logic and mathematics upon his further journey.'[1] He imagines his adopted neophyte standing before his chosen building, drinking in his first impression of size, strength and sublimity and pondering on the 'simplicity, nobility of proportions, symmetry and propriety' revealed before him. But despite these qualities architecture is only the antechamber, so to speak, to the nobler art of sculpture. For architecture is purely abstract, a matter of 'lines, surfaces and masses', and as such stands 'outside the portals of true art', whereas sculpture is Nature, Truth and Beauty.

For us the significant points about this passage are, first, that architecture is the lowest rung on the ladder of the arts, which ascends through sculpture, painting, music to the apotheosis of poetry; and secondly, that for Herder at this time (1769) architecture meant classical architecture pure and simple. The qualities he adduces as characteristic of the art are precisely those of Winckelmann's neoclassic ideal of Noble Simplicity and Serene Greatness. Such predilections left little room for the appreciation of Gothic architecture. That this was indeed Herder's attitude can be amply borne out by a vast number of pejorative references to Gothic throughout his works, mainly in the form of metaphorical comparisons.[2]

But Herder's attitude to Gothic was not entirely negative. From certain passages it is evident that he was sensitive to an air of sublimity which at times he associated with Gothic architecture. The most unequivocal references in this respect occur early in his literary career. In his first major published work, the *Fragmente über die neuere*

---

[1] iv. 124.
[2] A large number of these have been conveniently collected in an article by G. Lüdtke, 'Gothisch im 18. und 19. Jahrhundert'. *Zeitschrift für Deutsche Wortforschung*, iv. 133 ff. (Strasbourg, 1903).

deutsche Litteratur (1767) he regrets that the German language, though now a refined and polished instrument, is no longer 'the sublime Gothic edifice which it was in Luther's day'.[1] And in a well-known passage from his posthumously published *Journal meiner Reise im Jahre 1769* Herder describes how his first impressions of things always take on 'a Gothic greatness' and produce in him a thrill of sublimity: 'A feeling for the Sublime is, then, the natural bent of my mind . . . my life is a walk through Gothic arches . . . the prospect is always venerable and sublime.'[2]

The truth is that Herder's attitude to Gothic was ambivalent. On the one hand, Gothic could on occasion be sublime; on the other hand, it could be exactly the opposite. A good example of this double attitude is to be found in his *Auch eine Philosophie der Geschichte zur Bildung der Menschheit* (1774), where he describes the ecclesiastical system of the Middle Ages as a 'monstrous Gothic edifice! overladen, ponderous, gloomy, tasteless—the earth seems to sink under it— but how great! rich! well-contrived! powerful!'[3]

It must be said, however, that though there is certainly an element of ambivalence in Herder's attitude to Gothic, the negative references far outweigh the positive. The grounds of Herder's objections to the style are the familiar neo-classical ones: Gothic is barbarous;[4] taste-less;[5] overladen;[6] gloomy;[7] grotesque;[8] monstrous.[9]

It is also petty and trivial. In one of the *paralipomena* to the *Journal meiner Reise*, describing his disillusionment with the Paris opera, dated 2 December 1769, he writes of contemporary music: 'The time will come when our music will appear like our Gothic archi-tecture, ingenious in detail, but nothing when taken as a whole— nothing simple, human, or impressive about it.'[10]

It is also of course lacking in unity and harmony. This is the common burden of nearly all eighteenth-century criticism of Gothic, and Herder is no exception. He expresses himself particularly clearly on this point in the postscript to his essay on *Ossian und die Lieder alter Völker*, where he is discussing the unsatisfactory nature of most modern texts for musical setting, and exclaims: "What Gothic structures! How the

---

[1] i. 376. [2] iv. 438–9. [3] v. 522.
[4] e.g. iii. 299, 400, 401; v. 546; vi. 85.
[5] e.g. iii. 399, 413; iv. 216; v. 245, 359, 385, 522, 528, 534; viii. 91, 101, 136.
[6] e.g. iii. 300, 401; v. 203, 522, 528–9.
[7] e.g. iv. 456; v. 360, 522, 527; vi. 93, 163, 164.
[8] e.g. iv. 456; vi. 93, 164.
[9] e.g. iii. 413; v. 360, 522.   [10] iv. 479.

masses fall apart! Where is there any harmony? any transition? . . .
Where is there any true centre?"[1]

Twenty-five years later in the *Briefe zu Beförderung der Humanität*
(8. Sammlung, *1769*) he is still saying the same thing. The modern
Pindaric ode is 'a Gothic building, vast and incoherent, exaggerated
in its images, overladen with ornament, uneven and unharmonious
in the modulation of the rhythm'.[2]

Herder sometimes uses the term Gothic simply as a synonym for
bad or ugly. At one point in his travel diary he speaks of the influence
that first impressions exercise on our development:

> Let us use our senses in order to derive ideas of truth about everything,
> and not identify ourselves at the very first impression with what is ugly and false.
> It is hard to say what admirable results might follow if our first impressions
> were of the best in their kind. Our Gothic fables and old wives' tales are very
> bad first forms: our first impressions of churches and religion are Gothic,
> gloomy and often inclined to be grotesque and empty: our first pictorial
> images are from Nuremberg woodcuts, our first taste of literature from
> Magelone and other medieval romances; who ever thinks of seeing to it
> that our first musical tones are gently harmonious and melodic? Hence it
> comes about that our souls grow old in these Gothic forms instead of being
> brought up on ideas of beauty and enjoying their early youth in beauty's
> Paradise . . . What can one expect of a youthful soul, gothically corrupted
> (*Gothisch verdorben*) in history, art, science, and religion? And what might
> one not expect from one nourished on concepts of true beauty?[3]

Here, then, 'Gothic' is contrasted directly with 'beautiful' to suggest
something ugly, clumsy, gloomy, and old-fashioned.

In other places the antithesis is between Gothic and art. In the third
Wäldchen, for instance, Herder laments the lack of a national mythology
which could be put beside that of the ancients:

> The allegorical figures and fairy tales by means of which we express
> general ideas in our childhood are Gothic, often monstrous, and virtually
> never suitable for artistic representation. They have been introduced to us,
> not by the poets of Greece, but through Nordic fairy tales . . . In the course
> of the centuries even these have disappeared, and as far as art is concerned such
> Gothic forms of the imagination have been no loss.[4]

It is noteworthy that Herder never deals directly with the subject
of medieval architecture anywhere in his early writings, not even in
Auch eine Philosophie der Geschichte. The latter omission is especially
significant. After all to give an account of medieval civilization without
any consideration of the most impressive and tangible product of that
civilization is something of a feat. But the reason is not far to seek.
Auch eine Philosophie der Geschichte is in its essence a polemic against the

[1] v. 206. [2] xviii. 104. [3] iv. 456. [4] iii. 413.

Aufklärung, but in his views on medieval architecture Herder was in fact in agreement with the *Aufklärung*. To have admitted this would have considerably weakened the force of his argument. Therefore the safest thing to do was to leave out all reference to the subject. In these early writings, then, we can only divine Herder's attitude to Gothic from his metaphorical comparisons.

A certain change in this attitude becomes evident in the—very scanty—allusions to the matter in his *Ideen zur Philosophie der Geschichte der Menschheit* (4 vols. 1784–91). This is Herder's most ambitious work, and it preoccupied him for the greater part of the decade of the eighties. The *Ideen* summed up Herder's genetic view of history: the attempt to understand all phenomena in the light of their origin and of the geographical, historical and spiritual climate out of which they grew. In his section on the Middle Ages he mentions the subject of Gothic architecture on two occasions, though even here it is introduced in illustration of a thesis, and not for its own sake. First, when he is discussing the Papacy and its virtual monopoly of the cultural life of Europe, he instances Gothic architecture as one more example of the ecclesiastical stranglehold. It is seen to be just as much a product of its physical and spiritual environment as the hierarchy or the feudal system themselves. To this he adds a note calling for a history of medieval art, and especially of the various periods of Gothic architecture.

At the end of the last book Herder returns briefly to the subject of Gothic architecture in connection with the cultural activities of the medieval cities, for which he professes high admiration:

> Gothic architecture would never have flourished as it did, if the republics and wealthy mercantile cities had not tried to rival each other in their cathedrals and town halls, just as the Greek cities once did in their statues and temples ... It is the city constitutions and the spirit of the times which explain the better sort of Gothic architecture. For as men think, so do they build ... Monasteries or baronial castles could never have given rise to the boldest and most delicate Gothic architecture; that is the proud possession of the public corporations.[1]

This theory leads Herder to the eccentric view that the finest examples of Gothic are to be found, not in ecclesiastical, but in civic architecture. Gothic thus takes its place along with other manifestations of the medieval spirit in Herder's grand survey of history, but the place it takes there is a comparatively unimportant one and betrays little appreciation of its true significance in the medieval world.

[1] xiv. 488–9.

Above all Herder, the Lutheran pastor, shows no inkling of the religious significance of Gothic, even though he is well aware of its dependence on the ecclesiastical system of the Middle Ages. To the Romantic generation Gothic was the specifically Christian style. Herder evinces no more realization than Goethe of this cardinal aspect of the matter.

Nor does Gothic have any of the national or patriotic significance for Herder that it had for Goethe and the Romantics. For them Gothic architecture *was* German architecture, and one of the supreme manifestations of the German spirit. There is no hint of this in Herder. In so far as he ventures any opinion on the question of the origins of the style—a theme which was to exercise so deadly a fascination on his successors—he subscribes to the view propounded by Wren that much of what we call Gothic taste in architecture is really of Arabic origin, mixed with Greek elements, and that it came to the rest of Europe via Spain.

Herder expresses himself most unequivocally on the subject of Gothic architecture in a *paralipomenon* to Book xix on the Papacy, where he does his best to discredit the reputation of the medieval ecclesiastical system for furthering the cause of the arts and sciences. Small indeed, he says, was the contribution made by the churches and monasteries of the Middle Ages to either. 'The monastic architecture was rarely of a beautiful kind, and the fact that after centuries the more delicate Gothic taste arose in Europe was, it is true, manifested in churches and monasteries, but this was due not to bishops and monks, but to other effective causes. *Indeed, what a good thing it would have been if this taste had never been allowed to arise.*'[1]

This revealing remark speaks volumes for Herder's attitude towards Gothic architecture. Almost up to the very end of his life this attitude remained predominantly negative. The truth is that from beginning to end his tastes in architecture remained faithful to the Winckel-mannian views expressed in the fourth *Wäldchen*. In the literary sphere, for instance, he is never tired of exhorting his fellow countrymen to seek strength and inspiration in the treasures of their own past, instead of slavishly following foreign models. Never does he suggest that they should seek similar inspiration from the achievements of German medieval architecture.

But, strange to say, Herder's predominantly negative attitude to medieval architecture is in fact only a facet of his predominantly negative attitude to the Middle Ages altogether. One of the most

[1] xiv. 541.

6

curious phenomena in German literary history is the persistence, despite all the evidence to the contrary, of the legend of Herder's medievalism.[1] Started by Haym, it has been repeated parrot-like by one critic of Herder after the other, down to the present day.[2] But it is only necessary to read the actual text of Herder's writings to discover the truth for oneself—namely, that his utterances on the Middle Ages from the beginning to the end of his career are overwhelmingly negative in character. On closer inspection indeed Herder's supposed enthusiasm for the Middle Ages turns out, as in the case of Wackenroder later, to be largely a figment of nineteenth and twentieth century criticism.

Herder's early remarks on the subject differ in no respect from those of the most orthodox *Aufklärer*. To him, in the Riga period anyway, the Middle Ages were synonymous with superstition, priestcraft, ecclesiastical tyranny. Indeed his views were precisely what one would expect from a Lutheran pastor of the period. The pages of his early writings are sprinkled with such phrases as *Gotisch-papistischer Mönchsgeschmack, mittlere Barbarische Mönchszeiten, mittlere Gotisch-Barbarische Turnierzeiten, Barbarisch-Christlicher Mönchsgeschmack, Gothisch-Papistisch-Barbarisch, mittlere Gothische Barbarn.*[3]

Herder's supposed medievalism is primarily based on the passage on the Middle Ages in his *Auch eine Philosophie der Geschichte*. In this passage Herder is concerned with the Middle Ages—to which significantly only 8 pages out of a total of 109 are devoted—as a foil for the contemporary world of the 'enlightened' eighteenth century. The main purpose of the essay is to shake the conviction of the *Aufklärung* that the Age of Enlightenment represented the peak to which all past history had been tending, and for this purpose it was useful to point out that the Middle Ages were not necessarily as totally unredeemed as the *Aufklärung* believed.

Herder's endeavour, as one would expect, is to understand the medieval period, to place it in proper perspective within the procession of the ages, to appraise its function in the sequence of time. This function, in Herder's view, was to supply dynamic movement

---

[1] Cp. my paper 'The Legend of Herder's Medievalism', *Publications of the English Goethe Society*, New Series, vol. xxxiii. (1963).

[2] Honourable exceptions to this generalization are: Max Rouché, *La philosophie de l'histoire de Herder* (*Publications de la faculté des lettres de l'Université de Strasbourg*. Fascicule 93, Paris, 1940); Heinz Stolpe, *Die Auffassung des jungen Herder vom Mittelalter* (*Beiträge zur deutschen Klassik*, vol. i. Weimar, 1955); and G. A. Wells, *Herder and After. A Study in the Development of Sociology* (*Anglica Germanica*, vol. i. The Hague, 1959).

[3] Cp. iii. 399, 400, 401; v. 546.

and vitality to a world which was in danger of stagnation. In this period Fate wound up the clock of history which had begun to run down. This was the explanation of 'the eternal migrations of peoples, of the devastations, vassal wars and feuds, of the monastic armies, pilgrimages and crusades (*which I should be the last to defend*') (my italics).[1]

The main characteristic of the Middle Ages is the profusion, often the confusion, of their teeming life. 'It is just the lack of unity, the confusion, the rich superfluity of branches and twigs that constitute their nature'.[2]

It is true that to point the contrast with the failings of his own age Herder is ready enough to see good in the Middle Ages—within limits. He acknowledges elements of nobility and courage, of chastity and simplicity of manners, of pride of craftsmanship, self-reliance, sense of honour, and love of freedom. To quote the well-known words: 'However that may be, give us in many respects your devotion and superstition, darkness and ignorance, lawlessness and coarseness of manners, and take instead our light and unbelief, our enervated reserve and refinement, our philosophic indifference and human wretchedness!'[3]

This passage is nearly always interpreted as a proof of Herder's enthusiastic love for the Middle Ages. But after all *Aberglaube, Unwissenheit, Unordnung* and *Roheit* remain superstition, ignorance, lawlessness and coarseness, even though from some points of view (in manchem Betracht) and looked at from certain angles they had certain advantages over the defects of his own 'enlightened' age.

The truth of the matter is that Herder's remarks on the Middle Ages in *Auch eine Philosophie der Geschichte* have been misunderstood, because they have been judged solely in relation to his attack on the eighteenth century and not to what he has to say about other periods and cultures. It is thus made to appear almost as if he looked back nostalgically to the Middle Ages as the golden age of German history, in the way the Romantics were to do some three decades later. Nothing could be farther from the truth. Herder's real attitude to the Middle Ages can be summed up very simply: he did not, like some of his contemporaries, deny *all* merit to the period, for it was against his inmost conviction to deny all merit to *any* civilization. It was his belief that all civilizations, if understood in their own terms, in the light of their own conditioning factors, have their positive aspects. But this does not mean that some are not more positive than others.

[1] v. 526.   [2] v. 529.   [3] v. 526–7.

And assuredly the Middle Ages, in Herder's view, was one of the least positive.

No. Not the Middle Ages, but Greece was and always remained Herder's true ideal, even in the days of his most vehement Storm and Stress. Consider the glowing ardour with which he describes the Greek phase in world history in *Auch eine Philosophie der Geschichte*, and compare it with the conditions and reservations with which his praise of the Middle Ages is hedged about:

In the history of mankind Greece will eternally remain the place where mankind has experienced its fairest youth and bridal beauty . . . noble youth with fair anointed limbs, favourite of all the Graces, beloved of all the Muses, victor in Olympia and all the other games, spirit and body together one single flower in bloom![1]

And again:

Greece, type and exemplar of all beauty, grace and simplicity! Youthful blossoming of the human race—Oh, would that it could have lasted for ever![2]

In the *Ideen* Herder's picture of the Middle Ages is painted in more sombre colours. It is no longer his purpose to contrast the virility of the Middle Ages with the senility of his own, no longer his aim to discredit the *Aufklärung*, nor to exalt German vitality at the expense of French effeteness. Indeed his attitude in the *Ideen*, in the sections relating to the Middle Ages, is for the most part indistinguishable from that of the eighteenth-century *philosophes*. Once again the Middle Ages are 'those harsh, dark barbarous ages'[3] which form an even more glaring contrast than in *Auch eine Philosophie der Geschichte* to the glory that was Greece.

There are two main targets of Herder's attack in the medieval chapters of the *Ideen*, the despotism of the Princes and the despotism of the Church. The two were of course closely connected, because the secular despotism would never have maintained its position if it had not been based on the ecclesiastical despotism of the Roman Church, which it found ready-made, so to speak, awaiting it. Among other things, the dynastic and hierarchic system of the Middle Ages stifled the craftsman's pleasure in his work and his inventive spirit, and was responsible for the evils of serfdom. An offshoot of the hierarchic system, the monastic orders, meets with Herder's sternest disapproval. In this respect at any rate he is at one with Voltaire and Gibbon. However profitable the existence of these orders to the Papal power, their influence on the arts and sciences and on the body

---

[1] v. 495.   [2] v. 498.   [3] xiv. 413.

politic was deplorable. Even the adoption of Latin as the common language of educated Europe, a creation of the monastic system, brought much more harm than good. It prevented the natural and healthy development of the vernaculars, and excluded the common people, who were ignorant of it, from all part in public life.

But Herder reserved his strongest diatribes for yet another by-product of the ecclesiastical system, the Crusades. Indeed in his attitude to this manifestation of the medieval spirit he is more severe than the *Aufklärer* themselves, who despite reservations usually attributed to the Crusades a certain civilizing role.[1] Herder pours scorn on the benefits which the Crusades are commonly supposed to have brought medieval Europe in the sphere of commerce, in the institution of chivalry, in the rise of the Templars and other religious orders, in the corporate life of the towns and the emancipation of the peasants. Still less do the arts and sciences owe anything to this source. Herder ends his account of the evil effects of the Crusades on Europe with the significant words: 'Altogether, the degree of genuine and lasting good which a movement can bring forth is exactly proportionate to the amount of Reason which inspires it.'[2]

In general, it must be admitted, Herder's account of the Middle Ages in the *Ideen* is dark indeed. 'Europe was full of enslaved serfs, and the slavery which oppressed these people was all the harder, because it was a Christian slavery, regulated by political laws and blind tradition.'[3] No help for this state of affairs could be expected from Rome. On the contrary, 'the servants of the Church had them-selves participated in the secular rule and Rome itself was based on a host of spiritual slaves . . . the arts and sciences had disappeared, for under the bones of the martyrs, the peal of bells and organs, the smoke of incense and purgatorial prayers there was no room for the Muses. With their threats and penalties the hierarchy had stifled free thought, with their oppressive yoke they had paralysed every nobler form of activity. The sufferers were promised their reward in another world; the oppressors, in return for suitable bequests, were assured of absolu-tion in the hour of their death: the kingdom of God on earth was up for sale.'[4]

Herder's picture of the Middle Ages, then, is essentially that of a Europe groaning and festering under the stranglehold of the Roman Church—the typical image, that is to say, of the *Aufklärer* and Lutheran pastor of the eighteenth century.

---

[1] Cp. Rouché, op. cit. pp. 518–9.   [2] xiv. 476.
[3] xiv. 445–6.   [4] xiv. 446.

In this sombre portrait there are nevertheless certain lighter spots. Unlike most 'enlightened' historians, Herder has words of praise for medieval scholasticism. The disputations of the schools sharpened the wits of those who took part in them, gave room for elements of doubt at a time when doubt had no other outlet, and in this respect can even be said to have paved the way for the Reformation. Then there are the cities, which, as we have seen, Herder regarded as the true repositories of what civilization there was in the medieval period. The constitutions of the city guilds and corporations, the industry and skill of the city craftsmen, these were the oases of healthy life in the desert of ecclesiastical and secular despotism. The universities, too, were bulwarks of scholarship against the surrounding barbarism.

It is worth noting that in so far as Herder does present the Middle Ages in a favourable light in the *Ideen*, he treats them as an essentially French phenomenon. This is in contrast to *Auch eine Philosophie der Geschichte*, where they are envisaged in a primarily German context. In the earlier work there is a good deal of polemic against France as the home of the *Aufklärung*. Now France is saluted as the source of medieval culture in general and of medieval literature in particular. Nowhere did the literature of chivalry and romance flourish as in France. And this is only to be expected, for in no other land did the ideals and practice of chivalry blossom so brilliantly. The poetry of the Troubadours was both anterior and superior to that of the *Minnesänger*, who were a later and harsher echo of the Provençal poets. France was the home of scholasticism, Paris the intellectual centre of Europe. 'No wonder then that the French nation has become the vainest in Europe; almost from the birth of its monarchy it has lit the way for the rest of Europe and has set the tone in the most important changes that have occurred.'[1]

As Rouché suggests,[2] this sympathetic attitude towards France in the *Ideen* may well have been influenced by Herder's initial enthusiasm for the French Revolution. (The fourth part of the *Ideen*, from which all these references are taken, dates from 1791). In any case Herder's picture of the Middle Ages as something essentially French stands in glaring contrast to the Romantic conception of the Middle Ages as the specifically German epoch of world history.

It has been necessary to dwell at some length on Herder's attitude to the Middle Ages in general, for only then does his attitude towards medieval architecture become intelligible. It is now plain that his indifference to Gothic, far from standing out in startling contrast

---

[1] xiv. 465.   [2] Op. cit. p. 520.

to his attitude to other medieval phenomena, is itself part and parcel of his indifference to the Middle Ages altogether.[1]

There is only one passage in the whole of Herder's writings which shows a truly positive attitude towards medieval architecture, and that dates from the last year of his life. It is to be found in the essays on freemasonry—the *Freimaurergespräche*—which he wrote for his journal *Adrastea*. They form part of his conspectus of the intellectual and cultural achievements of the just ended eighteenth century. On the analogy of Lessing's *Ernst und Falk*, which was also devoted to the subject of freemasonry, Herder expressed his views in the form of a series of dialogues. The first appeared in the eighth part of the *Adrastea*;[2] the remaining three were first published from the *Nachlass* in Suphan's edition.[3]

Three books especially seem to have been instrumental in moving Herder to take a more favourable view of Gothic architecture at this juncture. The first of these was—strangely enough—Wren's *Parentalia*, the account of the great architect's life written by his son, which was well known in Germany and was actually translated into German. Wren's views on Gothic architecture expressed therein are on the whole decidedly negative; but the book nevertheless provided a welcome confirmation to Herder of his growing conviction that the origins of freemasonry were to be found in the masonic guilds of the Middle Ages, and that there was a close connection between fremasonry and the architecture to which these guilds gave rise. Herder quotes the passage in the section on Salisbury Cathedral which summarizes Wren's views on the Saracenic origin of Gothic. Wren talks of 'a Fraternity of Architects . . . who stiled themselves Freemasons, and ranged from one Nation to another, as they found Churches to be built.'[4] To this Horst, one of the characters in the dialogue, adds: 'All over the North we owe to them (i.e. the freemasons) so many vast and splendid edifices, which one cannot sufficiently wonder at and admire; in short it is to the freemasons that we owe the finest Gothic architecture.'[5]

Through the mouths of his interlocutors Herder expresses amazement at these 'wondrous structures of the masonic art'. They can only be explained in terms of the *Zeitgeist*; they are the product of the mental climate of the age that gave birth to them, and it is this that

---

[1] For a fuller discussion of Herder's relation to the Middle Ages, including his attitude to medieval literature, see my paper 'The Legend of Herder's Medievalism'.

[2] In April 1803, despite the date 1802 on the title page. Cp. Haym, op. cit., ii. 788–9 n.

[3] xxiv. 441–463.

[4] *Parentalia*, compiled by Christopher Wren (London, 1750), p. 306.   [5] xxiv. 138.

gives them their unity and coherence. 'The medieval builders built as they did, because they thought as they did. In this type of architecture everything coheres from base to pinnacle; altars, sepulchral monuments, sacred vessels, pictures, windows, all are harmonious throughout.'[1]

'Only a sacred brotherhood', his friend continues, 'could have produced such variety in a spirit of such simplicity: great and small, squat and lofty, fussy in detail and yet as far as the whole is concerned sublime above human kind. One must have endured and experienced much before attaining this nobility of feeling, this distillation of pure thought.'[2]

These and similar eulogies of Gothic architecture are inspired by James Murphy's volume of engravings of the Portuguese abbey of Batalha.[3] Horst quotes from Murphy's *Introductory Discourse on the Principles of Gothic Architecture*, referring *inter alia* to a passage in which Murphy commends the dim religious light cast by the stained glass windows of Gothic buildings. To this another interlocutor replies: 'I too commend it. Apart from a sacred grove, in which every tree spreads its shade as though it were an arch and soars up to the sky like a living pyramid, I know nothing which stirs solemn emotions and produces so magic an illusion as the best of these Gothic churches. In many a cathedral I have scarce been able to tear myself away from the pleasure of strolling about and dreaming away my time under the piers and vaults and arches. Where are the ages which built in such a style? Where are they gone?'[4]

Herder here repeats his appeal for a history of Gothic architecture, preferably by an Englishman. 'Let him investigate the history of these so-called Gothic buildings, weigh up their characteristics and merits and explain the origin of this impressive achievement of the Middle Ages, of which we are no longer capable.'[5]

The third book which influenced Herder's more favourable attitude to Gothic in the *Freimaurergespräche* was Frick's splendid engravings of the Marienburg in East Prussia, partly from drawings by Friedrich Gilly.[6] 'Let us', says one of the characters in the dialogue, 'rejoice at the rough vigour, the massive industry and intelligence of medieval architecture. With joy and amazement I have studied the views of the castle of Marienburg in Prussia; no order of knights builds like this any more.'[7]

---

[1] xiv. 459-60.   [2] xxiv. 460.
[3] *Plans, Elevations, Sections and Views of the Church of Batalha . . . to which is prefixed an Introductory Discourse on the Principles of Gothic Architecture* (London, 1795).
[4] xxiv. 459.   [5] xxiv. 461.   [6] See below pp. 265-6.   [7] xxiv. 461.

Even allowing for the fact that these utterances are put into the mouths of the various interlocutors in a dramatic dialogue and are not a direct expression of Herder's opinions, allowing also for the fact that they are an integral part of his general argument on the role of freemasonry in the Middle Ages and are introduced to support this argument, they nevertheless constitute a remarkably warm tribute to the impression created by great Gothic architecture, and stand in vivid contrast to his other utterances on the subject. It is a notable fact that this change in his opinion was brought about, not by any fresh contact with actual Gothic buildings, but by the perusal of the books of engravings we have just referred to. It is clear from the *Freimaurergespräche* that he was impressed by Murphy's introductory essay and had studied it carefully. Most of what his interlocutors say on the subject of Gothic architecture in the Fourth Dialogue is in fact an amplification of Murphy's words. Finally, one should bear in mind the date at which the *Freimaurergespräche* were written. The climate of opinion in the matter of Gothic architecture had changed much within the years which separate these passages from most of those we have quoted. For by 1803 the Gothic Revival in Germany was well under way.

2. THE YOUNG GOETHE

It has been necessary to dwell at some length on Herder's attitude towards Gothic, not because his own writings played a direct part in the Gothic Revival, but because of the vexed question of his influence on Goethe's main contribution to the movement, the essay on Strasbourg Minister entitled *Von Deutscher Baukunst*.

Herder met Goethe for the first time in Strasbourg in the autumn of 1770, and stayed on in the city till the following spring in order to undergo an eye operation. In *Dichtung und Wahrheit* Goethe has described for us the hours he spent at Herder's sickbed, discussing with him every subject under the sun. Herder was then twenty-six, Goethe twenty-one; and Herder was not only the older, but very much the more experienced of the two, both in life and literature. At this time it was Herder who gave and Goethe who took. There is no doubt that Goethe's essay *Von Deutscher Baukunst* was deeply influenced by what he learnt from Herder in Strasbourg, but the nature of this influence has often been misunderstood.

Goethe's essay is incomparably the most important document which we have yet encountered in the development of the Gothic Revival in Germany. It marks a milestone in the German—and not only the German—attitude towards medieval architecture. More than any other single factor it differentiates the course of the early Gothic Revival in Germany from that in England and other countries.

It is in many respects a surprising and paradoxical piece of work. In the first place, nothing in Goethe's previous aesthetic development prepares us for this dithyramb on Strasbourg Minster and its architect. His early taste in the visual arts had been formed in the first instance by the art of the Frankfurt painters who were employed by his father to embellish the walls of the renovated house in the Grosser Hirschgraben. These artists—F. W. Hirt, J. G. Trautmann, C. G. Schütz, Justus Juncker, and others—lived in the rococo period, but they did not paint rococo pictures. Despite individual differences they have in common a faithful realism in the Dutch manner. They consciously imitated the Dutch genre masters, but they were not mere imitators, any more than were Morland or Wilkie in this country. What they give us is an essentially bourgeois art, which has deliberately turned from the artificiality of the Rococo back to nature. The qualities of these pictures are simplicity, realism and a pleasing naturalness. Their aim, like that of their Dutch models, is truth rather than beauty: the opposite ideal, one might say, of the Rococo. In these pictures, then, Goethe found incorporated in however humble a form one of the guiding principles of his aesthetic life—truth to nature.

The next important step in Goethe's aesthetic development was his friendship during his student years in Leipzig with Adam Friedrich Oeser, to whose influence he pays such emphatic tribute in his letters. Oeser was director of the Academy of Art in Leipzig, and Goethe was one of his most faithful pupils during his years at the University. Now through his influence on Winckelmann during the crucial period in which the latter was writing his *Gedanken über die Nachahmung der Griechischen Werke in der Malerei und Bildhauerkunst* Oeser may be looked upon as the fountain-head of the neo-classicist movement in eighteenth-century Germany. Both in his teachings and in his own paintings this 'sworn enemy of shells and flourishes', as Goethe calls him, represented the first serious reaction against the rococo tradition. In place of the delicate artificiality of the Rococo, Oeser established, and never tired of preaching both by precept and example, the ideal of "edle Einfalt und stille Grösse" (noble simplicity and serene greatness) which he had himself imparted to Winckelmann. It is true that this early classicism of Oeser's is a very thin and feeble affair, but it was sufficiently revolutionary in its day to exercise a compelling influence on Goethe's aesthetic development.

Goethe summed up what Oeser had meant for him in the words: 'He taught me that the ideal of beauty is simplicity and serenity' (letter to P. E. Reich of 20 February 1770). Or, as he puts it in the letter to Friederike Oeser of 13 February 1770: 'There is after all nothing true but what is simple,' and in the same letter: 'What is most intolerable in a picture is lack of truth.'

What Oeser, then, had taught Goethe was the neo-classical ideal of beauty as something resident above all in simplicity, serenity and truth to nature. Moreover Oeser, like Winckelmann, held that these qualities had found their most perfect embodiment in the works of the ancients: 'The statues and larger sculptures of the ancients remain the basis and the summit of all knowledge of art.'[1] In other words, what Oeser taught Goethe were the aesthetic tenets which were to remain the core of his philosophy of art throughout his life.

Goethe continued to expound and apply Oeser's gospel after leaving Leipzig. He writes to his old master, lamenting the aesthetic obtuseness

[1] Carl Justi, *Winckelmann und seine Zeitgenossen*, 5th ed. (Cologne, 1956), i. 405.

of his Frankfurt milieu (24 November 1768): 'However I cannot help preaching the gospel of Good Taste.' Indeed, according to *Dichtung und Wahrheit* it was Goethe's proselytzing zeal in defence of Good Taste which led to the rupture with his father and his departure for Strasbourg. He had, he explains, exasperated Johann Kaspar by his incautious criticism of the interior arrangements and decorations of the renovated house in the Grosser Hirschgraben. It is symbolic that the particular objects of Goethe's disapproval were some mirror frames and Chinese wall-papers in the rococo style.

Up to the time of his departure for Strasbourg there is no evidence that Goethe had ever manifested the slightest interest in Gothic architecture. He had plenty of opportunity of seeing it; indeed it surrounded him on every hand. Frankfurt itself was still essentially a medieval city, and its most conspicuous landmark, the Gothic cathedral, though not a supreme masterpiece, was a respectable example of the style, and as far as its Late Gothic tower is concerned, something more. At least it in no way deserved to be included in Goethe's sweeping statement that before Strasbourg he had seen only 'clumsy buildings of this kind, without either good proportions or consistent design.'[1] And the cathedral is only the most conspicuous among a large number of Gothic churches which he must have passed every day of his youth. In Leipzig, too, he must have been familiar enough with the churches of St. Thomas and St. Nicholas and the other Gothic buildings of the city. But of all this there is no mention whatever in his writings. An interesting sidelight on his attitude to the Middle Ages at this time is thrown by a remark in a letter to his Leipzig friend Ernst Theodor Langer of 30 November 1769, where he says of the librarian at Mannheim that 'il ait quelque air sombre, que j'attribue à cette maudite étude du medium aevum.'[2]

Nothing, then, could be more sudden or unexpected than Goethe's paean on Strasbourg Minster in *Von Deutscher Baukunst*. What is the explanation of this apparently abrupt conversion to the Gothic style? The answer usually given to this question is contained in the one word: Herder. But this explanation can only be accepted with very considerable qualifications. It is certainly not true in the sense that Herder directed Goethe's attention to the merits of Gothic architecture in general or of Strasbourg Minster in particular. For, as we know, Herder's views on Gothic at this time did not differ materially from those of the strictest disciple of the *Aufklärung*. As for his views on

[1] *Dichtung und Wahrheit*, Book ix (WA I. 27, 274).
[2] *Briefe der Jahre 1764–1768 (Artemis-Ausgabe)*, p. 132.

Strasbourg, he writes some weeks after his arrival there: 'Strasbourg is, to put it mildly, the most wretched, the vilest, the most disagreeable place I know.'[1]

Nevertheless, though Herder had virtually no understanding of Gothic himself, he was, it would seem, the means, or one of the means, of helping Goethe to this understanding, or at least of determining the particular form this understanding was to take.

It is of course impossible to say when Goethe's enthusiasm for the minster was first awakened. According to *Von Deutscher Baukunst* (and the description in *Dichtung und Wahrheit*, written some forty years later, only amplifies what is said there) Goethe was profoundly impressed by the cathedral at first sight, though for some time he was unable to account for the depth of this impression.

It is nevertheless surprising, if the experience of the minster was as immediate and overwhelming as Goethe makes out, that there is no reference to it in his letters of the time. Soon after his arrival he writes to J. C. Limprecht on 19 April 1770, almost as tartly as Herder: 'I have now been here a fortnight, and I find Strasbourg not a jot better or worse than anywhere else in the world, that is to say—very mediocre.' On the other hand, another aesthetic experience of these same weeks, the tapestries woven from originals by Raphael which were hung in honour of Marie Antoinette's passage through the city, evoked an outcry of passionate enthusiasm in a letter to Langer. Of one of these, the School of Athens, he says: 'It leaves one speechless; but this I know, that I shall reckon a new epoch of my understanding from the moment that I first saw it.' Carried away by this second-hand experience of Renaissance art at its most classical, he exclaims: 'To Italy, Langer! To Italy!'[2] It is evident at least that if the Gothic cathedral had made any impression on him by this date (29 April 1770), it had not been strong enough to counterbalance the classical experience of Raphael's designs.

Whether Goethe's account of the *immediate* impact of the minster in *Von Deutscher Baukunst* can be taken quite literally is therefore doubtful, but there is no reason to suppose that a more gradual revelation of its significance had not come to him before Herder's arrival, five months later, in September 1770. We are in all probability justified in assuming that Goethe's initial discovery of Gothic architecture had nothing whatever to do with Herder. It was, as he describes it in the *Baukunst*, an entirely original experience. What Herder did was

---

[1] *Briefe an Johann Heinrich Merck*, ed. Karl Wagner (Darmstadt, 1835), p. 6.
[2] *Briefe der Jahre 1764–1768 (Artemis-Ausgabe)*, p. 139.

to influence profoundly Goethe's intellectual apprehension of this
direct aesthetic experience, and especially its formulation in *Von
Deutscher Baukunst*. For Goethe saw instinctively that Herder's ideas
on art and nature provided the key to a new comprehension of Gothic
architecture, and in *Von Deutscher Baukunst* he proceeded to apply
this key, which had been so strangely neglected by Herder himself.[1]

Von Deutscher Baukunst, apart from reviews in periodicals the
first of Goethe's prose works to appear in print, was published in
late October or early November 1772, though the date on the title-
page is 1773. The little brochure of sixteen pages appeared anonymously and without name of publisher or place of publication.
All that the title-page contains, apart from the title and the misleading
date is the dedication 'D. M. Ervini a Steinbach.' This is appropriate,
for the essay is above all a hymn, in the spirit of the *Sturm und Drang*,
to the creative genius of the architect of the cathedral. It is almost
certain that the essay was composed in one piece in the early autumn
of 1772, shortly before publication, i.e. a year after Goethe left Strasbourg, though in writing it he may of course have made use of notes
taken in Strasbourg itself.[2]

Von Deutscher Baukunst is divided into five short sections. The
first begins with Goethe's lament that he has been unable to find
Erwin's tombstone and his determination to erect one himself some day.

'But', he asks on second thoughts, 'what need have you of a monument!
You have built yourself the most glorious of monuments; and even if the
ants who crawl around it care nought for your name, you share that fate with
the architect who piled mountains to the clouds. To few has it been granted to
engender in the soul a Babel-thought, so complete, so sublime and so necessarily beautiful down to the smallest detail, like trees of God . . . What need
have you of a monument! and from me! . . . In face of the Colossus you have
created, the feeble apostles of Good Taste will always flinch and quail, and great-
hearted souls will recognize you for what you are without interpreter.'

It is already clear in the first few paragraphs of the essay that the
shadowy figure of the medieval architect Erwin von Steinbach

[1] Cp. N. Pevsner, 'Goethe e l'Architettura', *Palladio*, iv. 174 (October/December, 1951).

[2] For the arguments in favour of this dating see my paper 'On the Composition of
Goethe's *Von Deutscher Baukunst*', *Modern Language Review*, liv (October, 1959).

Cp. also the admirable edition of *Von Deutscher Baukunst* by Ernest Beutler (*Reihe
der Vorträge und Schriften des Freien Deutschen Hochstifts*, vol. 4, Munich, 1943) for a discussion of this and all other questions relating to the essay.

There are two recent English translations: one by Geoffrey Grigson in the *Architectural Review* (xcviii, 1945, pp. 155–9) and one by E. G. Holt in *Literary Sources of Art
History* (Princeton, 1947, pp. 542–4), to both of which I am indebted for certain
phrases in the passages I have translated.

has been transformed by the ardent young Goethe into a Promethean
genius in the purest spirit of the *Sturm und Drang*.

The second section is taken up, strangely enough, with a vehement
polemic against the Abbé Laugier, who is referred to throughout
as if he were a dyed-in-the-wool classicist of the most uncompromising
sort. We know that this was far from being the case, that in fact no
one in Europe before Goethe had shown such understanding of the
Gothic style as Laugier. The circumstance that he had singled out the
tower of Strasbourg Cathedral for special commendation makes it
all the odder that Goethe should have selected him as his chief target
of attack.

But Goethe was not concerned with the passages in Laugier's works
which deal with Gothic architecture. He refers only to the *Essai sur
l'architecture*, though, as we know, both the *Essai* (in Volkmann's
German translation) and the *Observations* were in his father's library.[1]
In fact his references seem to be confined to the first chapter of the
Essai, so that is is possible, as Beutler suggests,[2] that he never got as
far as the fourth chapter—on ecclesiastical architecture—where most
of Laugier's remarks on Gothic are to be found. Whatever the reason,
Goethe gives no indication that he was in any way aware of the Abbé's
positive attitude towards medieval architecture.

For Goethe Laugier was the embodiment of the academic pedant,
whose slavery to system and rule stood in the way of a creative and
vital approach to great art: 'If only you had *felt* more than measured, if only the spirit of the masses you were gazing at had entered into
you, then you would not merely have imitated others.' And again:
'To the genius principles are even more harmful than examples'—
which sounds like a variation on Young's comparison of the rules to
crutches, which are needful to the lame, but an impediment to the
strong. The true ground of Goethe's objections to Laugier is to be
found in the passionate revolt of the young generation—to whom,
as Faust was shortly to declare, 'Feeling is all'—against the coldly
sober approach of the *Aufklärung*.

There was, it is true, another element in Goethe's polemic against
Laugier. For the Abbé was suspect, just because he was a 'Welscher'.
Goethe at this time—no doubt under the influence of Herder—asso-
ciated academic pedantry in aesthetic matters especially with the
French, and so the anti-pedantry polemic was reinforced by the anti-
Gallic polemic, which runs like an undercurrent right through the
Baukunst.

[1] Cp. Beutler, ed. cit., p. 31.   [2] Ibid. p. 33.

Goethe ends the section by recapitulating the image of the tree of God as symbolizing the infinite variety and organic complexity of the great Gothic façade 'with its thousand branches, million twigs and leaves like the sand on the shore.'

This serves as a kind of bridge to the third section with its glowing account of the minster—the most splendid tribute paid to a Gothic building since the Middle Ages. Goethe begins by describing the unregenerate state of mind in which he approached the great church for the first time, with his head full of the well-worn prejudices of neoclassicism:

'On hearsay I paid deference to the harmony of the masses, the purity of the forms, and was a sworn enemy of the confused capriciousness of Gothic ornament. Under the heading 'Gothic' I heaped up as in a dictionary article[1] all the synonymous misunderstandings which had ever passed through my head, of the confused, disordered, unnatural, botched together, patched up, overladen. No wiser than a nation which calls the whole world outside itself barbarian, I designated as 'Gothic' everything which did not fit into my system, from the elaborate brightly coloured carvings and paintings with which our *bourgeois gentilshommes* decorate their houses to the solemn relics of our ancient German architecture, concerning which, on the score of a few bizarre curlicues, I joined in the general cry: Totally smothered in ornament! And so on my way to the minster I shuddered at the prospect of being confronted with a malformed curly-bristled monster.'

'How unexpected, then,' he continues, his prose taking wing as his rhapsodic excitement rises, 'was the feeling that seized me as I stood before it. An impression of oneness, wholeness and greatness filled my soul—an impression which, because it consisted of a thousand harmonizing details, I could savour and enjoy, but by no means understand or explain. They say that it is like this with the joys of heaven, and how often did I return to enjoy this heavenly-earthly bliss, to embrace the titanic spirit of our elder brethren in their works. How often did I return to contemplate its dignity and glory from every side, from far and near, in every light of the day. It is hard on the spirit of man when his brother's work is so exalted that he can only bow down and adore it. How often has twilight soothed my gaze-wearied eyes with its friendly peace, when it melted the countless parts into whole masses, and now these masses, simple and sublime, stood before my soul, and my spirit in its strength rapturously unfolded in simultaneous joy and understanding.'

Then Goethe is visited by the spirit of Erwin himself, who explains the functional purpose of these masses and proportions, lamenting the lack of the twin tower and of the five finials which should have crowned both towers. He is awakened from slumber by the cries of the birds who dwell in the thousand apertures of the minster and who now salute the rising sun.

[1] Goethe is obviously thinking here of the article on Gothic in Sulzer's *Allgemeine Theorie der schönen Künste*.

How freshly it gleamed towards me in the fragrant morning light, how joyfully I stretched out my arms towards it, and beheld the great harmonious masses alive in their countless tiny details; as in the works of eternal nature, down to the smallest fibre, all form, and all contributing to the whole; how lightly the stupendous building, so firmly based, rises into the air; how filigreed it all is, and yet for eternity!

There is much that is remarkable in this passage. Goethe has intuitively divined, as no one before him, the organic unity, the hidden symmetry, underlying the apparent capriciousness of a great Gothic building. He envisages it as a work of nature, as a living organism, in which all the parts, however multifarious, are functionally related to the whole. Thus at one stroke he rebuts the most persistent charge of neo-classicism, that Gothic is overladen. Like the works of nature the Gothic building possesses an 'inner form', evolved from within and not imposed from without—a concept which went back to Shaftesbury and which was to play a large part in Goethe's aesthetic development.

Goethe's emphasis on the naturalness of Gothic, on its consonance with nature, may have been partly an answer to the common contention of eighteenth-century aestheticians that it was unnatural and arbitrary. It may too owe something to Shaftesbury's comparison of the work of art to the self-sufficient whole of nature 'with due subjection and subordinacy of constituent parts.' But it also gave expression to one of Goethe's most deeply felt aesthetic beliefs, now and throughout his life—the close correspondence between the laws underlying nature and art. This conviction, which is here so clearly adumbrated, was to lead him under the influence of the works of Palladio which he saw on his Italian journey to the formulation that art is a 'second nature' governed by laws which are paralleled by those of the natural sciences.[1]

The fourth section of the Baukunst is no less revolutionary than the third. Here at last Goethe condescends to explain the provocative title of his hymn to the genius of Erwin: 'Of German Architecture'.

And now have I not reason to be indignant, holy Erwin, when the German art critic, on the word of envious neighbours, fails to recognize his advantage and belittles thy work with the meaningless word 'Gothic'. When he ought to thank God to be able to proclaim aloud: that is German architecture, our architecture, since the Italian can boast none of his own, still less the Frenchman.

[1] Cp. Goethes Werke (Hamburger Ausgabe), vol. xi (Italienische Reise), ed. H. v. Einem, pp. 565–6.

It is unnecessary to waste time on stressing the untenability of this claim. It is more relevant to remember that it was common form for the various nations of Europe to try and annex Gothic architecture during the Romantic period. In the early decades of the nineteenth century in England Gothic was regularly referred to as the English style.[1] It was only about 1830 that the French were able to prove that their own and nobody else's claim to the invention of Gothic was justified.[2] Even so the old legend persisted in places against all evidence to the contrary. As late as 1844 Gilbert Scott reports that the Germans 'were labouring under the old error that Gothic was the German (Alt Deutsch) style'.[3]

Goethe was the first German to proclaim that Gothic architecture was of German origin, and this faith, as we shall see, was to play a large part in the development of the Gothic Revival in Germany. Or, to put it in another way, Goethe was the first to associate Gothic architecture with the awakening impulses of German nationalism, as manifested in the effort of the *Sturm und Drang* to find in the German past a basis for their patriotic ideal. In this connection the reference to 'manly' Albrecht Dürer, later in the essay, is significant. He too, like Erwin, is a 'strong, rough, German soul'. Thus Erwin (d. 1316) anachronistically takes his place among the manly, honest, vigorous figures of the early sixteenth century—Luther, Götz, Sachs, Dürer—who seemed to the young Goethe (and Herder) representative of the German character at its best.

Goethe now proceeds to draw a distinction between what he calls 'beautiful' art and 'characteristic' art. He is here taking as his point of departure Sulzer's essay *Die schönen Künste in ihrem Ursprung, ihrer wahren Natur und besten Anwendung* (autumn 1772), to which Goethe devoted a devastating review in the *Frankfurter Gelehrten Anzeigen* for 18 December 1772 (a few weeks, that is to say, after the appearance of the *Baukunst*). Sulzer maintains that the origin and essence of art are to be found in the natural desire of man to embellish the objects that surround him. In other words he assigns a purely decorative value to art. Against what Goethe calls this 'feeble doctrine of modern pretty-prettiness' he opposes his ideal of characteristic art—'an art which is true and great, indeed often truer and greater than "beautiful" art itself. For there is a creative spirit in man, which will manifest itself immediately his conditions of life are secure. As soon as he has nothing to

---

[1] Cp. Sir Kenneth Clark, *The Gothic Revival* (rev. ed. London, 1950), p. 100.
[2] Cp. Frankl, op. cit. p. 499.
[3] Cp. Clark, op. cit. p. 247.

fear or worry about, this demi-god, active in his security, gropes round
for some material into which he can breathe his spirit. And thus the
savage adorns his coconuts, his feathers, and his body with grotesque
features, frightful shapes, and harsh colours. And even if this plastic
art consist of the most arbitrary and disproportioned forms, it will
nevertheless harmonize, for a single emotion has welded it into a
characteristic whole.' (In the last few sentences Goethe would seem
to have anticipated by more than a century some of the most significant developments of modern art.)

Characteristic art, then, 'is the only true art'. But here Goethe
adds a qualification. It is not enough that art should be characteristic;
the greatest art must accord with those proportions 'which alone
are beautiful and from eternity'. He does not deny, then, that there
are certain absolute norms of beauty; but the greatest characteristic
art will conform to these instinctively.

Such a work of characteristic art in the highest sense is Strasbourg
Minster, the sole creation, as Goethe believed, of the titanic genius
Erwin von Steinbach: 'Here stands his work; approach and acknow-
ledge the deepest sense of truth and beauty of proportions, emanating
from a strong rough German soul on the narrow gloomy monkish
stage of the *medium aevum*.'

It should be emphasized that the distinction between 'beautiful'
and 'characteristic' art by no means corresponds, as one might at
first sight be tempted to suppose, to that between Classical and Gothic.
The contrast Goethe is making is between imitative art and original
art, between an art which is the genuine expression of the artist's
character and an art which is purely decorative and superficial,
whether it be Gothic or Classical. In a letter written to his friend
J. G. Röderer shortly after his return to Frankfurt from Strasbourg
he expressly equates Erwin and Bramante.[1]

The brief final section, after a scornful glance at 'our *aevum*' with
its artificial and degenerate rococo art, concludes with a paean to the
creative genius of the artist, ending appropriately enough with the
Prometheus image which was the legacy of Shaftesbury to the *Sturm
und Drang*.

When one regards the essay as a whole, the first thing that strikes
one is that it is really very little concerned with Gothic architecture
as such. Many strands have gone to make up its complex web: the
polemic against Laugier, the polemic against Sulzer, the awakening
nationalism of the *Sturm und Drang*, the concept of genius inherited

[1] *Briefe der Jahre 1746–1786 (Artemis-Ausgabe)*, p. 161.

from Shaftesbury, Young and Herder, the concept of 'characteristic' art, the analogy between the work of art and the natural organism. In its emphasis on symmetry and proportion even the neo-classicism of Oeser plays its part.[1]

From one point of view the whole essay could be looked upon as a hymn to the original genius, and it is this above all, of course, which has stamped it as a product of Herder's impact on Goethe and as one of the most characteristic utterances of the *Sturm und Drang*. In Strasbourg Minster Goethe saw pre-eminently those qualities which were especially dear to the *Geniebewegung*, qualities moreover which dominated Goethe's own emotional life at the time he was writing the *Baukunst*—elemental power, superabundant creative energy, what he calls its 'titanic spirit'. In this instance the chosen vessel for these attributes was Erwin von Steinbach, whom Goethe, as we know, regarded as the author of the whole building. (He was in fact only responsible for the lower stages of the façade.) Erwin was conceived of by the young Goethe as a stupendous genius, who had created the cathedral ('your Colossus') just as Shakespeare had created *King Lear*. Hence the similarity between the *Baukunst* and that other nearly contemporary essay, which owed equally much to Herder, *Zum Schäkespears Tag*. Erwin, the spontaneous natural genius, is contrasted with the rule-and-system-ridden French classical architects in much the same way as Shakespeare, the elemental creative genius and despiser of the rules, is contrasted with the French classical dramatists in the Shakespeare essay. 'To the genius principles are even more harmful than examples' might apply to both. Erwin, we know, is another Götz or Dürer, with his 'strong, rough German soul'—another young Goethe, in fact. He, like Shakespeare, is the elemental genius, whose only teacher is Nature herself, the Promethean figure who bodied forth his creations on a colossal scale: original genius, creative genius, titanic genius all in one.

Other elements in the essay which betray the inspiration of Herder are the passage on characteristic art, which though entirely Goethean in its formulation, nevertheless goes back to Herder's views on the elemental qualities of primitive poetry; further, the strong nationalist currents in the essay, namely, the equation of Gothic with German and the anti-French polemic; so too the passage in the second section on the part played by the pillar and wall in Southern and Northern architecture respectively, which is exactly comparable to Herder's

[1] For this aspect of the essay see my paper 'Goethe and the Gothic Revival', *Publications of the English Goethe Society*, New Series, vol. xxv (1956).

discussion of the conditioning factors of Greek and Shakespearean drama in his Shakespeare essay. Finally, quite apart from the underlying ideas, the whole tone and manner of the essay owes much to Herder, both the emphasis on Feeling as opposed to Reason ('If only you had felt more than measured') and the rhapsodic style in which it is written.[1]

Nevertheless, when all is said and done, the fact remains that the core of the essay is not due to Herder or Oeser or anybody else, but is a personal vision of a great Gothic building, a vision which was unique in its time and an inspiration for later generations. To read *Von Deutscher Baukunst* after, say, Walpole's remarks on Gothic in his *Anecdotes of Painting* is itself like passing from Strawberry Hill to Strasbourg Cathedral. It is a question of attitude. From this point of view the degree of Goethe's understanding for the specific qualities of the Gothic style is irrelevant. What matters is that here, one feels, for the first time since the Middle Ages some one has stood before a great Gothic building and has seen it for what it is—one of the supreme achievements of the human spirit. 'It is hard on the spirit of man when his brother's work is so exalted that he can only bow down and adore it.' Such sentences mark a true revolution in the history of taste. At last Gothic has been accepted seriously and has been accepted wholeheartedly, without reservation or qualification. The Romantic Movement has begun. The fact that for nearly two hundred years now we have been accustomed to regard Gothic architecture in the light of Goethe's new Romantic attitude makes it difficult for us to realize the astounding originality of his achievement. Single-handed, so to speak, this young man of twenty-three made a clean sweep of the doubts and scruples of the neo-classical apologists and the modish triflings of the Rococo Gothicists, and gave expression to an attitude which was so far in advance of his day that decades had to pass before his example could bear fruit.

In one important respect, however, the attitude of *Von Deutscher Baukunst* to medieval architecture differs fundamentally from that of the Romantics. Throughout Goethe's essay there is no hint of the religious associations of Gothic which were to play so large a part in the later stages of the Gothic Revival. When he addresses the architect of the minster as 'heiliger Erwin', Goethe is thinking of him as a saint, not of God, but of Art. The minster, we remember, is saluted

---

[1] In this connection it is interesting to note that both Hamann and Sulzer assumed Herder to be the author of the essay. Cp. G. Witkowski's introduction to the reprint of *Von Deutscher Baukunst* in Kürschner's *Deutsche National-Litteratur*, vol. cvii. (Stuttgart, 1892), p. 161.

as a 'Babel-thought', erected, that is to say, rather in defiance of God than in his service. There is a total absence of the sense of religious awe, which the Romantics proper found inseparable from the columned and vaulted spaces of the Gothic interior. One obvious reason for this is that in the *Baukunst* Goethe is solely concerned with the exterior—indeed with the façade—of Strasbourg Cathedral. And it is the interior rather than the exterior of a Gothic church which stirs the sense of mystery and reverence. This argument of course works both ways: one could equally well maintain that Goethe omits all mention of the interior just because he was not susceptible to its numinous qualities.

Indeed it was perhaps just because the Gothic style had no religious connotation in Goethe's mind that he felt attracted to it. For, strange though it must seem to us, it is abundantly clear from the *Baukunst* that to Goethe at this time Gothic was, so to speak, a neutral style, without specifically religious implications. The reason for this is not far to seek. For the specifically religious style of Goethe's day was the Baroque, which was certainly one of his grounds for disliking it. The sometimes flamboyant and even morbid religiosity of ecclesiastical Baroque was naturally repellent to Goethe, who always retained a solid kernel of sober bourgeois Protestant *Aufklärung* in his intellectual make-up. It was in Goethe's eyes precisely the absence of the mystical, irrational element that made Gothic acceptable.

This indifference to the religious aspect of Gothic actually leads him to the paradoxical assertion that Erwin's creation was effected in direct opposition to the spirit of his age. To Goethe at this point— and indeed, essentially, at all points—of his development the Middle Ages were dark, monkish, and obscurantist. Against this background Erwin is presented as a champion of truth and light and of German *Treu' und Redlichkeit*, creating his masterpiece in the teeth of surrounding barbarism.

Quite apart from the wholeheartedness of its approach there is another respect in which *Von Deutscher Baukunst* represents a milestone in the acceptance of Gothic. The essay, as we have seen, shows no knowledge or understanding of the technical aspects of the style. It is *par excellence* the work of an amateur, in all senses of the word. Now hitherto the appreciations of Gothic, such as they were, had come from more or less professional circles—either from practising architects, like Soufflot or Weinlig, or at least from men who were well acquainted with the technicalities, like Laugier. Even Walpole and Gray were professional in comparison with the author of the Erwin essay. In Goethe we have the complete amateur—the precursor of how many others—without any professional knowledge of architecture at all. What he records in *Von Deutscher Baukunst* is a purely aesthetic experience—the direct impact of the great Gothic building on the imagination of the beholder, unfettered and uncomplicated by any intervening technical considerations. Was it not indeed Goethe's very innocence in this respect that enabled him to realize intuitively the sublime potentialities of a style hitherto regarded for the most part as a kind of amiable filigree?

Goethe's new-found enthusiasm for Gothic was not of long duration. It was an experience confined to this one Gothic building at this particular stage of his development, and not transferable to Gothic architecture in general. Otherwise he would surely have applied his new-won insight to the Gothic buildings of Frankfurt and its neighbourhood. But in fact there is little indication, apart from the *Baukunst* itself, that Gothic architecture had any serious meaning for Goethe from the day he left Strasbourg to that period of his old age when his interest was temporarily revived through the agency of the brothers Boisserée.

In a well-known passage in *Dichtung und Wahrheit* (Book xi) Goethe describes how the cast of a Corinthian capital in the Electoral Collection at Mannheim, which he visited on his way back to Frankfurt from Strasbourg in August 1771, already somewhat shook his 'faith in Nordic architecture'. Whether this incident should be classed as *Dichtung* or *Wahrheit* is not clear, since it has now come to light that Goethe actually visited the collection before, not after, his stay in Strasbourg, though it is possible of course that he paid more than one visit.[18] But in any case it is a symbolic recognition by the ageing Goethe of the extreme transience of his early 'Gothic' phase.

There are in fact only two utterances of the young Goethe, apart from the *Baukunst* itself, which betray any concern with Gothic architecture, and both of these refer to Strasbourg Cathedral. The first is contained in a letter to J. G. Röderer, which was written on 21 September 1771, just a month after his return to Frankfurt. Goethe writes to his Strasbourg friend, who was evidently contemplating architecture as a profession, that 'most of our architects are mere artisans', which is all right as far as everyday buildings are concerned, but great buildings call for great souls, 'like Erwin or Bramante'.

[18] Cp. H. Trevelyan, *Goethe and the Greeks* (Cambridge, 1941), pp. 38–39 n.

He then proceeds to explain that the minster, 'the greatest master-piece of German architecture', will show Röderer better than Goethe can that the great work differs from the petty work chiefly in its origina-lity and independence of others, so that it seems to exist from eternity. Goethe could not see, what it is so easy for us to see, that Strasbourg Minster is anything but original in this sense, and owes in fact most of its inspiration to French sources. What mattered to the young *Stürmer und Dränger* was that it was an expression of superabundant energy and power.

The second utterance on the minster is the little effusion, only a page or two in length, with the curious title, *Dritte Wallfahrt nach Erwins Grab* (Third Pilgrimage to Erwin's Grave). It was first published in that strange hotch-potch *Aus Goethes Brieftasche* in 1776, and records a visit paid to the minster on Goethe's return from his journey to Switzerland in July 1775. (The *second* pilgrimage had presumably taken place on the way to Switzerland in May, when he spent two days in Strasbourg). The *Wallfahrt* is modelled on manuals of devotion, such as he had no doubt seen at Maria Einsiedeln a few weeks before, and on the analogy of such booklets is divided into various sections: Preparation, Prayers, and Stations of the Cross. In this case the 'sta-tions' represent the stages of Goethe's ascent of the minster tower—three only instead of the usual fourteen, because, as the author explains, at that point his reflections were interrupted by the arrival of his friend and fellow poet Lenz.

The *Wallfahrt* is one of the most characteristic expressions of the expansive titanism of the *Sturm und Drang*. It has little to do with Erwin or his minster. Primarily it is an anti-philistine tract, another rhapsody to the power of genius and the creative spirit in face of the trivial medi-ocrity of what Goethe untranslatably calls the 'Welschen aller Völker'.

As Goethe stands once more beside the grave of Erwin, beneath the great architect's monument, he again salutes him as his 'saint', thank-ing God that he, Goethe, is still as susceptible to the Great and True as ever. He prays to the creative spirit, as it is manifested in the mighty building he is now ascending, which is a living unity, begotten not made, on a parallel with the sublime sights he had just witnessed in Switzerland—the falls of the Rhine, the eternal snow peaks, the wide shining lakes, and the towering cliffs and wild ravines of the Gotthard.

In the last paragraph Goethe sums up the result of his conversation with Lenz on the tower: 'With every step we became more convinced that creative power in the artist is an upswelling feeling for proportion, measurement, and propriety, and that only through these can an original work be produced, just as other creations are produced by their individual germinative force.'[1]

The minster, then, is still seen as an organic work of nature and as the product of Erwin's individual genius. But at the same time the last paragraph implies a distinct shift or return towards neo-classical values. In the *Baukunst* after all the stress on measurement was one of the points for which Laugier was most sternly rebuked.

In the Second Station of his Pilgrimage Goethe refers back to his Erwin essay as 'an obscurely intimate pamphlet, which was read and understood by few'. This is by no means an overstatement, for the immediate effect of the *Baukunst* on the contemporary attitude towards Gothic was negligible. And to judge from the reviews those who did read it were not much impressed. We know of at least five such notices, and considering the somewhat sibylline style in which the essay is written and the fact that it appeared anonymously, it is surprising that it received so many. The most favourable of them appeared, as we should expect, in the *Frankfurter Gelehrten Anzeigen* for 4 December 1772, the organ of the young *Stürmer und Dränger*, to which Goethe was at that time a regular contributor. The tone is positive throughout: 'We wish that similar writings of such a modest number of pages and so rich in content would come our way more often,' it begins. It proceeds to give a survey of the contents with liberal quotations from the more important passages, and ends: 'We commend this little book to all lovers of art, both on account of its principles and of the true genius which pervades every detail.'

Despite this Goethe refers to the reviewer, Christian Heinrich Schmid of Giessen, as a 'Scheisskerl' and his review as 'gesudelt' (letter to Kestner of 25 December 1772). What then must Goethe, enemy of the Rococo in every form, have thought of the notice in Wieland's *Teutscher Merkur* (June 1773) by the same reviewer, which found the pamphlet 'worth reading', but marred by stylistic 'flourishes which in architecture would be called curlicues'!

The longest and weightiest of the reviews appeared anonymously[2]

---

[1] WA I. 37, 325.

[2] Vol. xiv, pp. 287–94 (1773). The review has usually been attributed to the neo-classical Dresden architect Friedrich August Krubsacius, following P. Schumann, *Barock und Rokoko* (Leipzig, 1885). In his *Laugier and 18th Century French Theory* (London, 1962, pp. 190–1) Wolfgang Herrmann questions this attribution, the evidence for which is not stated by Schumann, and gives reasons for believing that J. G. Sulzer is more likely to have been the author.

in the *Neue Bibliothek der schönen Wissenschaften und der freyen Künste*. The review starts straightaway on an ominous note: 'We experienced a real pleasure in reading this little essay, but we must honestly admit that it was a somewhat malicious pleasure.' Apart from the pretentious obscurity of the style, what irritated the reviewer most was the fact that this anonymous tyro should have ventured to pronounce intuitive judgments on matters of which he had no professional knowledge. The reviewer does not deny 'the charm of delicate Gothic architecture', but objects to the author's semi-deification of Erwin: 'Does it really redound to the credit of the Germans, when things are said of them which can only move a foreigner to laughter?' He pours scorn on Goethe's belief in the German origin of the Gothic style, and points out that France, England and Italy have Gothic churches as beautiful as any in Germany. He ends: 'The author dispatches the despiser of Gothic architecture to Paris; would it not be a good thing for him to go there too?'

Despite its ironic tone the review is no more unfriendly than one would expect from a protagonist of the classical school, and some of the strictures are fair enough. The surprising thing really is that anyone should have bothered to review an obscure and anonymous pamphlet in defence of Gothic at such length (nearly seven pages) in one of the leading intellectual journals of the time.

The next stage in the history of the *Baukunst* was its inclusion in Herder's *Von Deutscher Art und Kunst* (1773). Despite its haphazard origins and humble format this little collection of essays by diverse hands was an epoch-making document in the development of German literature and taste in the eighteenth century. It has often been described as the manifesto or charter of the *Sturm und Drang*, and indeed one might go farther than this and claim it as the true starting point of the German Romantic movement. It contained two essays by Herder himself, one on Ossian and the folk-song and one on Shakespeare; these were followed by Goethe's *Von Deutscher Baukunst*, a translation of an essay on Gothic architecture by Paolo Frisi, and lastly by an essay on *Deutsche Geschichte*, excerpted from the preface to the History of Osnabrück by Justus Möser. Common to all the essays except Frisi's, even to the Shakespeare essay, was a patriotically-coloured revival of interest in the past.

It was doubtless the patriotic or nationalist element in Goethe's essay which appealed to Herder and decided him to include it in his collection, for as we know he was himself far from feeling any enthusiasm for medieval architecture. Herder in fact makes his attitude to the matter quite clear in a note which he appended to the *Baukunst* to explain that he was including Frisi's essay on Gothic as a kind of counterblast to Goethe's essay. He expresses the hope that it might perhaps give rise to a third and more objective statement which, Herder-like, would investigate the historical origins of Gothic architecture and decide what in it is geographically determined and an exception to the rules of classical beauty, or to what extent, on the contrary, it may represent a new type of beauty.

Paolo Frisi was an Italian mathematician of some eminence in his day and the author, among other things, of a *Saggio sopra l'architettura gotica* (Livorno, 1766), which is here translated. Certainly no greater contrast, both in style and in content, to Goethe's essay could be imagined. Not only is the author a declared enemy of the Gothic style, but his whole tone and approach, which is highly technical—indeed mathematical—in character, is at the opposite pole from Goethe's rhapsody.

From our point of view the importance of *Von Deutscher Art und Kunst* is that it rescued Goethe's essay from the complete oblivion that might otherwise have overtaken it. Herder's collection was noticed in six different journals, though it is true that the reviews were mainly concerned with his own contributions, and the *Baukunst* was only referred to incidentally, if at all. More important was that the pirates got on to the track of the work through Herder's compilation. It was included in the fourth volume of Christian Friedrich Himburg's pirated edition of Goethe's *Schriften* (1779) and also in the fourth volume of Christian Schmieder's equally unauthorized edition of 1780. Since Goethe himself did not reprint the *Baukunst* until 1824, we may well owe to Herder and the pirates the fact that the essay was not completely forgotten. To this day only five copies of the original edition have been located.[1]

The first sign we have that the seed of the *Baukunst* did not fall on wholly stony soil is to be found in Gottfried Huth's *Allgemeines Magazin für die bürgerliche Baukunst*.[2] Huth was Professor of Physics and Mathematics at Frankfurt-an-der-Oder, and his *Magazin* was the first German journal to be devoted solely to architecture. It only extended to four parts (1789–96), but in its day it discharged a useful function. It was addressed in the first place to practising architects, and its prime aim was to provide them with information of a practical

[1] Cp. Beutler, ed. cit., p. 24.
[2] Vol. i, Part i. pp. 84–91 (Weimar, 1789).

and technical kind, but it also contained articles of historical and aesthetic interest.

Among these latter Huth included a reprint of the *Baukunst*, which
he knew from Herder's collection. It is clear that he was primarily
impressed by its patriotic appeal. He presumes that 'it will scarcely
be known to many contemporary architects . . . nevertheless it would
be a pity if it were allowed to pass unnoticed by the profession . . .
the sentiments which find such strong and fine expression there deserve
to be taken to heart by everyone in whose veins flows German blood.'
And in a postscript he calls for 'a history of architecture among the
Germans, a history of German architecture'—the first time that this
cry had been raised in print,[1] and one that was not to be answered
till some thirty years later by C. L. Stieglitz's *Von Altdeutscher
Baukunst*.

This reprint of Goethe's essay is not the only sign that Huth was
interested in Gothic architecture. In fact the reprint is itself part of a
more general survey of the subject. Huth begins the discussion with a
reprint of Weinlig's letter on Gothic architecture in Rome. To this he
adds a note on the originality of the Gothic architects. 'The strength
of their genius impelled them to avoid the slavish path of imitation
and to develop independently their own imagination and inventive
capacity. Thus they drew up the plans for their buildings out
of their own heads, perfected and refined the same according to
their own thoughts, and so created their works as they thought fit,
in keeping with their own principles of perfection and beauty.' (This
is the most uncompromising statement of a view we have already
seen suggested by the French critics, such as Laugier). He continues:
'They were not without taste, rather they had a great deal of it,
but it was a taste which was based entirely on the civilization of its
age.'

Huth then appends to Weinlig's letter a passage from Frisi's essay
on Gothic—also taken from Herder's collection—and it is in answer
to this that he includes Goethe's *Baukunst*. He adds a note on its authorship: 'The author has not given his name, but connoisseurs of German
literature will have little difficulty in guessing it from the style and
vigour of expression which are peculiar to him.'

Further evidence of Huth's interest in Gothic is afforded by a
review of Louis-Sébastien Mercier's *Tableau de Paris* (1781), from which
he quotes an attack on French classical architecture, and adds: 'I
infinitely prefer the Gothic style; it is free and bold; it astonishes.

[1] Herder's similar appeal in the *Ideen* dates from 1791.

What a glorious monument of the past is the minster in Strasbourg! What boldness! What lightness!'[1]

Yet another reprint of the *Baukunst*, also taken from Herder's collection, is to be found in C. F. Cramer's translation of Jens Baggesen's *Labyrinthen* (1795). This is a diary of the Danish poet's travels in Germany, Switzerland, and France in 1789–90. Cramer reprints Goethe's essay in his translation as a counterweight to Baggesen's partly enthusiastic but intolerantly anti-Catholic account of Strasbourg Minster. He regrets in a footnote that Goethe had not included the essay in his collected works.[2]

These reprints provide evidence that the Erwin essay had not been completely forgotten. The time was now at hand when it was to find an echo at last in the new Romantic generation and thus make its contribution to the full tide of the Gothic Revival in Germany.

---

[1] For Huth see Beutler, ed. cit., pp. 64–66, and E. H. Lehmann, *Die Anfänge der Kunst-zeitschrift in Deutschland* (Leipzig, 1932), pp. 154–8.

[2] *Baggesen oder Das Labyrinth* (Altona and Leipzig, 1795), 5. Stück, pp. 480 ff.

3. HEINSE—FORSTER—NICOLAI

BETWEEN the publication of *Von Deutscher Baukunst* and the Romantic outburst at the turn of the century we have to record a few isolated instances of Gothic appreciation, which probably owe nothing to Goethe's essay. Like their predecessors they are mainly confined to the two outstanding monuments of German Gothic—Strasbourg and Cologne.

In July 1780 Wilhelm Heinse, the author of *Ardinghello*, passed through Strasbourg on his way to Italy. He recorded his impressions of the minster in the posthumously published diary of his Italian journey. This is in many respects a remarkable document of pre-Romantic Gothic appreciation. Heinse catches sight of the minster from afar, commanding the landscape 'like an enormous pine tree miraculously left over from the giant race of the primeval world'. And when he arrives in the city itself, this first impression is confirmed and reinforced. 'The minster tower has the most living form of any building I have ever seen. I obtained my first close view of it just as the sun had set. The openwork spire gave it the naturally jagged and airy appearance of a pine tree. And whence shall a tower have its origin in nature if not from a tall tree? And from what better than a pine or cedar?'[1]

It is impossible to say whether Heinse knew Goethe's essay; he may well have done so of course from Herder's *Von Deutscher Art und Kunst*. The diary passages on the minster provide no evidence either way. Though his comparison with the pine tree may remind one of Goethe's image of the soaring beech tree or the tree of God with its thousand branches, it would be pedantic to suppose that Heinse needed any prompting from Goethe to arrive at such a similitude.

In actual fact Heinse carries very much farther than Goethe the analogy between Gothic architecture and natural forms. He assumes without more ado that spires derive from pine trees, just as domes derive from lime or oak trees. In his view, without reproduction and imitation of nature there would be no art. Again, the interior of the minster is compared to a sacred grove; and the nave and aisles of the Gothic interior remind him, as they had reminded Laugier and others before him, of a triple avenue of lofty branching trees. The pillars

[1] Wilhelm Heinse, *Sämmtliche Schriften*, ed. Carl Schüddekopf, (10 vols. Leipzig, 1902–25), vii. 12–13.

are trunks which support a 'German', i.e. pointed, arch. The spaces between the trunks are illuminated by the stained glass windows which let through the light like airy branches. It is no exaggeration to say that in Heinse's description the whole building is dissolved into the plant forms of nature. In this he most notably anticipates the Gothic enthusiasts of the Romantic Movement.

Again it might be maintained that Heinse's remarks on Gothic proportions are not far removed from Goethe's concept of 'inner form', already adumbrated in the Erwin essay, but here too there is no reason to assume that Heinse derived it from Goethe. Every kind of living object, he argues, has its own appropriate proportions; thus the types of proportion are as manifold as the infinite variety of nature, and are by no manner of means confined to those of the Doric, Ionic, and Corinthian orders.

In any case the differences between Heinse's work and Goethe's are far more marked than any—probably chance—resemblances between them. The most obvious contrast is that whereas Goethe's essay had been concerned wholly with the outside of the cathedral, Heinse is mainly impressed by its inside. More important, Heinse, in strong contrast to Goethe, is clearly conscious of the religious atmosphere evoked by the Gothic interior. To step within the minster is like entering a sacred grove. The ancient stained glass windows suffuse the whole with a dim religious light, and the lighted candles in the choir, which, Heinse remarks, is 'lower and holier, narrower and darker' than the rest of the church, contribute to the impressive effect. In line with this is the passage in *Ardinghello* (1784), where he exalts the 'solemn Gothic cathedral with its vast free spaces' as the most fitting vehicle for communal worship, 'where the voice of the priest resounds like thunder, and the chorale of the congregation is raised in homage to the father of the universe like a storm of the sea, before which even the boldest unbeliever must quail'.[1] Heinse is the first German writer to draw attention to the spatial impressiveness of the Gothic interior.

Even in Italy Heinse's sensitiveness to medieval architecture finds expression. The Church of St. Francis at Assisi is 'a glorious Gothic building' and 'the vaults are masterly in their construction'. San Petronio in Bologna is another 'glorious Gothic building, sublime and spacious', and has the greatest harmony, serenity, and majesty of any church in that city. In Brescia he compares the seventeenth-century Duomo Nuovo with the very early Romanesque Duomo

[1] Heinse, ed. cit. iv. 31.

Vecchio, much to the disadvantage of the former. The Duomo Nuovo is built in the 'feeble over-polished manner of all modern art', whereas the old cathedral astonishes by the originality of its design and the excellence of its proportions.

Specially interesting are his remarks on the cathedral of Milan, the object of so much comment, both favourable and unfavourable, in the eighteenth century. His attitude is more divided in this case than in that of Strasbourg. On the one hand he admits that the cathedral always makes a very strong first impression on account of its colossal height and spaciousness and the dim light cast by the stained glass windows. On the other hand the excess of detail and decoration is displeasing. He compares the multitude of little pinnacles to a hedgehog's bristles, and declares that it would be hard to find anywhere such a vast collection of monstrosities as is provided by the statues of this church, both within and without.

Above all for Heinse the cathedral is 'the most glorious symbol of the Christian religion that I have seen ... One must admit that such a building stands in quite a different relationship to Christianity from St. Peter's or the Pantheon, where you can see at the first glance that the people who built or commissioned them were without a spark of religious conviction. The cathedral, on the other hand, with its sombre choir and sharp pointed arches and stupendous pillars and its nonsensical mass of decorative detail, is the very symbol of hell, death, damnation and a terrible God who punishes every little human failing with everlasting torments."[1]

Though it is certainly true that Heinse's interpretation of Christianity has—to put it mildly—little in common with that of the Romantics, this passage nevertheless forms a striking anticipation of the Romantic attitude towards Gothic as the specifically Christian style. It is paradoxical that Heinse, agnostic and hedonist, should have been the first writer in German literature to give expression to this particular, and most important, aspect of the Gothic Revival.

Altogether Heinse shows a surprising awareness of Gothic architecture for his time. In his Italian diary he seldom fails to comment on the medieval buildings in the places he passes through, sometimes adversely, more often favourably. But he remains a classicist at heart. He is tolerant, and more than tolerant, of Gothic and Romanesque, but it is the architecture of the Ancients and the Renaissance which stirs his enthusiasm.

[1] Ibid. pp. 231–2.

Heinse spent the later years of his life as librarian to the Elector of Mainz. One of his fellow librarians during the latter part of his tenure of office was a personage of much greater significance in the history of the Gothic Revival in Germany. This was Johann Georg Adam Forster, generally known as Georg Forster, who is incidentally one of the most fascinating figures in the field of Anglo-German literary relations in the eighteenth century. Descended from a Yorkshire family of Scottish origin which emigrated to Polish Prussia in the period of the Civil War, he was himself almost as much at home in England as in Germany and in the English as in the German language. He rightly finds his place in the *Dictionary of National Biography* as well as in the *Allgemeine Deutsche Biographie*. In his short life of thirty-nine years the parts he played were startlingly varied. Born near Danzig in 1754, he went to England as a boy of twelve, and at the age of eighteen he accompanied Captain Cook on his second voyage round the world. In his last years he was the leader of the Mainz revolutionaries and their representative at the National Convention. Between these two extremes he had taught natural history at Cassel and Vilna and succeeded Johannes von Müller as electoral librarian at Mainz. He was the intimate friend of Fritz Jacobi, Lichtenberg, Sömmering, and the young Humboldts, and on friendly terms with Goethe and Herder. He died in poverty and misery in Paris in 1794, deeply disillusioned by what he had seen at first hand of the Revolution for which he had sacrificed so much.[1]

To the literary historian Forster is well known as travel writer, essayist, and the master of an admirable prose style, but there is one aspect of his many-sided achievement which has not been sufficiently recognized—namely, his place in the development of German Romanticism. This is partly due, no doubt, to the fact that his most influential critics—Friedrich Schlegel, Gervinus, Hettner, Leitzmann—have chosen to lay emphasis on his classical qualities and affinities to the exclusion of his Romantic connections.

Forster's most obvious connection with the Romantic Movement is his translation of Kalidasa's *Sakontala* from the English version by Sir William Jones, which probably gave Goethe the idea for his *Vorspiel auf dem Theater* in *Faust* and helped to inspire Friedrich Schlegel and other Romantic writers with their interest in oriental literature. To

[1] For an account of Forster's life and significance see G. P. Gooch, *Germany and the French Revolution* (London, 1920), pp. 303–16; for his relationship to England and the English see my *German Travellers in England 1400–1800* (Oxford, 1953), pp. 192–7; and for his place in the Gothic Revival see my article 'Georg Forster and the Gothic Revival', *Modern Language Review*, vol. li (January, 1956).

this might be added the brilliant descriptions of the scenery and inhabitants of the South Seas in his *Voyage round the World*,[1] which
stimulated the fashionable primitivism of the time, even though Forster
himself was by no means a disciple of Rousseau. But the most important respect in which Forster may be said to have anticipated the Romantic Movement is in his enthusiastic appreciation of medieval
architecture.

Forster's share in the Gothic movement has been consistently under-
estimated, and deserves to be placed at last in its true perspective.
For if Goethe's rhapsody on Strasbourg Minster is the first milestone
in the history of the Gothic Revival in Germany, then Georg Forster's
observations in his *Ansichten vom Niederrhein* is the second. There is
little to prepare us in Forster's antecedents for the insight and enthusiasm of these utterances. During his English period (1766–78) his
views on the subject do not appear to have been in any way in advance
of his time. In his diary of a journey to Paris in 1777 he writes (in
English) of Notre Dame almost as if he were describing Strawberry
Hill:

> Notre Dame, the cathedral of Paris, is a large Gothick Building, richly
> ornamented on the outside with that species of childish fretwork which our
> modern Goths in England admire so much, and with clod-pole statues of
> kings, bishops and saints. The inside is very spacious but not pleasing to me.
> The pillars of Gothick architecture are such clumsy posts from which such
> spindleshanked branches rise to support a great Arch, that it makes one's
> head ache to look at it.[2]

At this stage, then, Forster does not even share the fashionable craze
for Rococo Gothic; his attitude, in fact, does not go beyond that of
the most bigoted anti-Goth, and might serve as an excellent example of
the orthodox neo-classical view.

When and how Forster's attitude to the Gothic style underwent the
transformation which is revealed in the *Ansichten* is not clear. The
letters and diaries of the intervening years do not help. The only
evidence, in fact, is negative. In the diary describing his journey
from Cassel to Vilna in 1784 he makes no reference to any Gothic
building, though he must have seen several noble examples of the
style. In Prague, for instance, he comments on the splendid baroque
interior of the Jesuit church, but passes over the choir of the cathedral

[1] Originally written and published in English (1777); German translation by Forster
and Rudolf Erich Raspe (1779).
[2] *Georg Forsters Tagebücher*, ed. Paul Zincke and Albert Leitzmann, *Deutsche Litteraturdenkmale des 18. und 19. Jahrhunderts*, No. 149 (Berlin, 1914), p. 23.

without a word. He is full of enthusiasm for Vienna and the Viennese, but there is no mention of St. Stephen's. The only feature of this diary which in any way prepares us for the change in Forster's attitude is a number of romantically heightened landscape descriptions, which show a predilection for 'Gothick' ingredients: ruined castles, moss-grown rocks, melancholy groves, and grottoes which send a thrill of awe down the spine of the beholder.[1] All this betrays clearly enough the Ossianic and sentimental fashions of the time and is far from imply-ing a capacity to appreciate Gothic architecture, but it does at least indicate a state of mind from which such a capacity might develop.

That Forster did in fact develop such a capacity is abundantly proved by the *Ansichten vom Niederrhein*,[2] which describes a journey through the Low Countries to England and France that he undertook in the company of his friend the young Alexander von Humboldt in the spring and summer of 1790. By general consent this is Forster's best book; it shows more convincingly than any of his other writings the breadth of vision and freshness of outlook which Friedrich Schlegel rightly applauds as his most characteristic quality.[3] He seems equally at ease whether he is discussing the history and politics of the countries he passes through or expatiating on their botanical and geological phenomena or their cultural achievements in literature and art. His remarks on Gothic architecture are mainly concentrated in two pass-ages—in his description of Cologne Cathedral (i. 70–73) and his account of the Oxford colleges (iii. 227–30). Taken together they constitute the most notable appreciation of medieval architecture to be found in German literature between Goethe's *Von Deutscher Baukunst* and the *Reisebriefe* of Friedrich Schlegel.

The primary impression awakened in Forster by the sight of Cologne Cathedral—as in Goethe by that of Strasbourg—is the sense of the sublime: 'Whenever I visit Cologne I always return to this glorious temple in order to feel the thrill of the sublime'—the very opposite, therefore, of the current eighteenth-century view of Gothic as some-thing trivial and fussy. It is the imaginative boldness of the Gothic builders that contributes most forcibly to this sublimity: 'The Gothic style, however lacking in proportion it may be, seizes the imagination in an irresistible manner. With what ease these slender columns

---

[1] e.g. his descriptions of the environs of Dresden (ibid. pp. 115–6); the Saxon Switzer-land (pp. 120–3); the view from the Cobenzl (pp. 177–9).

[2] *Ansichten vom Niederrhein, von Brabant, Flandern, Holland, England und Frankreich, im April, Mai und Junius 1790* (3 vols. Berlin, 1791–4).

[3] Cp. *Charakteristiken und Kritiken* by August Wilhelm and Friedrich Schlegel (2 vols. Königsberg, 1801), i. 93.

shoot upwards to the sky! By what power of magic do their lofty branches meet to form the bold pointed arch?' In this bold imaginative quality Forster sees the essential virtue of Gothic in contrast to the formal perfection of the classical style: 'In face of the Gothic pillars which taken singly would sway like reeds and only when united in large numbers to a central shaft are sufficiently massive to sustain their upright growth—under their arches which rest as it were on nothing and hover in the air like the shady tree-top vaulting of the forest: here our senses exult in the overweening boldness of the artist's achievement.' Thus the contrast between apparent fragility and actual strength, which so distressed the neo-classicists, has now become a matter for congratulation.

This leads Forster to a further contrast between Classical and Gothic architecture, which touches on a fundamental distinction between Classical and Romantic art altogether: 'Greek architecture seems to be related to everything that exists, to everything human; Gothic buildings, on the other hand, are like phenomena out of another world, like fairy palaces, set there to provide evidence of the creative power in man, which is able to pursue an isolated thought to its utmost limit and to reach sublimity even though by an eccentric path.' What is this but another way of saying what August Wilhelm Schlegel expressed some twenty years later in the famous definition in his Vienna lectures on dramatic art and literature: 'The poetry of the ancients was one of possession, whereas ours is a poetry of longing; the former stands firm on the ground of the present, the latter alternates between memory and surmise.'[1]

This passage is of special interest in that here for the first time in the Gothic movement Forster sounds what one might call the transcendental note—the suggestion of otherworldiness, of visionary magic. This was to play a large part in the Romantic conception of Gothic; it is a quality which is singularly absent from the realized projects of the Gothic Revivalists, both in Germany and England, though it is often characteristic of their unrealized projects, for example in the Gothic sketches of Schinkel and Pugin.

It is no great step from this transcendental note to the even more specifically Romantic concept of Gothic architecture as the expression of the Infinite. It was this concatenation of ideas which was to give the Gothic style its peculiar significance for the Romantic generation, and in this respect, too, Forster was the first to anticipate the Romantics. It is the vertical emphasis of the style, the upward surge of the

[1] *Ueber dramatische Kunst und Litteratur* (3 vols. Heidelberg, 1809–11), i. 24.

pillars and walls, which suggests to Forster this particular association of ideas: 'Even though the infinity of the universe cannot be symbolized in a finite space, nevertheless in this bold soaring of the pillars and walls one senses that restlessly dynamic element which the imagination so easily expands into the illimitable.'

In his description of Cologne Cathedral Forster gives vivid expression to the analogy between Gothic architecture and the plant forms of nature. Goethe had likened the exterior of Strasbourg Minster to a mighty tree; Forster, the professional naturalist, repeats the simile in somewhat different form and in more precise detail with reference to the interior of Cologne Cathedral: 'There they stand in their tremendous height, the group of slender columns, like the trees of a primeval forest; only at their topmost summit are they split into a cluster of branches, which interlaced with their neighbours form vaults of pointed arches, so lofty that they are beyond the reach almost of the spectator's gaze.' He is still more forcibly impressed by this resemblance when he sees the staircase of Christ Church hall at Oxford, where 'the centre of the vault rests on a fragile slender pillar, the branches of which spread out aloft in delicate arches like a palm tree'.

Though Forster carries on several ideas which had already been suggested in *Von Deutscher Baukunst*, there is no indication that he was acquainted with the essay. The tone of the two works is entirely different. Goethe's is a rhapsody in honour of Erwin von Steinbach; Forster's is both less personal and less lyrical. Despite the eloquence of his language, it is a sober attempt to appraise the distinctive features of the Gothic style. Moreover, it is noteworthy that two of the cardinal points of Goethe's essay find no echo in the *Ansichten*. Forster has nothing to say of the organic unity, of the harmony in diversity, of Gothic architecture, which is so strongly emphasized in *Von Deutscher Baukunst*. Nor does he share Goethe's belief in the German nature and origin of Gothic, a belief which, as we know, was to triumph over all evidence to the contrary until well into the nineteenth century. With his cosmopolitan background Forster forms an honourable exception to this Gothic chauvinism, which was of course by no means confined to Germany.

Then again Forster's attitude to Gothic was much more catholic than Goethe's. Goethe's admiration was confined to one Gothic building; Forster on the other hand—and he is the first German, with the possible exception of Heinse, of whom one can say this—obviously had an appreciation for the Gothic style as such. He has words of commendation for most of the Gothic buildings, both ecclesiastical and secular, which he passes in his travels. It is true that his feeling for the genuine article was not always impeccable, as witness his enthusiasm over Hawksmoor's rather unhappy towers at All Souls, which he compares to tall cypress trees in their 'simplicity and slender boldness'.

Forster, like Heinse, has an eye for the Gothic landscape. Take for instance his description of Oxford: 'Let him who wishes to see well-preserved Gothic buildings come here. Except for London, Oxford is perhaps the most handsome of all English cities from the distance—and, I am almost tempted to say, from near at hand as well. A forest of Gothic spires soars up from the shady alleys and meadows beside the Kam and Isid [sic].'

Yet despite his wide appreciation of Gothic Forster is by no means an uncritical admirer of the style. Of the Gothic tower of the Hôtel de Ville in Brussels he writes: 'This tower has more simplicity than Gothic buildings usually have; the multiplicity of little pinnacles and individual details does not prevent the eye from receiving a single strong impression of height soaring upwards lightly and boldly. It will always remain a blemish of Gothic architecture that its shapes appear prickly and as it were split into pieces, that its forms and proportions are too sharp, angular and elongated, and provide no rest to the eye.'[1]

The latter part of this passage is a compendium of objections already familiar to us from the anti-Gothic camp. At heart indeed Forster—like Heinse—remains a classicist. Though Gothic rouses his admiration and awe, it is classical, indeed neo-classical, architecture which elicits his affection. Note, for instance, his observations on the neo-classical church of St. Jacques in Brussels: 'Here both the eye and the spirit are at rest; here one feels at home; here there is nothing dark, naught of the awfully sublime. Here we have greatness, surrounded by a pleasing grace, by beauty and love.'[2] It is the same contrast which had struck him so forcibly at Cologne between the human reference of classical forms and the otherworldliness of Gothic.

Forster's classical preferences become more obvious in his judgements on pictorial art. Here he follows wholeheartedly the line of Winckelmann, Oeser, Mengs and the later Goethe. To him, as to them all, Raphael was indisputably the greatest of all painters. He is emphatically on the side of 'beautiful art' as opposed to 'characteristic art'.

---

[1] Briefe und Tagebücher Georg Forsters von seiner Reise am Niederrhein, in England und Frankreich im Frühjahr 1790, ed. Albert Leitzmann (Halle, 1893), p. 155.

[2] Ansichten, i. 492.

Thus the Flemish primitives are crude, distorted, ugly, and not worth the serious consideration of a man of taste. For the most part he ignores them completely, though virtually every church and gallery he visited in Brabant and Flanders had examples to show. He passes through Bruges without a reference to Memling, and of the Van Eyck altarpiece in Ghent all he has to say is: 'The composition, as one would expect of that period, is lacking both in order and clarity and in impressiveness of effect. Despite the care that has been expended on it, the drawing is stiff and incorrect; perspective and poise are entirely absent; the colours are harsh and bright and without shadow.' And lest one should suppose that this negative attitude towards Gothic painting applies only to the Netherlands school, he adds: 'But even in Italy people painted in this manner before Perugino.'[1] It is all the more remarkable that anyone who was so firmly rooted in the neoclassical tradition as far as painting is concerned should have shown such an unusual degree of feeling for Gothic architecture.

In the realm of the visual arts Forster has been called the last of the classicists.[2] He was also in some important respects the first of the Romantics. In several ways his conception of Gothic is more "romantic" than Goethe's. The note of otherworldliness, the association between Gothic and the longing for the Infinite, the likening of the Gothic interior to the primeval forest—all these constitute a notable anticipation of Romantic attitudes. And finally Forster was the first writer of the eighteenth century to formulate that wish-dream of German Romanticism: the call for the completion of Cologne Cathedral. 'It is much to be regretted', he says, 'that so splendid a structure should remain incomplete. If the mere visualization of the completed design can have so profound an effect on our imagination, what would not the effect of the reality be?'[3] The Romantics were to prove not unmindful of the debt they owed to Georg Forster.

A somewhat unexpected epilogue to this chapter is provided by Friedrich Nicolai's remarks on Gothic buildings in his journal of a tour through Germany and Switzerland undertaken in the year 1781.[4] It is an interesting comment on conventionally accepted literary

[1] Ibid. ii. 207.
[2] Cp. W. Waetzoldt, *Deutsche Kunsthistoriker* (2 vols. Leipzig, 1921), i. 212.
[3] *Ansichten*, i. 73.
[4] *Beschreibung einer Reise durch Deutschland und die Schweiz, im Jahre* 1781 (12 vols. Berlin and Stettin, 1783–96).

reputations that Nicolai, the arch *Aufklärer*, the sworn foe of everything Romantic, the butt of Goethe and Schiller, of Tieck and the
Schlegels, for his last-ditch rationalism, does in fact display considerably
more understanding of medieval architecture than either Herder or
Wackenroder, the supposed inaugurators of Romantic medievalism.

Like Herder's, Nicolai's attitude to Gothic is to some extent ambivalent, but in sum it is a great deal more positive than his. In a
letter to Herder of 19 November 1771 he makes an interesting comparison between Gothic architecture and 'our great geniuses, who
corrupt our taste and poetry' (he is evidently thinking chiefly of
Klopstock's Odes, which he has sent Herder for review). The fault
of both is their insistence on being original. Thus instead of following
the Greeks, who had exhausted the possibilities of 'proportions which
are pleasing to the eye and which at the same time possess both stability
and charm', the Goths strained after new effects. In consequence
'their architecture has neither the appearance of firmness nor of
charm, though it is both bold and singular This is the true image of
our poets, who do not wish to owe anything to their masters.'[1]

There is certainly nothing unorthodox here, but if we turn to
Nicolai's travel journal, written some twelve years later, we shall
be surprised indeed by the tone of his observations on the great
Gothic churches that came his way. His most explicit comments on
the subject are aroused by the spectacle of St. Stephen's in Vienna.
He begins his remarks by quoting with disapproval Dr. Burney's
description of the cathedral as 'a dark, dirty, and dismal old Gothic
building'.[2] 'One could not', writes Nicolai, 'make a more inept
judgment . . . on me the interior of St. Stephen's created quite the
opposite impression. The imposing and yet harmonious effect, vast
and yet stable, the twilit dimness of the lighting which reigns therein—
all this awoke in me sensations of astonishment and awe whenever
I entered the building.'[3]

Nicolai asks himself why St. Stephen's made a greater impression
on him than Strasbourg Minster and finds the answer partly in the
fact that the minster lacks the suggestive half light of Vienna's cathedral, partly that the choir of Strasbourg has been painted white and
gold in the modern fashion, and partly that St. Stephen's is larger and
loftier than Strasbourg. On the other hand nothing could excel the

---

[1] *Herders Briefwechsel mit Nicolai*, ed. O. Hoffmann (Berlin, 1887), p. 66.
[2] Charles Burney, *The Present State of Music in Germany, the Netherlands, and the
United Provinces* (2 vols. London, 1773), i. 239.
[3] Nicolai, op. cit. ii. 654-5.

beauty of the minster tower. 'There is something ineffable about the proportions of the tower, which holds and satisfies the spectator to such an extent that finally he cannot turn away from it. And the indescribable delicacy of the openwork carving combined with such evident stability gives it precedence over all similar structures.' Most beautiful of all is the sight of the setting sun shining through the interstices of the spire: 'then indeed one is lost in enchantment at this admirable masterpiece of German architecture, which in its kind is beyond compare.'[1]

Finally, Nicolai is the only eighteenth-century writer I know of apart from Goethe who laments the anonymity of the great medieval masters. When he comes to deal with Ulm Minster he notes with scorn that the name of the patrician who laid the foundation stone, but not that of the architect, has been recorded for all time, 'as if the great artist who first conceived in his mind the idea and the plan of this building and had the courage to carry it out were not on a totally different level from Ludwig Kraft and his empty ceremony'. None of the architects of the minster is known by name 'except Matthäus Enziger, who died in 1483 and was therefore probably the builder of the tower. His name along with that of Erwin and Johannes von Steinbach and David Hülz at Strasbourg, and of Georg Hauser and Anton Pilgram in Vienna deserves to be held in honour by posterity.'[2]

[1] Ibid. ii. 657–8.   [2] Ibid. ix. 26–7.

PART THREE

THE ROMANTIC MOVEMENT

THE ROMANTIC MOVEMENT

THE revival of interest in medieval architecture during the German Romantic period was of course just one facet of the revival of interest in the Middle Ages altogether. It is usually asserted—and with justice on the whole—that medievalism played a larger part in the German Romantic movement that in its English counterpart. Heine even went so far as to claim that the Romantic school in Germany was "naught else than the reawakening of the poetry of the Middle Ages, as it manifested itself in the songs, sculpture, and architecture, in the art and life of that period".[1]

Nevertheless it should be emphasized that this study is not a history of Romantic medievalism—for that several volumes would be necessary—but of one particular aspect of it. In consequence, many writers who are of the utmost importance for the development of Romantic medievalism will find little or no mention here, for the simple reason that they were not interested in the architecture of the Middle Ages, or at least did not express this interest in their writings.

Thus Tieck, who might be called the father of Romantic medievalism and who would occupy a foremost place in any history of the subject, is only represented here by a few pages, and the same is true of Brentano. Other writers who made important contributions—such as Novalis, Arnim, Uhland, Fouqué, or the brothers Grimm—do not appear at all.

Despite the name, the same considerations apply to the so-called Gothic novels, which made a contribution of a sort to Romantic medievalism in general, but nothing to the Gothic Revival in particular. Indeed in German—where they are referred to, more accurately, as *Schauerromane* or *Ritter- und Räuberromane*—they do not even have the name in common.[2] With this *caveat* we can proceed on our way.

---

[1] *Heines Sämtliche Werke*, ed. Ernst Elster (7 vols. Leipzig, 1887–90) v. 217.
[2] Cp. J. W. Appel, *Die Ritter-, Räuber- und Schauerromantik* (Leipzig, 1859); Carl Müller-Fraureuth, *Die Ritter- und Räuberromane* (Halle, 1894); Hansjörg Garte, *Kunstform Schauerroman* (Leipzig, 1935).

1. WACKENRODER

UNTIL the end of the eighteenth century the interest in the Middle Ages had been fitful and sporadic. The initiative of Bodmer, Breitinger, and Christoph Heinrich Myller had fallen on stony ground. Casparson, Oberlin, Justus Möser, and Johannes von Müller remained isolated figures. As we have seen, neither Herder nor Goethe was interested in the Middle Ages as such. For them the great age of the German past was the age of Dürer, Sachs, and Luther, of Götz von Berlichingen and Faust—the German Renaissance in fact. Not till the last years of the century can one speak of a revival of interest in the Middle Ages proper.

Now it is a commonplace of German literary history that this revival of interest in the Middle Ages was due in the first place to Wilhelm Heinrich Wackenroder and the small collection of his essays with the picturesque title *Herzensergiessungen eines kunstliebenden Klosterbruders* (1797). Wackenroder is usually credited with having been an enthusiastic admirer of both medieval painting and medieval architecture, and of having started the fashion for the Italian Pre-Raphaelites and the German Primitives. This legend—for legend it is[1]—was inaugurated by Goethe and his friend Heinrich Meyer in their famous attack on German Romantic painting in the essay 'Neu-deutsche religios-patriotische Kunst' (1817), and was given its most uncompromising expression in Heine's *Die Romantische Schule*.[2]

In actual fact Wackenroder had little interest in the Middle Ages—German or any other—in the sphere of the visual arts,[3] and his place in the development of Romantic medievalism has been consistently misrepresented. It has been claimed, for instance, that the *Herzensergiessungen* are the lineal descendant of *Von Deutscher Baukunst*, in the sense that the enthusiastic medievalism displayed in Goethe's essay lay dormant in the intervening decades until it was revived by Wackenroder.[4] This is to pile Pelion on Ossa in the way of misunderstanding,

---

[1] Cp. my article 'Wackenroder and the Middle Ages', *Modern Language Review*, vol. L (April, 1955).

[2] Heine, ed. cit. v. 235.

[3] Wackenroder's interest in German medieval literature, which is not in dispute, has been investigated by A. Gillies, 'Wackenroder's Apprenticeship to Literature: his Teachers and their Influence', *German Studies presented to H. G. Fiedler* (Oxford, 1938) and the same author's edition of the *Herzensergiessungen* (Oxford, 1948), pp. xiv–xx.

[4] Cp. G. Witkowski's introduction to the reprint of *Von Deutscher Baukunst* in Kürschner's *Deutsche National-Litteratur*, vol. cvii (Stuttgart, 1892), p. 169.

for, as we know, *Von Deutscher Baukunst* betrays contempt rather than enthusiasm for the Middle Ages, while the *Herzensergiessungen* is a paean not to the Middle Ages but to the Italian Renaissance.

The most reliable indication of Wackenroder's real attitude to medieval art and architecture is to be found in the long journal-letters written to his parents during the summer semester and vacation of 1793, which he spent with his friend Tieck at Erlangen. These diaries give a detailed and conscientious account of the various tours which he made—with, or more usually without, Tieck—through the Franconian countryside. They provide an almost continuous record of Wackenroder's aesthetic and other experiences during what was perhaps the most impressionable period of his brief life. Here, if anywhere, we can expect to find the immediate and genuine expression of his aesthetic attitude.

From our point of view these diaries are as instructive for what they omit as for what they include. In his account of Bamberg, for instance, this is all he has to say of the magnificent array of medieval sculpture which embellishes the cathedral: 'Inside, the cathedral contains an indescribable wealth of old pictures, tombs, bas-reliefs, &c., such as are to be found in all Catholic churches, though not always in such quantities.'[1] In general he finds the Gothic stone and wood carvings in the Bamberg churches to be 'ugly' and 'clumsy'[2] just as the medieval glass in the Lorenzkirche in Nuremberg is 'unsightly'.[3]

Medieval painting seems to have meant as little to Wackenroder as medieval sculpture. On the so-called Bamberger Altar, dated 1429, one of the acknowledged masterpieces of German medieval art, his only comment is: 'The figures are stiff, and have a golden halo round their heads, which merges very strangely into the gold background.'[4] Despite its qualifications, the most positive utterance on medieval painting to be found in all Wackenroder's writings occurs in his description of the fourteenth- and fifteenth-century pictures in Kloster Heilsbronn: 'This church is well worth seeing on account of the many ancient pictures by the fathers of German painting, which, it is true, are in part more faulty, stiff, and tasteless than the experiments of a tyro, in part however please the eye by their simple and modest dignity, by their unalloyed and unaffected naturalness of poise and expression, and by the noble folds of the garments.'[5]

---

[1] Wackenroder, *Reisebriefe*, ed. H. Höhn (Berlin, 1938), p. 119.
[2] Ibid. p. 130.   [3] Ibid. p. 187.   [4] Ibid. p. 139.
[5] Ibid. p. 211. Incidentally it is interesting to note that many years before this date (in 1781) an enthusiastic account of Grünewald's Isenheim altarpiece had been written by Goethe's Strasbourg friend Franz Christian Lerse, who is so attractively described in

Wackenroder's observations on medieval architecture are few and perfunctory and partly at any rate couched in the language—one might almost say jargon—of eighteenth-century neo-classicism. The noble exterior of Bamberg Cathedral is, somewhat disconcertingly, likened to a pastry cook's confection, and the churches of Nuremberg are 'black' and 'overladen'. Nevertheless he seems to have been genuinely impressed by the most beautiful of them, the Lorenzkirche, 'which is internally the most venerable, quaint and ancient church I know,'[1] But that is all. He shows no appreciation for the specific qualities of Gothic architecture, no sense of the revelation of a whole new world of beauty, such as had found expression years before in Goethe's *Von Deutscher Baukunst* or more recently in Forster's *Ansichten vom Niederrhein*.

The evidence of the Franconian diaries, then, as far as Wackenroder's medievalism is concerned, is mainly negative. But—it might be objected—Wackenroder was only twenty at the time he wrote them, and for his maturer views on the subject one must look to his later essays in the *Herzensergiessungen* and its posthumous sequel, the *Phantasien über die Kunst*. And yet the actual text of the essays gives even less justification for his reputation as a pioneer of medievalism in the arts.

For the fact of the matter is that the Middle Ages play an utterly insignificant role in the *Herzensergiessungen*. Medieval art proper—the paintings of the Italian Pre-Raphaelites and the German Primitives, Gothic or Romanesque sculpture or architecture—is barely mentioned in their pages. The misunderstanding on this point is all the more surprising in view of the reiterated emphasis with which Wackenroder enunciated his opinion that the Italian Renaissance, and not the Middle Ages, was the Golden Age of Art. In his essay on the death of Francia, for instance, he salutes the Renaissance as 'the true Heroic Age of Art', in which the divine frenzy which now flickers feebly in a few isolated individuals then inflamed the hearts of all and sundry. So far is Wackenroder from extolling medieval art that he refers to the Renaissance in the same essay as the period in which the art of painting rose like a phoenix from its ashes, and to Francia himself as belonging to the *first* generation of noble Italian

the Alsatian chapters of *Dichtung und Wahrheit*. This is the first known description of Grünewald's masterpiece and shows very much more feeling for medieval art than anything Wackenroder wrote on the subject. Cp. W. Waetzoldt, *Deutsche Kunstwerke beschrieben von deutschen Dichtern* (Leipzig, 1940), pp. 40ff. and Louis Kübler, *Unterlinden-Museum zu Colmar* (4th ed. Colmar/Paris, 1962), p. 19.

[1] Ibid. p. 186.

painters, who deserve all the more respect, 'since they founded a quite new and brilliant realm *on the ruins of barbarism*'.[1]

The Michelangelo essay is still more emphatic on this point. In the last paragraph of the essay Wackenroder states unequivocally that the age of Michelangelo is the 'beginning of Italian painting and the true age of the original artist. Who painted like Correggio before Correggio? like Raphael before Raphael?' All subsequent painting has been in greater or less degree an imitation of these First Originals. 'And whom,' he concludes 'did these ancestors themselves imitate? They produced this new and glorious art entirely out of themselves.'[2] In other words, for Wackenroder Italian painting begins with Michelangelo, Raphael and Correggio.

The passages which are most frequently adduced in support of Wackenroder's medievalism occur in the essay on 'Allgemeinheit, Toleranz und Menschenliebe in der Kunst' and in the Dürer essay. From the first:

To God the Gothic temple is as pleasing as the temple of the Greeks; and the crude war music of savages is no less acceptable to him than elaborate anthems and chorales.

Why do you not condemn the Red Indian for speaking his own language instead of ours? And yet you would condemn the Middle Ages for not building Greek temples.[3]

These sentences, detached from their context, are commonly taken as a plea for Gothic architecture and a claim for its equation with the classical style. But this is to put an emphasis on the words which is not warranted by the context and which falsifies their real import. From this context it is clear that these passages are not a specific plea for medieval architecture at all, but a general plea for that universal tolerance in matters of art which is the theme of the essay. This is made evident by the second half of the first sentence: 'And the crude war music of savages is no less acceptable to him than elaborate anthems and chorales.' In other words, *all* forms of art, whatever their provenance and character, are equally pleasing to God. Or, to put it in a slightly different way: all beauty is one, however, varied its expression. Hence it is as illogical to condemn the Middle Ages for not building Greek temples as it would be to censure the Red Indian for not speaking German.

[1] Wackenroder, *Werke und Briefe*, ed. H. Höhn (Berlin, 1938), p. 20.

[2] Ibid. pp. 87–88. It is interesting to compare this statement with the words of Friedrich Schlegel—the true apostle of the primitives in Germany—in his *Europa*: 'Titian, Correggio, Julio Romano, Andrea del Sarto, &c., das sind für mich die letzten Maler.' (*Kritische Friedrich-Schlegel-Ausgabe*, Abt. I, vol. 4, p. 13).

[3] Wackenroder, *Werke und Briefe*, ed. cit., pp. 52–53.

Precisely the same argument lies at the root of the Dürer essay, on which the claim for Wackenroder's medievalism is chiefly based:

Not only under Italian skies, majestic domes and Corinthian columns, but also under pointed arches, grotesquely decorated buildings and Gothic towers does true art flourish.[1]

It is this sentence above all others which has led to the misunderstanding concerning Wackenroder's aesthetic position. Time and again it is cited as a proof of his advocacy of medievalism, of the equation of Gothic and classical art. But this again is a distortion of Wackenroder's meaning which could only have arisen by isolating the passage from its context. It follows immediately on the comparison between the art of Raphael and that of Dürer, and the danger of making such comparisons in any narrow or invidious sense: 'Heaven has distributed its gifts among the great artists of the earth in such a way that it is incumbent upon us to pause before each in turn and pay each one a share of our tribute.'[2] All that the sentence is really saying, therefore, is that Dürer is a genuine artist as well as Raphael. The contrast, in fact, is a geographical one—a contrast between Italian and German art, not, as is usually supposed, between classical art and the art of the Middle Ages. The qualities, for instance, which Wackenroder attributes to Dürer's art—its realism, psychological truth, its raciness and manly strength, its human dignity and seriousness—have nothing specifically medieval about them, but are in Wackenroder's view typical of the German character at its finest. The sense of the passage is best summed up, indeed, in Wackenroder's succinct query earlier in the essay: 'Are not Rome and Germany on one and the same earth?'[3]

In the whole of the *Herzensergiessungen* there are only two passages which have any concern with the Middle Ages or medieval art. The first is the introduction to the Dürer essay, which we shall deal with later; and the other is the essay entitled 'Die Malerchronik', in which Wackenroder retells from the pages of Vasari and others anecdotes from the lives of the Italian painters, among whom he mentions several of the Pre-Raphaelites—Giotto, Lippo di Dalmasio, Fra Angelico, Spinello, and even Cimabue. But in these anecdotes he is in no way concerned with the aesthetic qualities of their art. He is principally interested in them as exemplifications of his favourite thesis—that the lives of the old Italian painters were inspired by the same piety as their pictures. Nevertheless this is the only passage in his writings which shows that Wackenroder was even aware of the existence of Italian medieval painting.

[1] Ibid. p. 66.   [2] loc. cit.   [3] Ibid. p. 58.

If we now sum up the evidence provided by the diaries and essays, it is hard to escape the conclusion that Wackenroder had in fact very little understanding of, or interest in, medieval art or architecture. Of medieval Italian painting (as apart from the painters) he has literally nothing to say, which is after all not surprising, since he had probably never seen any.[1] But of German medieval art and architecture, which he had seen on a considerable scale, he has also very little to say, and what he does say is for the most part pejorative. Only for the very latest phase of German Gothic art, which is already merging into Renaissance, does he manifest a certain feeling.

The legend of Wackenroder's medievalism first received currency, as we have indicated, in the essay on 'Neu-deutsche religios-patriotische Kunst', which was written by Heinrich Meyer in the closest collaboration with Goethe and was published by the latter in the second number of his periodical *Kunst und Altherthum* in 1817. Meyer begins his argument with an attempt to trace the origins of the enthusiasm for the old masters of the fourteenth and fifteenth centuries now so prevalent among the Romantic painters. After mentioning various pioneers in this direction in the eighteenth century, he goes on to consider the *Herzensergiessungen*. 'This book', he says, 'was well received and much read in Germany, and soon found its way to Rome, where without doubt it made a very great impression. With burning eloquence the author called for a warmer veneration for the older masters, set up their manner of painting as the best of models, and spoke of their works as if in them the highest peak of art had been achieved.'[2] It is clear from the preceding paragraphs of the essay that when Meyer talks of the 'older masters' he is referring to the Italian Pre-Raphaelites, the primitives of the fourteenth and fifteenth centuries. Here, then, we have for the first time the definite assertion that Wackenroder took the medieval painters as his ideal and that to this extent he was responsible for the neo-medievalism of German Romantic art.

Now, as we know, such a conclusion is in no way warranted by the actual text of Wackenroder's writings. The explanation of the misunderstanding must be sought in the artistic developments of the time. As Meyer states, the *Herzensergiessungen* "soon found its way to Rome, where without doubt it made a very great impression". Meyer is here alluding to the German Nazarene painters, who aimed at a school of art which should both live and paint as far as possible

[1] None of the galleries which Wackenroder visited—Dresden, Pommersfelden, Cassel, Salzdahlum—contained, as far as I know, any examples of Pre-Raphaelite painting at this time.   [2] WA I. 49 (i), 33.

in the spirit of the Pre-Raphaelite masters. In this endeavour they were undoubtedly inspired by the example of the *Klosterbruder*, and it is easy to see how this misinterpretation of Wackenroder's gospel arose. For the atmosphere of naive piety, of childlike reverence and simplicity, with which Wackenroder infuses his account of the great masters of the Italian—and German—Renaissance is in fact much more appropriate to the painters of the Middle Ages. He writes of Raphael and Michelangelo in terms which we should now apply, if at all, to Fra Angelico or Giotto. It was a simple step, then, for the Nazarene painters, in the interest of their own ideal, to displace this attitude from the Renaissance, where it was ludicrously inappropriate, to the sphere where it more or less belonged—to the art and artists of the Middle Ages. We are thus presented with the curious paradox that Wackenroder, who had himself little feeling for medieval art, did in fact have a considerable influence on the development of Romantic medievalism through the misinterpretation of his gospel by the Nazarene painters.[1]

But this is by no means the whole story of Wackenroder's influence on Romantic medievalism. For however little understanding he may have had of medieval art or architecture proper, he did, it is obvious, have considerable feeling for what one might loosely call a medieval atmosphere—for the quaint, the old-world, the Urban Picturesque. And in this respect at least Wackenroder was a pioneer and an innovator. It is not always realized how comparatively recent is this taste for the Urban Picturesque—in contradistinction to the taste for the Rural Picturesque, which antedates it by many decades both in Germany and England.

The taste for the Urban Picturesque must not be confused with the antiquarian interest in the relics of the past, which had long existed in both countries, as is witnessed by many a dusty folio from the sixteenth, seventeenth and eighteenth centuries. The essential difference between the two is that the former is aesthetic and sentimental, whereas the latter is historical in character.

To the German eighteenth century the Middle Ages were a living reality in a way which has no parallel in this country. Unspoilt medieval towns were the rule rather than the exception, towns which had altered astonishingly little from medieval times either architecturally or hygienically. To the eighteenth-century German, therefore, the Middle Ages meant dark and narrow streets, evil smells,

[1] For a fuller account of Wackenroder's aesthetic position see my article 'Wackenroder and the Middle Ages', *Modern Language Review*, vol. L. (April, 1955); for the Nazarene painters see Keith Andrews, *The Nazarenes* (Oxford, 1964).

inadequately lit houses and mouldering churches. And this applied
to large cities like Frankfurt and Cologne as well as to the Rothen-
burgs and Dinkelsbühls, which have retained their medieval character
almost intact to this day. Goethe has preserved for us the medieval
character of eighteenth-century Frankfurt both in *Dichtung und
Wahrheit* and in *Faust;* Georg Forster admired Cologne Cathedral,
but felt only disgust for the narrow stinking streets of the medieval
city. Thus though the Middle Ages were certainly a living reality
to the eighteenth-century Germans, they were a living reality which
was almost entirely bad.[1]

Nothing could illustrate more aptly the contrast between Wackenroder's new attitude to the medieval town and that of his eighteenth-
century predecessors than an account of Nuremberg written in
1786 by a Saxon clergyman, who happened to be the great grand-
father of the Germanist Erich Schmidt:

Nuremberg makes a good impression from the distance owing to its many
towers, but the nearer one approaches the less it pleases, because of its old-
world Gothic character which everywhere predominates. The narrow streets
are almost all dark and crooked, the houses tall, brightly coloured and painted
with tasteless figures and very often embellished with images of the saints;
the interiors are badly planned. The Rathaus, the Sebald-, Lorenz-, and Egidien-
kirchen, the deutsche Ordenshaus, the citadel, the great Spital with the Church
of the Holy Spirit, what frightful masses of stone they represent! The boldness
and eccentricity of the old and especially Gothic architecture filled me with
amazement, but nowhere did it make a pleasant impression on me. When I
entered the Sebalduskirche I thought I had come to an abode of bats, so power-
fully did it stink of these vermin, and so gloomy and hostile to man did it seem.
Ohe jam satis est, I thought, and had no mind to see any more churches; however, I did go into the Lorenzkirche, which was not much better.[2]

And now compare with this Wackenroder's reaction as recorded in
the diaries of his visits to this same city of Nuremberg only seven
years later. He is obviously delighted with the old-world atmosphere
of the place, with what he himself describes as its quaint (aben-
teuerlich) and romantic appearance. 'This city', he exclaims, 'never
ceases to fill me with amazement; because one does not see a single
new building, but only old ones from the tenth century on. Thus
one is completely transported into the olden times and is always
expecting to meet a knight or a monk, or a citizen in ancient costume,
for modern clothes do not fit at all with the style of the architecture.'[3]

[1] Cp. Wolfram von den Steinen, 'Mittelalter und Goethezeit', *Historische Zeitschrift*,
vol. 183 (April, 1957), pp. 252–5.
[2] E. Schmidt, 'Die Entdeckung Nürnbergs' from *Charakteristiken*, First Series (Berlin,
1886), p. 42.   [3] Wackenroder, *Reisebriefe*, ed. cit. p. 89.

Or again: 'Both the exterior and interior of almost every house seem to me to be without a trace of modern taste. Not a single new-fangled façade. The house doors are often small and dark and nearly always shut. You ring and the door opens; you make your way through dark recesses up a dilapidated staircase and find even people like Herr von Murr and Herr Panzer in rooms filled with books sitting at windows with little round panes which look on to the courtyard or a narrow alley.'[1]

Such passages as these form the background of the famous opening paragraph of the Dürer essay in the *Herzensergiessungen:*

Nuremberg, thou once world-famous city! How gladly did I wander through thy crooked alleys; with what childlike love I contemplated thy old-world houses and churches, which so firmly bear the stamp of our old native art! How deeply do I love the products of that age, which bear so racy, strong, and genuine a character! ... How often have I conjured up that age in thought when I sat in thy venerable libraries, Nuremberg, in some narrow corner dimly lit by the little round-paned windows and brooded over the folios of the worthy Hans Sachs or over other old, yellow, worm-eaten papers;—or when I wandered under the bold vaults of thy sombre churches, where the daylight wonderfully illuminates all the ancient carvings and pictures through brightly painted windows.

It would be hard to find a neater example of the contrasted attitudes of *Aufklärung* and *Romantik* to the medieval or old-world city than the above accounts of Nuremberg. Wackenroder appears to take delight in those very aspects of the scene which had most repelled eighteenth century taste. It is precisely the narrow winding streets, the old world buildings, the grotesque paintings, the dim-lit rooms, the creaking staircases and musty churches that appeal to him. This love of the past for its own sake, just because it is past, is something new. With Wackenroder it has the freshness of a discovery; he must not be held responsible for the excesses of sentimentality to which this cult was to lead.

Now though the taste for the Urban Picturesque is something quite different from the Gothic Revival proper it undoubtedly had an influence on it. For in popular estimation anyway the Urban Picturesque was more or less identified with the Medieval Picturesque, and the taste for it did much to predispose people in favour of a so-called 'medieval' atmosphere, which was conducive in its turn to a taste for Gothic architecture. In this respect, then, Wackenroder may truly be said to have made a contribution—even if indirect—to the Gothic Revival in Germany.

[1] Ibid. pp. 73–74.

2. TIECK

ACCORDING to Rudolf Köpke's biography of Tieck, which was largely based on the poet's own observations, Tieck shared to the full Wackenroder's enthusiasm for the old-world atmosphere of Nuremberg. This enthusiasm, it is true, does not find expression in the essays which he contributed to the *Herzensergiessungen* and the *Phantasien über die Kunst*. But many years later in the introduction to the first volume of *Phantasus* (Berlin, 1812), he looks back (through the person of Ernest) to 'the beloved city, in which Dürer had worked, where the churches, the glorious Rathaus and many a private collection preserved traces of his workmanship, as did the Johannis-Kirchhof his corpse; how gladly did I roam through winding alleys, over bridges and squares, where fountains and artistic objects of every kind reminded me of Germany's noble past.'[1]

The opening chapter of Tieck's novel *Franz Sternbalds Wanderungen. Eine altdeutsche Geschichte* (1798) contains a faint echo of this early Nuremberg experience. But of much more interest from our point of view is the account of Sternbald's visit to Strasbourg. Tieck's hero, a pupil of Dürer, passes through the city on his way to Italy, and there has a discussion on the merits of the minster with the sculptor Bolz, who is on the return journey from Italy to Nuremberg. They see the spire towering up in the distance, and Bolz, who has just been expressing a very low opinion of German art, exclaims: 'The minster is certainly a work that does the Germans credit!' 'But this does not fit in with your ideas about the Ideal and Sublime', interjects Sterbald. 'Why should I bother about my ideas?', replies the sculptor, 'I kneel in thought before the spirit who designed and carried out this mighty structure. Verily, it was no common soul who ventured thus to plant this tree with its branches, twigs and leaves, its rock-like masses approaching ever nearer to the clouds, and to conjure up as if by magic a work that is, as it were, an image of infinity.'[2]

The resemblance between these words and certain passages in *Von Deutscher Baukunst* (especially 1,3 and 11,) is striking, and there can be little doubt from this and many other indications that Tieck

[1] *Phantasus* (Berlin, 1812), i. 9.
[2] *Franz Sternbalds Wanderungen*, Deutsche National-Litteratur, vol. cxlv. pp. 269–70.

did in fact borrow from Goethe's essay in his account of the minster in *Franz Sternbalds Wanderungen*. Indeed the *Baukunst* would seem to have been one of the main sources for his description of a building which after all he had never set eyes upon at the time of writing. The whole passage is, one could say, not so much an imitation, as a set of variations on the theme of Goethe's Erwin.

Sternbald's reply to Bolz's words is couched in even more enthusiastic terms. In this passage indeed Sternbald-Tieck shows himself to be the most wholehearted admirer of Gothic we have yet encountered. Here for the first time we meet the note of *Schwärmerei* which was to become so characteristic of the Gothic Revival in the next decades. Goethe and Forster had at the most equated Gothic and Classical; Tieck comes down unequivocally on the Gothic side. Let all who dare to prate of Greek and Roman architecture, he cries, come to Strasbourg. There it stands, the minster, in all its glory, and needs no defence beyond its own presence. Impatiently he dismisses the whole neo-classic tradition of Taste and Noble Simplicity. The sublimity of this great Gothic building is an unique sublimity, which cannot be achieved by any other style of architecture. Its perfect symmetry, its aspiration towards the Infinite, coupled with its inner harmony and logic, are proof of this. Furthermore (and this is something new in the eighteenth-century interpretation of Gothic) it is a symbol of the Spirit of Man, of his unity in diversity, of the boldness of his heavenward aspirations, of his power of endurance and the mystery of his fate. He who can remain indifferent or hostile in the face of this achievement is no better than Peter when he denied Our Lord.

Curiously enough, the patriotic note is almost entirely absent from this passage in the original version of *Sternbald*. This is all the stranger, since it is a characteristic both of *Von Deutscher Baukunst* and of Wackenroder's essay on Dürer. Tieck himself evidently noticed this omission when he came to revise his novel for the collected edition of his works in 1843. Sternbald's reply to Bolz now begins: 'How glad I am that it has been granted me to see this monument of German art and sublimity! How eloquently does the name of Erwin resound through the world, and in face of this achievement how deeply do we sense the immortality of the human spirit.'[1] And after Sternbald has finished his observations, a speech of Bolz is interpolated, which would be hard to beat for Gothic chauvinism: 'It is true that these Gothic structures, which perhaps belong to the Germans alone, must make immortal the name of the German people . . . Perhaps

[1] *Schriften* (20 vols. Berlin, 1828–46), xvi. 222.

we shall discover some day that all the glorious buildings of this type in England, Spain and France have been erected by German masters.'[1] These words, it must be remembered, were written in 1843, some two years, that is to say, after Franz Mertens had demonstrated for those who had ears to hear that Gothic was a French, not a German invention.

The testimony to Tieck's interest in Gothc architecture is not exhausted by this brief passage from his early *Künstlerroman*. There is also his poem *Strassburgs Münster*, which dates from 1805–6, in which he compares the mighty structure to the Falls of Schaffhausen, with its soaring jets of stone, tender as a dream, sublimer than the pyramids, an eternal monument to the greatness of the human spirit. And in the introduction to the first volume of *Phantasus*, from which we have already quoted, Tieck pays a tribute to those pioneers who first drew attention to the greatness of German medieval art and architecture, mentioning in particular the Goethe of *Von Deutscher Baukunst* ('which I have never been able to read without emotion'), the *Blätter von deutscher Art und Kunst*, the *Klosterbruder* and Friedrich Schlegel.

[1] Ibid. p. 224.

3. BRENTANO

MENTION should here be made of another Romantic effusion on Strasbourg Minster, written in its first form some four or five years later than Tieck's *Sternbald*. This is to be found in Brentano's *Aus der Chronika eines fahrenden Schülers*. The *Chronika* first saw the light in 1818, but it had been begun as early as 1802. The original version, from which we here quote, was discovered in 1874 and was first published in 1880–1 in the *Stimmen aus Maria-Laach*.

Unlike Tieck's tribute, Brentano's account of the minster owes nothing to Goethe's essay. Nor can it be said to demonstrate any particular understanding of Gothic architecture. The description is put into the mouth of Brentano's young wandering scholar Johannes, and is confined to the tower. He is strolling round the garden of his lodging early on a bright summer morning, when he suddenly becomes aware of the minster tower soaring upwards to the clouds. He is struck, almost alarmed, by the sight. Not even Nature herself in her most romantic moods had impressed him so profoundly: 'I realized with astonishment how I had sat under lofty oaks in sombre forests and by plunging waterfalls in lonely valleys . . . and yet had not felt myself so moved as by the sight of the minster tower . . . When I beheld this stupendous tower with its many pillars, pinnacles and embellishments rising out of each other, and which are as transparent as the skeleton of a leaf, then it seemed to me like the dream of a profound architect, at which he would himself be startled, if on waking he were forced to realize his dream in stone.'[1]

In contrast to Tieck, it is not the soulfulness, but the soullessness of the tower that strikes and disturbs him: 'It stands there proud and solid without heart or understanding, as if it had grown out of itself and owed nothing to any man—that is what made the sight so shattering to me, since after all the flowers and trees and even the hard rocks seem to have a soul which breathes and feels like man, rejoicing with him in spring and mourning with him in winter; and yet I could not take my eyes off it.'[2]

Brentano's is an isolated voice, for from Goethe's *Baukunst* on

[1] *Brentanos Werke*, ed. Max Preitz, *Meyers Klassiker-Ausgaben* (3 vols. Leipzig and Vienna, 1914), i. 381.
[2] loc. cit.

it was precisely the organic or, as it was later to be called, the 'vegetable' aspect of the style, in other words its affinity with the phenomena of nature, which most fascinated the Gothic enthusiasts.

The *Chronika* is set in the year 1358, one of the first German Romantic tales therefore, after Novalis's *Heinrich von Ofterdingen*, to be placed in the Middle Ages proper. It is in many ways an interesting example of Romantic medievalism in its early phase, with its fairy-tale quality, slightly archaic style and supposedly medieval atmosphere of naive piety and childlike simplicity. For us its interest lies in the fact that an appreciation of a Gothic building should be introduced into a work of fiction as an integral part of this atmosphere. It may well be that Brentano had been moved to do so in the first place by the example of *Franz Sternbalds Wanderungen*, though the world of Tieck's novel is the Renaissance, not the Middle Ages.

4. SCHELLING

A NOTABLE exception to the Gothic enthusiasms of the Romantics is provided by the philosopher Schelling. His views on the subject are contained in the posthumously published lectures on the Philosophy of Art, originally delivered in Jena in the winter semester of 1802–3, and repeated in Würzburg in 1804–5.

Schelling's observations on Gothic form part of his contention that architecture is an allegory of the organic expressed in an inorganic medium, and of the corollary thereto, that its prototype is the organism of plants. Now no other style of architecture illustrates this truth so patently as Gothic, for in it the plant world is reproduced without any modification at the hands of art. 'One has only to look at a genuine example of Gothic architecture in order to recognize in all its shapes the unaltered forms of the plant.'[1] Thus the most distinctive characteristic of a Gothic building—for example, Strasbourg Minster—is the narrowness of the base in relation to its size and height. In this it is like a huge tree, which ramifies from a relatively slender trunk into an enormous crown, stretching out its twigs and branches on every side into the air. These twigs and branches are represented by the numberless turrets, pinnacles and other excrescences, and the analogy is rendered still more precise by the masses of carved foliage which proliferate over the Gothic church. The chapels, &c., which cluster round the base of the building are an indication of the spreading roots of the mighty tree. This same plant form is to be observed in all the ramifications of the Gothic church—in the cloisters, for instance, whose vaulted roofs reproduce the intertwined overhanging branches of an avenue of trees.

But all this should not be taken to imply that Schelling approves of Gothic architecture. Quite the contrary in fact. Gothic, it is true, imitates vegetable nature (thereby apparently fulfilling his definition of what architecture should be), but it does so in a crude and purely naturalistic way, where art plays no part. (One is inclined to ask what Gothic buildings, if any, Schelling had actually seen!)

In sharp contrast to this is 'the higher imitation of plant forms in the nobler type of architecture'. Schelling takes the example of the

[1] *Friedrich Wilhelm Joseph von Schellings Sämmtliche Werke*, ed. K. F. A. Schelling (Stuttgart and Augsburg, 1859), Abteilung I. vol, v, p. 584.

Doric column, which imitates nature only indirectly in that it imitates the trunk of a tree after it has been felled and shaped by man. Thus Gothic, because it represents the tree in its natural state, has to narrow the base and expand the upper part, whereas the Doric column, like the felled trunk, is broader at the base and narrower at the top. 'Here art expresses nature more perfectly and, as it were, improves it. It removes what is superfluous and purely individual and leaves only what is significant.'[1] We are back at Wickelmann and Mengs and the pure milk of the neo-classic word.

Schelling's attitude to Gothic is curious, indeed unique. He attaches even more importance to the 'vegetable' element in the style than either his predecessors (Goethe, Heinse, Forster) or his Romantic successors (Friedrich Schlegel, Boisserée, Büsching, Görres); but whereas for all of them without exception the 'vegetabilism' of Gothic was one of its most admired and attractive qualities, for Schelling it is a proof of its inferiority to the classical style. None of the anti-Goths of the eighteenth century had put forward this particular argument.

In his whole discussion of architecture Schelling takes Greek architecture as the norm, more or less equating it indeed with architecture altogether. It is clear that his attitude towards Gothic is essentially that of the eighteenth-century neo-classicists: good architecture is classical architecture, from which Gothic is an unfortunate aberration.

This rejection of Gothic is strange in a leading figure of the Romantic movement. It is all the stranger in one whose definition of beauty was: the representation of the Infinite in finite terms ('Das Unendliche endlich dargestellt'). For most of the Romantic Gothicists the main appeal of Gothic resided in the belief that it was precisely this.[2]

[1] Ibid. pp. 586–7.
[2] Later Schelling seems to have modified his objections to Gothic. At least he showed considerable interest in the projects of Sulpiz Boisserée. Cp. SB i. 86–9.

5. FRIEDRICH SCHLEGEL

THE Romantic approaches to Gothic which we have so far been considering have been tentative only. The first member of the Romantic generation to concern himself seriously with medieval architecture was Friedrich Schlegel in his *Briefe auf einer Reise durch die Niederlande, Rheingegenden, die Schweiz, und einen Theil von Frankreich.* These travel letters were first published in Schlegel's *Poetisches Taschenbuch auf das Jahr 1806*, and were then reprinted in a considerably amplified form and with a new title, *Grundzüge der gothischen Baukunst*, in the sixth volume of his *Sämmtliche Werke* (Vienna, 1823).[1] The greater part of the *Briefe* describes his journey from Paris to Cologne in the spring of 1804, and was written in the summer and autumn of that year.[2]

Friedrich Schlegel had been resident in Paris since June 1802, and since the autumn of 1803 he had been living in the closest touch with the brothers Boisserée, who had come to Paris chiefly in order to study the German and Flemish medieval paintings then exhibited in the galleries of the Louvre. Under their influence Schlegel devoted himself intensively to the study of this hitherto neglected field of European art, and the result of this preoccupation is to be seen in the last two essays on the Paris collections (*Zweiter* and *Dritter Nachtrag alter Gemälde*) in his periodical *Europa*. The Boisserées accompanied Friedrich Schlegel on his journey to Cologne in 1804; indeed it was on their invitation that he decided to settle in that city. We cannot doubt that his views on Gothic architecture were profoundly influenced by their constant companionship before, during and after this journey.

Schlegel's *Briefe*, along with Goethe's *Von Deutscher Baukunst* and Forster's *Ansichten vom Niederrhein*, are the most important landmarks in the rediscovery and rehabilitation of German medieval

[1] Both versions are included in the text of the *Kritische Friedrich-Schlegel-Ausgabe*, Abteilung I. Band 4, *Ansichten und Ideen von der christlichen Kunst*, ed. Hans Eichner (Munich, &c., 1959), to which volume all page references refer unless otherwise stated.

[2] This is made evident in a reference on p. 185 to medieval paintings in the churches and private collections of Cologne, from which it emerges that the *Briefe* (up to the end of the description of Cologne on p. 186) were written *before* the *Zweiter* and *Dritter Nachtrag alter Gemälde*, which we know to have been composed in the first half of September 1804 (Cp. SB i. 30). The rest of the *Briefe*, describing a journey to Switzerland via the Rhine and Strasbourg and back through Paris in the autumn and winter of 1804-5, were written after his return to Cologne in March 1805.

architecture. The significance of Schlegel's letters, to put it in a nut-shell, lies in the fact that through them the Gothic Revival became firmly anchored as a constituent part of the German Romantic move-ment. Friedrich Schlegel was the first to realize fully the relevance of Gothic architecture to the Romantic spirit, the first to recognize its pre-eminence as an expression of that medievalism which meant so much to the Romantic generation. As he was to put it later in his Vienna lectures: 'The spirit of the Middle Ages in general, and of the German Middle Ages in particular, finds more complete expression in the monuments of so-called Gothic architecture than anywhere else.'[1] All this is implicit in the *Briefe* of 1804, but it is only in the revised version of 1823 that it is explicitly stated.

In other respects, too, the *Briefe* represent a milestone in the develop-ment of the Gothic Revival in Germany. In the first place, they are the first publication of any length in German literature to deal pre-dominantly with the subject of medieval architecture. Schlegel's observations are couched in the form of a travel diary, and though many subjects are touched on in the course of the journey, the theme of medieval architecture is so consistently in the foreground that when he came to revise the letters for the collected edition of his works he rechristened them, as we have seen, *Grundzüge der gothischen Baukunst*. It is true that this title is misleading, for there is nothing systematic about Schlegel's observations even in the revised version. Nevertheless this travel diary represents the first serious and sustained attempt in German literature to investigate the nature and origin of Gothic architecture.

In the second place, the *Briefe* introduce us at last to the Gothic Revival proper as opposed to its preliminaries. Tentative beginnings are over; it is the full flood at last. The acceptance of Gothic is now complete. Friedrich Schlegel's admiration for the style is unbounded. It is implied, if not actually stated, that it is superior, profounder, more significant, and more sublime than the classical mode.

It is evident that Schlegel was familiar with *Von Deutscher Baukunst* and with the *Ansichten vom Niederrhein*, and that he is indebted to both his predecessors for some of his basic conceptions and formulations. Indeed one could say that Schlegel's diary is the first work to show the influence of Goethe's essay in a fruitful and creative way. Time and again the *Reisebriefe*, both in their thought and in their expression, remind one of passages in the *Baukunst*. It is clear that Goethe's essay was at least one of the factors which opened Schlegel's eyes to the world of Gothic architecture.

As for Forster's book, quite apart from similarities of thought and expression, Schlegel is following the example of the *Ansichten* in the very form of his work—the travel journal as a vehicle for aesthetic observations. Furthermore, Schlegel's diary covers much of the same ground as Forster's—Brabant and the Rhineland. And finally he follows Forster in concentrating on Cologne Cathedral as the out-standing monument of Gothic architecture.

A more pervasive influence, and one more difficult to assess, is that of the brothers Boisserée. It is safe to say that but for Friedrich's intimate friendship with the brothers the *Briefe* would never have been written, or at least not in their present form. For left to his own resources he had little feeling or understanding for architecture in any shape.[1] His natural taste was for painting rather than architec-ture, as is amply testified both by the greater bulk and the greater merit of his writings on the subject. There is a significant entry in Sulpiz Boisserée's fragmentary autobiography, describing how he introduced Schlegel to the cathedral of Notre Dame, which 'as a result of some preconceived idea he had left unregarded.'[2] In other words, Friedrich Schlegel, the declared apostle of Romantic medieval-ism, had been living in Paris for well over a year without even bother-ing to look at one of the greatest monuments of European Gothic.

Boisserée relates how deeply impressed Schlegel was by his visit to the cathedral under the aegis of the brothers, and proceeds:

His attention was thoroughly roused when we promised him a still higher enjoyment from the many old architectural monuments in the Netherlands, in Cologne, and in the Rhineland generally. All this awakened in our friend the wish to become acquainted with these districts . . . and at the end of April 1804 he accompanied us through Belgium to Aachen and from there via Düsseldorf to Cologne. The *Briefe auf einer Reise durch die Niederlande*, &c., which were published in the *Poetisches Taschenbuch für 1806*, owe their origin for the most part to this journey.[3]

It is clear, then, that Schlegel's conversion to Gothic was directly due to the Boisserées. Nor can we have any doubt that the Gothic monuments they passed on their way from Paris to Cologne were the subject of the closest discussion between the friends, and that this consultation was continued in Cologne, when Friedrich came to

[1] Cp. Hans Eichner's introduction to vol. 4, p. xxx.
[2] SB i. 27.   [3] SB i. 27–28.

compose his observations with the help of the notes he had taken on the journey.[1] In fact we may look upon the *Reisebriefe* as the first shot fired in the campaign of the Boisserée-Schlegel circle for a greater understanding of medieval architecture. As far as the content of the letters is concerned, we shall not go far wrong if we regard them as virtually a work of collaboration between Friedrich Schlegel and the brothers Boisserée, though the brilliant formulation of his ideas is of course entirely Schlegel's. These remarks no longer apply to the additions of the 1823 version, for in the interval Schlegel had developed his own theories on medieval architecture, in isolation, more or less, from his friends.

Another debt, acknowledged by Friedrich himself in a footnote to the section on Cologne, was to the antiquarian and historian of Cologne, Ferdinand Franz Wallraf. Wallraf, though his tastes were anchored in eighteenth-century classicism, was one of the first to show understanding and appreciation for the medieval antiquities of his native city. Friedrich gratefully admits how much his own observations on Cologne owe to Wallraf's help and calls upon him to write a history of Gothic architecture, 'for which it would be difficult to find anyone more thoroughly equipped'.[2]

Wallraf had been Rector of Cologne University during the occupation of the city by the French troops and it was due to his courageous intervention that the stained glass windows and statues of the cathedral had been saved from the revolutionary mob in 1794. Today he is chiefly remembered as a collector of German primitives, especially of the Rhineland school, and in this respect he was a pioneer and a forerunner of the Boisserées, though his methods were unsystematic and haphazard in comparison with theirs. There are many testimonies, including Goethe's, to the hopeless confusion that prevailed in his vast collections. All was grist to his mill—not only medieval paintings, but Roman antiquities, coins, gems, armour, engravings, manuscripts, incunabula, fossils and minerals. He bequeathed this miscellaneous but valuable material to his native city, and this formed the core of what was later to become the world-famous Wallraf-Richartz Museum.[3]

---

[1] This supposition is corroborated by a sentence in a letter of Boisserée to Friedrich Schlegel (13 February 1811): 'Ich sah mich bei diesem Brief immer auf dem Standpunkt, als führe ich ein Gespräch mit Ihnen, wie damals, als Sie Ihre Briefe über die altdeutsche Baukunst schrieben.' (SB i. 106).

[2] *Schlegel*, p. 176 n.

[3] For Wallraf see L. Ennen, *Zeitbilder aus der neueren Geschichte der Stadt Köln, mit besonderer Rücksicht auf Ferdinand Franz Wallraf*, (Cologne, 1857).

In attempting to assess Friedrich Schlegel's contribution to the Gothic Revival in Germany it is important to distinguish clearly between the two versions of his travel letters. The 1823 version contains both revisions and additions, some of considerable length and import. Hitherto accounts of Schlegel's attitude towards medieval architecture have failed to discriminate between these two versions, with the result that he has been credited with holding opinions in 1804 which actually date from almost twenty years later. And in these twenty years much had happened both in the development of the Gothic Revival and in the development of Friedrich Schlegel. In particular he had become a Catholic and had developed to the full the ideas on 'Christian Art', towards which he was only feeling his way in 1804. Indicatively, the volume of his collected works which contains the *Grundzüge der gothischen Baukunst* (and the *Gemäldebeschreibungen aus Paris und den Niederlanden*) is entitled *Ansichten und Ideen von der christlichen Kunst*.

What, then, were Friedrich Schlegel's views on Gothic in 1804, as revealed by his travel letters in the *Poetisches Taschenbuch*? In the first place, he uses the term 'Gothic' to cover the whole period of medieval architecture. As an alternative he advocates the term 'German' architecture; he bases this usage, not on Goethe, but on the art historian Fiorillo, who had argued in its favour in his history of painting and elsewhere, on the ground that this architecture was common to all the 'German' peoples, and that the most important examples of the style in Italy, France, and Spain (England is not mentioned) were built by German architects.[1] But Friedrich's use of the term is ambiguous, since sometimes he seems to apply it only to the later medieval (i.e. Gothic) style. In any case he is convinced that Gothic is German in another and deeper sense: 'Every nation, every land and clime has its own specific and uniquely appropriate architecture',[2] and the style that is native and natural to the German lands is Gothic.

For Friedrich Schlegel the most distinguishing characteristic of Gothic architecture lies in its affinity with, and imitation of, the multifarious phenomena of nature, and especially of vegetable nature. Here, of course, he is following both Goethe and Forster. No doubt he is referring directly to the *Ansichten* when he states that the clustered pillars of Cologne Cathedral have been 'not inaptly compared with the proud vaulting of a lofty avenue of trees'.[3] But Schlegel pursues the analogy far more thoroughly and gives it a much wider application

---

[1] See below, p. 239.   [2] *Schlegel*, p. 174.   [3] Ibid. p. 178.

than either of his predecessors. Indeed this feeling for nature and its expression in architecture is for him the very essence of the Gothic spirit.

It is Cologne Cathedral that calls forth his most detailed and eloquent treatment of this point, but the theme recurs in various contexts throughout the diary. Thus the exterior of the cathedral and its elaborate system of buttresses with all their turrets, pinnacles and other embellishments is like nothing so much as a forest, whereas the interior with its clustered pillars and leafy capitals and branching vaults has, as we know, been compared to an avenue of trees. Others again have imagined a resemblance to the column-like formations of basaltic rocks,[1] and from near at hand the whole structure reminds Schlegel of an enormous piece of crystallization. He sums up, in terms that recall Goethe's later morphological writings as well as the oft-quoted passage from the third section of the *Baukunst*:

In a word these miracles of art, in respect of their organic complexity and inexhaustible wealth of forms, most resemble the works and products of nature herself; at least the impression they make is the same, and just as the structure, tissue and growth of a living organism appears inexhaustibly rich to the investigator, so too does the formal complexity of such an architectural creation. Everything is shaped and moulded and embellished, and ever more lofty and mighty forms and decorations arise from the primary and smaller ones. Moreover these forms are themselves borrowed from the plant world.

The essence of Gothic architecture consists therefore in the power of creating, like nature herself, an infinite multiplicity of forms and of flower-like decorations. Hence the inexhaustible and countless repetitions of the same decorative details; hence the vegetable element. And hence too the deeply moving and mysterious power of this architecture, and its capacity to charm and delight and at the same time to evoke our amazement at its sublimity.[2]

This leads Friedrich Schlegel to the specifically Romantic concept, already adumbrated by Forster, of Gothic as the expression of the Infinite: 'Gothic architecture has the highest possible significance, for, in contrast to painting, which can only give us faint, uncertain, ambiguous and remote indications of the divine, it can represent and realize the Infinite through the mere imitation of nature's bounty— *even without reference to the ideas and mysteries of Christianity*, which have nevertheless had a considerable influence on the origin and development of ecclesiastical architecture.'[3] It was this vision of Gothic

[1] e.g. J. D. Fiorillo, *Kleine Schriften*, I, 151–2 (Göttingen, 1803), which refers in this connection to Fingal's Cave.

[2] *Schlegel*, pp. 179–80.

[3] Ibid. p. 180. Somewhat surprisingly the sentence which I have italicized was left unaltered in the 1823 version.

as the direct and concrete expression of the Infinite which made it especially dear to the Romantic generation.

If the translation into architectural terms of the infinite abundance of nature is the primary achievement of Gothic, a second and more surprising characteristic is the simplicity and purity of proportions, the hidden symmetry, of the Gothic style at its best, qualities which seem at first sight to be scarcely compatible with its richness of decoration and multiplicity of detail. It is the Hôtel de Ville at Louvain which first calls forth Schlegel's enthusiasm on this point: 'What particularly distinguishes this building along with its extreme delicacy and wealth of detail is its beautiful simplicity and purity of proportions. For it is quite mistaken to suppose that these latter qualities have been entirely banished from Gothic architecture.'[1]

Cologne Cathedral confirms on a larger scale what Schlegel had sensed in Louvain:

The vastness of this sublime torso fills everyone with amazement, and especially the height of the choir vaulting evokes admiration from all who behold it. But the most striking point to anyone who has had the opportunity of studying with care a number of monuments of Gothic architecture is the beauty of the proportions, the simplicity, the harmony despite the delicacy of detail, the lightness despite the bulk. This impression is sensed by everyone who has a feeling for such things; but it is not possible to describe or explain this feeling further, only exact measurements and comparisons with other buildings of a similar kind would be able to throw light on the secret of that symmetry which is yet so obvious to more delicate perceptions.[2]

We are inevitably reminded of the terms in which Goethe describes his first impression of Strasbourg Minster, the mysterious sense of unity and harmony despite the thousand details, the contrast between mighty size and fragile delicacy. This stress on the proportions, the harmony and simplicity of Gothic is what most differentiates the attitude of the nineteenth century from that of the eighteenth on the subject. The very qualities whose supposed lack had roused the gravest disapproval in the neo-classic critic are now triumphantly vindicated as leading characteristics of the style. It was the genius—truly an 'original genius'—of the young Goethe which first divined this 'inner form'. Here as in many other matters Schlegel is following in his wake, amplifying and defining more closely what had been first suggested in *Von Deutscher Baukunst*.

In other respects, however, Schlegel strikes out entirely fresh ground. Hitherto the understanding which in varying degrees had been

[1] Ibid. p. 167.   [2] Ibid. p. 177.

extended to Gothic architecture in the course of the eighteenth century had not embraced Gothic sculpture or church fitments. Wackenroder has some rather equivocal remarks on the stained glass windows of the Lorenzkirche in Nuremberg; otherwise this so conspicuous ingredient of Gothic churches had also escaped notice. In these fields Schlegel is a pioneer. His remarks on medieval sculpture in connection with the tombs of the Frankish kings in St. Denis show a surprising insight into this aspect of medieval art. He stresses the intimate relationship between medieval sculpture and the building of which it forms an integral part, and shows how its particular characteristics are determined by this fact. Thus its predominantly vertical character, the disproportionately narrow and elongated figures, are part and parcel of the extreme verticality of Gothic architecture.[1] 'Just imagine', he says to reinforce his point, 'a marble figure with the full round proportions of classical art attached to a slender soaring Gothic pillar and you will feel at once how inappropriate it is'. After admitting that the medieval sandstone sculptures can never have the natural smoothness and vitality of marble, nor its delicacy of outline, he goes on: 'But the skilful workmanship of the close-fitting garments, the straight and simple stance, and the innocent and pious truth of the facial expression can raise such sculptures to the rank of significant and beautiful decorative objects.'[2] Friedrich Schlegel was the first to realize the significant part played by sculpture in the Gothic system. At least he was the first to express it in print, for here as always it is impossible to determine how much of his insight is due to the Boisserées.

Similarly, no one before him had written with such rapture of the effect of Gothic glass. Thus of the west window of St. Gudule's in Brussels:

How is it possible to describe the splendour and the magical impression of such a window when the light is just right, neither too dazzlingly bright nor too dim. It is like a heavenly tapestry of precious stones and crystals, like the brightly shimmering surface of a sea of fiery flowers, in whose rippling waves all the secrets of colour and light float past our eyes in ever new and mysterious combinations.[3]

It is a tribute to Schlegel's powers of discrimination that in discussing

---

[1] Cp. F. Hemsterhuis, *Lettre sur la sculpture*, (Amsterdam, 1769), p. 20, for an explanation of the same phenomenon more in accord with the age of Enlightenment: 'The Christian sculptor had recourse to starving beggars for his models, and being accustomed to study these emaciated bodies in order to carve his saints and martyrs, the proportions of his figures became in general excessively elongated.'

[2] *Schlegel*, p. 158.   [3] Ibid. p. 166.

the glass in the Cologne churches he is inclined to give the preference, as far as the colour effect is concerned, to the thirteenth-century glass of St. Cunibert's rather than to the fifteenth-century glass in the cathedral.

But Friedrich Schlegel's most weighty claim to originality lies in his treatment of Romanesque architecture. Neither Goethe, nor Forster, nor with the single exception of C. L. Stieglitz[1] any other German writer on Gothic before Schlegel had apparently realized that there were two styles of medieval architecture. Here, for the first time, in his consideration of the Cologne churches, a serious attempt is made to define the characteristics of the Romanesque style and to show in what respects it differs from Gothic.

He states categorically: 'There are two completely different epochs in Gothic architecture: an older, which owing to its resemblance to the Constantinian-Byzantine Christian style might be called the Helleniz-ing; and the perfected later style, which is incomparably more accom-plished and which is in reality German'.[2] He then goes on to consider the characteristics of some of the Romanesque churches of Cologne: St. Gereon, St. Aposteln, St. Cunibert, St. Severin, St. Martin. He notes the arrangement of the Romanesque system of towers and choirs, aisles and ambulatories, which give the impression, not of a single church, but of a series of churches rising out of each other, and comes to the conclusion that the essential feature of Romanesque is its intricately interrelated multiplicity. He has words of special appre-ciation for St. Gereon, praising its harmonious proportions and decora-tive simplicity. He notes that animal motifs are only used for sub-ordinate purposes, such as gargoyles, and that the plant motifs, so characteristic of the Gothic style, are here almost completely absent. The capitals of the Romanesque pillars are usually plain, without em-bellishment except for their gilding. But there also exists a type of column peculiar to Romanesque, namely the squat basalt columns to be seen in the apsidal galleries of the choirs, and also in windows and cloisters, usually double, occasionally even quadruple, whose capitals are sometimes plain, sometimes a pattern of birds, dragons and other figures intertwined with foliage. These remarks reveal keen observation in a virtually unexplored field, though Schlegel is aware that he is merely treading on the fringe of the subject. 'All this', he says, 'must first be defined and clarified by means of drawings and measurements.'[3] Thus he points the way which Sulpiz Boisserée

[1] See below, p. 245.   [2] *Schlegel*, p. 180.   [3] Ibid. p. 184.

was later to follow in his *Denkmale der Baukunst vom 7. bis zum 13. Jahrhundert am Nieder-Rhein.*

Schlegel makes various attempts to investigate the origin of medieval architecture. He is quite clear in his mind that the dividing line between medieval and ancient architecture is a religious one. 'Gothic', in his wide sense of the term, is the specifically Christian style. This is for us so obvious a truism that it scarcely needs assertion. Yet Friedrich Schlegel was the first writer in German literature to formulate it clearly and unambiguously. As we have seen, there had been no hint of it either in *Von Deutscher Baukunst* or in Forster's *Ansichten*. Heinse, it is true, had recognized the religious appropriateness of the style, but Schlegel was the first to see the origin and meaning of medieval architecture in specifically Christian terms. 'With Christianity since Constantine an entirely new idea and significance came into architecture, which extended its influence right through the Middle Ages.'[1]

Thus Schlegel emphatically rejects the notion of an Arabic origin for the Gothic style. The supposed resemblance between Gothic towers and Moorish minarets is an illusion; it is far more likely, if one bears in mind the more massive type of tower to be found in some medieval churches, that they derive from the medieval castle.

More than this, the deepest meaning of Gothic architecture is to be found in the Christian symbolism which lies at its root. 'The chief aim of the Gothic builders was to express an idea, and one cannot doubt that they often had the definite and conscious intention of representing and indicating in the visible building the spiritual idea of the Church itself, whether the Church militant or the Church triumphant.'[2]

It is in such a passage as the above, written, it should be noted, four years before Schlegel's conversion, that one seems to hear most clearly the voice of the brothers Boisserée, who were fervent Catholics by upbringing and conviction. It is noteworthy that the Gothic appreciations with which we have been dealing hitherto have all come from the Protestant, or at least non-Catholic camp. It was the main historical significance of the Schlegel-Boisserée circle in the development of the Gothic Revival in Germany that they approached medieval architecture, not only from a specifically Christian, but from a specifically Catholic point of view. To them Gothic was the Catholic style *par excellence*, and could only be properly understood as the symbolic expression of the Catholic faith. Hence the close connection between

[1] Ibid. p. 169.   [2] Ibid. p. 166.

the Gothic Revival and the catholicizing tendencies of the German Romantic movement.

This represented a revolution in architectural taste, for hitherto for some two hundred years the specifically Catholic style had been Baroque. Though there are many magnificent examples of Protestant Baroque, such as the Frauenkirche in Dresden or St. Paul's in London, the style in its ecclesiastical aspect had originated and mainly flourished in the Catholic lands. Up till the time of the Boisserées in Germany it was Baroque, not Gothic, which seemed the natural vehicle for Catholic faith and ritual.

This shift in significance was of course part of the Catholic medievalism which played so large a role in the German Romantic movement. Through the influence of Novalis, Tieck and others the Middle Ages had begun to take the place of the ancient world as an aesthetic ideal. It was only natural, then, that the religion of the Middle Ages, as they conceived it, should have exercised a powerful fascination over the Romantic imagination, and finally that the architecture which provided a framework and a habitation for that religion should have ousted Baroque as the specifically Catholic style. After all, Baroque was the Catholic expression of divided Christendom, Gothic of united Christendom; and we know from Novalis's essay *Die Christenheit oder Europa* how much the idea of united Christendom meant to the Romantic generation.

It is noteworthy that Schlegel's romantic patriotism interferes on occasion with his aesthetic judgment on Gothic architecture. For since Gothic is a fundamentally Germanic art, it follows that its finest examples will be found on Germanic soil—unless, like Milan, they have been built elsewhere by German architects. Thus he is remarkably cool in his judgment of Notre Dame: its site is unfortunate, the towers incomplete, its dimensions quite inadequate to the vast city that surrounds it, the interior spoilt by tasteless modernization. Even more remarkable is his indifference to Rheims, of which all he has to say is: 'The church at Rheims seems to be in a still older style that that in Paris, still more elaborately decorated, but rougher in workmanship; nor are the towers complete, though they seem to be somewhat further advanced than those of Notre Dame.'[1]

The first Gothic structure to move him to enthusiasm is the openwork tower of Cambrai Cathdral. 'What a strange way of building!'

[1] Ibid. p. 159.

he exclaims, as though he had become fully aware of the Gothic style for the first time, only to add a few lines further on less convincingly: 'I have a great predilection for Gothic architecture; wherever I have come across any monument or relic of this style I have studied it with the closest attention, for it seems to me that its deep meaning and real significance have not been at all understood so far.'[1]

The Netherlands, he says at one point, are the real home of the Gothic style, and he is loud in praise of St. Gudule in Brussels and above all of the Hôtel de Ville in Louvain. But his highest enthusiasm is reserved for Cologne. His style here takes on a new warmth, like that of Goethe when he comes to write of Strasbourg in *Dichtung und Wahrheit*. As far as ancient monuments are concerned, and especially the monuments of medieval architecture, Cologne is truly 'of tounes A per se'. Every period and variety can be studied there, and a historian of medieval architecture would find in this city alone all that he needed.

Of course the most remarkable of these monuments is the cathedral, and 'if it were completed, then Gothic architecture in this stupendous structure could bear comparison with the proudest monuments of modern or ancient Rome'.[2] Like Forster and others before him Schlegel places Cologne Cathedral at the summit of Gothic achievement. 'Even in its incomplete state it is superior to what can be seen elsewhere on account of its dimensions and still more of the beauty of the style . . . it is certain that in comparison with Cologne most Gothic churches, however justly famous, appear either somewhat crude and cumbrous, or else overladen and trivial.'[3]

As we have already pointed out, one of the peculiarities of the Gothic Revival in Germany is this concentration from the outset on two monuments—Cologne and Strasbourg—almost to the exclusion of all others. After all Germany is rich in Gothic buildings of singular beauty, though perhaps not so rich as France or England. Freiburg, Ulm, Oppenheim, Nuremberg, Halberstadt, Marburg, Dinkelsbühl, immediately spring to mind, and very many others could easily be added to the list. But you could almost divide the Gothic enthusiasts in Germany into one of two camps: those who prefer Strasbourg to Cologne (like Goethe), and—a much larger camp—those who prefer Cologne to Strasbourg. Friedrich Schlegel very definitely belongs to the latter. After his raptures on Cologne his observations on Strasbourg are comparatively cool. Though 'the world-famous Minster (by which he seems to mean the tower and façade only) certainly deserves

---

[1] Ibid. p. 160.   [2] Ibid. p. 177.   [3] Ibid. pp. 177–8.

its fame and is indisputably one of the foremost monuments of Gothic architecture, the church itself is disproportionately small and undistinguished'. Moreover the plant-like blossoming of Cologne is here replaced by 'arbitrary arabesques' (i.e. geometrical patterns) which give 'the whole and many of the parts the appearance of a stupendous artificial clock or some other artificial iron-work rather than that of an organic growth in stone'.[1]

When Friedrich Schlegel came to revise his travel letters for the first collected edition of his works in 1823 his first aim was to emphasize the part played by Gothic as the central theme of the diary. He did this, first, by rechristening the letters *Grundzüge der gothischen Baukunst;* and, secondly, by interpolating several entirely new passages, some of considerable length, almost all of which deal exclusively with the subject of medieval architecture. These interpolations have the effect of fundamentally modifying the impression left by the 1804 version. In a word, what had been only implicit in the *Reisebriefe*—the significance of Gothic architecture for the Romantic movement—is here made explicit. In the *Poetisches Taschenbuch* the word 'Romantic' does not once occur; in the *Grundzüge* Gothic is hailed as the essentially Romantic art. Secondly, as we should expect, the element of Catholic symbolism is more clearly emphasized than in the *Reisebriefe;* and thirdly, since 1804 Schlegel has considerably revised his ideas on the significance of the term 'Gothic'.

Above all, almost all of these interpolated passages lay stress on an aspect of Gothic architecture which though already implicit in Goethe's Erwin essay and explicit in Forster's *Ansichten* had been omitted entirely from the 1804 version: namely, the element of imaginative boldness. In this element Friedrich Schlegel now sees, as Forster had done before him, the essential characteristic of the Gothic style, 'which has distinguished it in all its phases from the time of Theodorich on'.[2] Moreover it is this quality which entitles Gothic architecture to be considered the Romantic style *par excellence*, for imaginative power is the essential feature of Romantic art altogether, and especially of medieval art in all its manifestations, 'both in the poetry and architecture of the Middle Ages, in the Orient no less than in the Catholic West'.[3] And so Schlegel now actually adopts the term 'Romantic architecture' to designate what we should call Gothic architecture—as opposed to the 'Old-christian' or Romanesque style—because

[1] Ibid. p. 192.   [2] Ibid. pp. 190–1.   [3] Ibid. p. 172.

in the later style 'that element of the boldest architectural imagination first attained its fullest development'.[1]

Very closely related to this imaginative splendour is the deep feeling for nature, which in Schlegel's view is something peculiarly German and which finds expression primarily in that imitation of plant forms in their infinite abundance and complexity to which we have so often referred. This is 'the root and the living spring from which all else has proceeded'.[2]

Schlegel is now led to revise and amplify his ideas on the use of the term 'Gothic' as applied to medieval architecture in all its forms. In 1804, it will be remembered, he had advocated the term 'German' as an alternative to 'Gothic' on the grounds that the style was common to all the 'German' peoples and that the most important examples of the style in other countries had been built by German architects. He now definitely opts for the term 'Gothic', which he uses as an equivalent for Germanic, including thereunder all the Germanic peoples, 'for with the Goths begins the dominating influence of the Germanic race and the German spirit in history, both in the customs and politics of the west, and in its art and poetry'. The term 'German architecture' (*pace* Goethe) cannot possibly be applied to a style 'which has flourished throughout all those lands which were once ruled by the Goths, from the extreme east to the far west of the Christian Occident'.[3] But the reasons for equating Gothic and Germanic are by no means purely geographical or historical, for Schlegel believes that the really distinguishing characteristics of medieval architecture are inherently Germanic (or even German) qualities.

The longest of the 1823 interpolations is occasioned by the sight of the Rhine castles perched so perilously on the tops of precipitous cliffs. This moves Schlegel to postulate yet another explanation for the origin of medieval architecture, for these castles reveal the same imaginative boldness which had impressed him so much in the Gothic churches he had visited. Moreover the Germans (*vide* Tacitus) had possessed castles from the earliest times; they thus represent the earliest type of Germanic architecture, from which all other types have developed—including Gothic, which owes much to them, not in details, but in the exercise of the architectural audacity common to both.

In rereading his *Poetisches Taschenbuch* Schlegel evidently felt the need to define more precisely the distinction between the 'Old Christian' and the 'Romantic' styles of medieval architecture. He

[1] Ibid. p. 163.   [2] Ibid. p. 191.   [3] Ibid. p. 162.

now introduces a quite new concept of 'geometrical beauty' as the essential feature of the earlier style. Such a church as St. Gereon, for instances, has a basic scheme of geometrical shapes—triangle, square, cross, rotunda, star-like hexagon and other polygonal figures—which give the whole building what he calls a 'sidereal form' (siderische Gestaltung). Such a form the Friedrich Schlegel of 1823 finds truly appropriate for a church, in that it is a consecrated building which 'should as it were present an image of the eternal structure of heaven in miniature'. This geometrical and sidereal element plays only a small part in the later phase of medieval architecture, where of all these forms only that of the cross remains truly visible, 'and even it is clothed in the richest embellishment and as if entwined with blossoming roses'.[1]

One of the most significant of the 1823 interpolations deals with an English book on Gothic which Schlegel professes to have found on his return to Paris in November 1804. Actually the book to which he refers, without giving name or author, is Sir James Hall's *Essay on the Origin, History and Principles of Gothic Architecture*, which was first published in 1813.[2] The author of this publication believes the origin of Gothic to lie in a deliberate imitation of primitive withy huts and basket work. To Schlegel such a purely naturalistic explanation is anathema. To combat it he points out that this naturalism is lacking in Romanesque, from which after all the Gothic style developed. What Schlegel, the German, is here maintaining is the primacy of spirit over matter in the genesis of the most spiritual of all architectural styles.

Schlegel has of course increased his knowledge of the architectural background in the twenty years or so that had elapsed since the writing of the *Reisebriefe*. He is aware of the variations of, and transitions between, the two main styles of medieval architecture, and mentions specifically the Moorish Gothic of Spain and Portugal, the peculiar style of the Templars' churches, the 'old Italian' marble churches, and the castle-like churches in certain districts of Germany. All this moves him to call for a comprehensive history of Gothic architecture, 'which after so many preliminary studies should be quite feasible, provided

[1] Ibid. p. 185.
[2] Hall's *Essay* had been discussed in detail by J. Büsching in the *Wiener Jahrbücher der Literatur* (vol. ix, 1820) and in his *Versuch einer Einleitung in die Geschichte der Altdeutschen Baukunst* (1821). Schlegel may well have derived his knowledge of Hall's arguments from Büsching's accounts, which dealt specifically with the theory of the derivation of Gothic from withy work and which had appeared shortly before he began to revise his *Reisebriefe* for his collected works.

that the basic idea of the whole has been properly understood and established'.[1]

Schlegel ends the 1823 version with a somewhat pessimistic post-script. 'Will the time never come', he asks, 'when Art shall again ennoble and permeate all aspects of life, as it did with the Greeks and, in a different way, in the Catholic Middle Ages?'[2] Architecture is the mother of the arts and any real advance must proceed from that quarter. Rococo Gothic castles may be all right in England, but Schlegel is not in favour of a serious application of neo-Gothic. Instead he envisages the possibility of building churches in a neo-Romanesque style, "as well planned as the originals and perhaps even finer in execution".[3] However the present age is more inclined to leave the old churches to decay than to spend money on building new ones. As far as architecture is concerned, we have only the memory of the grand old days and the hope of a better future.

In the interval between the two versions of the travel letters Friedrich Schlegel had returned briefly to the subject of Gothic architecture in his Vienna lectures of 1812 on the *Geschichte der alten und neuen Litteratur*. In the eighth lecture he makes a comparison between the monuments of Gothic architecture and the medieval romances, the points of resemblance being 'the noble but simple idea which underlies the whole, and also the wealth of decorative detail'. It is here that Schlegel states his conviction that 'the spirit of the Middle Ages in general, and of the German Middle Ages in particular, finds more complete expression in the monuments of so-called Gothic architecture than anywhere else'.[4]

What Schlegel chooses to emphasize in this passage is the element of Christian symbolism in Gothic architecture. Indeed this particular aspect is more clearly and eloquently expressed here than in the *Grundzüge* of 1823. No one knows, he says, speaking of the great Gothic cathedrals, who were the authors of these marvellous structures, but whoever they were their purpose was 'not merely to heap stones one upon another, but to express great thoughts therein'. Architecture cannot represent nature directly. 'Thus all architecture must make use of symbols, and this is especially true of the Christian architecture of the German Middle Ages.'[5] The most obvious of these symbols is the depiction of the soul's aspiration to God by means of the soaring

---

[1] *Schlegel*, p. 193. [2] Ibid. pp. 203-4. [3] Ibid. p. 204.
[4] *Schlegel*, Abt. I. Vol. vi. p. 202.   [5] Ibid. p. 203.

verticality of the pillars, arches and vaults. But for that matter every detail of a Gothic church is charged with symbolic meaning, from the position of the altar, the arrangement and number of the doors and towers, to the cruciform plan. He ends this brief excursus by asserting that the basic figure in all Gothic decoration is the rose, from which is derived the peculiar form of windows, doors, towers, and flower and leaf ornamentation.

6. AUGUST WILHELM SCHLEGEL

IN comparison with Friedrich Schlegel's contribution to the revival of interest in medieval architecture in Germany, that of his brother August Wilhelm is surprisingly meagre, though his contribution to the literary side of Romantic medievalism is of course immense. Wilhelm Schlegel had no more natural feeling for architecture than his brother, and the drive towards the art and architecture of the Middle Ages, which was supplied in Friedrich's case by the friendship and counsel of the Boisserées, was lacking with him.

There are indeed only two passages in his voluminous works which deal specifically with medieval architecture, and both of them are rather perfunctory in nature. The first occurs in the first series of Berlin lectures, *Über schöne Litteratur und Kunst*, which were delivered in the winter semester of 1801–2, and which were devoted to general aesthetic problems. Though the lectures were enormously popular, most of them, including the one in question, were never printed in Schlegel's lifetime, nor indeed did they see the light until they were published from the original manuscripts by Jakob Minor in 1884.[1]

The lectures are partly written out in full, partly only sketched under headings, and the passage on Gothic architecture unfortunately belongs to the latter group.[2] According to these headings Schlegel began by discussing the origin of Gothic, which incidentally he considered to be an unsatisfactory term. Evidently he subscribed to the theory of a Saracenic or Indian origin. The style in its purest form is to be found only in Germany, France and England; Italian Gothic is a hybrid. Then comes the cardinal question, which shows clearly enough that Wilhelm was not prepared to go as far along the road of Gothic appreciation as his brother: 'Whether the Gothic style has any artistic value, since it is diametrically opposed to the Greek?' Greek architecture has an absolute validity, Gothic only a partial, i.e. its principles are valid only for a particular epoch and code of manners and for a particular religion. The basic principle of Gothic architecture is multiplicity, just as simplicity is that of Greek.

Wilhelm Schlegel returned to the subject of Gothic architecture

---

[1] *Deutsche Litteraturdenkmale des 18. und 19. Jahrhunderts*, vols. xvii–xix.
[2] Ibid. xvii. 181–2.

in the lectures on the theory and history of the plastic arts (*Über Theorie und Geschichte der bildenden Künste*) which he held in Berlin in the summer of 1827.[1] In the sixteenth lecture he deals with the general theme of art in the service of the Christian religion, in which Gothic architecture inevitably plans an important part. In this passage he gives an explanation for the loftiness of Gothic churches which is surely unique. It is due, he says, to the invention of the organ, which 'demanded a greater height in the vaulting of the building . . . Thus arose the lofty vaults and arches of the cathedrals, those magic structures, in which the laws of gravity appear to have been rescinded'.[2] Gothic architecture is the most brilliant and original creation of the Middle Ages and no more borrowed from the Mohammedans (he has evidently changed his opinion on this point since the Berlin lecture of 1801–2) than are the songs of the Troubadours from the Moors. It should really be called 'German' architecture, but since the Goths were the most important of the Germanic tribes of the *Völkerwanderung*, the misleading but old-established term 'Gothic' may be retained.

Wilhelm Schlegel's observations on the origin and development of the Gothic style are superficial in the extreme. One must remember that these lectures date from 1827, from a time, that is to say, when the Gothic Revival was already firmly established and many excellent studies of the subject, including his brother's, had long been available.

Apart from these two passages, which deal directly with Gothic architecture, there are two incidental references to the subject in his writings.[3] One is from the Berlin lectures *Über schöne Litteratur und Kunst* (second course, 1802–3). Schlegel is arguing the inferiority of modern architecture to ancient, especially in the matter of firmness and solidity, in which we are surpassed, not only by Egyptian, Greek and Roman, but even by Gothic architecture, 'which often seems to approach the limits of the possible . . . and shooting up in stems, saplings, branches, leaves and tendrils, represents as it were a "vegetable" architecture'.[4]

The other passage is more important, because of the wide currency it attained in the Romantic period. This is the famous comparison at the beginning of the lectures *Über dramatische Kunst und Literatur*

---

[1] Extracts from these lectures are reprinted in *Deutsche Litteraturdenkmale*, xvii. pp. xxxi–lxiv.

[2] Ibid. pp. xlii–xliii.

[3] For the sake of completeness there should perhaps be added his sonnet on Milan Cathedral, written in 1805 (*Poetische Werke*, Pt. I. p. 332, Heidelberg, 1811).

[4] *Deutsche Litteraturdenkmale*, xviii. 42.

(delivered in Vienna in the winter of 1807–8 and published in Heidelberg in 1809–11) between ancient and modern art and literature,
in which Schlegel finds the essential character of ancient (or classical)
art to be 'plastisch' and of modern (or Romantic) art to be 'pittoresk'.
To illustrate his point he takes an example from architecture. 'In
the Middle Ages there prevailed a style of architecture, which especially
in the last centuries of that era was carried to the utmost degree of
perfection; and which, whether justly or unjustly, has been called
Gothic architecture.'[1] At the Renaissance the enthusiasts of the classical style condemned Gothic architecture root and branch as tasteless,
gloomy and barbarous. Such an attitude was perhaps pardonable in
the Italians, with whom classical art lay so to speak in the blood:

But we Northerners are not so easily to be talked out of the powerful,
solemn impressions which seize upon the mind at entering a Gothic cathedral.
We feel, on the contrary, a strong desire to investigate and to justify the source
of this impression. A very slight attention will convince us that Gothic architecture displays not only an extraordinary degree of mechanical skill, but
also a marvellous power of invention; and, on a closer examination, we shall
recognize its profound significance and that it constitutes in itself a complete
and self-subsistent system just as much as the Greek. And now to apply the
comparison: the Pantheon is not more different from Westminster Abbey or
St. Stephen's in Vienna than the structure of a tragedy of Sophocles from that
of a drama of Shakespeare. The comparison between these wonderful productions of poetry and architecture might no doubt be carried farther. But
does our admiration of the one compel us to depreciate the other? Can we
not admit that each is great and admirable in its kind, although the one is and
is meant to be, quite different from the other?[2]

Owing to the popularity of Schlegel's Vienna lectures, this unequivocal acceptance of Gothic as the equal of classical architecture,
despite, or rather because of, the fundamental differences between
them, and above all the recognition that this antithesis was just part
of the wider antithesis between Classical and Romantic art altogether
must be accounted one of the most influential pronouncements on the
subject in the Romantic period.

[1] A. W. Schlegel, *A Course of Lectures in Dramatic Art and Literature*, translated by J.
Black, revised by A. J. W. Morrison, *Bohn's Standard Library* (London, 1846), p. 22.
Apart from a few minor alterations I have used Black's translation for this and the following extract.
[2] Ibid. p. 23.

7. CARL RITTER

FRIEDRICH Schlegel's *Briefe auf einer Reise* were to remain for many years to come the most stimulating and eloquent discussion of Gothic architecture that had yet appeared in Germany. Few writers on the subject within the next decade or two failed to pay tribute—acknowledged or unacknowledged—to their penetrating insights and brilliant formulations.[1] One of the first to show their influence was the great geographer Carl Ritter, who published a brief account of the ancient monuments of Cologne in the *Rheinisches Archiv für Geschichte und Litteratur*.[2] Ritter's essay, entitled 'Die Ruinen am Rhein', is a reprint of a lecture delivered in Frankfurt in 1808.

Ritter divides his survey into three sections: first, the Roman period from the birth of Christ till 600; second, the period from 600 to the death of Conrad III of Hohenstaufen (i.e. Romanesque); and third, the period from 1153–1350.

We need not concern ourselves with the first section. The Romanesque period is divided by Ritter into an early (Carolingian) and a later phase. To the first he assigns St. Maria im Capitol and St. Martin. He has few good words for this early phase of Romanesque: 'This architecture is without any nobility; coarse as the solid sandstone from which it is hewn, its form is what you would expect of the rough age and people that produced it.'[3]

Ritter makes a wide distinction between these buildings and those of the later phase, such as the Apostelnkirche or St. Gereon. These churches are thoroughly deserving of the admiration of posterity. Even from a distance their exterior makes a noble and dignified impression, and the nearer one gets to them the more complex and richly elaborate are they seen to be. Further contemplation will reveal a mysterious unity beneath all this diversity, a unity attained by a kind of mystic mathematics—through repetition, that is to say, of the sacred numbers 3, 7, &c. in the various parts of the building.

[1] Cp., for example, Tieck's letter to Friedrich Schlegel of 4 September 1806, in which he warmly congratulates Schlegel on the *Briefe auf einer Reise*, which will help to destroy the 'old barbarism' of neo-classicism, and which 'have won you many friends among younger architectects'. (*Ludwig Tieck und die Brüder Schlegel*. Briefe mit Einleitung und Anmerkungen herausgegeben von H. Lüdeke. Frankfurt, 1930, p. 158.)
[2] Jahrgang 1810, Bd. i. Heft 3, pp. 199–220.
[3] Ibid. p. 206.

Ritter takes over Friedrich Schlegel's nomenclature in adopting the terms 'Hellenizing' or 'Byzantine' for what we should call 'Romanesque'. Indeed at every turn there is evidence enough that he was deeply steeped in the *Reisebriefe*. Like Schlegel, Ritter is impressed by the galleries of short double columns, which form the chief exterior decoration of these Rhenish Romanesque churches and give them their characteristic appearance. Like Schlegel, too, he notes the absence of the 'vegetable' element in this older phase of medieval architecture.

But Ritter goes well beyond Schlegel in his appreciation of Romanesque. His description of St. Gereon is, it is safe to claim, the most enthusiastic tribute to the effect of a Romanesque building which had yet appeared in German, though it must be admitted that this effect was evoked by the decoration of the interior rather than by its architecture.

The pillars are painted in the loveliest lapis lazuli and are encircled with broad gold bands up to the capitals. From the latter the azure ribs run to meet in a radiant sun, which forms the centre of the vault; all around you see grey and azure ribs and bands entwined with gilded laurel branches, and studded with golden stars, and the bright vault itself resembles the vault of heaven: it too is adorned with countless silver stars . . . If the sun is shining when one enters this sacred hall, it is as if the heavens opened with their diurnal and nocturnal splendour; and the pious believer who kneels on consecrated ground by the High Altar under the protection of so many hundred saints, while around and above him the sacred building shines in the glory of all the colours of the rainbow, must experience a foretaste of the joys of heaven.[1]

When Ritter comes to deal with his third section, the Gothic architecture of the twelfth to fourteenth centuries, he sees it in the context of all the other glorious manifestations of this so unjustly neglected period. Above all this style is the expression of the faith of the Middle Ages, the symbol of the 'mysterious, sublime and all-merciful triune God, whose stronghold is the earth and whose throne the heavens'.[2]

Now, as it happens, no city in Germany is so rich as Cologne in monuments of this greatest period of medieval art, and the greatest of these monuments is of course the cathedral. Cologne Cathedral is both older and finer than its brethren in Strasbourg, Vienna and Milan, and, if completed, 'it would be famed throughout the world as one of the sublimest monuments of the human spirit'.[3]

At this point, instead of describing it in his own words, he interpolates Schlegel's account of the building and his definition of the essential characteristics of the Gothic style. This long quotation (two

[1] Ibid. pp. 209–10.   [2] Ibid. p. 212.   [3] loc. cit.

pages out of an essay of twenty) is as striking a tribute as one could wish to the prestige of the *Reisebriefe* in the Gothic field.

Ritter amplifies Schlegel's description on certain points. He reinforces the latter's hint about the influence of Christian symbolism on the Gothic style; and he stresses the symmetry of the system of pillars and the strict unity underlying the whole. His most original contribution is on the subject of stained glass windows, an aspect of Gothic architecture to which his predecessors, even Friedrich Schlegel, had paid comparatively little attention. Ritter is the first to note explicitly one of the fundamental characteristics of Gothic architecture: the dissolution of the wall space into a mere framework for the coloured glass. He writes, for instance, of the windows of the choir aisles of the cathedral: 'The space they occupy is much more extensive than that of the walls and pillars of the church themselves. Indeed it is as if the latter were raised only in order to form a framework for these radiant paintings in glass, so thin and delicate do their shafts appear to the eye.'[1]

He compares the clerestory windows of the choir to magnificent tapestries, each entirely different from the other: 'Here the glass as a material substance disappears entirely; it was treated by the medieval artists solely as a medium through which the world of light was revealed in all its beauty, as the solar radiance is revealed in the rainbow . . . The whole style is a triumph of form over matter, of construction over mass.'[2] And he marvels how anything so fragile could have withstood for so many centuries all the hazards of wind and weather.

Though Ritter's essay is brief in compass, it is an interesting example of the stimulating effect of Friedrich Schlegel's *Briefe*. It also contains insights into aspects of medieval architecture hitherto unnoted at this stage of the Gothic Revival in Germany.

[1] Ibid., p. 217.   [2] Ibid. p. 218.

PART FOUR

GOETHE AND BOISSERÉE

1. THE BROTHERS BOISSERÉE

IN the previous chapters we have seen how much of Friedrich Schlegel's understanding of medieval architecture was due to his friendship with the brothers Boisserée. It is now time to turn our attention more exclusively to these remarkable figures, for with them we reach the central point of our whole enquiry. Sulpiz Boisserée especially is one of the most significant, and incidentally one of the most attractive, personalities of the Romantic period in Germany. Because his work lay outside the main stream of Romantic literature, his place in the German Romantic movement has not been estimated at its true value. His achievement deserves to rank beside, if not above, other great landmarks of German Romanticism like the Schlegel–Tieck translation of Shakespeare, *Des Knaben Wunderhorn* and Grimm's fairy tales. For to Boisserée, more than to any other man, is due not only the revival of interest in, but to a large extent the actual preservation of, the treasures of German medieval art and architecture at a time when they were in danger of being lost to the world for ever.

Despite their name the Boisserées, as Sulpiz is careful to explain in the first sentence of his autobiographical fragment, were not of French origin. On the father's side they came from the neighbourhood of Liége. Their mother was a Brentano, daughter of a wealthy Cologne merchant of Italian origin and his German wife. The brothers, then, were only one quarter German, but their family had long been settled in Cologne and ranked among its wealthiest and most respected citizens. Sulpiz, the second youngest of a family of eleven, was born in 1783, and his brother Melchior in 1786.

In early childhood, as he tells us in his autobiography, Sulpiz's love for medieval architecture had been awakened by the sight of the cathedral and the other noble medieval churches of Cologne. He had been confirmed in this taste by Georg Forster's eloquent account of Cologne Cathedral in his *Ansichten vom Niederrhein*, and by a tour he made through Brabant and Flanders in 1802, on which, with the *Ansichten* as his guide, he saw many examples of medieval architecture which filled him with enthusiasm.

Shortly after this he was introduced by his friend Johann Baptist Bertram, a young law student of intellectual and aesthetic taste some seven years his senior, to the latest publications in the sphere of art criticism and the new Romantic literature. He mentions by name the *Propyläen*, the *Herzensergiessungen*, *Franz Sternbalds Wanderungen*, the *Phantasien über die Kunst*, August Wilhelm Schlegel's poems, and Friedrich Schlegel's *Europa*. These writings played their part in turning his attention more intensively to the field of the visual arts. Some time before this indeed Sulpiz had decided, partly on Bertram's advice, to give up his career in the family business in order to study at Jena. Melchior, now and always his devoted friend and collaborator, resolved to follow his example. However, a month or two before the autumn term was due to begin Bertram, the third partner in this life-long trio, proposed that the three of them should first pay a short visit to Paris. At this time, the autumn of 1803, the French capital had become the centre of attraction for all lovers of art, owing to the great collections of Italian and Netherlandish paintings abducted by Napoleon from the lands he had conquered, which were now assembled in the Louvre.

They arrived in Paris on 20 September 1803. Soon afterwards Sulpiz became indisposed, and it was too late for them now to reach Jena in time for the winter semester. In the meantime they had made the acquaintance of Friedrich Schlegel, who was then living with Dorothea Veit at 19 rue de Clichy, where in the previous winter Friedrich had held a course of private lectures on the history of German literature for the benefit of some of his compatriots resident in Paris. And now, since Jena was impossible, they decided to let Friedrich Schlegel be their university. And so they joined his household in the rue de Clichy and became enthusiastic attendants at his lectures in the ensuing winter and spring. We have already seen that the intellectual intercourse between Schegel and the Boisserées was by no means entirely one-sided and that their friendship was to have important consequences for Friedrich's aesthetic and spiritual development.[1]

On their return to Cologne in the spring of 1804 the close association between the Boisserée-Bertram trio and Friedrich and Dorothea was maintained. Though they no longer all lived under the same roof, Friedrich continued to hold private lecture courses on philosophy and world history, which were faithfully attended by the Boisserées and Bertram, and they continued to share their mutual interest in the art and architecture of the Middle Ages. 'At that time', writes

[1] For eye-witness accounts of the Schlegel household in the rue de Clichy see the memoirs of Helmina von Chézy, *Unvergessenes* (Leipzig, 1858), i. 247 ff. and SB i. 23 ff.

Sulpiz, 'we really lived only with Schlegel and his wife; we saw them every day and often more than once'.[1]

Since the brothers had left for Paris in the autumn of 1803 the process of secularization under the Napoleonic decrees had made ruthless advances. Many churches and monastic establishments had been closed or demolished. The contents—including their art treasures—had either been confiscated by the state or sold for a pittance to any rag and bone man willing to buy. Sulpiz describes in his autobiographical fragment how soon after his return to Cologne, as they were walking over the Neumarkt one day with Friedrich Schlegel, they met a man trundling a wheelbarrow loaded with junk, among which was an old picture with golden haloes which caught their attention.

The painting, which represented Christ carrying the Cross with the weeping women and Veronica, seemed not without merit. I had noticed it first, and enquired for the owner, who lived close by; he did not know what to do with the large canvas and was glad to be rid of it for the agreed price. We were now faced with the problem of housing it; in order to avoid ridicule and fuss, we decided to convey the dusty antique into our parental home through a back entrance. When we arrived there our old grandmother appeared by chance at the door, and after she had contemplated the painting for a while, she said to the somewhat shamefaced new owner: 'That is an impressive picture you've bought and you've done well to acquire it.' Her words were like a benediction on our future endeavours.[2]

Such was the small beginning of the famous Boisserée Collection. Soon they had managed to rescue many a valuable and beautiful example of medieval art from destruction, and to build up the first systematic collection of German medieval paintings, especially of the Lower Rhenish school. Sulpiz describes how here and there the old paintings did duty as window shutters, dovecots, table tops or sheds. There were even instances of uncomfortably large canvases being forced upon scrap-iron coopers as a condition of trade, and of dirty and dusty old pictures in the cloisters of secularized monasteries being used for fuel.

But it was probably only relatively inferior works of art that suffered this humiliating fate; the finest examples even of the primitives (such as Stefan Lochner's Adoration) were preserved from the general destruction by the prestige that still clung to them from the past. And when the new baroque taste drove them from the high altar and main body of the church to the side chapels, chapter houses,

[1] SB i. 32.   [2] Ibid. p. 30.

vestries and treasuries, though little regarded, they were on the whole well preserved.

In this activity the three enthusiasts remained inseparable, each contributing his particular talent to the common task. Bertram had the sharpest eye for a picture's quality; Melchior had the best business brain; Sulpiz, the real leader, was the most gifted as a historian of art. He soon, for instance, became aware that the Cologne school of painting did not begin, as had hitherto been supposed, contemporaneously with the Van Eycks in Flanders, but long before. In Sulpiz's eyes the early Rhenish primitives, like the contemporary Italian paintings, had a marked affinity with Byzantine art, in consequence of which he called them by the somewhat strange term 'neugriechisch' (neo-Greek), which we can take to be more or less synonymous with our Romanesque.

This view was further confirmed by the archaic nature of the frescoes which came to light during the demolition of many Cologne churches and monastic buildings at this time. Sulpiz vividly describes how on the collapse of the supporting pillars 'we saw the plaster ceiling detach itself from the walls and vaults, under which the painted surfaces appeared as in a lightning flash, before disappearing for ever. If often happened, moreover, that through the shock the plaster ceiling which had hidden the old paintings fell down from adjoining parts of the building and that these remained a few days before they too were demolished. The frescoes which were revealed to us in this strange and tragic fashion consisted for the most part of single figures on monochrome red, blue or other backgrounds.'[1]

And then Sulpiz Boisserée's medieval interests took a new direction, of the profoundest significance for the purposes of this study. In his own words:

In the winter of 1808 a tremendous fermentation took place within me. Schlegel's lectures were ended; the concern with the arts, the collection of old German paintings, the study of art history, and especially the study of medieval architecture had come to mean ever more to me. Now at the beginning of this year I started to take measurements of the cathedral, and I began to dream passionately of a work which should represent by means of plates this so sadly interrupted monument of German greatness in its completed shape.[2]

And so began a project which was to be the main preoccupation of Sulpiz Boisserée's existence for the rest of his life. At first his dream seems to have been confined to the idea of producing a series of engravings of the cathedral as it would have appeared if completed,

[1] Ibid. p. 37.   [2] Ibid. p. 42.

together with a brief introduction on the nature and history of Gothic architecture. Only gradually was this comparatively unambitious project transmogrified into the stupendous vision of the actual completion of the building, not on paper, but in stone. Thus at long last, and largely through the tireless efforts and dogged patience of this one dedicated spirit, was to be accomplished a task which had been the ideal of so many lovers of medieval architecture from Crombach on.[1]

But not only was this project to remain the central preoccupation of Sulpiz Boisserée, it was also to constitute the central preoccupation and rallying point of the Gothic Revival in Germany altogether. It was invested with a symbolic significance, gathering in unto itself all the many strands of Romantic sentiment which had accumulated round the Gothic movement in the preceding decades. In the English Revival there was nothing quite comparable to this symbolic focal point; perhaps Barry's Houses of Parliament is the nearest parallel.

It is important to realize what exactly existed of Cologne cathedral at the time Sulpiz Boisserée took up his self-appointed task. The chequered history of this famous structure might serve as a kind of running commentary on the fluctuations of taste towards Gothic architecture throughout the centuries. Begun in 1248, in the finest flowering of Gothic genius, the choir of the cathedral was completed by 1322. At this point the initial impulse seems to have flagged; between this date and the final cessation of work on the building in 1560 nothing further was brought to completion; but some of the north aisle was vaulted and the pillars of the nave and transepts were carried up to the height of the aisle capitals, the south west tower was raised to one third of its total height and the north west tower just high enough to act as a terminal to the north aisle, and the nave and aisles, as far as they extended, were covered over with a provisional roof. Then in 1560, after a considerable period in which very little had been added to the building, the work finally ceased completely, chisel and hammer were silent, and the medieval crane on the torso of the south-west tower remained poised in air for the better part of three long centuries—a standing reproach and exhortation to the succeeding generations.

Already in 1654 Crombach had made his appeal for the completion

[1] Cp. Helene Rosenau, *Der Kölner Dom* (Cologne, 1931), p. 159: 'So ist der Name Sulpiz Boisserée in bestimmendem Mass mit der Neuerweckung des Baubetriebes verknüpft, ihm, nicht den Dombaumeistern, sind die tragenden Impulse zuzuschreiben.'

of the work, but the call lay unheeded. Far from completing the work
the eighteenth century did what it could to destroy the effect of what
was already there. The medieval belfry turret on the roof of the choir
was removed; the tabernacle, which in size and delicacy of carving
must almost have rivalled Adam Kraft's masterpiece in the Lorenzkirche in Nuremberg, was hacked to pieces and shoved into the Rhine
as rubble; the interior was whitewashed and the medieval glass removed from the windows. The lowest point in the fortunes of the
Cathedral was reached after the French occupation of the city in
1794. In November 1796 the services were discontinued at the behest
of the French authorities and the building was commandeered by the
revolutionary army as a corn and forage store. In the next year it was
used as quarters for Austrian prisoners of war. Finally, as a result of
the Napoleonic concordat of 1801, the archbishopric was dissolved
and the Cathedral degraded to the position of a mere parish church.
Indeed it was lucky to escape total demolition, a course seriously
recommended by the then Bishop of Aachen. Even so the state of
the fabric was growing yearly more dangerous, for as a result of the
French occupation and the secularization decrees neither the municipal
nor the ecclesiastical authorities were in a position to finance the most
elementary and essential repairs.

Such then was the state of affairs when Sulpiz Boisserée began
his activities in the winter of 1808. For the next few years he was
absorbed in studying and measuring the details and proportions of the
existing building, and in deducing from them and from Crombach's
engraving of the original design for the western towers those parts of
the edifice which were left uncompleted when work stopped in the
sixteenth century. Sulpiz spared neither trouble nor expense in the
realization of his vision. He enlisted the services of a marine engineer to
ensure absolute accuracy with the measurements, and two artists,
Angelo Quaglio and Maximilian Heinrich Fuchs, to execute the drawings. By the spring of 1810 the most important of the drawings were
finished, including views of the cathedral from the south side, both
as it was and as it would be if completed, also a cross section of the
choir and the ground plan of the whole. With this the first stage of
Sulpiz's project had been completed.

The next stage was to secure influential support for his enterprise,
and in this endeavour he was as untiring as in his more purely artistic
labours. The first step was to exchange Cologne, French-occupied
and isolated from the rest of Germany, for Heidelberg, then at the
height of its fame as an intellectual and cultural centre. Thither

then he moved in the spring of 1810, along with his inseparable companions, Bertram and Melchior, and his portfolio of drawings. The collection of German primitives followed bit by bit.

Sulpiz lost no time in spreading his gospel. Already on the way to Heidelberg he made a halt in Frankfurt in order to show his drawings to the influential Karl von Dalberg, Archbishop of Mainz and Primate of the Confederation of the Rhine. A few months later he is displaying them to the appreciative Schelling in Stuttgart, and even to the Queen of Württemberg, 'who as an English princess has a great love for Gothic . . . she much enjoyed looking at the drawings, which vividly reminded her of her fatherland and especially of Windsor'.[1]

But these were all comparatively small fry; Sulpiz had more important fish in view. There was one man above all others whose prestige was so great, whose authority in aesthetic matters was so decisive, that if he could be won over for Sulpiz's projects, then indeed the prospects for their success would be immeasurably heightened. And so he conceived the apparently foolhardy idea of approaching the apostle of classicism, who had shown for so many years now the most uncompromising hostility to every form of medieval art. Sulpiz however, in reliance on the justice of his cause and his own powers of persuasion and tact, was undismayed at the prospect. But before we embark on the fascinating story of Goethe's relationship to Sulpiz Boisserée and Romantic medievalism, we must return briefly to his attitude to Gothic architecture in the forty-odd years that had elapsed since his youthful enthusiasm for Strasbourg Minster.

[1] SB i. 87–88.

2. THE CLASSICAL GOETHE

WE have seen how, according to *Dichtung und Wahrheit*, Goethe's new-found enthusiasm for 'Nordic architecture' was already shaken by the sight of a Corinthian capital in the Mannheim Collection in August 1771. Certainly there is little indication, apart from the *Baukunst* itself and its curious sequel, the *Dritte Wallfahrt nach Erwins Grabe*, that Gothic architecture had much significance for Goethe for a period of some forty years after his departure from Strasbourg.

It is true that in *Dichtung und Wahrheit*, after describing his impressions of Strasbourg Minster, Goethe seems to imply that he felt similar emotions for the cathedrals of Cologne and Freiburg: 'When I consider the interest which drew me to these old monuments, when I reflect on the time which I devoted to Strasbourg Minster alone, the attention with which I later contemplated the cathedrals in Cologne and Freiburg, and the increasing value I put upon these buildings, then I could blame myself for having entirely lost sight of them subsequently and, attracted by a more highly developed art, left them completely in the background.'[1]

This passage presumably refers to Goethe's visit to Cologne in the summer of 1774 during his Rhine tour with Lavater and Basedow, and to a visit to Freiburg on his way to Switzerland with the Stolbergs in May 1775.[2] It is, however, significant that there is no reference to either of these Gothic experiences in the letters of the time; and the only other reference to the Cologne visit in *Dichtung und Wahrheit* itself does not testify to any great interest in the cathedral. He begins by saying: 'The cathedral ruin (for an unfinished work is a kind of ruin) awoke the feelings familiar to me from Strasbourg.' But in fact, as he then clearly states, what he did actually feel in face of the cathedral torso was discomfort and confusion. He regretted the lack of any reliable guide to explain to him the relationship between the original plan and what had actually been carried out, 'such as has now been supplied by the industry and patience of our friends. In company, it is true, I admired these remarkable halls and pillars, but

[1] WA I. 27, 278.
[2] Goethe passed through Cologne in November 1792 on his way from Coblenz to the Jacobis in Düsseldorf, but neither his letters and diaries, nor the *Kampagne in Frankreich* make any reference to the visit; he also travelled through Freiburg in 1779 on his way to Switzerland with Karl August, but this visit has left equally little trace in his writings.

when I was alone I always felt depressed at the sight of this famous building interrupted before it was half finished. Yet another example of a stupendous concept not brought to completion!'[1]

The key to the passage lies in the words 'such as has now been supplied by the industry and patience of our friends'. In other words the whole paragraph is part of Goethe's graceful tribute to the work of the brothers Boisserée, and is written, as is the account of Strasbourg Minster itself, with this in view. In these circumstances, and written as it is some forty years after the events it describes, it cannot be accepted as proof of any particular interest on Goethe's part for the cathedrals of either Cologne or Freiburg in his *Sturm und Drang* period. Any interest he felt in these structures was to come to him much later through the agency of Sulpiz Boisserée.

Before Goethe's departure for Weimar, then, there is no indication that he felt enthusiastically about any Gothic building other than Strasbourg Minster. But at least there is no abuse of Gothic, whereas from his arrival in Weimar until his meeting with Boisserée there is scarcely a reference to medieval architecture which is not abusive. The one notable exception is a passage in a letter to Frau von Stein of 25 September 1779, describing his impressions of the Romanesque cathedral at Speyer. Clearly Goethe did not yet realize that there was such a thing as a Romanesque style, differing essentially from the style of Strasbourg or Cologne; what he does realize—in striking contrast to his attitude in the Erwin essay—is that medieval churches altogether are peculiarly calculated to awaken feelings of religious devotion; 'They assemble the congregation within the confines of their simple and noble forms, and in their high vaulted roofs the spirit can expand and soar, without however entirely losing itself in the Infinite, as happens in the face of nature.'

Otherwise Goethe's attitude towards medieval architecture, as towards every aspect of medievalism, during this long period is almost unrelievedly negative. Until his departure for Italy in September 1786 there is no evidence apart from the passage on Speyer just quoted, that he gave a thought to the subject. Thuringia after all is not a region in which Gothic monuments obtrude themselves on the attention.

Still less of course was his journey to Italy calculated to make him think kindly of medieval architecture. The references to the subject in the diaries and letters of the time are as rare as they are devastating. As far as architecture is concerned, Italy meant to Goethe the ancients

[1] WA I. 28, 284-5.

and Palladio. The tables are now completely turned on the Strasbourg experience. It is the architecture of Greece and Rome and of the Italian Renaissance which is *naturwahr* and *naturgesetzlich*, i.e. true to nature and ruled by laws which are in consonance with the laws of nature; it is Gothic which is unnatural and arbitrary. In this of course Goethe has returned to the orthodox neo-classical view.

Take, for instance, his reflections on seeing the Roman aqueduct at Spoleto: 'This is the third piece of ancient architecture that I have seen; again everything is so beautifully natural, functional and true. What a feeling they had for the sublime! . . . I have always hated the trivial and arbitrary.'[1]

This feeling for the *Naturgesetzlichkeit* of classical art receives its most unambiguous formulation in the *Italienische Reise* under the date 6 September 1787: 'These sublime works of art are at the same time supreme works of nature produced by man in accordance with nature's laws; everything arbitrary or fanciful is eliminated. All is Necessity, is God.' Whether these words occur in the original letter (burnt by Goethe in 1829 along with the other documents relating to the second stay in Rome) or were first added when he came to compile this final section of the *Italienische Reise* (1819–29) we do not know. In any case they admirably sum up his views on the subject.

Similarly with Palladio, for whom Goethe's enthusiasm was unbounded. 'Palladio has opened to me the way to all art and life,' he writes to Frau von Stein.[2] For Palladio, that 'divine and glorious' genius, had, like the ancients, revealed to Goethe an art which was 'true' and 'noble' and utterly without caprice. He compares him in this respect with Raphael: 'There was not a trace of the arbitrary about them; their greatness resides in the fact that they knew the laws and limitations of their art to the fullest extent and moved easily within them.'[3]

With these views on the absolute pre-eminence of classical art it is perhaps surprising that Goethe's comments on medieval buildings in his Italian letters and diaries are not more virulent than they are. There are in fact only three points at which he gives expression to his distaste. (Strangely enough—and this is seldom realized—the most abusive remarks on Gothic in the *Italienische Reise* all belong to the period in which the first part was compiled, i.e. November and December 1814, and not to the period of the journey itself.)

[1] *Tagebücher und Briefe Goethes aus Italien an Frau von Stein und Herder, Schriften der Goethe-Gesellschaft* (Weimar, 1886), ii. 209.
[2] Ibid. p. 139.   [3] Ibid. pp. 190–1.

Goethe's unfavourable comment was called forth in the first place by St. Mark's and the Doge's palace in Venice. Of the former he writes that 'the style is a worthy expression of all the nonsense which was ever taught or acted within its walls', and the façade he compares to a 'colossal crab'. The Doge's palace is 'the oddest thing ever produced by the human spirit', and the stocky truncated pillars of its colonnade suggest to him the ingenious idea that the architects of this period may have taken as their model ancient ruins which were half buried in the soil. His second object of disapprobation was the church of St. Francis in Assisi, which he left on one side in his eagerness to reach the Roman Temple of Minerva, lest, as he puts it, his imagination should be corrupted by the sight. And thirdly Milan Cathedral, which he visited on his return journey to Weimar, and of which he wrote to the Duke on 23 May 1788: 'Yesterday I visted the cathedral, in order to build which a whole marble mountain has been forced into the most absurd forms. The poor stones are still being tortured daily, for this non-sense or poor-sense is by no means completed.'

The revolution in Goethe's attitude towards Gothic architecture is very clearly illustrated in the little essay, simply entitled 'Baukunst' (1788), which he contributed to Wieland's *Teutscher Merkur* in 1788-9 along with several other short essays on aesthetic subjects. They appeared under the general title *Zur Theorie der bildenden Kunst*, and may be considered as a summing up of his Italian experiences in the artistic sphere.

In this essay Goethe is concerned to prove that the form of the stone temples of ancient Greece derives from more primitive temples built of wood. In order to show that the transference of stylistic peculiarities from one material to another is by no means confined to this instance he adduces the example of Gothic architecture which, according to this view, owed its origin to an imitation in stone and on a grand scale of the wood carvings 'with which in the earliest times the shrines, altars and chapels were decorated, and which at a later period, when the power and wealth of the church had increased, were stuck on with all their scrolls, shafts and fillets to the exteriors of Nordic walls, under the impression that gables and shapeless towers were in this way beautified.'[1]

At this point, then, Goethe has reverted to the filigree argument of the neo-classicists. Indeed the view of Gothic which he now holds is the precise opposite of that of the author of the Erwin essay, for whom the minster was something sublime and noble and the expression

[1] WA I. 47, 64.

of a 'titan spirit'. Above all it was a living organism, an organic whole. Now Gothic is 'multiplizierte Kleinheit', without relationship between the parts, and Gothic ornament is neither functional nor organic, but is merely 'stuck on' as a superficial embellishment.

At no period of his life was Goethe so far removed from the spirit of the Gothic Revival as in the twenty years which succeeded his return from Italy. This was the epoch of the *Propyläen* and the Weimar prize competitions, of the 'Weimarischen Kunstfreunde', and the ascendency of the arch-classicist, Heinrich Meyer. During this period he was committed almost wholly, at least as far as the visual arts are concerned, to the narrowest type of neo-classicism—an aesthetic attitude, however barren, which he defended against the vital forces of Romanticism with stubborn tenacity. We need go no farther than the winning results of the Weimar prize competitions to be convinced of the essential sterility of his aesthetic gospel at this time.[1] This gospel, as expressed in the introduction to the *Propyläen* and in the Laokoon and Winckelmann essays, was, to put it in a nutshell, that the only valid criterion of art was that of ancient Greece.

Goethe expresses his view on the pre-eminence of classical art over all other schools, and particularly over all primitive schools, with uncompromising clarity in the Advertisement to the first three parts of the *Propyläen* which he wrote for Cotta's *Allgemeine Zeitung* (29 April 1799): 'In our opinion students of art devote far too much time to the Egyptian, archaic Greek, Italian primitive, and especially the German primitive schools of art, which are for the most part merely of historical significance, and seldom have any claim to a higher aesthetic interest, and which in comparison with the free greatness of perfect [i.e. classical] works of art are like spelling compared with reading or stuttering with reciting and declaiming.'[2]

One of Goethe's most significant utterances on the subject during his classical period is to be found in a passage added to an article of Meyer's in the *Propyläen* on 'Lehranstalten, zu Gunsten der bildenden Künste'. (Goethe was addicted to airing his anti-Romantic sentiments by the method of interpolating passages in Meyer's essays, e.g. his attacks on Tieck and Wackenroder).[3] Meyer has been describing the admiration aroused in us by 'beautiful' works of art and the pity and contempt engendered by 'formlessness and bad taste'. At this point

---

[1] For Goethe's prize competitions see W. Scheidig, *Goethes Preisaufgaben für bildende Künstler 1799–1805, Schriften der Goethe-Gesellschaft* (Weimar, 1958), lvii.

[2] WA I. 47, 41–42.

[3] See my article 'Wackenroder and the Middle Ages', *Modern Language Review*, vol. L (April, 1955), pp. 165–6.

Goethe interpolates the sentence: 'Who has ever felt his mind in-spired to a free and active serenity in a barbarous building, in the gloomy aisles of a Gothic church or a medieval castle?'[1]

This highly characteristic sentence illustrates better perhaps than any other single utterance of Goethe's classical period the core of his attitude towards medieval architecture. Gothic is barbarous just be-cause it is 'gloomy', just because it is at the opposite pole of that 'free and active serenity' which remained his ideal both in life and art.

The whole paragraph, of which this forms one sentence, is illumina-ting for Goethe's attitude at this time. For though the rest of it was actually written by Meyer, we know that the entire essay, like all Meyer's contributions to the *Propyläen*, was composed in the closest collaboration with Goethe. (In this case two of the three manuscripts of the essay were carefully gone through and corrected by the poet). Meyer continues thus, after Goethe's interpolation: 'Only those who find a melancholy satisfaction in imagining ghosts, in experiencing chill shudders amid the smell of mould and corruption will feel a mournful pleasure in such buildings; any healthy and vigorous soul will escape from such a hole at the earliest possible moment, glad to breathe fresh air again and to be able to congratulate himself that the times which produced such places are long past.'[2] The 'Weimarischen Kunstfreunde' have here returned to the attitude of the Gothic poets of the early eighteenth century, for whom Gothic architecture meant moss-grown ruins and decay. But where *they* found in the Gothic mood the thrill of the exotic, Meyer finds only matter for disgust. The taste for Gothic is stamped as morbid; the healthy person will turn his back on it and breathe a sigh of relief that the Middle Ages are over and done with for ever.

Goethe's noble essay, 'Winckelmann und sein Jahrhundert', may be regarded as the peak and climax of his classicism, a defiant challenge in praise of those eternal values of the Beautiful, the Good and the True, which he felt to be threatened by the rising tide of Romanticism. The year in which it appeared (1805) was also that in which he had regretfully and resentfully brought to a close the series of Weimar prize competitions, and to some extent the Winckelmann essay may be looked upon as an answer to this event.

But however complete the picture of Goethe's classicism may seem between his return from Italy and his meeting with Sulpiz Boisserée, one must not forget the strange, the almost unbelievable achievement

[1] WA I. 47, 333.
[2] *Propyläen*, Bd. ii. Stück ii. p. 5 (Tübingen, 1799).

of the completion of the First Part of *Faust*. It is not always sufficiently
realized that more than half of the most romantic of Goethe's works
was written in the middle of his most rigidly classical period. No
adequate explanation of this astonishing fact has ever been forthcoming, though it is easy to name a number of contributory factors,
such as the insistence of Schiller and the desire to round off outstanding
fragments for the new Cotta edition of his works. All Goethe himself
has to say on the matter is that he turned to the idea of completing the
fragment of *Faust* in a period of restless inactivity while waiting to set
out on his abortive journey to Italy in the summer of 1797. It was, he
says, a suitable piece of work in the circumstances, because the individual scenes could be composed separately and in different moods,
provided they were subordinated to the spirit and tone of the whole.
It was his recent preoccupation with the ballad as a poetic genre that
had brought him back to this 'Dunst- und Nebelweg' (Letter to
Schiller of 22 June 1797). A few days later (27 June) he is still referring
to it as a 'barbarous composition', whose parts—'for it will always
remain a fragment'—he will do his best to render 'charming', 'entertaining', and 'thought-provoking'. Strange terms, surely, to
apply to such passages as Faust's suicide monologue or the revised
version of the final prison scene!

It is true, of course, that the more essentially 'romantic' portions
of the poem had been written long before and that some of the
apparently romantic scenes of the newly written portions, such as the
Walpurgisnacht, betray an ironic detachment which is not quite in tune
with the scenes of the *Urfaust*. Nevertheless the fact that from 1797
to 1808 (though mainly from 1797 to 1801) Goethe was occupied off
and on with the completion of this 'barbarous' composition, and that
the finished work leaves so few traces of his classical tastes and convictions is indeed amazing. In any case it is enough to prepare one for
the emergence in the years to come of an attitude more tolerant to
romanticism and to the medievalism that accompanied it.

In this context it is interesting to remark that in some notes on
Magdeburg Cathedral made in 1805 Goethe is not without words of
appreciation for certain aspects of the medieval tombs: that of the
Empress Edith, for example, 'probably dating from the second half
of the fifteenth century. The face damaged, but like the hands very
natural, serene and noble'; and of the Archbishop Friedrich (d. 1464):
'The face a bit polished and worn, but carved with truth and dignity
in a half realistic, half conventionalized style.'[1]

[1] WA I. 48, 242–3.

A further slight loosening up of the rigidity of Goethe's classicism in these years is to be seen perhaps in his tolerant interest in folk poetry, as shown, for instance, in the warm-hearted review of *Des Knaben Wunderhorn* in the *Jenaische Allgemeine Zeitung* for 21 January 1806. But the first unmistakable public sign that Goethe's classicism was not impregnable was the notice of a book of Dürer drawings in the same journal for 19 March 1808 and 18 April 1809. This review was actually written by Heinrich Meyer, but it contained two short interpolations by Goethe, and the style is such that until Meyer's original manuscript was discovered it was always taken for granted that the review as a whole was the work of the poet. It is yet another example of the intimate collaboration of the 'Weimarischen Kunstfreunde'. The subject of the review is Dürer's marginal illustrations (1515) to the Emperor Maximilian's Prayer Book, which had been recently discovered in the Royal Library at Munich and reproduced in part by the lithographer Strixner. It is true that these drawings constitute a 'Dürer without tears', so to speak, whose delicate charm and ingenious arrangement round the borders of the text could hardly fail to please even the most hardened classicist. However, in view of the fact that only a few years before (1801) Goethe had accused Dürer of never being able to rise to the 'idea of harmonious beauty' and of possessing a 'gloomy, formless and undisciplined imagination',[1] the degree of his enthusiasm is surprising. Of one of the plates Goethe-Meyer writes: 'In addition to the dignity of the whole, and the splendid relationship of the parts, the way the composition fits into the available space could not be bettered; or rather, it seems to be as much a part of it, and to grow out of it as immediately as do those admired Fates of Raphael on one of the pilasters of the Vatican *Loggie*.'[2] The comparison with the adored Raphael is especially significant in this connection.

Moreover the excellence of Dürer's drawings reflects glory on the whole age that produced them: 'When one considers that these drawings are marginal decorations of a book of devotions, one cannot help feeling veneration and respect for an epoch in which so much art and love of art prevailed as to bring forth such works.'[3]

The second part of the review, written a year later, contains an even more enthusiastic tribute: 'Our aim has been attained if we have succeeded in drawing the attention of the public to this valuable legacy of a great age and a great and glorious artist, who has brought honour

---

[1] Ibid. p. 208.
[2] Quoted from R. Benz, *Goethe und die romantische Kunst*, p. 149.   [3] Ibid. p. 153.

to the German nation and whose name will be mentioned with respect
so long as true taste and culture have not been completely extin-
guished.'[1]

To these signs of a reawakened interest in, and more tolerant attitude
towards, the German past must be added Goethe's preoccupation
with the *Nibelungenlied* and other Middle High German poems, as
recorded in the *Annalen* for 1806–9 and in the letters, diaries, and conversations of the time. His interest had been stirred by F. H. von der
Hagen's semi-modernized version of the poem, a copy of which he
had sent to Goethe. Goethe replied on 18 October 1807 in surprisingly
enthusiastic terms: 'In my view *das Lied der Nibelungen*, as far as its
matter and content is concerned, can be placed alongside the best we
possess in the way of poetry.' In the autumn of 1808 Goethe read the
poem, with impromptu translation and comments, to the ladies of
his *Mittwochgesellschaft*, and in a letter to Knebel of 25 November
1808 he writes: 'The value of the poem increases the more one reads
it and it is well worth the trouble to set down its merits in black and
white . . . altogether I do not allow myself to be put off by the fact
that our modern religiose Middle Agers are responsible for encouraging
much that is regrettable, for through their zeal and enthusiasm a lot of
invaluable material has come to light.'

But the most remarkable instance of Goethe's new-found tolerance
towards Romantic medievalism is provided by his novel *Die Wahlverwandtschaften*, which was written in this same year of 1808 and in
the following year. We have already had occasion to refer to this work
in connection with the fashion for English landscape gardening, of
which the park which forms its background can be considered an
example. But *Die Wahlverwandtschaften* has a more intimate connection
with the Gothic Revival. For among the wide-scale improvements and
alterations to the estate, which form a kind of ground-bass to the other
themes and motifs of the novel, is included the restoration and redecor-
ation of the medieval parish church. The work is carried out by a
young architect whose tastes lie clearly in the direction of the Gothic
Revivalists. Jakob Grimm was the first to suggest that in drawing
this character Goethe had in mind Daniel Engelhard, a young architect from Cassel who visited Goethe in Weimar in 1809 and 1811
and who was deeply interested in medieval art and architecture.[2]
Goethe seems to accept this identification in his reference to Engel-
hardt's visit in the *Annalen* for 1811.

The restoration of the church forms an actual and symbolic

[1] Ibid. p. 154.   [2] Cp. *Goethes Werke* (*Hamburger Ausgabe*), vi. 641.

background to much of the second part of the novel. Goethe describes it as a well-proportioned structure, built and decorated in the 'German' style ('nach deutscher Art und Kunst') several centuries ago. 'It still made a dignified and agreeable impression on the spectator, although the new internal arrangements for the Protestant form of worship had deprived it of something of its majesty and peace.'[1]

The young architect had no difficulty in persuading Charlotte to allow him to undertake the restoration of both the exterior and interior in medieval style. While investigating the fabric he discovers to his astonishment a neglected side-chapel 'whose proportions were still more delicate and ingenious and whose detail was still more charming and intricate than the rest of the church. At the same time it contained many a carved and painted relic of that older form of service, in which the various festivals of the Church were celebrated by means of such visible symbols as these. The architect could not resist the idea of including the chapel in his plan and of restoring this narrow space as a monument to the taste of former times. Already in imagination he had covered the blank spaces of the walls with suitable embellishments, and was delighted at this opportunity of exercising his pictorial talent'.[2]

In the evenings the architect entertained Charlotte and Ottilie by displaying an array of prehistoric objects from Nordic burial sites, and by showing them his collection of old engravings. The climax was provided by a portfolio of quite special interest:

For the most part it contained only outlined figures, but because they had been traced directly from the originals they had retained completely their old-world character, and attractive indeed did the specators find this. Purity of spirit was common to all these figures; they all deserved to be called good, if not noble. Serene contemplation, willing acknowledgement of a divine Presence above us, quiet devotion and expectation found expression in all their faces and gestures. The old man with the bald pate, the curly-haired boy, the cheerful youth, the serious man, the transfigured saint, the floating angel: all seemed rapt in innocent contentment and pious anticipation. Their meanest action had an element of the divine, and each might have been partaking in some act of worship.[3]

There can be not doubt as to what sort of pictures Goethe has in mind. They were clearly medieval Primitives; whether Italian, Flemish or German is not specified. From the terms in which they are described one would be tempted to think of certain works of Stefan Lochner and other painters of the Cologne school. Goethe had never

[1] WA I. 20, 208. [2] Ibid. p. 209. [3] Ibid. p. 211.

seen any such paintings at the time the novel was written, but Engelhard, who had been in touch with Wallraf and the Boisserées in Cologne, certainly had. It is natural to suppose that this passage owes its character, partly in any case, to Goethe's conversations with Engelhard in Weimar in the New Year of 1809.

The architect now proposed to paint the walls of the chapel with figures based on these medieval drawings, much as the Nazarene painters were to do in Rome and elsewhere. When the chapel is finally completed, Ottilie pays it a visit and is duly surprised and delighted by what meets her eyes. "Through the single high window fell a solemn many-coloured light; for it had been charmingly put together from pieces of coloured glass. By this means an exotic and individual character was imparted to the whole. The beauty of the vault and the walls was heightened by the pattern of the floor, which was made of specially prepared tiles."[1]

Of course these Gothic elements are not here for their own sake. The medieval atmosphere is deliberately introduced as the symbolic milieu, the appropriate element, in which Ottilie moves and has her being. This is made clear by repeated indications. The qualities attributed to the medieval pictures in the architect's portfolio are a reflection of the saintly aura which surrounds Ottilie in the later chapters of the novel. Most people, we are told, look upon such a world—the world of medieval faith and devotion—as a vanished Golden Age, a Paradise Lost. 'Only Ottilie perhaps was in a position to feel herself among her kindred.'[2] This is a deliberate anticipation of the scene where Ottilie, on the architect's insistence, takes the part of the Virgin Mother in the *tableau vivant* of the Nativity, where she is described in terms strongly reminiscent of the portfolio drawings. Again the figures painted by the architect on the vault of the chapel come to bear an ever closer resemblance to Ottilie, until it seemed 'as if Ottilie herself were looking down from the heavenly spaces'.[3] When the chapel is finished, Ottilie feels a peculiar mystical affinity with the little building, as though she were already its rightful possessor and were half aware of the destiny which was to make it her eternal home.

All this prepares us for Ottilie's apotheosis, for the strange happenings during the funeral procession and the last visit of the architect at nightfall to the chapel, where Ottilie lies under the glass lid of her coffin guarded by the faithful Nanny. Never, it seemed to the architect, had the ancient building appeared more mysterious and venerable than at this moment, in the dim light shed by the solitary lamp.

[1] Ibid. pp. 220-1.   [2] Ibid. p. 211.   [3] Ibid. p. 219.

Certainly the Pre-Raphaelite or Nazarene atmosphere in which all this is conceived comes unexpectedly from the author of the Winckelmann essay and of the attacks on 'neukatholische Sentimentalität' and 'das klosterbrudisirende, sternbaldisirende Unwesen'.[1] No wonder the Romantics were surprised. Most of them were enthusiastic in their reception of the novel.[2] Zacharias Werner even went so far as to claim in a letter to Goethe that it was responsible for his conversion to Catholicism.[3]

[1] WA I. 48, 122. [2] Cp. *Goethes Werke* (Hamburger Ausgabe), vi. 627-53.
[3] Ibid. pp. 646-7.

3. THE MEETING OF GOETHE AND BOISSERÉE

THE signs we have noted of a greater tolerance on Goethe's part towards certain aspects of Romantic medievalism do not of course count for much against the prevailing background of his persistent neo-classicism. Nevertheless they were sufficient to embolden Sulpiz Boisserée to beard the lion in his den.

His first step was to enlist the help of his friend of many years' standing, Karl Friedrich Reinhard, a diplomat of Swabian origin in the service of Napoleon, who was also a close friend of Goethe's. At Sulpiz's request Reinhard wrote to Goethe on 16 April 1810, recommending his young friend to the poet's notice and incidentally conveying Sulpiz's wish to be allowed to display his drawings of Cologne cathedral in person. Goethe's response to this request was not altogether encouraging. For the name of Boisserée was already known to him, but unfortunately it carried with it the association with Friedrich Schlegel, who had told him of the brothers and their crusade for medieval German art on his visit to Weimar in 1808. Since this was just after Friedrich's conversion, a more inauspicious moment for introducing the subject to the 'old pagan' could hardly have been conceived. According to Schlegel's own account in his letter to Sulpiz Boisserée of 9 May 1808 Goethe had been not unfavourably impressed. But it is clear from Goethe's reply to Reinhard of 22 April 1810 that the connection with Friedrich Schlegel was far from being a recommendation in his eyes: 'I would not at present advise the young man of whom you speak to undertake the journey to us. I am extremely busy . . . now if your young man were to meet me in such a state of confusion he would gain even less pleasure and profit than he would be likely to do in any case. For, as you yourself know best, a pupil of Friedrich Schlegel would have to spend a good deal of time in my neighbourhood and beneficent spirits would have to equip both of us with special patience, if any real good were to come of it.' He does not, however, discourage the idea of a visit altogether, but suggests that if it does take place, it should be postponed till later, when Sulpiz could be assured of a friendly reception for Reinhard's sake and 'even in matters with which I am normally out of sympathy he shall find more patience and consideration than I usually exercise'.

Despite the reserved, not to say discouraging, tone of this reply, Sulpiz decided to send the six completed drawings of the cathedral for Goethe's inspection before his impending departure for Carlsbad. He accompanied the drawings with a long letter (8 May 1810), giving a full and detailed account of his plans and projects, including a sketch of the history of the cathedral and other information useful for a proper understanding of the drawings. In the course of the letter he gives renewed expression to his conviction that the cathedral greatly surpasses all other Gothic buildings known to him 'on account of the noble unity which prevails so consistently through all its multiplicity of form'. He thanks Goethe for his invitation to visit him later in the year and expresses the 'pious hope' that in the following year Goethe will be able to visit the Boisserée Collection in Heidelberg. Finally, he adds an extremely tactful postscript: 'When I remember the architect in Die Wahlverwandtschaften I feel sure you will not take it amiss if I beg you to see that the drawings are packed with especial care'[1]— thereby ensuring at one stroke that his portfolio should receive the consideration due to it, that Goethe should realize that he was a devoted admirer of his works, and, still more important, that the poet should thus be reminded of his own unexpected understanding for the cause of medieval art as manifested in the activities and opinions of the architect in question.

To this Goethe replied more warmly than might have been expected, saying that both the drawings and the accompanying letter had given him and his friends much pleasure and that he hoped to see Sulpiz in Weimar in the autumn.

Much more explicit and highly significant for Goethe's unvarnished views on medieval architecture at this period is his letter to Reinhard of 14 May 1810, in which he makes it clear that he has nothing against the study of medieval art and architecture, provided the approach is historical and not aesthetic. With this qualification Goethe has only praise for Boisserée's efforts, and confesses that the ground plan of the cathedral is one of the most interesting architectural objects that he has encountered for many a day. In words reminiscent of the Erwin essay he proceeds: 'The perspective drawing gives a good idea of the difficulty of completing so tremendous an undertaking, and one sees with astonishment and awe the legend of the Tower of Babel re-enacted on the banks of the Rhine.' All the more praiseworthy, then, is Boisserée's conjectural restoration of the missing sections of the whole.

[1] SB ii. 6.

'Thus far', says Goethe, 'the genuine and unhesitating approval' which one must extend to Sulpiz and his friends. The rest of the letter was intended for Reinhard's eyes alone. 'Certainly', he proceeds, 'one needs to be inspired by a passionate one-sidedness in order to be able to produce something of this sort'. And then comes a sentence which though intended for Reinhard's exclusive consumption was nevertheless included by him in the extracts from Goethe's letter which he communicated to Sulpiz: 'I too used to be interested in these things and indulged in a similar kind of idolatry for Strasbourg Minster, whose façade I still consider to be a grander conception than that of Cologne Cathedral.' (This last point was, as we shall see, specially unwelcome to Sulpiz.)

Goethe goes on expressly to revoke the most controversial point of the Erwin essay: 'Strangest of all seems to me now the German patriotism which insisted in claiming this obviously Saracenic plant as a product of our native soil.' And then in words which give a much more accurate picture of Goethe's attitude to the Middle Ages than the passages intended for Boisserée's encouragement, he compares the whole field of Gothic architecture to 'a caterpillar or cocoon state, in which even the early Italian artists were wrapped, until at last by conceiving St. Peter's Michelangelo broke through the husk and was revealed to the world in all his splendour'.

Not unnaturally Sulpiz was delighted with Goethe's reception of his work and projects as expressed in the passages communicated by Reinhard. It seemed almost as if the most formidable of neo-classicists had capitulated at the very first contact with medieval art. Obviously Reinhard was somewhat disturbed at this misunderstanding, which was due, as he saw, to Goethe's considerate request that he should withhold from Sulpiz the more critical passages in his letter. 'The young man', he writes to Goethe, 'jumped straight to the conclusion that you see the whole matter with *his* eyes. He thinks that it has struck you like some great experience of which you long ago had a youthful dream, but which has never come your way again.'[1] Moreover Sulpiz ventures to hope that Goethe will be persuaded to write the first public announcement of his book of drawings for Cotta's *Morgenblatt*, and in that case will he please *not* suggest, as he did in his letter to Reinhard, that the façade of Strasbourg is superior to that of Cologne.

[1] *Briefwechsel zwischen Goethe und Reinhard in den Jahren 1807 bis 1832* (Stuttgart and Tübingen, 1850), p. 85.

To this Goethe replies in no uncertain terms on 22 July 1810:

In the first place, I must beg you to give a clear and sufficient explanation to our young friend in Heidelberg, so that he may understand my attitude in the matter. Otherwise if he were only to discover my real views when we meet, it might give rise to an awkward situation. What he and his artists have achieved one can praise unconditionally. The treatment of the subject is excellent; *the subject itself, however, only has value for us in its proper place, as a document of a particular stage of human culture.* (My italics.) It is true that if these good young people did not treat such an intermediate epoch as the highest and ultimate, where would they derive the courage to undertake such an infinitely laborious task? If the Knight did not believe his Lady to be fairer than all others, would he be ready to fight dragons and monsters on her behalf?

I have often enough in my life had similar experiences with young people, so that recently I have kept away entirely, even from the better sort. They credit *us* with influence and *themselves* with insight, and their secret intention is to exploit the former for the sake of the latter. There is no real mutual confidence in the matter. I do not blame them, but I neither wish myself to be the victim of an amiable self-deception, nor to further other people's aims against my own convictions.

Gothic art and architecture, then, have only a historical importance; not, like classical art, an intrinsic one. However, let the young have their illusions if they want, says Goethe, so long as they do not try to write my name on their banner.

Some two months later, in a letter to Reinhard of 7 October 1810, Goethe returns to the charge: 'I am quite willing to put up with this whole retrograde tendency towards the Middle Ages and to the antiquated altogether, partly because thirty or forty years ago we ourselves followed the same tendency, and partly because I am convinced that some good will come of it; only they must not press me too closely and importunately.'

Goethe is obviously determined to be fair, but the best that he can really find to say of the medieval revival is that it may lead the younger generation 'to higher regions of art'. In other words, the main justification for the study of medieval art is that it may serve to lead one back to classical art! 'It will, it is true, take some decades before this phase has been worked through, and I am of the opinion that one neither can nor should accelerate its development and declension. All really capable individuals will solve this problem in their own way.' (i.e. the stronger spirits will grow out of their Romantic teething troubles.)

In view of all these outbursts and reservations it is perhaps surprising that the meeting between Sulpiz Boisserée and Goethe ever took place. However, in a letter of 23 January 1811 to Reinhard Goethe renews his invitation to Sulpiz for the 'good season', and on 3 May 1811, at long last and after so many preliminaries, Sulpiz and his portfolio arrived in Weimar.

What followed is described for us with wonderful vividness and detail in Sulpiz's letters and diaries of the time. It is the story of the gradual overcoming of Goethe's firmly entrenched prejudices through the infinite tact, patience and enthusiasm of this singularly charming young man.

Sulpiz reports the somewhat inauspicious first encounter in a letter to his brother Melchior in Heidelberg:

I have just come from Goethe, who received me very coldly and stiffly; I did not allow myself to be put out and continued to be polite without being obsequious. The old gentleman kept me waiting for a while and then appeared with powdered hair and full insignia; his manner of addressing me could not have been more stiffly distant. I conveyed various greetings to him: 'Thank you, thank you.' Then we came to the drawings, the contract with Cotta, &c.: 'Yes, yes, quite so, hem, hem.' We proceeded to the work itself, to the fate of medieval architecture and its history . . . to all of which he listened as if he'd like to eat me alive. It was only when we came to speak of the old painters that he thawed a little . . . He asked about Van Eyck, confessed that he had never set eyes on anything of his . . . I was as fair and objective in every respect as you would expect me to be, but also as frank and definite as possible and did not let myself be at all put out of countenance by his reserve or his 'yes, yes, exactly, how interesting'.

Sulpiz sums up his impression of this first meeting in the words: 'On departure he gave me either one or two fingers, I am not sure which, but I think we will soon achieve the whole hand.' And three days later he is able to record: 'I am getting on splendidly with the old gentleman; the first day I only got one finger, the second I already had his whole arm.'[1]

On 7 May Sulpiz reports to Bertram, beginning with a word of caution, lest they should be too carried away by Goethe's unexpectedly favourable attitude towards their aims and endeavours: 'Despite these momentary attacks of youthful enthusiasm one must not forget that he is an old gentleman from whom one cannot expect any really active cooperation.' Nevertheless many points have been won already, however much at times against Goethe's own will. He has dropped his objection to the German origin of Gothic architecture, and has relinquished his so regrettable preference for Strasbourg over Cologne. 'When I was alone with him on Tuesday and showed

[1] SB i. 111–13.

him the drawings he sometimes positively growled at me like a wounded bear; you saw how he battled with himself and blamed himself for ever having failed to recognize such greatness.'[1]

And in his diary for 8th May Sulpiz is already able to announce that victory is won: 'After lunch we sat alone; he praised my work with all possible warmth and emphasis. I had the elevating sense of the victory of a great and noble cause over the prejudices of one of the most intelligent of men, with whom in the last few days I have had to wage a regular battle . . . I experienced the noble joy, which is so seldom vouchsafed to us in life, of seeing one of the greatest of men recant an error, through which he had been untrue to himself.'[2] And it is touching to read how the naive enthusiasm and sincerity of the warm-hearted Sulpiz finally moved the old man to embrace him with tears in his eyes.

The outward and visible sign of Sulpiz's triumph was an exhibition of his drawings arranged by Goethe at the Weimar court. He has left us an amusing account of this notable occasion in a letter to Melchior. Sulpiz brought along not only his drawings of Cologne Cathedral, but also plans and drawings of other Gothic churches—including Strasbourg, Milan, Vienna, Rheims, Batalha—for comparison. Goethe evidently spared no pains to make the occasion a success; clad though he was in full court dress, he helped Sulpiz personally with unpacking and arranging the exhibits. About twenty-five to thirty people were present, including the Weimar and Coburg ducal families and the poet Wieland. Goethe did his best to explain how remarkable and important it all was, 'though his sense of dignity made him somewhat stiff and perhaps embarrassed in this company'. The Duchess and the Dowager-Duchess of Weimar showed an intelligent interest, 'but the Duke behaved somewhat like a cavalry officer, and looked like one too; however he made the best of the situation, and asked a great many rather inconsequent questions, by no means as intelligently as the ladies . . . In the innocence of his heart he gave expression to the view that it was a great pity that Cologne Cathedral had lost the Rubens St. Peter, for it was so entirely in harmony with the spirit of this great building, and intended for it! I glanced at the old gentleman, who was standing beside the Duke, looking as if he had been turned to stone, and made no comment on this piece of Serene Wisdom.'

When it was over, Goethe and his protégé returned home satisfied with the day's work—'like the Italian opera director, who called out

---

[1] Ibid. p. 117.   [2] Ibid. p. 118.

at the opening performance, before the curtain had quite reached the floor: *Dio sia laudato che passato senza scandalo!*[1]

So began the friendship of Goethe and Boisserée, which was to develop into one of the most intimate relationships of the poet's later years, and which was unique in its kind. No one among Goethe's younger friends succeeded in winning his confidence so completely. Apart from Sulpiz's natural tact and charm what attracted Goethe to him in the first place was doubtless his naive and disinterested enthusiasm for his ideal. This selflessness, this extroverted concentration of his energies on a definite object outside himself, was a welcome contrast in Goethe's eyes to the morbid subjectivism of so many of the Romantic generation. Here was a romanticism which could not be dismissed as 'krank'. Through Boisserée Goethe was able to make his closest approach to German romanticism—even to certain aspects of it, patriotic and religious, which were furthest from his normal predilections.

On Goethe's part the relationship was a mixture of paternal affection for the enthusiastic young man and genuine interest in his ideas and plans. On Boisserée's side it was a combination of admiration for Goethe's greatness, of affection in response to Goethe's own affectionate attitude towards him, and of gratitude for Goethe's help towards the realization of his ambitions. With all his admiration for Goethe Boisserée never surrendered his own very different standpoint. It was this independence of spirit, perhaps more than anything else, which commanded Goethe's respect and formed the basis of their good relationship.

It is necessary to stress the warmth and depth of Goethe's feeling for Boisserée, for it is this in large part which explains his apparent conversion to medieval art and architecture in the years following the meeting with his young friend. This was no more a true conversion than had been the early enthusiasm for Strasbourg Minster. It was partly a genuine historical interest in the subject and partly a desire to encourage the younger generation, of whom Boisserée was the most persuasive and likeable representative he had met.

In just over a week, then, the ice had been completely broken. Through his tact and youthful ardour Boisserée had quite won over the old poet, if not to his own point of view, at least to a state of readiness to assist him as far as possible with his projects for the revival of

[1] Ibid. p. 123.

interest in the German art and architecture of the Middle Ages. Boisserée is already on such easy terms that he does not scruple to remind Goethe of 'the equivocal reputation he had gained by suppressing his address on Strasbourg Minster', at the same time complimenting him on his youthful receptiveness for spheres of interest usually alien to his way of thinking, as in the recent instance of the Dürer drawings. 'He had already told me a few days previously' he writes to Melchior, 'that there was something to be said for living into old age, since otherwise he would never really have got to know Dürer. He did not expressly apply this remark to the field of architecture, but in everything he said and did he showed me only too clearly how glad he was to have lived long enough to become properly acquainted with German medieval architecture.'[1]

After his departure from Weimar Boisserée continued his correspondence with Goethe in the warmest terms. 'Since my brief visit to you in Weimar,' he writes on 29 July 1811, 'I feel like someone who has found a long dreamed-of treasure and then straightway lost it again; it is the only way I can describe the relationship that has opened between us . . . In view of my love for the German past how could I help feeling moved to the depths of my soul by you—you who are the greatest German of your time and who were the first to revive the spirit of the German past, and were thus the originator of all our present endeavours to do likewise and to appreciate and preserve the achievements of our forefathers.'[2]

If Goethe's own letters of the time give us a less rhapsodic picture of the relationship, it is nevertheless clear that he has been most favourably impressed by Boisserée and is anxious to give him what help he can. For as he puts it in a letter to Reinhard of 8 May 1811, written during Boisserée's visit: 'If one does not want to become entirely cut off from the world, one must take the young people as one finds them and keep in with some of them in order to discover what the others are doing.' And in another letter to Reinhard, written from Carlsbad on 8 June 1811, he refers to his new friend thus: 'I got on very well with Herr Sulpice . . . I found him well versed in all the matters which interest him, and as far as the history of architecture and painting is concerned I believe him to be on the right path.' Goethe confesses that the meeting with Boisserée has stirred his old interest in the architecture of the Middle Ages and that he has learnt much from his conversations with him. He adds that he has been much attracted by his natural good manners and intelligence, and that

[1] Ibid. pp. 123–4. [2] SB ii. 13–14.

his interest in him has been increased by the very fact that he is a Catholic.

On 8 August Goethe writes to Boisserée in answer to his letter of 29 July already quoted: 'You may be sure that I was very sorry to miss you in Carlsbad. I cannot always reciprocate the good opinion which young men have of me, because they are apt to follow paths which lead too far away from my own. It was therefore all the pleasanter for me to make your acquaintance, for your general attitude is entirely congenial to me and your special field of study is one which I love and in which I am glad to be instructed by others, since I have been prevented from pursuing it myself through time and circumstances. Let us therefore always remain in contact and let me know from time to time how you are getting on.'

When Boisserée had left Weimar for Leipzig Goethe had given him a cordially worded introduction to his publisher Cotta in the hope of awakening his professional interest in the young man's drawings of Cologne Cathedral. But Cotta was too depressed by the political and international situation to undertake so ambitious a publication at that juncture. This made Sulpiz all the more anxious to obtain from Goethe some kind of public recognition of his work, and in his letter of 17 June he does not hesitate to remind him of the 'friendly promise' which he had apparently made him in Weimar. Goethe replies on 26 June that Sulpiz can rest assured that he has not forgotten his promise, but begs for time, in order that the projected statement may appear 'in the right place'.

The truth was that Goethe had already decided to include his public commendation in *Dichtung und Wahrheit*, on which he was now working. The relevant passage appeared, most appropriately, at the end of his description of Strasbourg Minster in Part Two (Book IX), which was published in October 1812. The tribute is ingeniously introduced as an illustration of the motto prefixed to the second part: 'Was man in der Jugend wünscht, hat man im Alter die Fülle.' (What one longs for in youth, in old age one has in plenty).

Goethe, in a passage already quoted, reflects on the time and energy he had expended in his youth on Strasbourg Minster and other Gothic buildings and is half inclined to regret his subsequent neglect of such interests. But when he observes the passionate devotion which is now given to such objects by members of the younger generation he is encouraged to feel that his early endeavours have not been in vain. 'In this connection I would specially single out the valiant Sulpiz Boisserée, who is tirelessly engaged on a magnificent series of engravings of

Cologne Cathedral, depicting this building as a model of those stupendous conceptions which strove Babel-like to reach the heavens, but which were so out of proportion to the means available that they necessarily failed to reach completion.' Goethe then calls for support from the wealthy and influential for such ventures as this, so that we can form a just estimate of the noble spirit and soaring ambitions of our forefathers. With a reference to the detailed history of medieval architecture planned by 'our active young friend' Goethe concludes the passage: 'When the results of these patriotic endeavours are made public, I for my part will be able to repeat with true contentment the words of the motto: what one longs for in youth, in old age one has in plenty.'[1]

Sulpiz acknowledges Goethe's generous tribute in suitably grateful terms. And indeed he had every reason to be satisfied with the manner of Goethe's public recognition of his project, published as it was, not in the comparative obscurity of some periodical review, but enshrined for ever at a central point of one of his major works—a work, moreover, which was calculated to arouse the greatest interest in the intellectual world of its day and thus to guarantee to Sulpiz the very maximum of publicity.

For that matter the whole long passage on Strasbourg Minster in the ninth book of *Dichtung und Wahrheit* can be considered as an indirect tribute on Goethe's part to the efforts and ambitions of his young friend. It was Sulpiz after all who had reawakened Goethe's long-lost interest in Gothic architecture, and we may be sure that but for his stimulus the minster would have played a very much less conspicuous role in the Strasbourg section of his autobiography. It is a significant fact that there is no allusion whatever to the minster in the two original 'Schemata' for *Dichtung und Wahrheit*, dating from October 1809 and May 1810 respectively.[2] The first reference is in a diary entry for 16 March 1811, by which time Goethe was already engaged on the first draft of the work. By a happy chance the section dealing with the minster is one of the few fragments of this first draft which have come down to us. Although this fragment predates the actual meeting with Sulpiz, it is clear that the stimulus behind it, and possibly even the decision to include the minster in his autobiography at all, came from his correspondence with his protégé in the preceding year and especially from his detailed perusal of the drawings of Cologne Cathedral.

---

[1] WA I. 27, 279–80.

[2] For Schema I see WA I. 26, 349–64; for Schema II see *Goethe-Jahrbuch* (1907), xxviii. 9–17. Cp. also Kurt Jahn, *Goethes Dichtung und Wahrheit* (Halle, 1908), pp. 143 ff.

The draft opens unequivocally: 'Among the things which preoccupied me most during my stay in Strasbourg the minster took almost the first place. It was the first dignified and imposing work of art which I had ever set eyes on. From the very start it made a strong impression on me, which only increased with greater familiarity.'[1]

Developing a theme which had been lightly sketched in *Von Deutscher Baukunst*, when the spirit of Erwin explains the functional necessity of his dispositions (III. 2), Goethe now attempts a detailed functional analysis and explanation of the main features of the façade of the Christian church in general. Such a façade will be divided both horizontally and vertically according to the arrangement of the doors and windows into three sections, making nine compartments in all. To these must be added two towers, which were originally used as belfries, but which grew ever loftier, until in the later Christian churches they almost entirely lost their original function and served only to announce the existence of the church to the distant traveller.

The next task of the Christian architect was to lighten the mass of the wall surface by frequent perforations and to diversify it by elaborate ornamentation. This brings us to Strasbourg Minster in particular which, according to Goethe, is unique in the perfection of its proportions and in the harmony of its details.

The rest of the draft passage is concerned with a matter which was only hinted at in the Erwin essay. In the third section of the latter Goethe, or rather the spirit of Erwin, refers to 'the mysterious forces which were intended to raise those two towers high in the air, of which alas one only stands sadly there, without the five-pinnacled crown which I destined for it.' In the draft Goethe describes how his intuitive assumption that the design of the tower demanded these five culminating finials was triumphantly vindicated by the original plan, which was revealed to him by an official of the cathedral and which showed the towers completed in this way. Goethe traced a copy of the plan on transparent paper with the idea of having it engraved, 'but nothing came of it, as of so much else; perhaps, however, this honour will now be accorded to Strasbourg Minster, an honour which it deserves as much as—and perhaps even more than—Cologne Cathedral'.[2]

When we compare this draft with *Von Deutscher Baukunst* the main impression must be that there is really very little in common between them. There was in fact comparatively little of the Erwin rhapsody which Goethe could utilize for his present purpose. The *Leitmotive*

---

[1] WA I. 27, 400.   [2] Ibid. p. 403.

of the *Baukunst*—'innere Form', the organic unity of the building, the constant comparison with the creations of nature, the homage to the original genius of Erwin—all these are conspicuously absent from the draft. Nor do the concepts of 'characteristic art' or of Gothic as a specifically German product play any part. Still less of course is there any trace of the polemical elements (anti-Laugier, anti-Sulzer, anti-French) which took up so much space in *Von Deutscher Baukunst*.

All Goethe appears to have taken from the *Baukunst* are some hints from his description of the minster in III. 2 and II. 10. The points recognizably suggested by III. 2 are the functional explanation of the façade, the emphasis on the fine proportions of the whole and the parts, and the passage on the missing finials; II. 10 contributed the passage on the multiplication of detail as a means of lightening and diversifying the monotony of the wall space. Few though these points of resemblance may be, they are enough to show that Goethe reread the old essay before composing this draft for the Strasbourg section of his autobiography.

The draft passage on the minster dates, as we have said, from March 1811. It was not till the beginning of September 1812 that Goethe rewrote the passage for inclusion in the final version of *Dichtung und Wahrheit*, Part Two, which appeared at the end of October of that year.[1] In the long interval that elapsed between first draft and final version there had occurred the meeting of Goethe and Boisserée and the revival of Goethe's interest in medieval architecture. When he came to reconsider the minster passage he evidently decided that it would have to be completely rewritten. In the first place he now felt very differently about the subject from what he had done eighteen months before. Though it would be an exaggeration to claim that he had been converted to Boisserée's point of view, his interest in medieval art and architecture had been thoroughly roused by his young friend's learning and enthusiasm. The account of the minster was now itself to be a kind of indirect tribute to the aims and achievements of the Boisserées. It must therefore occupy a much more prominent part in the Strasbourg narrative than was originally intended, and—equally important—it must be several degrees warmer in tone. Moreover Goethe was now very much better equipped to write on the subject. Sulpiz had brought with him to Weimar drawings and plans of Strasbourg as well as of Cologne, and we know that the merits and demerits of the minster had been under close discussion.[2] In

[1] Cp. diary entries for September 1st, 4th and 5th (WA III. 4, 317–19).
[2] Cp. diary entry for 10 May 1811 (WA III. 4, 204) and SB i. 117.

addition Goethe had had the benefit of Sulpiz's long and detailed dis-
quisitions on the nature, history and development of medieval architecture in general. In consequence of all this the minster finally became
one of the three main themes, along with Herder and Friederike
Brion, of the whole Strasbourg episode.

By now indeed Goethe had decided to give the minster, and more
especially the tower of the minster, a symbolic value, quite apart
from its strictly architectural significance. It dominates the Strasbourg
chapters much as the actual tower dominates the Strasbourg landscape.
It has become the outward and visible sign of the new life and inspiration, of the immense extension of experience, which Strasbourg
brought him. It has become too a symbol of the new patriotism, of the
reaction against the values of French civilization, which characterized
the *Sturm und Drang*.

When Goethe came to write the final version in September 1812 he
split up the minster theme into three main sections, thus greatly rein-
forcing its significance for the Strasbourg chapters. The first section
gives the minster pride of place as the opening scene of the whole
Strasbourg drama. For as soon as he had arrived, says Goethe, he
hurried to the cathedral to see at close quarters what had long been a
conspicuous feature of the landscape as he approached the city.
And then in words obviously suggested by the third section of *Von
Deutscher Baukunst* he proceeds: 'When I first caught sight of this
Colossus through the narrow alley and then stood in the all too confined space in front of it, it made on me an impression of a quite
peculiar kind which I felt incapable of analysing on the spot.'[1]
After further contemplation he came to the conclusion that this pecu-
liarity consisted in the combination in the same building of the
Sublime and the Charming. 'However I made no attempt to resolve
this paradox, but allowed this so astonishing monument by its very
presence to continue working quietly upon me.'[2]

There he leaves the matter for the time being, and it is not till
he has described for us his daily table companions, his studies and general milieu that he returns to the subject of the minster. This time he
settles down to the subject in earnest, and gives a detailed analysis
of the dispositions of the façade. The object of this carefully reasoned
disquisition is to explain the contradictory sensations of his first
impression. This analysis is in essence an amplification—a considerable
amplification—of the corresponding passage in the first draft. As

[1] WA I, 27, 229.   [2] Ibid. p. 231.

there he divides the façade into nine compartments, the separate features of which are all determined by their functional uses.

Whereas, Goethe argues, it is the arrangement of the masses and the relation of the parts to the whole which give a building Sublimity, it is the treatment of the details which give it Charm. 'It is precisely in this respect that the work under discussion satisfies us in the highest degree, for every single detail is completely appropriate to the part it adorns, is subordinated to it and seems indeed to have grown out of it.' The details, however, are not only appropriate, they are also functional: 'The apertures in the wall, the solid parts of the same, the buttresses, each has its particular character which proceeds from its particular use. This special character is communicated step by step to the subordinate parts, so that the decoration is harmonious throughout; everything, both great and small, is in its right place.'[1]

Goethe then proceeds to give examples of what he means with a precision of detail which bears eloquent testimony to the teachings of Sulpiz Boisserée:

I need only mention the portals receding in perspective into the thickness of the walls with the infinitely elaborate ornamentation of their pillars and pointed arches; or the circular rose-window and the outline of its tracery; or the slim reed-like columns of the perpendicular sub-divisions. Let me remind you of the gradually receding buttresses with their slender little pointed structures, light-pillared and canopied, intended to protect the statues of the saints, and all striving heavenwards; and of the way every rib, every boss has the form of a flower cluster or spray of leaves or of some other natural object turned to stone . . . I realize that my estimate of this work of architecture may appear exaggerated to some; for I myself, though strongly attracted to it from the start, nevertheless took a long time to become thoroughly aware of its merits.[2]

This last sentence leads Goethe to consider his attitude towards Gothic before the revelation of Strasbourg Minster:

Having grown up among enemies of Gothic architecture, I had nourished a dislike of its frequently overladen and confused ornamentation, the arbitrary character of which increased the repugnance which I in any case felt for the religious gloom characteristic of this style. I was confirmed in this distaste, since I had hitherto come across only inferior examples of the style, without either good proportions or artistic consistency. In this instance, however, I felt I had experienced a new revelation, since none of these defects were visible, but on the contrary the very opposite qualities forced themselves on my notice.[3]

Finally he records how, inspired by the German origins of the

[1] Ibid. p. 273.   [2] Ibid. pp. 273–4.   [3] Ibid. p. 274.

minster and its architect, he ventured to substitute the term 'German architecture' for the discredited appellation 'Gothic', and how he subsequently gave expression to his patriotic feelings in the Erwin essay.

With this he breaks off his account of the minster and only takes it up again at the end of Book XI, on the eve of his departure from Strasbourg and his final farewell to Friederike Brion. At this point he inserts the story of his intuitive completion of the minster tower which had formed the second half of the draft fragment. But whereas the first half of the draft with its analysis of the façade had been very considerably amplified in *Dichtung und Wahrheit*, this second half has been compressed. Otherwise the account in Book XI keeps fairly close to the original draft. Only at the end the invidious reference to Cologne Cathedral has been omitted out of deference to Sulpiz Boisserée.

If we compare the account of the minster in *Dichtung und Wahrheit* with that in *Von Deutscher Baukunst* we shall find the differences to be even more striking than were those between the draft of 1811 and the early essay. It is indeed the difference between the young and the old Goethe altogether. In 1770 Strasbourg Minster had been a passionate personal experience of the most intimate kind, perhaps the only architectural experience of Goethe's life to which he reacted with spontaneous enthusiasm and immediacy.[1] Now forty years later it is an experience of the long past to be analyzed and dissected with the detachment of old age. Where *Von Deutscher Baukunst* had been a paean to the original genius of the architect, *Dichtung und Wahrheit* is a sober analysis of the architecture.

On the other hand there is still no consideration of the interior, nor for that matter of any other Gothic building. Goethe still writes as though Strasbourg was the only Gothic church in the world. Nor—despite the ministrations of Boisserée—is there any suggestion of the religious implications of Gothic architecture. Indeed the passages on the minster show very little more understanding for the specific nature of Gothic than does *Von Deutscher Baukunst*. The main point is that *Dichtung und Wahrheit* endeavours to find a rationalistic explanation for the intuitive perceptions of the Erwin essay. In addition, the *Dichtung und Wahrheit* passages show a heightened awareness of the character of the decorative detail and of the manner in which the underlying unity is attained, and for these insights he is no doubt

---

[1] Cp. N. Pevsner, 'Goethe e l'Archittetura', *Palladio*, iv. 174 ff. (October/December, 1951).

indebted to his young mentor. But of the essential characteristics of the Gothic style (as we understand them nowadays, and even as they were understood in Goethe's day by such men as C. L. Stieglitz, Georg Moller and Sulpiz Boisserée himself) Goethe shows no more apprehension than in his early essay. The façade is still seen essentially in terms of Oeser's neo-classicism—harmonious proportions and pleasing grace.

Nevertheless the tone of Goethe's remarks in his autobiography presents an astonishing contrast to the views on Gothic architecture which he had been expressing for the preceding thirty-five years or so. One has only to compare his positive treatment of the decorative detail in the *Dichtung und Wahrheit* passage with his remarks in the 1788 'Baukunst' essay, where Gothic ornamentation is condemned as something 'stuck on' superficially, without sense or proportion. It is true of course that Goethe is here consciously attempting to recapture the mood of forty years before, and it would certainly be a mistake to assume that the account in *Dichtung und Wahrheit* fully and correctly represents his attitude to Gothic at the time of writing. At the same time his high valuation of the building is defended and explained with so compelling a logic that the reader is insensibly persuaded that the author is indeed conveying his present views. This at any rate was the effect on his contemporaries. After the long sojourn *in partibus infidelium* the account of the minster in *Dichtung und Wahrheit* inevitably created the impression that Goethe had at last seen the error of his ways and returned to the Gothic fold.

4. RHINE, MAIN AND NECKAR

WITH Goethe's public acknowledgement of his aims and achievements in *Dichtung und Wahrheit*, Sulpiz Boisserée could justly claim that the second stage of his enterprise—the enlistment of public support for his projects—had been successfully accomplished. The next milestone in the relations between the two men was Goethe's visits to Rhine, Main and Neckar in the summers of 1814 and 1815. The significance of these journeys for Goethe's poetic development, the part they played in the composition of the *West-östlicher Divan*, the relationship with Marianne von Willemer—all this is a commonplace of German literary history. Less well known is the contribution they made to Goethe's reawakened interest in medieval art and architecture.

For years Sulpiz had been begging Goethe to visit Heidelberg and see with his own eyes the collection of German and Flemish primitives which the brothers Boisserée and their friend Bertram had been patiently and skilfully acquiring in the course of the previous ten years. In 1814 the international situation, which rendered Goethe's customary visits to the Bohemian spas inadvisable, gave Sulpiz the opportunity he had been waiting for. Goethe—partly at least as a result of his young friend's insistence—was persuaded to exchange Carlsbad for Wiesbaden on this occasion, and from there he paid his long planned visit to Heidelberg.

Goethe stayed with the Boisserées for over a fortnight from 24 September to 9 October, and the faithful trio did everything they could to make the visit a success. He was given a large room immediately adjoining the picture gallery, and according to Sulpiz he was in the gallery by eight o'clock every morning and stayed there without interruption till lunch time, absorbed in the contemplation of the paintings. Bertram has described how he had the pictures placed for him one by one on an easel, so that he could concentrate on each one separately, undisturbed by its neighbours.

Goethe had at this time never seen a Van Eyck, and apart from Cranach and a few Dürers no early German paintings either. Thus he was confronted Cortes-like with a new and virgin world, and the immediate effect was overwhelming: 'My friends', he exclaimed again and again, 'what fools we are, what fools we are! We dare to think we're superior to our ancestors. By heaven, they (i.e. the Primitives) were in a different class from us! Why, they are beyond all praise! The kings and princes and all the nations of the earth should come and pay them homage.'[1]

Goethe was specially impressed by Rogier van der Weyden's *Adoration of the Kings*, which was at this time ascribed by the Boisserées to Van Eyck, asserting in terms which he was otherwise accustomed to reserve for the products of classical art: 'That is the purest truth and nature.' On another occasion he declared that he had deliberately cut himself off from the younger generation in order to protect himself from all impressions of a novel or disturbing kind, and now he suddenly found himself face to face with a totally unfamiliar world of forms and colours, which forced him out of the rut of his old views and prejudices into an unqualified enthusiasm for what he saw.

So much for Goethe's reactions as reported by others. That the accounts are not exaggerated is shown by his own words in the diary letters to Christiane which he wrote during his visit: 'Sunday 25 September. Began to study the old masterpieces of the Netherlands. One must admit that they are well worth a pilgrimage. I only wish that all my friends could see them.' On 28 September, speaking of Van der Weyden's *Adoration* and *St. Luke*: 'Even when one has seen them often, it is hard to believe that such pictures are really possible.' And of the collection as a whole he writes on 1 October: 'The pictures surpass in splendour one's wildest dreams.'

In a letter to Reinhard of 8 October 1814 Goethe sums up his impressions of the Boisserées and their achievement: 'You know my young hosts and have long been on intimate terms with them. It is hard to say what one should admire most about them, their true affection for a worthy cause, or their persistence in furthering it . . . I have already been here twelve days. First one is astonished, then one admires, then one discriminates; but it is only when one has left that one will really know what has been permanently gained, but also what has slipped one's grasp.'

On parting from Heidelberg he writes to Christiane on 8 October: 'Unwillingly I took leave of the rooms which contain so many treasures. They are so perfect that one cannot help wishing to have them always before one's eyes.'

It has often been remarked that the Rhine, Main and Neckar journeys of 1814 and 1815 constitute a kind of second youth in Goethe's

[1] SB i. 234.

development, second only to the Italian journey in their rejuvenating influence on his emotional and intellectual life. Many years later he spoke of them to Eckermann (11 March 1828) as examples of that 'temporary rejuvenation', that 'repeated puberty', which occurs to 'specially gifted people even during their old age'. The two respects in which this rejuvenation made itself felt most obviously were of course Goethe's passionate relationship with Marianne von Willemer and his lyrical productivity in the *Divan* poems. But another and scarcely less striking example of it was the freshness and enthusiasm of his reception of the Flemish and German primitives in the Boisserée Collection.

So absorbing was this revelation of medieval art that medieval architecture—which always remained Sulpiz's primary concern, for the picture collection was mainly Melchior's responsibility—was obliged to take second place during the Heidelberg visit. Nevertheless Sulpiz's portfolio was not forgotten. Several mornings towards the end of Goethe's stay were devoted to detailed study and discussion of Cologne Cathedral and the development of Gothic architecture. On leaving Heidelberg on 9 October Sulpiz accompanied him as far as Darmstadt, where he introduced him to Georg Moller, who had recently discovered the original elevation of the north tower of Cologne Cathedral. It was, according to Sulpiz, at least partly Goethe's good offices which moved Moller to adopt a cooperative attitude about the new discovery and to allow Sulpiz to make a trace copy of the original for his own purposes.

And here they parted, Goethe proceeding to Frankfurt, where he stayed for over a fortnight before returning to Weimar. Sulpiz writes: 'I was sad indeed to part from our old friend, especially when he had driven off and I remained alone behind with nothing but my reflections on what he had meant to us and what we had had from him during these memorable days.'[1] Goethe notes, more laconically but no less cordially, in a letter to Christiane of 11 October: 'I have seldom undertaken anything so successful as this expedition to Heidelberg.' Goethe had indeed been deeply impressed, and Sulpiz had won from him the promise that he would himself write an account of the Collection and of the efforts of the Boisserées in the cause of medieval art and architecture.

What Goethe's apparent conversion to medieval art meant to the Romantics and the friends of 'Christian art' it is easy to imagine. We get a glimpse of it in a letter to Sulpiz from a friend in Cologne,

[1] SB i. 227.

describing Max von Schenkendorf's reaction: 'Schenkendorf has been describing to me with loving ardour Goethe's conversion when confronted with your pictures, and I can imagine the scene as if I had been present. What a miracle! What a phenomenon! Is it not as if the three heathen kings at the manger of the Saviour had been joined by a fourth who also brought his gift, knelt down before the new-born Child, and made his offering and believed, and then spread the gospel among his brothers, farther and ever farther . . . And so shall the Propyläen crumble and with them the heathen idols in the Elegies, and who knows whether instead of Iphigenie a great and glorious Christian heroine shall not crown Goethe with the garland of immortality!'[1]

But the Romantics, and especially the Catholic Romantics, were too optimistic. Goethe's conversion to the cause of medieval art and architecture was a good deal less thorough-going than they supposed. Once removed from the stimulating presence of the Boisserées and of the pictures themselves he reverted to the benevolent but detached approach which had underlain his attitude to their endeavours all along. We need not doubt that this cooler attitude was reinforced by his renewed intercourse with Heinrich Meyer, whom he saw much of on his return to Weimar, and whose influence was always exerted in keeping Goethe as far as possible to the strictly classical path. There are indeed clear indications that Goethe felt that he had allowed himself to be carried away too far in the direction of Romantic medievalism by the siren tones of the Boisserée household and that the inevitable reaction was now setting in. There is, for instance, the letter of 9 November to his old friend Knebel, written within a fortnight of his return to Weimar, in which he says of his recent journey: 'I have feasted at the Homeric as well as at the Nibelungen table, but for my part found nothing more congenial than Nature in her depth and breadth and perpetual vitality, as she is to be found in the works of the Greek poets and sculptors.'

Symptomatic too is Goethe's letter to Sulpiz, thanking him for his hospitality. In the first place, the letter was not written till 19 November, well over a month after they had parted and over three weeks after he had returned to Weimar. And the tone of the letter is by no means as enthusiastic as one might have expected in the circumstances. In retrospect the most tangible gain of the Heidelberg experience now seems to Goethe to be the increased understanding of his own collection of prints and drawings of the later Netherlandish

[1] Ibid. pp. 239-40.

painters, such as Rubens and Rembrandt, which the acquaintance
with their medieval forbears had afforded. It may too, he suggests,
have served to correct a certain one-sidedness in his earlier aesthetic
attitude.

This last remark is made apropos of the *Italienische Reise*, and it is
in this quarter that the most evident signs of Goethe's reaction are
to be seen. For it was during these months of November and December
1814 that he was engaged in revising and arranging the letters and
diaries of his journey from Carlsbad to Rome, precisely that section
of the book which contains the adverse remarks on Gothic architecture
which were added during the final compilation. It is remarkable how
this final version goes out of its way to emphasize the distaste for
Gothic which finds only an occasional hint in the original diaries and
letters of 1786. In his description of Palladio's Basilica in Vicenza,
for instance, he has added to the account in the original *Tagebuch*
the words: 'Here too unfortunately I find next to each other both
what I am fleeing from and what I seek.'[1] What he seeks is the classical
beauty of Palladio, what he flees is the Gothic of the Palazzo della
Ragione. In the *Italienische Reise* he passes by the church of St. Francis
in Assisi in favour of the Temple of Minerva, as in the *Tagebuch*, but
this time 'with aversion'.[2]

The most notable of these inserted passages is the famous outburst
vis-à-vis the cast of a fragment of a Roman temple in the Palazzo
Farsetti in Venice: 'That is to be sure, something very different
from our huddled saints of the Gothic style, piled up on top of one
another on little corbels, something very different from our tobacco-
pipe columns, spiky pinnacles and foliated crockets; from all taste
for these I am now, thank God, set free for ever.'[3]

It is true that Goethe is here ostensibly projecting himself back
into the state of mind of 1786; but, one may ask, why was it necessary
retrospectively and gratuitously to stress in this way his anti-Gothic
attitude at the time of the Italian journey? The passage is all the more
surprising in that it selects for contumely the very details of Gothic
decoration which he had extolled only two years before in his description of Strasbourg Minster in *Dichtung und Wahrheit*. It is impossible
to avoid the impression that this and the other anti-Gothic touches
in the *Italienische Reise* were deliberately inserted in November and
December 1814 as a kind of self-defence against becoming too deeply
involved in the Romantic medievalism of the Boisserées.

Goethe must have realized that the passage would be painful to the

---

[1] WA I. 30, 79.   [2] Ibid. p. 182.   [3] Ibid. p. 135.

faithful Sulpiz. The following summer he brought up the subject of the *Italienische Reise* in a conversation recorded by Sulpiz in his diary (8 August 1815): 'Italienische Reise. Pleasure in architecture, purely personal passion for Palladio; Palladio, Palladio, and nothing but Palladio . . . Rage and hatred against Gothic architecture; he will omit this passage for my sake, so that I may see what a good fellow he is. People being what they are would be sure to misunderstand it. In any case the composition will be all the better for its omission'.[1] Presumably the item referred to is the tobacco-pipe passage. If so, Goethe either changed his mind or forgot his resolution, for when the first volume of the *Italienische Reise* appeared in 1816 the offending entry was still there.

In the first few months of 1815 there is little evidence from the letters and diaries that Goethe was concerned with the revelation of medieval art which had been vouchsafed to him in the previous autumn. We hear no more, for instance, of the promised article on the Boisserée Collection. He was fully occupied, as we know, not with medieval art, but with Hafiz and the *West-östlicher Divan*, not to mention the *Italienische Reise* and the preparation of the new collected edition of his works.

The only utterance of significance on the subject in this period occurs in a letter of 10 May 1815 to the architect Ludwig Friedrich Catel, thanking him for his *Grundzüge einer Theorie der Bauart protestantischer Kirchen*. In this letter Goethe expresses his sympathy with the historical study of medieval architecture, but rejects absolutely the attempt to apply a medieval style to contemporary buildings. 'Certainly one ought to value highly the old German style of architecture, to preserve its memory, study it historically, and learn much from it, especially in the technical sphere; but no attempt should be made to erect new buildings in this taste and style.'

These brief sentences are the concentrated essence of a much more detailed draft letter to Catel, which for some reason or other (perhaps because he felt diffident about obtruding his views on a professional architect) he never sent, but which constitutes one of Goethe's clearest and wisest statements on the subject of the Gothic Revival.

He begins by thanking Catel for reintroducing him to the realm of architecture, 'in which I formerly tarried so passionately, but which at present I only enter momentarily and from time to time as an alien visitor'. He then applauds the patriotic efforts of the brothers Boisserée and their like on behalf of German medieval architecture.

[1] SB i. 264.

'But', he proceeds, 'the more we are enabled by such endeavours to reach a historical and critical appreciation of these edifices, the less shall we be inclined to employ these obsolete and antiquated forms in contemporary architecture. The present fashion in this respect has arisen from the mistaken tendency to try and reproduce what one admires, even under totally differing circumstances. When one reflects that pinnacles and pointed arches tend to attract the type of morbid imagination which delights in the vague and formless, when one considers that this astounding style was first reintroduced in the shape of garden follies, then the impropriety of using such forms, however respectable in themselves, for higher purposes is immediately obvious.'

But Goethe comes nearer the heart of the matter in the following paragraph, where he voices very eloquently one of the most telling arguments against the whole Gothic Revival, namely the fundamental contrast between the technical conditions of the Middle Ages and those of modern times. 'Least of all do people seem to realize that the architects of the thirteenth century had at their disposal an enormous reservoir of technical skill, the last trace of which has now disappeared.'[1] Where, he asks, are the masons' guilds with their archives and secret traditions, where the cunning artists in stone and glass, who existed in their thousands in those centuries? In such conditions it becomes intelligible that an exceptional individual like the architect of Cologne Cathedral could plan the whole tremendous structure down to the smallest detail *aus einem Guss*, but in these days we should be lucky if we could scrape together the hundred thousandth part of it.

It is significant that Goethe does not mention the weightiest of all arguments against the Gothic Revival: namely the spiritual discrepancy—more important even than the technical discrepancy— between the Middle Ages and today. It is the background of a universally accepted religious faith which alone makes intelligible the stupendous achievements of medieval architecture. With the spirit lacking, the builder buildeth but in vain. But to this aspect of the matter the 'old pagan' of Weimar was—perhaps deliberately—blind.

On 24 May 1815 Goethe left Weimar for his second journey to the Rhine and Main. He stayed first in Wiesbaden, whence at the end of July he made an excursion down the valley of the Lahn to Nassau. Here he visited Freiherr vom Stein, who proposed that together they should make an impromptu journey down the Rhine to Cologne. And so, on 26 July 1815, Goethe for the third time set eyes on the cathedral. What he thought of the building, to which under the aegis of the

[1] WA IV, 25, 410–11.

Boisserées he had devoted so much thought and study for the last four years, we do not know. Neither the diaries nor letters of the time throw any light on the matter, and even the *Annalen* for 1815 have nothing of significance to say. Nevertheless this joint visit with Stein was to have important consequences as far as Goethe's part in the Gothic Revival was concerned.

The poet and patriot Ernst Moritz Arndt happened to be in Cologne at the time and—long afterwards, it is true—described his meeting with the two:

We went to the cathedral. Stein greeted us in the most friendly manner. And whom do you think we saw with him? There stood the other greatest German of the nineteenth century, Wolfgang Goethe, contemplating the *Dombild*.[1] Stein whispered to us: 'Be careful, my good friends, to keep off politics! He can't bear that! I know we can't agree with him there, but we must respect his greatness.' It was wonderful to see these two Germans walking side by side with such mutual esteem.[2]

In the absence of Boisserée Goethe and Stein were shown round the city by Wallraf, whose collection of German Primitives was only less remarkable than that of the brothers in Heidelberg, and by Maximilian Fuchs, the architect-draughtsman who collaborated with Sulpiz in his drawings of the cathedral. Amongst other things they were taken to see the paintings and manuscripts of Rektor G. K. Fochem, who has left a lively account of the visit: 'Herr von Stein and Goethe, accompanied by Wallraf and Fuchs, paid me a call of an hour and a half. Goethe held forth the whole time to Stein.' The visitors praised his medieval treasures, but characteristically their real enthusiasm was reserved for a painting by Raphael. 'They sat down, stood up, sat down again; Goethe shook his head and finished off by saying that it was a magnificent picture—and all this in the presence of Wallraf and Fuchs!' Nevertheless Goethe was loud in his praise of Fochem's efforts on behalf of German medieval art: 'It is beginning to dawn, and yours is the credit for breaking through the mists'— an odd sentiment from the protagonist of classical clarity and the sworn foe of medieval obscurity. Fochem ends his account with the words: 'I have only one thing to say against them: they were impolite

[1] The *Dombild* was the appellation given for convenience by Boisserée and his contemporaries to the painting of the Adoration of the Kings by Stefan Lochner which now stands in the Marienkapelle of Cologne Cathedral. It was removed to the cathedral in 1810 from the comparative obscurity of the Ratskapelle at the instigation of Sulpiz Boisserée, who attributed the painting at the time to Meister Wilhelm von Köln.
[2] Arndt, *Meine Wanderungen und Wandelungen mit dem Reichsfreiherrn Heinrich Karl Friedrich von Stein* (Berlin, 1858), pp. 224-5.

enough to stand on my silk-upholstered chairs in their muddy boots in order to get a closer view of the pictures.'[1]

There was a symbolic quality in this visit of the two greatest Germans of their day to one of the greatest monuments of the German Middle Ages at this precise moment of time, when the Rhinelands had been finally freed from the Napoleonic yoke and a wave of patriotic enthusiasm for the German past was sweeping the country. That this symbolic quality was felt at the time is indicated in Goethe's letter of 1 August to his son, in which he speaks of the enthusiastic, indeed fanatical reception which was accorded him. 'That I made this journey precisely at this moment has given much food for thought; strangely enough it was quite unpremeditated, but it will certainly not remain without result.'

Sulpiz Boisserée at least was in no doubt as to the symbolic value of Goethe's adherence to the cause at this juncture. On 25 June he had urged him to visit Heidelberg now that the Battle of Waterloo had finally settled Napoleon's fate. The movements of the Imperial armies had brought with them the happy result for the Boisserées that the most distinguished and influential personalities, Prince Metternich, the Archduke Johann, and Kaiser Franz himself, had visited their collection and manifested the most gratifying approval. Their interest and support raised Sulpiz's hopes that the restoration of peace after the long years of war and unrest would mean offical recognition for the patriotic endeavours of themselves and their fellow enthusiasts:

It is precisely in this respect that we should so specially welcome your visit. Even those who are well disposed to our cause lack a universally recognized authority who would provide a sanction for their judgment. You alone can give them this by publicly declaring your views on German medieval art. Nothing we ourselves write on the subject can really fulfil this aim. The expert who praises his own subject is always to some degree suspect . . . Therefore we beg you to carry out the promise you gave us last year. In this way you will be able to achieve something for the German past, and incidentally for us, which will redound to your credit both with contemporaries and posterity. Perhaps the moment will never recur when this can be accomplished with such ease and success.[16]

Sulpiz's appeal was to be answered, but not quite in the way he had envisaged. On 31 July Goethe is back in Wiesbaden, where he was shortly joined by his young friend, who was to remain at his side until 9 October, and whose detailed diary of these weeks provides us with an invaluable record of Goethe's preoccupations during this critical period of his life. Sulpiz alone of all his friends was aware of what

[1] *Goethes Gespräche, Artemis-Ausgabe*, xxii. 794–5.   [2] SB ii. 63.

Marianne Willemer meant to Goethe at this time, and of her intimate connection with the poems of the *Divan*. To no other male friend, at any rate of his later years, did Goethe reveal his heart with so much candour. Sulpiz was worthy of his trust: the secret of the *Divan* he took with him to the grave.

Sulpiz's diary opens with the words: 'Lunch with Goethe, cheerful, cordial reception. Stein has asked him to write a memorandum for Hardenberg on artistic and antiquarian matters; he wants to consult me about this.'[1] In other words, the concrete result of the joint visit to Cologne was a proposal on Stein's part that Goethe should address himself directly to the Prussian chancellor in order to draw the attention of the authorities to the artistic and historical monuments of their newly-acquired Rhineland province. After decades of French occupation the whole administration of the Rhinelands was in a state of chaos and desperately in need of reorganization. To bring about this reorganization in the cultural sphere was one of the aims of Freiherr vom Stein, and the real motive behind the joint expedition to Cologne and the proposal of the Hardenberg memorandum was to enlist Goethe's help in this endeavour.

He seems to have embraced the idea with enthusiasm. During the next few weeks the diaries of both Goethe and Boisserée contain frequent references to the progress of the work. The plan was to write a description of the objects of artistic and archaeological interest which Goethe had met with in the course of his journey—beginning with Cologne, proceeding down the Rhine, and concluding with an account of the Boisserée Collection in Heidelberg. Sulpiz made himself directly responsible for the portion dealing with his collection, but in fact the whole essay must be regarded as a work of collaboration between the two friends, for at every point, as is clear from the diaries, Goethe sought his assistance over details of the itinerary.

It is touching to think that during these weeks when Goethe, as we know, was so deeply preoccupied with Marianne Willemer and the *Divan* poems he should still have had time to spare for Sulpiz and the cause of medieval art in the Rhinelands. There are, it is true, occasional indications that he was anxious not to become too involved in Sulpiz's plans and undertakings. When his friend told him that Count Solms, Governor-General of the Lower Rhine, had asked him for his views on the preservation of German medieval antiquities, Goethe replied: 'Well, that's fine; you've set the ball rolling, and you don't really need me any more. If you could leave me out of your

[1] SB i. 249.

calculations, I should be grateful.'[1] But Sulpiz was not to be put off so easily, and the following weeks show the two friends as busy as ever with the memorandum. Goethe had by now come to the conclusion that the most effective course would be to present the work, not as an official document, but as an essay addressed to the public at large, of which he would send copies to Hardenberg and Metternich.

On 18 September the two friends set off for Heidelberg, spending two nights in Darmstadt on the way, where they called on that important figure of the German Gothic Revival Georg Moller, who showed them his plans and drawings of Strasbourg and Freiburg Minsters. In Heidelberg Goethe lodged with the Boisserées as in the previous year. Three days after their arrival they were joined unexpectedly by the Willemers and on 28 September for one night by Karl August, who was shown round the collection—not very willingly, according to Bertram—by Goethe.

Goethe's second visit to Heidelberg in the autumn of 1815 seems to have taken place under less happy auspices than that of the previous summer. It is clear from Sulpiz's diary that he was much distracted during these weeks—partly by the Duke's visit, but more especially by his feelings for Marianne Willemer. Sulpiz has little to report this time of his reactions to the Flemish and German primitives, though other eye-witnesses make it clear that he was still capable of being deeply impressed by them. The Hamburg bookseller Friedrich Perthes, for instance, records Goethe's exclamation on seeing Memling's St. Christopher: 'If I were not such an old pagan, that picture would convert me!'[2] And Wilhelm Grimm reports the most surprisingly positive of all Goethe's utterances on medieval art; 'Goethe sat long in silence in front of Van Eyck's [i.e. Van der Weyden's] great picture, but said nothing about it all day, until he went for his afternoon walk, when he remarked: "I have written many poems in my life, among which are a few good ones and many mediocre ones; and there is Van Eyck who paints a picture which is worth more than all my works put together".'[3]

Amid his other concerns Sulpiz's work on Cologne Cathedral was not forgotten. Goethe goes so far as to declare that the plan of the cathedral has given him an entirely new insight into the art of architecture. He understands now why Sulpiz exalts it over all other Gothic monuments, because it embodies a principle—though

---

[1] Ibid. p. 274.   [2] *Goethes Gespräche*, ed. cit., p. 851.   [3] Ibid. pp. 851–2.

he does not specify what it is—which has been carried through the whole building with the utmost consistency.

On 6 October Goethe's restlessness decided him to return home at once, and next day he set off, Sulpiz accompanying him as far as Würzburg. The reason Goethe gave to Cotta and the Duke for this unexpected decision—the Duke had invited Goethe to join him in Frankfurt—was the need to finish off without delay the essay on the antiquities of Rhine and Main. Sulpiz in his diary gives the impression that it was nervousness about his health and unwillingness to be involved in the social round of the Duke's party. It is, however, generally—and no doubt rightly—assumed that the deeper motive for Goethe's sudden flight from Rhine, Main and Neckar was the growing tension of his relationship with Marianne, which was so inextricably associated in his mind with these regions and which would have been subjected to a new and agonizing strain by a renewed meeting with her in Frankfurt.[1] The essay was an added incentive and above all a convenient excuse for his hasty return to Weimar.

So ended Goethe's second journey to the Rhine: the climax, one may say, both of his relationship to Sulpiz Boisserée and of his relationship to the Romantic Movement altogether. It was many years before Sulpiz was to meet him again, and in the long absence the friendship inevitably grew less intimate. Away from the brothers and their infectious enthusiasm Goethe soon returned to his lifelong predilection for classical art, and though he always retained a friendly interest in their efforts and in those of other workers in the same field, he was never again to identify himself so closely with Romantic medievalism as on the Rhine journeys of 1814 and 1815.

The aesthetic and intellectual harvest of these journeys was concentrated into the essay which eventually appeared under the title *Ueber Kunst und Alterthum in den Rhein und Mayn Gegenden*. Back in Weimar Goethe concentrated his energies on finishing the essay as soon as possible. For days on end the entries in the diary begin with the laconic 'Kunst und Alterthum', varied only by 'Kunst und Alterthum. Divan'. For the next weeks and months his literary energies were divided between these two legacies of the Rhine journeys.

The spirit in which Goethe attacked the essay is well expressed in a letter of 12 November 1815 to the sculptor Johann Gottfried Schadow: 'I assure you that my sole source of satisfaction at the moment is . . . to contribute to the cause of the arts and sciences to the

[1] Cp. E. Beutler, 'Die Boisserée-Gespräche von 1815 und die Entstehung des Gingo-biloba-Gedichtes', *Essays um Goethe* (3rd ed., Wiesbaden, 1946, 2 vols.), i. 311 ff.

best of my ability in the purified air and on the liberated soil of Germany.'

In these months in fact Goethe was more affected by the wave of patriotic enthusiasm which swept the country after the liberation of German soil from the Napoleonic yoke than is always realized. He had been genuinely moved by the concern of Freiherr vom Stein for the preservation of the national heritage in the Rhinelands and even by the Romantic vision of medieval art which inspired the Boisserées. He was glad to play a modest part in the patriotic movement, a part which consisted primarily in lending the weight of his authority to the campaign for the preservation of the artistic treasures of the Rhinelands. And so he could write with conviction to Sulpiz shortly after his return to Weimar (23 October) with reference to the essay: 'It would be strange indeed if our laudable aim should fail in its effect and the modest patriotic flames which we are kindling on so many peaks and hills of Rhine and Main should not also arouse patriotic emotions.'

Nevertheless, though Goethe was genuinely in sympathy with the patriotic aims of the Romantic medievalists at this juncture, the decision to make a public confession of his views on the subject was due primarily to his desire to assist his friend Sulpiz. So he writes to Knebel on 21 October that he has undertaken the essay 'more for others' sake than my own'. And to Zelter on 29th October: 'True, it is not my way to intervene actively in the problems of the day, but on this occasion I was invited so earnestly and appealingly to undertake this task that I could not refuse. In actual fact I am merely playing the part of editor, by acting as the channel for the views, wishes and hopes of certain good and sensible people.'

Though Goethe had abandoned his original aim of compiling an official memorandum in favour of an appeal to the educated public in general, the essay still had a certain official connection. For the Prussian Minster of the Interior, K. F. von Schuckmann, applied to Goethe for his views on the cultural situation in the Rhinelands, and in reply Goethe sent him the proofs of the essay as they became available, together with supplementary notes. Schuckmann had been moved to make this request by Staatsrat Süvern of the Ministry of Education in Berlin. All this is evidence of the sense of responsibility for the cultural welfare of the new-won Rhenish provinces manifested by the Prussian authorities. It is in this context of widespread patriotic endeavour that Goethe's essay on *Kunst und Alterthum* should be read.

The composition took him much longer than he had originally

RHINE, MAIN AND NECKAR

contemplated. The essay was finally completed on 27 February 1816, but it was not till the beginning of June that he was able to send the first printed copies to Stein, Schuckmann and Sulpiz Boisserée. To the latter he wrote on 8 June 1816: 'Look kindly upon these sheets as written chiefly for your sake.'

During the course of composition Goethe had decided to issue the essay as the first number of a periodical to be entitled *Ueber Kunst und Alterthum in den Rhein und Mayn Gegenden*, which was to be devoted to the historical, archeological, artistic and scientific monuments and institutions of the Rhineland. As we shall see, the character of the journal was considerably modified as the years went by.

The *Kunst und Alterthum* essay takes the form of a travel journal condensing the impressions of both journeys into one. Goethe himself wished it to be considered as 'a part of my biography' (letter to Cotta of 6 December 1815). It is probably the least well-known of his autobiographical writings, and indeed its literary merit is small. But from the standpoint of the history of taste and of Goethe's aesthetic development its interest is considerable. For it constitutes his most important public utterance on the subject of German medieval art and architecture and his closest approach to the ideals and endeavours of Romantic medievalism.

The very title-page is a striking example of this approach. It was—*mirabile dictu*—designed by the arch-classicist Heinrich Meyer, and represents the sun of Christian art breaking through the dark clouds of anti-medievalism to illuminate two figures clad in what is meant to be medieval garb, standing beneath Gothic canopies. In the foreground, also lit by the triumphant sun, are a number of objects, partly antique, but including conspicuously the medieval symbols of sword and crozier.

In keeping with this symbolic introduction, the essay is in fact mainly concerned with the medieval antiquities of the Rhinelands and the best way of preserving them. Thus, however miscellaneous the journal was to become in its later career, in the first instance the 'Alterthum' of the title connoted medieval antiquity, and not, as is often supposed, the antiquity of Greece and Rome.

From our point of view the most interesting section of the essay is that devoted to Cologne Cathedral. For here a definite and serious proposal for the completion of the medieval torso is publicly mooted. After lamenting the uncompleted state of the building, Goethe praises in the warmest terms the 'quiet but indestructible patriotism' of the brothers Boisserée in proceeding, despite the difficulties of the times,

with their great task of fulfilling, at least on paper, the original intentions of the medieval master. Now that the way has been so well prepared, has not the time come, he asks, to set about the completion of
the work, no longer on paper, but in stone? Such a proposal, however,
raises in an acute form the question of finance. For the past twenty
years there has not even been enough money available to keep the
building in repair. The first necessity, therefore, is to establish a fund
for this purpose. But the only way to preserve the Cathedral satisfactorily is to complete it, for how else are the craftsmen to obtain the
necessary practise in their craft? Whatever is done, should be done
boldly and imaginatively, which means among other things having
the courage to face up to the difficulties inherent in such a project.

The longest and in itself the most valuable section of the *Kunst
und Alterthum* essay is the chapter entitled 'Heidelberg'. This section
is devoted exclusively to the Boisserée Collection—or rather, not so
much to the collection itself as to the historical development of the
art of the Lower Rhine and the Netherlands (between which schools
no real distinction is made either by Goethe or the Boisserées), from
its supposedly Byzantine origins down to Jan van Scorel and Rembrandt. All this is based of course on material supplied by Sulpiz
Boisserée, though Goethe has used his source very freely.[1]

In a last section of the essay Goethe gives a brief review of the latest
happenings of interest in the sphere of art, and especially of medieval
art: the progress of Sulpiz's labours, Georg Moller's publications on
German medieval architecture, the return of medieval manuscripts
to Heidelberg, and above all the discovery by Sulpiz in Paris of a
medieval elevation of the north west tower of Cologne Cathedral,
felicitously complementing the plan of the south west tower discovered
by Moller in Darmstadt.

Although Sulpiz acknowledges politely enough the copy of *Kunst
und Alterthum* sent him by Goethe, it is doubtful whether he and his
friends can really have been satisfied with it, or at least with the section relating to their collection. In the first place the detached, not to
say ironic tone of parts of Goethe's survey can hardly have been to
their liking. The following account of the fundamental beliefs of the
Christian faith, for example, must surely have caused the pious Sulpiz
a certain raising of the eyebrows:

The new religion acknowledges a supreme God, not as regally conceived

---

[1] For an account of Goethe's use of his sources in the *Kunst und Alterthum* essay see
WA I. 34 (ii), 36 ff. and E. v. d. Hagen, *Goethe als Herausgeber von 'Kunst und Alterthum'
und seine Mitarbeiter* (Berlin, 1912), pp. 25 ff.

as Zeus, but more humanly; for he is the Father of a mysterious Son, whose function it is to represent the moral qualities of the Godhead on earth. These two are joined by an innocent fluttering Dove, thus forming a miraculous trefoil, around which a chorus of blessed spirits are gathered in innumerable gradations. It is possible to venerate the mother of the aforementioned Son as the purest of women; for the combination of virginity and motherhood is already to be found in pagan antiquity. She is accompanied by an old man, but the mésalliance is approved on high, in order that the new-born God shall for the sake of appearances and for his own well-being be provided with an earthly father.[1]

Positive though the tone of the essay is towards medieval art on the whole, it naturally lacks the immediacy and fervour of Goethe's response in presence of the pictures themselves, as this is recorded in his letters and in the testimony of others. Of the 'great Eyck', for instance, which according to Bertram and Wilhelm Grimm had evoked such passionate enthusiasm, he still writes respectfully, but somewhat equivocally. On the one hand, 'we do not hesitate for one moment to place our Eyck in the first class of those whom Nature has gifted with artistic capacities'; but on the other hand, 'though Van Eyck's compositions have the greatest truth and charm, they do not satisfy the strictest canons of art'.[2]

The truth is that on his return to Weimar Goethe began to experience the same reaction against his own involvement with the ideals and ambitions of the Romantic medievalists as he had undergone in the previous year, and there are signs of this in the essay itself. He is moved, for instance, to a vigorous protest against a somewhat hysterical article by Wallraf on the *Kölner Dombild* of Stefan Lochner, which had appeared in the *Taschenbuch für Freunde altdeutscher Zeit und Kunst* (1816). After acknowledging the picture to be the 'axis of the Lower Rhenish school of art' he continues: 'It is to be desired, however, that its actual merits should be established from a historical and critical point of view, for at present it is the object of so much adulation that I fear it will soon be as much obscured in the mind's eye by such effusions as it was formerly hidden from the physical eye by the soot of lamps and candles.'[3] And in similar tone he ends the Heidelberg section with a plea for an objective historical approach to the subject of German medieval art: 'In this way we shall be happy to honour the German art of the fifteenth and sixteenth centuries, and the froth of uncritical admiration, which has already proved nauseating to the true lover of art, will gradually subside.'[4]

The same reaction is visible in Goethe's letters of the time. He

[1] WA I. 34 (i), 161. [2] Ibid. pp. 181–2. [3] Ibid. p. 178. [4] Ibid. p. 190.

complains to Cotta on 6 December 1815 that the essay is keeping him
from other work. To Georg Moller he writes on 10 November 1815
to thank him for the first two instalments of his *Denkmäler der deutschen
Baukunst*. This letter is a specially clear example of Goethe's attitude
towards the Gothic Revival. First, he praises Moller warmly for his
efforts in making known 'the aesthetic value of those ancient and
worthy buildings by means of a historical approach' and no less for
his merits in warning the German public against the attempt to resur-
rect the spirit of past ages in contemporary architecture. He compli-
ments him on the discovery of the medieval plan, 'a great find, which,
like everything which benefits the cause of Cologne Cathedral,
cannot be praised too highly'. The Cathedral should serve, he says,
as a pattern of excellence, by which other works in the same style
may be judged, and so 'in future we shall no longer rave over inferior
work out of a confused feeling of patriotic prejudice'.

Still more explicit is a letter to Zelter of 11 March 1816:

> If I had recognized the import of these pages (i.e. *Kunst und Alterthum*)
> earlier, I should have refused to have anything to do with the whole business . . .
> On the other hand I must gratefully acknowledge that without this pressing
> invitation I should never have understood the way in which art was kept
> alive right through the ages of barbarism, nor should I have realized what is
> now being done both nationally and regionally to preserve the past. There is
> a lot of stuff here which is palatable only if approached intellectually, for even
> absurdity pleases, if we can understand what it is trying to say.

It is clear that by the time Goethe had finished writing his survey
he had become more than a little tired of the subject of medieval art.
The Rhine and Main essay had occupied the whole of the first number
of *Kunst und Alterthum*. The second number, which appeared in April
1817, reflects very distinctly the ambivalence of Goethe's feelings on
the subject. For the first item of the new number constitutes the most
formidable of all his attacks on the neo-medievalists—the essay,
namely, with the ominous title 'Neu-deutsche religios-patriotische
Kunst'; but this is immediately followed by the most curious and charming of his flirtations with Romantic medievalism.

When staying in Wiesbaden in the summer of 1814 he visited the
chapel of St. Roch near Bingen, where he witnessed the celebrations
attending its restoration after the Napoleonic wars. It is a description
of this occasion which Goethe published in the second number of
Kunst und Alterthum under the title 'Sanct Rochus-Fest zu Bingen'.
But he did more than describe it; he made a vow to present a picture
of the saint to the chapel, and the vow was duly fulfilled in time for the

saint's name-day on 16 August 1816. Goethe himself made the first sketch for the picture, which was then drawn in outline by Meyer and finally painted in oils by Louise Seidler. The painting—an engraving of which prefaced the second number of the journal—represents the saint as he is about to set forth on his pilgrimage, distributing the last of his worldly goods to two young children. The tone of the whole is gentle and charming, the style of the drawing graceful and slightly sentimental in the pseudo-classical manner of the Weimar prize competitions. Nothing less medieval could be imagined. It is significant, for instance, that all reference to the more gruesome or superstitious aspects of the legend are scrupulously avoided. Was Goethe deliberately trying to show by example how a Christian theme, if it must be the subject of art at all, can best be treated so as not to offend classical susceptibilities? Whether this was the real motive for his action, or whether it was merely a gracious commemoration of the happy days he had spent in the Rheingau in the summer of 1814, this gratuitous excursion into the world of Catholic legend is one of the strangest episodes of Goethe's later years.

That the first motive was the operative one is strongly suggested by the juxtaposition with the polemic against the Nazarenes. 'Neudeutsche religios-patriotische Kunst' was signed 'W.K.F.' (i.e. Weimarische Kunstfreunde) and was actually written by Meyer, but we know from Goethe's diaries and correspondence[1] that this polite but frontal attack on the Romantic school of art was evolved in the closest collaboration between the two old friends, as is obvious in any case from the style of Meyer's essay. Goethe's letters make it clear that he identified himself completely with the views expressed therein, and this is acknowledged by the editors of the Weimarer Ausgabe by the inclusion of the essay among Goethe's *Schriften zur Kunst*. For that matter it is acknowledged by Goethe himself in that the essay was signed not 'H. Meyer', but 'W.K.F.'

The essay begins straightway on an ominous note: 'As is well known to all those who are interested in art, many worthy artists and intelligent art lovers at the present time are obsessed by a passion for the venerable, naive, but somewhat crude taste which characterized the masters of the fourteenth and fifteenth centuries.'[2] Nevertheless the essay is not, as the title might lead one to suppose, a violent polemic against Romantic art, but a conscientious, if unsympathetic attempt to trace the genesis and development of the taste for medieval, religious and patriotic elements in contemporary painting.

[2] Cp. WA III. 5, 246–8; IV. 27, 138, 170–1, 276–7.   [3] WA I. 49 (i), 23.

The author does not deny that the old masters (by which he means primarily the Italian Pre-Raphaelites) had their merits, but he is quite clear that they are anything but satisfactory models for present-day painters. All the more as these modern enthusiasts (he is thinking of Wackenroder and Tieck, and of their disciples, the Nazarene painters) tend to confuse art with religion, and to find the presence of the latter an excuse for neglecting the rules of the former. Having followed the development of this tendency up to 1806 or so, in the course of which tribute is paid to the 'authoritative' influence of Friedrich Schlegel's *Europa* essays, he shows how henceforth this 'love for the antiquated' took on a specifically patriotic form, especially in the field of architecture: 'Never were the old so-called Gothic buildings more zealously studied and extolled, never was what is truly admirable in them so generously overpraised; one might well call this period the epoch of their apotheosis.'[1]

However, modern attempts to imitate these Gothic buildings have not progressed very far for lack of the necessary craftsmanship. 'And thus there are artistic as well as technical reasons, ethical as well as mechanical, why it is utterly impossible to return completely to the spirit of past ages and to reproduce their peculiar quality.' And here the author returns to the favourite thesis of the 'W.K.F.' If there must be imitation, then let it be imitation of the ancients: 'From all this it is clear that as far as art is concerned the only sure and reasonable way is to concern onself exclusively with the study of ancient Greek art and with what has approximated to it in modern times, whereas it is always dangerous and perverse to look for other models.'[2]

There is much in all this which was calculated to grate harshly enough on the ears of the Heidelberg circle. It is indeed as if the Boisserées and all they stood for had never been and Goethe had returned to the uncompromising neo-classicism of 1805. In the concluding paragraphs of the essay the author strives to make some amends by paying tribute to the endeavours of the Boisserées and others in the interest of medieval art and architecture. And the essay ends with the somewhat two-edged admission that the patriotic movement in art is only a part or a consequence of the general patriotic movement of the time, and as such the more readily to be palliated. Just as the exaggerated chauvinism of the War of Liberation may be expected, now the goal has been reached, to develop into a dignified self-respect, so in the realm of art the 'constricting imitation of the old masters'

[1] Ibid. p. 43.   [2] Ibid., pp. 51–52.

will, it is to be hoped, give way to a reasoned and scholarly appraisal of their qualities. The same applies *mutatis mutandis* to the sentimental religiosity which is the prime target of the 'W.K.F.' throughout the essay.

One would have thought enough had now been said against the Romantic position in art. But no. In reading through the essay Goethe evidently felt that Meyer's formulations were too mild. Something more was needed. And so in a brief conclusion to this number of *Kunst und Alterthum* Goethe returns to the fray with a gratuitously offensive attack on the 'sickly *Klosterbruder* and his like', who are capable, it seems, of any nonsense, however revolting and absurd. In token of this he appends a description of a Dante illustration by Julius Schoppe, which he had not even seen, but of which he had received a distorted account from friends in Berlin. As an example of the sort of thing Goethe imagined he was fighting against in Romantic art the description is worth reproducing: 'Life size figure with green skin. From the decapitated neck spurts forth a fountain of blood; the hand of the outstretched right arm holds the head by the hair; the head, lit by an internal glow, serves as a lantern, the light of which suffuses the figure.'[1] The injustice of this attack, both on the memory of Wackenroder and on the equally innocent Schoppe, moved Achim von Arnim to write Goethe a vigorous protest.[2] To this letter Goethe made no reply.

And what of Sulpiz Boisserée? If this was Arnim's reaction, it is not difficult to imagine what Goethe's young friend must have thought of Meyer's effusion. And yet Goethe seems to have half persuaded himself that Sulpiz was on his side against the sentimental religiosity which he presumed to be a leading characteristic of Nazarene art. Thus he writes to Sulpiz on 7 August 1816, as if there were no difference between them on the point: 'The religious sentimentalists and poet-asters had to be attacked: for their double and triple botchings muti-late, indeed destroy, everything good. In the second number [of *Kunst und Alterthum*], on which I have been working for the last fort-night, we shall go one better.' This is the first indication of the coming storm.

On 27 September he reverts still more vigorously to the point: 'The second number of *Rhein und Mayn* will open with an essay on the history of the new sentimentally religious Non-Art from the eighties onwards. It will bring us many a dirty look, but that doesn't matter! Unless some contemporary makes a record of it, no one will

[1] Ibid. p. 60.   [2] Cp. Benz, op. cit. pp. 233–4.

understand this plague in fifty years. In the tone of our attack we will show the utmost consideration, but the thing itself cannot be sufficiently castigated.'

On 16 December he mentions the ominous title for the first time and adds: 'I hope that the essay will be found to be just and fair. Those connoisseurs who save and collect the old masters are highly praised; the artists who try to reproduce the old style will find themselves confronted with a mirror, to which we have tried to give a right good gloss.' Finally, on 27 May 1817, Goethe sends him the much-delayed issue: 'Here then is the second number of *Rhein und Mayn*. May it accord with your views and aims.' A pious hope, which he can surely not have seriously entertained!

Sulpiz's reply on 23rd June leaves no doubt of his feelings on the matter, though he tries to soften the edge of his disapproval by drawing a sharp distinction—which we know to be totally unjustified—between Goethe's views and those of 'W.K.F.' Sulpiz concentrates his protest on Goethe-Meyer's insistence on imitation of the ancients as the sole road to salvation in matters of art. On the contrary, he says, 'nothing genuine can ever spring from the imitation of works of art, whatever the models may be. The only way to salvation is and remains the free imitation of Nature. Every nation and every age must be content with that which the gods and fate—to speak in heathen terms—have apportioned it. But how different are all our conditions of life, is our whole milieu, from that of the Greeks!'[1]

However, Sulpiz is not without hope that the situation may nevertheless be turned to the advantage of the Heidelberger: 'We now have a double and triple reason for hoping that you will continue your account of our collection. That would provide the most simple and natural method of removing misunderstandings.'[2] But this detailed description of the collection, which had been publicly announced in both the first and second numbers of *Kunst und Alterthum* and referred to over and again in Goethe's correspondence with Sulpiz, was never to be realized—to the lasting disappointment and annoyance of the Boisserées.

The most serious reply to Meyer's essay was provided by the Munich Germanist, B. J. Docen, in the *Jahrbücher der Litteratur*.[3] Docen's reply is calm and objective in tone. It points out that the taste for Christian and medieval German themes and style amongst the younger painters received its first impulse from literary, not artistic sources; in the first place, indeed, from none other than Goethe himself, long

---

[1] SB ii. 174.   [2] loc. cit.   [3] *Jahrbücher der Litteratur* (Vienna, 1819), viii. 277–99.

before the more recent initiatives of Wackenroder, Tieck and the Schlegels. (Incidentally Docen is one of the first to appreciate at its true value the effect of the *Herzensergiessungen* on the artistic developments of the first decades of the nineteenth century in Germany.) It was Goethe, too, who in his early writings (*Von Deutscher Baukunst, Nach Falconet und Über Falconet*, and his 'Kunstgedichte') laid such vivid stress on that very originality of the artist which is so painfully incompatible with the imitation of ancient models recommended by the 'W.K.F.'

Friedrich Schlegel's article on the exhibition of German art in Rome in the spring of 1819 in the preceding volume of the same periodical could also be looked upon as an indirect reply to the Meyer essay, in so far as it stoutly champions the merits of the Nazarene painters.

An amusing postscript to this whole episode is provided by Meyer's visit to the Heidelberg Collection in the autumn of 1817, during which he underwent a similar conversion to what Goethe had experienced three years before. Sulpiz reports thereon in a letter to Goethe of 19 October 1817:

> As to Hofrat Meyer, it was a great joy for us to hear him making his confession before the works of the misjudged painters, although to be sure it would have been better still if there had been no cause for him to make one . . . From all that he said it was clear that he had not credited what you had told him; indeed of Memling's head of Christ he expressly admitted that if you had seen the picture first and had said to him exactly what he himself now thinks about it, he would not have believed you. His verdict was that without exaggeration this work combines the merits of Leonardo and Titian.[1]

One might have thought that Goethe's spleen against the 'Frömmler' would have been sufficiently allayed by Meyer's essay and his own postscript thereto. But on the contrary, their publication seems to have been the signal for an almost hysterical outburst of virulence on Goethe's part. His indignation was evidently fanned by the approbation of friends like J. F. Rochlitz, Zelter and Schadow,[2] and he is full of the necessity for returning still more vehemently to the charge. Thus in a letter to Rochlitz of 1 June 1817, thanking him for particulars about the 'geistige Onanie' of the Romantic painters and begging for more, he says: 'We mean to let fly remorselessly against their false, morbid and basically hypocritical maxims, and, as you quite rightly advise, go on repeating the effective arguments against them *ad infinitum.*' And a few weeks later to Meyer (4 July 1817) with equal bellicosity: 'Our bomb could not have gone off more

[1] SB ii. 195–6. [2] Cp. Benz, op. cit. pp. 234 ff.

15

accurately and opportunely. The Nazarenes, I am informed, are running about like ants whose nest has been disturbed. They are trying to build it up again, but we won't give them time to do so. I've got some good ideas which should not fail of their effect.'

But in fact nothing came of these threats. Whatever he thought and said in private, Goethe made no further attempt to influence the aesthetic tendencies of the time as far as the Romantic painters were concerned. Only in the *Annalen* for 1820 is there a last rumbling of the old resentment.

It should be emphasized that Goethe's indignation was directed, not against medieval art—and still less medieval architecture—as such, but only against the, as it seemed to him, uncritical enthusiasm shown for it by the Romantic medievalists, and above all it was directed against the sentimental religiosity and the Catholicizing tendencies which Goethe imputed to the Nazarene painters. That this was so is illustrated by this same second number of *Kunst und Alterthum*, which along with Meyer's broadside also contains an article by Sulpiz Boisserée on the restoration work at Strasbourg Minster and Cologne Cathedral, with a postscript by Goethe on the first four parts of Moller's *Denkmäler*.

The third number of *Kunst und Alterthum* (1817) contains a short supplement to the Rochus-Fest essay, 'Im Rheingau Herbsttage', which reverts to Goethe's Rhineland journey of 1814. Otherwise there is nothing in the number to justify the old title *Ueber Kunst und Alterthum in den Rhein- und Mayn-Gegenden*. In the next number, the first of the second volume, Goethe has drawn the logical conclusion, and henceforth the periodical is entitled simply *Kunst und Alterthum* and deals with any topics of an artistic nature in which he happens to be interested, without special reference either to medieval art or to the antiquities of the Rhineland. The greater part of his *Schriften zur Kunst* appeared from now on in its pages, and most of these were concerned with Classical or Renaissance art.

5. *VON DEUTSCHER BAUKUNST 1823*

Goethe's later preoccupation with medieval art and architecture was concentrated in three distinct phases: first, the meeting with Sulpiz Boisserée in 1811; secondly, the Rhine journeys of 1814 and 1815; and thirdly, the period succeeding the publication of Boisserée's *Domwerk*[1] in 1823–4. In all three cases the preoccupation was intimately connected with his friendship with Sulpiz Boisserée.

After almost incredible delays Sulpiz's master work began to appear at last in September 1823, some fifteen years after its original conception. Sulpiz sent Goethe six engravings in proof in November 1822. Goethe thanked him on 22 December in terms of the warmest appreciation for this product of so many years of devoted toil and perseverance; and well he might, for the *Ansichten, Risse und einzelne Theile des Doms von Köln* remains to this day one of the most superb examples of its kind.

Its value is enhanced for Goethe by the memories it evokes of the past, both of the far distant past in Strasbourg and of the more recent past with Sulpiz Boisserée in Frankfurt and Heidelberg. He crowns his commendation with the statement, so especially sweet in Sulpiz's ears, that Cologne Cathedral is 'certainly the most sublime example of its kind, which in itself provides a sufficient measuring rod for all other similar buildings'.

In the process of showing off the splendid plates to all and sundry— 'princes and princesses, artists and laymen'—Goethe's old interest in these matters began to stir creatively. This interest, he says, will gradually take literary shape, 'and when I am able to settle down to it properly, I shall read your essay and then something worthwhile will surely emerge'. This is the first intimation of what was to become *Von Deutscher Baukunst 1823*.

Shortly after this Goethe fell seriously ill, and we hear no more of the *Baukunst* essay until 22 March 1823. On that day, while he is still convalescing, his diary notes: 'Reflected on German Architecture, with reference to an essay for Boisserées.' The diary entries for the next few days make it clear that he prepared himself for writing the

[1] The *Domwerk* was the convenient abbreviation used by Boisserée and his friends for the book of engravings of Cologne Cathedral entitled *Ansichten, Risse und einzelne Theile des Doms von Köln*.

essay by reading J. G. Büsching's *Versuch einer Einleitung in die Geschichte der Altdeutschen Baukunst* (1821). He began composing the essay on 24 March, and it was finished in fair copy on the 27th. On the next day he notes that he has had a copy made of 'Von deutscher Baukunst von 1773', and that he has been studying Moller's *Denkmäler der deutschen Baukunst*.

On 10 April he wrote to Sulpiz: 'Soon after my recovery I returned to the subject of our Old-German architecture, and these reflections gave birth to a little essay, for which I wish your approval. In my view the public, whose interest in these matters has begun to cool, needs a fresh reminder. In the last number [of *Kunst und Alterthum*] there was a general advertisement of the contents of your work; this time the intention is to supply a short introductory preface.' The essay duly appeared in June 1823 in *Kunst und Alterthum* IV, 2.

These various references serve to emphasize the close connection between *Von Deutscher Baukunst 1823* and Sulpiz's *Domwerk*. This is indeed obvious enough from the essay itself, which is essentially, as Goethe says, a preface to Sulpiz's work. But it is also a review, a retrospective account, of the changes that had come over Goethe's own attitude, and over the attitude of successive generations, towards medieval architecture since his first venture into this field some fifty years before. It is this which gives the essay its main interest for us. For between them the two essays *Von Deutscher Baukunst* cover almost the whole period of that revolution of taste which forms the subject of this study.

The comparison with the Erwin essay is forced upon us by the very title, which proclaims unequivocally Goethe's renewed adherence to the nomenclature he had introduced fifty years before. He makes no attempt to defend the usage in the essay itself. But that he laid some stress on the point is clear from a letter he wrote to Büsching on 31 January 1822, in which he deplores the tendency in some quarters to reintroduce the term 'Gothic' instead of 'German'.

The most obvious parallel between the two essays is the introduction into the discussion of a French critic of Gothic architecture: Laugier in 1772, François Blondel the elder in 1823. But his attitude to the two is itself a measure of the distance he had travelled in these fifty years. In 1772 Laugier is violently attacked for his neo-classic insistence on rules and proportions. In 1823 Goethe quotes Blondel with approval just because of his assertion that any beauty Gothic buildings do possess is due to the 'symmetry and proportion of the whole to the parts and of the parts to each other'. Moreover if one investigates

the matter closely, says Blondel, one will find that these proportions 'are the same on the whole as those of buildings which
are constructed according to the rules of good [i.e. classical] architecture'.[1]

Goethe then recalls his early enthusiasm for Strasbourg Minster,
which was due, he now declares, to his unconscious apprehension of
Blondel's insight that the beauty of Gothic architecture lies in its
approximation to the rules of classical architecture. There is, as we
have pointed out elsewhere,[2] a good deal of truth in this interpretation
of his early attitude, but it is one which Goethe himself would have
repudiated indignantly in 1772. For it is clear from the whole tone of
the Erwin essay that he considers 'German' architecture to be based
on principles of its own, fundamentally different from those of classical
architecture, but equally valid; and—as a corollary—that it is a fatal
mistake to try and apply the criteria of the one to the other. This
insight—the first and most axiomatic step towards the appreciation
of Gothic architecture—is here by implication reversed.

In another respect, however, the 1823 essay shows the enlightening
effect of the years of friendship with Sulpiz Boisserée. In 1772 Strasbourg
Minster is presented as the titanic creation of the individual genius
Erwin; now the Gothic style is seen to be a collective style, the joint
product of countless artists and craftsmen and closely bound up with
Christian ceremonial.

After quoting the Blondel passage Goethe turns to the main burden
of his essay, his commendation of the efforts of the Boisserées and other
enthusiasts in the cause of medieval architecture. He begins by pointing
the contrast between the indifference of the preceding centuries and
the enthusiasm of the present day among young and old alike—an
enthusiasm moreover which found expression not only in studying
the Gothic monuments of the past, but even in applying the style to
modern buildings. Goethe then proceeds to give a brief summary of
his own attitude to medieval architecture from Strasbourg on: 'After
my departure from Strasbourg I saw no more important or imposing
works of this kind; the impression died away and I could scarcely
remember the state of mind in which the sight of such a building had
aroused such lively enthusiasm. My stay in Italy could not do anything
to reawaken these feelings, especially as the modern alterations to
Milan Cathedral concealed the old character of the building. And so

[1] WA I. 49 (ii), 160.
[2] Cp. my paper 'Goethe and the Gothic Revival', *Publications of the English Goethe
Society*, New Series, vol. xxv. (1956).

for many years I lived apart, if not estranged, from this branch of art.'[1]

Then in 1810 came the relationship with the brothers Boisserée and the drawings of Cologne Cathedral; they introduced him to a building 'which careful study reveals to be pre-eminent over all others in its kind'. As a result of his renewed interest in these matters he finally 'found himself quite at home again' in the world of Gothic architecture. Nevertheless, 'in view of its nature, and especially of my age and situation, it was the historical aspect of this whole matter which assumed the greatest importance for me'. And this serves to introduce the work of his friends, which was contributing so much precisely to the historical understanding of the subject.

First he devotes a paragraph to a warm appreciation of the work of Georg Moller, whose discovery of the original plan of Cologne Cathedral had given a new impetus to such medieval studies and whose *Denkmäler der deutschen Baukunst* provide so admirable a conspectus of the rise and fall of the Gothic style. He then passes on to the Boisserées, whose work is deserving of 'the same attention and sympathy' as that of Moller—a sentence which Sulpiz must surely have read with mixed feelings. Great though the profit was which Goethe derived from such studies, his appreciation of Gothic architecture was still more effectively furthered by the visit which he paid to Cologne Cathedral in the company of Freiherr vom Stein. His description of this event accords closely with the account of his visit to the cathedral in 1774 in the fourteenth book of *Dichtung und Wahrheit*. In both cases he lays stress on the sense of spiritual discomfort ('Apprehension' is the word he uses in the essay) aroused in him by the sight of the stupendous torso, symbol, as it seemed to him, of man's limitations and inadequacy. 'Even the interior of the cathedral, to be frank, makes an inharmonious, though imposing, impression; only when we enter the choir, which charms us with its unexpected harmony and perfection, do we experience a thrill of joy and wonder and find our yearning more than fulfilled.'[2]

But any feelings of discomfort aroused by the incomplete state of the building can at least be alleviated by a study of the plans and drawings of the brothers Boisserée, which will enable the spectator, or even the reader at a distance, to follow the intentions of the medieval architects and to complete in imagination what the medieval builders left undone. Thus he can convince himself that Cologne Cathedral represents the 'highest peak to which this style of architecture has

[1] WA I. 49 (ii), 162.   [2] Ibid. p. 165.

ever attained . . . I at least congratulate myself on having reached this degree of clarity after fifty years' effort through the labours of patriotically minded, ingenious and indefatigable young men.'[1]

Goethe's renewed interest in the 'German architecture of the twelfth [sic] century' often brought to mind, he says, his early affection for Strasbourg Minster and the essay in which he gave expression to it. Nor does he need to feel ashamed of this early production, 'for I had after all sensed the inner proportions of the whole, I had traced the development of the individual decorative details out of this whole, and after long and repeated contemplation had found that the one apparently completed tower nevertheless lacked its proper termination . . . And even though the style of the essay was somewhat obscure, this may well be forgiven it, since it was trying to express something which is in fact inexpressible.'[2]

All this is leading up to the announcement in the last paragraph of his intention to issue at last a reprint of the Erwin essay. His decision to take this step was primarily due to the initiative of the Breslau Germanist, J. G. Büsching, whose Versuch einer Einleitung in die Geschichte der Altdeutschen Baukunst takes the Erwin essay as its starting point and who wrote to Goethe exhorting him to reprint it in an édition de luxe—an interesting testimony to the esteem in which the Romantic generation held Goethe's early essay as the Magna Carta of the medieval and patriotic revival.[3]

And so in the next number of Kunst und Alterthum (IV. 3, 1824) it duly appeared, somewhat incongruously sandwiched between Goethe's Paria poems and his article on a Titian engraving—and in anything but a de luxe format. From there in 1830 the essay found its way for the first time into an authorized collection of Goethe's works—in volume 39 of the Ausgabe letzter Hand.

Thus Von Deutscher Baukunst 1823 is not only an introduction to Boisserée's Ansichten, but also to the reprint of the Erwin essay. In this way, as he says, he will make crystal clear the difference between the first sprouting and the final fruit. He uses the same botanical metaphor to Sulpiz Boisserée in a letter of 12 December 1823, when announcing the forthcoming reprint of 'those early enthusiastically written pages of 1772, in which one may observe not without astonishment the first cotyledons of the tree which has continued to grow and spread so profusely for so many years'. Here then Goethe

[1] Ibid. pp. 165–6.   [2] Ibid. p. 166.
[3] Cp. E. Beutler, Von Deutscher Baukunst, pp. 72–73.

explicitly recognizes his own early essay as the first germ of the Gothic Revival in Germany.

Goethe was accustomed at this time to use botanical metaphors when discussing the subject of Gothic architecture, as of most other things. Thus when introducing Eckermann to the theme (21 October 1823) he speaks to him in terms reminiscent of his own *Metamorphose der Pflanzen:* 'In the works of Old-German architecture we see the flowering of an exceptional state of affairs. Anyone who encounters such a flowering unprepared can only be astonished at it; but he who contemplates the secret inner life of the plant, the play of forces and the gradual development of the flower, will see the matter with quite different eyes; he will understand what he sees.'

Owing to Sulpiz's absence in Paris in connection with the printing and publication of the *Domwerk* he did not see the essay until the late autumn. He thanked Goethe for the 'benevolent recognition of my own and others' work', but exhorted him to find time to make a summary of his own essay on Gothic architecture which he had written for the *Ansichten*. He had sent the manuscript to Goethe in May 1821 with a request for stylistic suggestions. Goethe was enthusiastic: 'The essay has turned out splendidly; I read it, as one reads novels, without interruption from beginning to end' (10 July 1821). On 23 July he writes that Meyer and Riemer were also enthusiastic, and that he would try and publish a summary of the work.

Goethe in fact was never to make the promised summary, any more than he was to write the promised account of the Boisserée Collection. This was a perpetual source of irritation to Sulpiz, though he did not allow it to impair the fundamental cordiality of their relationship. On 22 August 1824, for instance, he writes to thank Goethe for the repeated laudatory notices of the Cologne engravings which had appeared in *Kunst und Alterthum*, 'but I cannot disguise the fact that it would have given me even more pleasure if you had pronounced your judgment on my accompanying essay, for the public and I myself are very anxious to know in some detail what you think of my work, not to mention that such a verdict from you would be useful and beneficial to my personal circumstances'.[1]

However, Goethe was not to be bullied, even by Sulpiz Boisserée, though he did from time to time publish short critical notices in *Kunst und Alterthum* of the new instalments of the *Domwerk* and of Strixner's lithographs of the Boisserée Collection. Most of these were actually written by Meyer; the only one of interest from our point of

[1] SB ii. 374.

view is an article by Goethe on the Cologne Carnival which is appended
to a review of the first two instalments of the *Domwerk* in *Kunst
und Alterthum* (V, 1, 1824). After referring to the Cathedral as 'perhaps
the most admirable and magnificent product of the artistic intelligence
which has ever been erected on earth', he goes on to make the following highly significant and characteristic comparison between it and
the Carnival: 'Both of them, true to themselves, are organically
self-sufficient, stupendous and tiny; like elephant and ant, both
living beings and in this sense comparable to each other, the one
raising its mass into the air, the other teeming with motion at its
feet.'[1]

With these words, then, Goethe returns to the concept of Gothic
as a living organism which had underlain the Erwin essay, a conception
which is already implied in the conversation with Eckermann quoted
above. The passage is also reminiscent of Goethe's essay on the
Roman Carnival, with its basic idea of the popular festival as a
product of nature, subject to the same laws of freedom and necessity
which apply equally to the products of nature and art and human
society.[2]

Goethe also published in *Kunst und Alterthum* a number of articles
and reviews, either by himself or Meyer, on other examples of medieval
architecture, e.g. on the Marienburg, apropos of Büsching's work on
the subject published in 1823 (KA IV, 3); on Moller's engravings of
Freiburg Cathedral (KA VI, 2); and on F. H. Müller's book on the
Katharinenkirche at Oppenheim (KA V, 2 and VI, 2). The second
notice of Müller's work was written by Goethe in the spring of 1828
and represents his last public utterance on the subject of medieval
architecture. The closing sentences of this very brief review have
indeed a valedictory ring: 'Two further instalments should complete
this work before the end of the year. Now that Boisserée's work on
Cologne Cathedral and Moller's on Freiburg are nearing their end,
we shall at last have the clearest picture of how in a dark and turbulent
age the most colossal architectural conceptions were evolved for
the highest purposes and with the most edifying effects, and how
Proportion and Harmony attempted to establish and extend their
realm in that most unpropitious of epochs.'[3]

In this last sentence of Goethe's last public utterance on the subject
we have a recapitulation of the main motifs of his attitude towards
medieval architecture, motifs which recur again and again in his

[1] WA I. 49 (ii), 187. [2] Cp. *Goethes Werke* (*Hamburger Ausgabe*), xi. 563–4.
[3] WA I. 49 (ii), 190.

writings from the Erwin essay on: namely, his recognition of the imaginative boldness of the Gothic builders and of their merit in preserving in some fashion at least the classical virtues of harmony and proportion throughout the black night of the Middle Ages—a coda, then, brief but fitting, to this particular preoccupation, which had spanned so great an arc of Goethe's life.

His last public utterance on medieval architecture? In the Second Part of *Faust* occur the following lines, spoken by the astrologer, who is describing the magical transformation scene before the invocation of Helena:

> Durch Wunderkraft erscheint allhier zur Schau,
> Massiv genug, ein alter Tempelbau.
> Dem Atlas gleich, der einst den Himmel trug,
> Stehn reihenweis der Säulen hier genug;
> Sie mögen wohl der Felsenlast genügen,
> Da zweie schon ein gross Gebäude trügen.

To which the architect replies:

> Das wär' antik! Ich wüsst' es nicht zu preisen,
> Es sollte plump und überlästig heissen.
> Roh nennt man edel, unbehülflich gross.
> Schmalpfeiler lieb' ich, strebend, grenzenlos;
> Spitzbögiger Zenith erhebt den Geist;
> Solch ein Gebäu erbaut uns allermeist.[1]

Now this scene was also written in 1828. If this is really Goethe's last word on the subject, it is of course a piece of gentle persiflage directed against the Gothic enthusiasts.

It remains to record two private utterances of Goethe on Gothic architecture, which date from the last years of his life, one favourable, one unfavourable. Eckermann reports a conversation on 11 March 1828, in which Goethe argued that the hallmark of genius lay in its lasting power as a source of inspiration to others. He instances Mozart in the sphere of music, Phidias, Raphael, Dürer, and Holbein in the visual arts, to prove his point. Similarly 'the man who first invented the forms and proportions of Old-German architecture, so that in the course of time a Strasbourg Minster and a Cologne Cathedral became possible, was also a genius, for his conceptions have continued to exercise a creative influence down to the present day'.

The last recorded utterance by Goethe on the subject of Gothic architecture occurs in a conversation with Kanzler von Müller (6 June

---

[1] Act I. lines 6403–14. Translation on p. 309 below.

1830). Müller had expressed surprise that August von Goethe's letters from Milan contained no mention of the cathedral, to which Goethe replies: 'He knows quite well that it is of no interest to me . . . For me nothing of that sort stands the test any longer except the choir of Cologne; not even the minster itself.'[1] Goethe's last word on Gothic, then, is a negative one, though at the same time it bears witness to Sulpiz Boisserée's advocacy of the supreme merits of Cologne over all other Gothic buildings.

After Sulpiz's farewell to Goethe at Würzburg in October 1815 the two friends did not meet again for over ten years. It is difficult to realize that despite the intimacy and cordiality of a correspondence extending over almost twenty-two years, Sulpiz actually met Goethe on only four occasions: May 1811 in Weimar; September–October 1814 in Heidelberg; August–October 1815 in Wiesbaden, Frankfurt, Heidelberg; and finally in Weimar again from 17 May to 2 June 1826. From Sulpiz's diary of this last visit it seems that things did not always run as smoothly as they had done in the Heidelberg days. For despite a cordial reception, Goethe seems to have been for much of the time in a decidedly cantankerous mood: '20 May. Renewed abuse. Paris, German and French party spirit, princely caprice, decline of taste, stupidities of every kind, &c., &c. . . . With all this sarcasm I felt almost as if I were on the Blocksberg.'[2] Or again (23 May) Goethe suggests that Sulpiz should write a continuation of his article on the Boisserée Collection for *Kunst und Alterthum*. To which Sulpiz adds the comment (omitted in Mathilde Boisserée's edition of the diary): 'Anger and suspicion aroused by this suggestion.'[3] Clearly Goethe's failure to write his own article on the subject had wounded deeply.

Nevertheless Goethe for his part was evidently delighted to see Sulpiz again, and very reluctant to lose him. The account of his desperate efforts to persuade his friend to stay on a little longer is touching indeed: 'I had the greatest difficulty in tearing myself away from the old man; although I had delayed my departure three times, he repeatedly begged me to stay. "We shall never be as young again; you have no idea how much good your visit has done me; the longer you stay the better it turns out." . . . His farewell was as cordial as his reception, the splendid old man's eyes filled with tears and I tore myself quickly from his arms.'[4] They were never to meet again.

The diary, though humanly of great interest, contains nothing to our special purpose. Nor, essentially, does the correspondence from this

---

[1] *Goethes Gespräche*, ed. cit. xxiii. 709.
[2] Ibid. p. 433.   [3] Ibid. p. 435.   [4] Ibid. p. 438.

time on to Goethe's death, though it bears witness to his continuing interest in Sulpiz's work and includes some charming tributes to the depth of their friendship. There is much talk of the *Domwerk* up to the very end. In sending Goethe a late instalment thereof Sulpiz says: 'Only three plates are now lacking to complete the whole; I could not wait for these, I was too anxious to share with you my joy over the impending completion of this laborious undertaking, at whose inception twenty years ago you so kindly lent your support, thereby laying the basis of the relationship which has united us in loyal and affectionate friendship ever since.'[1] And on receiving the final instalment Goethe replies on 27 September 1831: 'I feel most deeply what the completion of this achievement signifies. My own productions after all call for no special technical resources outside myself, whereas yours demand craftsmanship of the very highest order.'

Sulpiz's last letter to his old friend of 7 March 1832 appropriately announces the despatch of the remaining text of the *Domschrift:* 'I should be very grateful if, when you feel in the mood for it, you would take another look at the engravings and have the commentary read aloud to you at the same time. You could then tell me how far I have succeeded in solving my task.'[2] But to this letter there was no reply; a fortnight later Goethe was dead.

What then did Goethe's contribution to the Gothic Revival amount to? It falls, as we have seen, essentially into two phases, separated by a wide span of time: the Strasbourg experience and its formulation in *Von Deutscher Baukunst*, and his support of Sulpiz Boisserée.

What, in the first place, did the preoccupation with medieval architecture mean to Goethe himself? Above all, the experience of Strasbourg Minster confirmed some of the basic concepts which were to accompany him through life and prove most fruitful in his creative development as poet and thinker: especially the concepts of 'inner form', of 'characteristic' art, and of the work of art as a living organism, *eine andre Natur*. Also Strasbourg Minster meant to him liberation from the world of Rococo and from the narrower aspects of the *Aufklärung* into the tumultuous creativity of the *Sturm und Drang*, and—which is very much the same thing—it signified the turning away from the French present to the German past.

To the later Goethe Gothic meant none of these things. What had been a deeply personal experience to the young Strasbourg student

[1] SB ii. 554.   [2] Ibid. p. 591.

had become something quite impersonal—a subject for detached and critical investigation, a phase, and not a very desirable phase, in the history of taste. In other words Goethe has reverted to the attitude of Herder towards the Middle Ages. It is true that the art of the Flemish primitives had moved him to genuine enthusiasm, but his feeling for medieval architecture seems to have been cooler than for medieval painting. Nevertheless, in order to assist Sulpiz Boisserée, he was ready to go to considerable lengths in his advocacy of the efforts of the Romantic medievalists. Indeed his attitude towards the Gothic Revival in his later years was a product of, and can only be judged in the light of, his relationship with his young friend. Through this relationship Goethe acquired a living contact with the Romantic generation which he would otherwise have lacked and which to some extent gave the lie to the oft-repeated accusation that he was indifferent to the ideals and enthusiasms of the contemporary world. In his advocacy of the Boisserées, Moller, Büsching and their friends he made his nearest approach to the patriotic movement of his time.

So much, then, for the significance of the Gothic Revival to Goethe. What was the significance of Goethe to the Gothic Revival? As we have seen, *Von Deutscher Baukunst*, whatever the limitations of its understanding of the specific qualities of the Gothic style, is a document of importance not only in the history of the Gothic Revival in Germany, but in the history of taste altogether. Its tone of whole-hearted acceptance, its awe-struck sense of the stupendous achievement of the medieval builders, distinguish it from all previous utterances on the subject. It was the first expression of the Romantic attitude towards Gothic, and as such it was only logical that the Romantics should have regarded it as the foundation stone of the Gothic Revival.

This brings us to a fundamental question: were the Gothic Revival-ists inspired by *Von Deutscher Baukunst*, or was it, on the contrary, their own independent enthusiasm for Gothic which led to the redis-covery of Goethe's essay? It is not easy to answer this question. It is, it is true, unlikely that the course of the Gothic Revival in Germany would have been very different if the Erwin essay had never been writ-ten, or had been—as it nearly was—lost in oblivion. On the other hand there is no doubt that the Romantics looked back to it as a kind of charter of the Revival, and especially of its patriotic aspect. We have seen how deeply the conviction of the German origin and character of Gothic architecture was held. This was an integral part of the Roman-tic exaltation of the German past, and especially of the German Middle Ages, of the feeling in fact that the Middle Ages as such were something specifically German. From this of course it followed that the most impressive product of the Middle Ages—Gothic architecture—should also be German.

Goethe's later preoccupation with Gothic under the aegis of Sulpiz Boisserée, despite its benevolent intentions, could not have a comparable significance to that of the Erwin essay. Nevertheless his constant advocacy of the ideals and projects of Boisserée and his fellow-enthusiasts, Moller, Büsching, and other medievalists in the field of the visual arts—an advocacy extending over a period of almost twenty years—was no mean contribution to the cause of the Gothic Revival. Especially the splendid passages on Strasbourg Minster in *Dichtung und Wahrheit* could not fail to be a source of encouragement to the Gothic enthusiasts, who now found the uncompromising foe of the 'age of barbarism' so unexpectedly on their side.

It would, however, be absurd to claim that Goethe's advocacy had a decisive influence on the Gothic Revival in Germany. Apart from all else, it came too late. The battle was already won. By the second decade of the nineteenth century the propagandist efforts of Friedrich Schlegel and the Boisserée's had already borne ample fruit; Romantic medievalism in the literary sphere was in full swing; *Taschenbücher* and *Damenkalender* were popularizing the medievalist tendencies, including that of medieval architecture; antiquarians and topographers were producing engravings of medieval buildings on every side; Romantic painters like Caspar David Friedrich were evolving visions of Gothic landscape; and the architects themselves were making increasing use of the neo-Gothic style. On the gathering momentum of this development Goethe's somewhat tentative intervention could in the nature of things make comparatively little impact.

PART FIVE

THE TRIUMPH OF GOTHIC

THE TRIUMPH OF GOTHIC

THIS section of our study gathers together under one head a wide and varied miscellany of contributions to the background of the Gothic Revival in Germany, dating from the first decades—mainly the second decade—of the nineteenth century. Common to the great majority of them is an unbounded enthusiasm for the Gothic style, an enthusiasm which is intimately bound up with the religious and patriotic attitudes engendered by the Romantic movement.

These manifestations of the triumph of Gothic are so multifarious that it is hardly possible to treat them on a purely chronological basis. It is more convenient to consider them according to various categories—art historians, *Germanisten*, archaeologists, &c. But first we must deal with two individual figures, a philosopher and an architect, who each in his way illustrates the culmination of the Romantic attitude towards Gothic.

1. HEGEL

HEGEL's views on Gothic architecture are to be found in his *Vorlesungen über die Aesthetik*, which in the form in which they have come down to us date mainly from 1820.[1] His survey of the subject is dominated by the view (1) that Gothic is the essentially Romantic and (2) the essentially Christian style of architecture, and (3)—a corollary of 2— it is above all other styles the symbolic expression of the Infinite. None of these points is new, but never before had they been stated with such clarity and force. Though he makes no reference to any of his predecessors except Goethe, Hegel's bold and assured survey of the whole subject in a few pages of concentrated prose rests ultimately on the labours and percipience of a long line of Gothic enthusiasts.

Hegel starts his chapter on Gothic architecture, which he entitles simply 'Die romantische Architektur', with the bold statement, which might be taken as the motto of this study: 'The Gothic architecture of the Middle Ages forms the characteristic centre of the essentially Romantic.'[2] For Hegel, then, Gothic is not only Romantic architecture *per se*, but it is the central manifestation of Romanticism altogether. He goes on to say that the change in attitude towards the Gothic style in recent times, which was due in the first place to the young Goethe, consists above all in the recognition that the 'magnificent structures' of the Middle Ages are the true expression of the spirit of Christianity.

The core of Hegel's argument is that all the characteristic features of the Gothic style derive from the needs and aspirations of the Christian soul, both the desire to shut itself off from the world in order to concentrate on its inner devotion, and, equally, the desire to expand outwards and upwards to the Infinite. The first part of the antithesis finds expression in the enclosed character of the Gothic church as opposed to the 'open serenity' of the classical temple. Thus the porticos and colonnades of the latter are transposed to the interior of the building in the form of vestibules, aisles, ambulatories, and so on. Further, the stained glass windows create the dim religious light which emphasizes this sequestration from the outside world.

Similarly, the second part of the antithesis, the striving towards the

[1] Cp. the preface to the three volume edition of H. G. Hotho (Berlin, 1835–8).
[2] Ed. cit. ii. 332.

Infinite, finds expression in the emphasis on the Pointed, in the shape of pinnacles, triangular forms and pointed arches, in strong contrast to the horizontal emphasis of classical architecture.

A corollary of all this is that in 'Romantic' architecture it is the interior which is more important, as is demonstrated by the fact that it visibly determines the form of the exterior. In the Gothic church the practical aspect of the architecture (enclosure through side walls and roof, supporting pillars and beams, &c.) is subsidiary. If one enters a medieval cathedral, one is not so much reminded of the stability and mechanical function of the pillars and the vaults they support as of the interlacing arches of forest trees. It is as if the walls and pillars had an independent life of their own, just as the branches of a tree appear to be, not borne by the trunk, but themselves a continuation of it. This gives the pillars a totally different character from the columns of classical architecture, which are visibly there to carry a horizontal weight. In Gothic, on the contrary, all the emphasis is on the upward thrust, and the pointed arches appear to the eye to be a mere continuation of the pillars, uninterrupted by the capitals, which sometimes, e.g. in many Dutch Gothic churches, are in any case lacking. This soaring upwards of the slender pillars lifts the Christian soul above earthly things to find its rest in God.

A noteworthy point is that in this discussion of the interior Hegel makes it clear that he is thinking throughout of the Gothic church as a vehicle for Catholic, and not Protestant worship. In fact at one point he contrasts the Gothic church with 'the box-like character of our Protestant churches, which are only built to house a congregation.'[1] The equation of Gothic and Catholic is not surprising in such writers as Friedrich Schlegel or Sulpiz Boisserée, but it is unexpected in the Protestant Hegel, and especially so at this comparatively late date.

When Hegel turns to consider the exterior of the Gothic church he illustrates in detail his thesis that the main features thereof are simply a reflection of the interior. Thus the cruciform shape, the arrangement of the portals and windows in the façade, all betray and are conditioned by the form and character of the interior. Nevertheless it has a certain independent existence of its own, as witness the system of buttresses (though this too, of course, is an indication of the interior arrangement of the pillars). And the vertical surge is even more marked outside than inside, for here there is no vaulted roof to inhibit it. It finds expression in the infinite multiplicity of finials and pinnacles, in the acute triangles above the portals and

[1] Ibid. p. 333.

windows, and in the steep gables of the roof. Above all, of course, it finds expression in the mighty steeples, the culmination of this whole system of verticality.

It is this stress on verticality which, in Hegel's view, accounts for the important role played by ornament in Gothic architecture. The desire of the Gothic architects to make the masses appear vaster, and especially higher, than they really are impels them to divide up their surfaces into forms which are themselves expressive of the upward surge, i.e. pillars, pointed arches, acute triangles, all on a miniature scale. But this infinite multiplicity of detail does not interfere with the clear articulation of the masses and proportions. Here, as always, the Gothic church is a symbol of the Christian soul in prayer which on the one hand reaches out to infinity and on the other remains concentrated on 'das Kleine und Kleinliche'. Another characteristic of Gothic decoration, its delicacy and apparent fragility, Hegel interprets as a part of the general Romantic tendency to idealize or spiritualize the material.

Finally, Gothic ornamentation tends towards the organic; hence the foliage and flower carvings, the animal and human forms, realistic or grotesque, characteristic of the Gothic style. This too Hegel sees as an example of the Romantic imagination at work, with its richness of invention and tendency to strange combinations of heterogeneous elements.

2. SCHINKEL

PERHAPS the best example of the penetration of Romantic sentiment into the architectural sphere is to be found in the work of Carl Friedrich Schinkel. Schinkel, the most distinguished German architect of the early nineteenth century, is chiefly renowned—and rightly so—for his great neo-classical designs, such as the Neue Wache, the Altes Museum and Schauspielhaus in Berlin, and the Nikolaikirche in Potsdam; but like most architects of this period he also made his contribution to the Gothic Revival. In this he was following in the footsteps of his master, Friedrich Gilly, who doubtless influenced the Gothic or Romantic side of his achievement through his drawings of the Marienburg, as he certainly influenced him in his classical projects. His first designs were all in the classical mode, but an early interest in Gothic is testified by the letters and diaries of his journey to Italy in 1803-4, where he writes with enthusiasm of the cathedral in Prague and the Stefanskirche in Vienna and the 'Saracenic' architecture of Sicily.

Schinkel returned from his travels to Berlin in January 1805 to find that the political and economic situation was extremely unfavourable to the architect. There was very little building in Prussia between this date and the end of the war in 1815. During this stage he was forced to turn to painting for his livelihood, mainly landscape compositions which had hitherto been purely ancillary to his architectural designs. This is also Schinkel's most truly Romantic phase, the height of which may be dated from about 1810 to 1815, in which he produced a series of 'Gothic' landscapes, rather in the manner of Caspar David Friedrich, by whose paintings he was profoundly influenced. These pictures of Schinkel—both paintings and drawings—have the same intense visionary character as Friedrich's work, though they are, perhaps, less nostalgically Romantic. His Gothic buildings are usually completed structures, not ruinous symbols of the transience of all things, as with Friedrich. And yet these Gothic structures are fantastic enough in all conscience. There is, for instance, the strange drawing of the Gothic cathedral, more like Kubla's pleasure-dome than any Gothic building known to man, rising spectrally out of the surrounding trees, entitled 'Abend'; or the better known 'Mittel-alterliche Stadt am Wasser' with its stupendous but highly unorthodox medieval fane towering above the stream below.[1] The Gothic of these works is Romantic in the extreme; it is a dream-picture of the Middle Ages, as phantasmal, as far removed from reality, as any Romantic evocation of Tieck or Novalis.

Indeed there is a strong literary quality about these paintings and drawings. A good example of this is the lithograph entitled 'Dom hinter Bäumen' with the characteristically Romantic legend: 'Attempt to express the pleasant yearning melancholy which fills the heart at the sound of divine worship proceeding from a church.'[2] Schinkel was in fact in close contact with the Romantic writers, especially Arnim and Brentano. The latter had an immense admiration for him, describing him in a letter to Wilhelm Grimm as 'one of the greatest landscape painters, draughtsmen and architects who have ever lived'.[3] He was a member of the Christlich-deutsche Tischgesellschaft, to which Kleist, Arnim, Brentano and Fouqué also belonged. And when Brentano offered his Märchen to the publisher Reimer in 1816, he warmly recommended Schinkel as his illustrator. In the same year Schinkel was commissioned by E. T. A. Hoffmann to design sets for the latter's opera Undine, and in 1818 he did the same for a production of Kleist's Das Käthchen von Heilbronn.

But the most remarkable example of the close bond between Romantic literature and the Gothic Revival is not a painting, in which after all imagination could wander at will, but an architectural design, which was meant to be carried out in stone and mortar. This is Schinkel's project for a mausoleum for Queen Louisa of Prussia, which dates from 1810. He accompanied the design with a commentary, which was intended to make quite clear to the spectator the mood in which it should be approached. It is characteristic of the literary nature of Schinkel's attitude to Gothic at this time that he should have felt that the design alone could not speak for itself. As one reads the description, one is involuntarily reminded of the account of Ottilie's chapel in Die Wahlverwandtschaften:

In the midst of a chamber, whose vaulted roof and supporting pillars create the impression of a grove of palms, a sarcophagus stands on a flight of steps, embellished with many sprouting leaves, lilies and roses. Here rests the recumbent statue of the Queen with a crown upon her head. At her head stand two angels with outspread wings and palm branches in their hands, their feet resting on lilies; they scatter flowers and gaze gently at the face of the Queen. At her

[1] Cp. A. Grisebach, Carl Friedrich Schinkel (Leipzig, 1924), pp. 50 and 39 respectively.
[2] Ibid. p. 53.
[3] Cp. R. Steig, Clemens Brentano und die Brüder Grimm (Stuttgart and Berlin, 1914), p. 203.

feet another angel kneels on a calyx and gazes heavenwards in rapturous contemplation of the transfigured spirit of the departed.

Light falls through the windows which surround the sarcophagus on three sides; the stained glass suffuses the whole mausoleum, which is built of white marble, with a soft rosy glow. In front of this hall is a portico, surrounded by trees of the darkest hue; you ascend the steps and enter with a gentle thrill of awe into the darkness of the vestibule, from which through three high openings you look into the hall of palms, where the deceased surrounded by angels rests peacefully in the clear rose of dawn.[1]

One could hardly go farther than this in the permeation of architecture with Romantic sentiment. It is a translation into the medium of words of the atmosphere of Schinkel's own Gothic landscapes with an admixture perhaps of Philipp Otto Runge's flower designs.

Schinkel prefaces his description of the mausoleum with a disquisition on the nature of architecture in general and of Gothic architecture in particular. Here again he shows how deeply his attitude to Gothic is coloured by Romantic thinking and especially by the writings of Friedrich Schlegel. The kernel of his argument is the typically Romantic thesis that the aim of Gothic is the expression of an idea, whereas classical architecture is based on purely material considerations. Hence from the outset Gothic 'is higher in its principles than the architecture of the ancients.'[2]

Schinkel reinforces his argument with a brief review of the progress of architecture through the ages. Thus the architecture of Greece and Rome was followed by an age of barbarism, which in its turn was brought to a close by the union of Christianity with the German Genius. For the Germans with their native originality and inborn love of freedom were able to revolutionize the art of vaulting which they had inherited from the Romans (who had invented it, but had been unable to develop it). The German medieval architects succeeded in making it the expression of ideas which derived equally from the native colour of German thought and from the world concept of Christianity. With the system of Gothic vaulting, which combined the minimum of material with the maximum of extension, the spirit attained complete dominion over matter. 'From henceforth', says Schinkel, in terms which almost seem to anticipate Worringer, 'matter presented no obstacle to the architectural expression of the deepest and highest concepts of which human nature is capable'.[3]

---

[1] *Aus Schinkel's Nachlass*, ed. Alfred Freiherr von Wolzogen (Berlin, 1862–4, 4 vols.), iii. 161–2.

[2] Ibid. p. 158 n. [3] Ibid. p. 157.

PLATE 4

'Abend' by *Carl Friedrich Schinkel*

PLATE 5

Schinkel's Design for a Mausoleum for Queen Louisa of Prussia

Gothic, then, in Schinkel's view, is at the same time the specifically Christian and the specifically German architecture, 'although for centuries now unhappy circumstances have seduced the Germans from their natural bent and driven them to follow foreign influences all too slavishly'—a strange sentence surely to come from the pen of the greatest of German neo-classical architects. It is moreover the specifically religious architecture altogether, 'the outward and visible sign of that which unites Man to God and the transcendental world'.[1]

It was the German architects of the Middle Ages who created the appropriate forms to express the ideas of 'sublimity, solemnity and soaring aspiration, and above all of that deep organic spiritual unity which produces perfection. In this way the effect and the immediate influence of every separate part on the building as a whole is made clearly visible. It was precisely this which was completely lacking in the ancient buildings, since with them the prevailing unity is simply a combination of physical requirements, and not a true spiritual fusion of all the parts in the whole.'[2]

Gothic architecture, then, is the expression of an idea, and Schinkel follows up his general remarks on Gothic with an explanation of the particular idea which he aimed to express in his design for the mausoleum. It was the Christian concept of death as the translation to a happier state, which stands in direct contradiction to the ideas of Greece and Rome on the subject. Therefore the architecture of Greece and Rome would be totally inappropriate for his purpose. We must create our own style, and for this the Middle Ages point the way.

Schinkel's commentary on his mausoleum design is one of the most fascinating documents of the Gothic Revival in Germany. No other writer, not even Friedrich Schlegel or Hegel, shows more clearly and convincingly how deeply the spirit and philosophy of the German Romantic movement had penetrated the architectural field. At one point or other of his commentary Schinkel gives voice to the following characteristically and essentially Romantic conceptions of Gothic:

(1) Gothic is the expression of an idea.
(2) Gothic is the triumph of spirit over matter.
(3) Gothic is the art of the transcendental.
(4) Gothic is the specifically Christian architecture.
(5) Gothic is the specifically German architecture.
(6) The unity of Gothic is an inner and organic unity.

[1] Ibid. p. 158.　[2] loc. cit.

(7) And finally, and for all these reasons, Gothic architecture is superior to Classical.

Schinkel believed that only a Gothic design could do justice to the purpose he had in view. Not so King Frederick William III, who preferred the idea of a small temple in classical style. This was actually erected to the plans of Heinrich Gentz in the park of the Palace of Charlottenburg, and—strangely enough, in view of all that has been said—Gentz was assisted in the carrying out of his design by Schinkel himself. The latter also designed a more modest monument to the Queen in cast-iron Gothic, which was erected at Gransee.

With the coming of peace Schinkel was able to return to his more purely architectural activities. From 1816 on begins the long series of masterpieces in neo-classical style which changed the face of Berlin and made Schinkel the greatest exponent of the 'Prussian style' in architecture. But it would be a mistake to suppose that he had now turned his back on Gothic. Right up to the end of his life he kept returning to it in his designs. The most remarkable of these is his project for a cathedral on the Leipziger Platz in Berlin as a national memorial to the War of Liberation. With its western towers and eastern dome and flat-roofed nave it is as fantastic a vision of Gothic as any to be found in his 'Gothic' landscapes, and one can only be grateful that it was never carried out. In the accompanying explanatory text Schinkel refers to the 'altdeutsche Bauart' as a style which yet remains to be perfected by the intermingling of classical elements, and evidence of this ideal of a synthetic style is to be found in most of his Gothic designs. Here, for instance, it is shown in the lack of buttresses, the avoidance of a pointed roof, and the mounting of the whole structure on a raised stone terrace or substructure. Thus Schinkel's neo-Gothic is anything but historically correct or pure. It retains a neo-classicistic element in the proportions and at the same time a Romantic or picturesque quality, which differentiate it sharply from the work of the 'correct' neo-Gothicists of the later nineteenth century.

Schinkel's grandiose scheme for a national cathedral came to nothing. Instead he had to be content with the modest little Gothic cast-iron monument to the War of Liberation on the Kreuzberg in the outskirts of Berlin. The visionary radiance which is so strong an element in Schinkel's Gothic designs and landscapes is singularly absent in his realized Gothic projects, which are apt to be austere, if not arid, like the Friedrich Werdersche Kirche in Berlin, or else lifeless imitations of English castle Gothic, like the Babelsberger Schloss near Potsdam.

In addition to his ever increasing architectural commitments Schinkel devoted much skill and energy in the years following 1815 to the designing of stage settings for the Berlin State Theatres. The most famous of these are his superb designs for *Die Zauberflöte* (1815), in which the architecture is a kind of romanticized Egyptian, but in several of his other sets he gave eloquent expression to his Gothic leanings. Perhaps the most striking of his Gothic settings are those of Rheims Cathedral, designed for Schiller's *Die Jungfrau von Orleans* (1825), and some of the sets for Hofmann's *Undine* (1816) and for *Das Käthchen von Heilbronn* (1818). Strangely enough, the Gothic of these theatrical designs is on the whole less 'theatrical' than that of his landscapes and unrealized architectural designs. The Gothic stage designs of Schinkel—and of the less gifted but equally Gothic sets of the Romantic painter Carl Blechen—are a testimony to the popularization of Gothic taste in the second and third decades of the nineteenth century. They in their turn contributed no doubt to the further spread and final triumph of this taste in the succeeding decades.[1]

---

[1] For a detailed account and illustrations of Schinkel's neo-Gothic buildings see *Karl Friedrich Schinkel. Sein Lebenswerk*, ed. Paul Ortwin Rave (Berlin, 1939). 10 vols. have appeared up to 1960.

(a) Fiorillo

Germany was the first country in Europe to develop the study of the history of art as an academic discipline—some one hundred and fifty years before we did so in England. It is therefore of some relevance to our purpose to enquire into the contribution of the German art historians to the Gothic Revival.

The first German *Kunsthistoriker* in the modern sense of the word was Johann Dominicus Fiorillo, who taught drawing and the history of art in Göttingen from 1781 until his death forty years later. From 1813 onwards he was Professor of Art History in the University. Fiorillo possessed the same kind of significance for the Romantic generation as Oeser had done for that of Winckelmann and Goethe. Tieck and Wackenroder were among his pupils, and he was on friendly terms with Wilhelm Schlegel, who helped him with the style of his history of art. This, his major achievement, occupied the greater part of his active life. It is in nine volumes: the first five (*Geschichte der zeichnenden Künste von ihrer Wiederauflebung bis auf die neuesten Zeiten*, Göttingen, 1798–1808) deal with the art of Italy, France, Spain and Great Britain, and the remainder (*Geschichte der zeichnenden Künste in Deutschland und den Vereinigten Niederlanden*, Hanover, 1815–20) with Germany and the Netherlands. This was to be the standard German history of art for many years to come, the first of any consequence since Sandrart's *Teutsche Akademie*, which it effectively supplanted. Above all, it was the source from which the Romantic generation derived its knowledge of art and architecture.

The first part of his history, written between 1798 and 1808, is very little concerned with medieval architecture, or indeed with architecture at all. These volumes are almost exclusively devoted to painting. His main interest is in the artists of the sixteenth and seventeenth centuries in Italy and France, though he refers tolerantly to such Pre-Raphaelites as Cimabue, Giotto and Masaccio. Apart from his advocacy of the term 'German' for Gothic, and his assertion that the Gothic churches of Europe were built by German architects, there was little or nothing in these volumes that could interest the Gothic enthusiast.

It is a very different matter with the volumes on Germany and the

Netherlands. But here it is not so much a question of Fiorillo teaching the Romantics to appreciate medieval art and architecture as *vice versa*. Between the appearance of the last volume of the first part of his history in 1808 and the first volume of the second part in 1815 much had been written in praise of medieval architecture, and the climate of opinion was fast changing in favour of the Middle Ages. In these volumes Fiorillo is deeply indebted to both Friedrich Schlegel and Carl Ritter.

The first two volumes deal with the medieval period, and are largely concerned with German Gothic architecture; indeed they provide the first thorough survey of medieval architecture throughout the German-speaking lands—including Austria and Bohemia—which had yet appeared. (The arrangement is according to provinces, and Switzerland is included in vol. 4.)

The artistic chauvinism which is hinted at in the first part of Fiorillo's history is carried much farther in these later volumes. He is now more than ever convinced of the German origin of Gothic architecture:

As soon as Germany had become an independent Empire, architecture, which had early developed on Byzantine and Roman lines, now took on a quite peculiar character which one can only call *German*. This style persisted until the fifteenth century, and spread from Germany into other European countries. Everywhere the great German architects found imitators and admirers; under the supervision, or with the help, of German masters splendid cathedral churches arose in Italy, in Florence, Pisa, Assisi, Orvieto and Milan. In Spain the cathedral of Toledo owed its first embellishments to German artists and the greatest French architect of the Middle Ages, Jean de Montreuil, was in all probability an Alsatian by birth and trained in a German school.[1]

As for the English, if they are so blinded by national pride as to imagine that they possess an indigenous architecture of their own, let them remember the archbishop of York, who had the minster embellished in the German manner as early as the reign of William the Conqueror. This astonishing statement is based on a reference in Thomas Stubbs's *Chronicles of the Archbishops of York* to the crucifix surmounting the rood screen in York Minster as being 'opere Teutonico'. In other words, the fact that the minster possessed a crucifix fabricated by German gold and silversmiths was sufficient to prove that Gothic is a German invention!

Fiorillo's chapter on Cologne is compounded of extracts from

---

[1] Fiorillo, *Geschichte der zeichnenden Künste in Deutschland und den Vereinigten Niederlanden*, ii. 269–72. By Jean de Montreuil Fiorillo means Pierre de Montreuil, who was not an Alsatian, but a native of Montreuil-sous-Bois on the outskirts of Paris.

Ritter's essay on the *Ruinen am Rhein*, J. F. Benzenberg's *Der Dom in Coln* (see below), and Friedrich Schlegel's *Dritter Nachtrag alter Germälde*, with only a few additions of his own.

The fourth volume (1820) contains a section on the present state of painting, which takes as its point of departure the Goethe-Meyer essay on 'Neudeutsche religios-patriotische Kunst'. Fiorillo agrees with Goethe-Meyer that the taste for medieval art has been greatly stimulated by the *Herzensergiessungen*. He describes how Tieck and Wackenroder had attended his lectures on the history of art in Göttingen: 'Tieck had a sharp penetrating mind, which took in everything at the first glance; he made very few notes. Wackenroder, on the other hand, could not put down enough on paper, and in addition to attending my lectures he would come to my house to inspect my engravings, books and other rare works, and note down this and that.'[1] Other works he mentions as having contributed to this same taste are *Franz Sternbalds Wanderungen*, the *Phantasien über die Kunst* and the poems of Wilhelm Schlegel, especially his *Bund der Kirche mit den Künsten*.

Fiorillo makes a long quotation from Friedrich Schlegel's *Europa* essays, commending the old German masters as models. But he himself is unable to accept the Nazarene position. He has shown, he says, that in the Middle Ages Germany possessed artists in every sphere who were in no way inferior to those of other nations; moreover he has demonstrated that Catholic Christianity has done more than anything else to help the arts and equally that the Reformation was unfavourable to them—'but to embrace the new doctrines and the new principles, that I cannot do'. And in an appendix on Friedrich Schlegel's essay on the Nazarene exhibition in Rome in 1819 he sums up his feelings about the German Primitives in the sentence: 'One should not despise the Old German paintings, rather should one admire them in their kind; but one should not exalt them above all others, as many people have done.'[2]

Fundamentally, Fiorillo's attitude to both medieval and neo-medieval art is identical with that of 'W.K.F.' in the *Kunst und Alterthum* essay, which he deeply admired and of which he, like most people, assumed Goethe to be the author. He was himself very far from being a Romantic medievalist, and yet his work certainly made its contribution to the medievalizing tendencies of the time. As we have seen, his history of German art was inspired by an ardent patriotism, which was meat and drink to the Romantic medievalists.

---

[1] Ibid. iv. 83.   [2] Ibid. iv. 116.

Indeed Fiorillo makes it clear in the preface to his first volume (1815) that a principal reason for undertaking the work was the desire to satisfy the newly awakened interest in medieval German art. Though his survey of German Gothic is rather in the nature of an inventory, it is clear that he has a sincere, if discriminating, admiration for the style. And for its highest achievements his praise is unstinted. Of Strasbourg he writes: 'The height of the heaven-scaling tower, the harmony of all its parts, the delicacy of the sculptures and the boldness of the vaulting make this monument an object of astonishment which is unique in Europe.'[1]

(b) Rumohr

Fiorillo's most brilliant pupil was the art historian Carl Friedrich von Rumohr. Rumohr has been described as the first in the series of professional art historians of the nineteenth century and at the same time the last of the great art historical dillettantes of the eighteenth century.[2] Descended from a noble Holstein family and plentifully endowed with private means, he had a milieu and horizon wider than that of the average German Gelehrte. He was in touch with the Romantics—both writers, such as Tieck, the Schlegels, Schelling, Steffens, and Bettina von Arnim; and artists, such as Cornelius, Veit, and Overbeck; as well as with the Humboldts and Goethe, with Niebuhr and Platen. He was the author of a novel and of several Novellen, of a cookery book and a treatise on etiquette, as well as of his masterpiece, the Italienische Forschungen (3 vols. 1827–31). In this book for the first time in German literature the Italian painters of the Middle Ages were accorded their due place in the history of art.

On Rumohr's gravestone in Dresden his friend and patron King Christian VII of Denmark saluted him as the 'founder of the deeper study of the art history of the Middle Ages'. The tribute was deserved, but Rumohr's attitude to the Middle Ages was very different from that of the Romantic medievalists. It was not a sentimental love of the past or an equally sentimental religiosity which turned his attention to the medieval field, but the scientific urge to explore and assess a neglected period in the history of art. His method is scholarly, documentary, objective; his style factual and somewhat arid.

Rumohr's chief writings on the subject of medieval German architecture are to be found in Friedrich Schlegel's Deutsches Museum (vols. 3 and 4, 1813). They fall into three parts: (1) a fragmentary history of German art in the tenth century; (2) a long essay in two

[1] Ibid. i. 359. [2] Cp. W. Waetzoldt, Deutsche Kunsthistoriker, i. 292.

sections on the origin of Gothic architecture; (3) an essay on the antiquities of Lower Saxony. Like Friedrich Schlegel, Rumohr rejects the term 'German' in favour of 'Gothic', however illogical and misleading the latter may be. He admits that the Germans have had an important share in the development of the Gothic style, whereas the Goths had none whatever. But the term 'Gothic' has become generally accepted in the best antiquarian works of all European nations, so that to introduce the term 'German' at this stage would only make confusion worse confounded.[1] As to the question of origin, Rumohr is largely concerned to controvert the theory of a Moorish or oriental source for Romanesque architecture. He asserts that he knows of no Christian monument in Europe before the twelfth century which shows any trace of oriental influence. Romanesque— or 'romano-barbarisch', as he calls it—is a debased development of late Roman architecture. Gothic architecture, on the other hand, is in part a natural development from early Romanesque and partly a product of oriental influence, infiltrating by way of the Crusades and the Venetian trade with Egypt and India.

Rumohr's essay is not concerned with value judgments. What he thinks of Gothic architecture, how high he rates it as an aesthetic manifestation, what it means to him personally are not indicated. From the point of view of this study, therefore, its significance is only subsidiary, though it does of course provide evidence of the growth of a serious interest in the whole subject of medieval architecture at this time.

Rumohr's third essay in the *Deutsches Museum* gives a detailed description of the medieval monuments of Lower Saxony, Mecklenburg and Schleswig, especially the churches of Lübeck and Hamburg. Though he is still more concerned with questions of date and origin than with aesthetic valuation, Rumohr does express appreciation for some of the works under review, such as the Marienkirche in Lübeck. Altogether this article must have been one of the first to draw attention to the merits and peculiarities of North German *Backsteingotik* (brick Gothic). It must also have been one of the first to demonstrate that there is such a thing as a specifically Romanesque style of sculpture. Though sometimes appreciative, Rumohr is never enthusiastic. Throughout he remains detached and objective. In this he is as far removed from Romantic medievalism as in the fact that for him Gothic does not appear to have any religious or philosophic significance.

[1] In his *Italienische Forschungen*, however, he proposes the term 'germanische Architectur' for Gothic and 'vorgermanische architectur' for Romanesque.

(c) Costenoble

The first book in German to be devoted exclusively to the subject of Gothic architecture was J. C. Costenoble's *Ueber altdeutsche Architektur und deren Ursprung* (Halle, 1812). Costenoble was a practising architect, and his approach is a practical one. The main body of the work is highly technical, consisting of a detailed consideration of the nature, origin and development of the various components of the Gothic system: vaulting, pointed arches, pillars, towers, buttresses and so on. Curiously enough he makes virtually no reference to specific buildings, which tends to render his treatment of the subject dry in the extreme.

However, more general considerations are broached in a brief introduction and a fairly lengthy appendix. Costenoble is here mainly concerned to investigate the origins of the Gothic style. His views on the matter can be subsumed under two headings: Gothic is German, and Gothic is not an imitation of anything else.

The very title of this first independent study of Gothic architecture in Germany indicates without more ado that Costenoble shares Goethe's equation of Gothic with German. He is indeed one of the most uncompromising supporters of this theory. In his view Old German architecture arose spontaneously in Germany in the eighth and ninth centuries, making its appearance along with the introduction of Christianity, with which religion it is intimately bound up. It grew naturally out of the methods of wood construction in use at that time. The forms of this architecture, originally rough and clumsy, gradually grew more refined, until they reached the perfect style of the twelfth, thirteenth and fourteenth centuries. Costenoble, then, does not recognize any division into what we should call Romanesque and Gothic as far as Germany is concerned; instead there is a process of gradual development without any recognizable break. But this state of affairs is peculiar to Germany. In Italy there was first the truly Gothic (*altgothisch*) style, i.e. the clumsy imitation of debased Roman buildings by the Goths and other Germanic tribes; and, secondly, the 'German' (or *neugotisch*) architecture introduced by German architects in the thirteenth century. The same division applies *mutatis mutandis* to France, Spain, and England. In all these countries the Gothic style, as we understand the term, was introduced from Germany.

Costenoble arrives at his conviction of the spontaneous German origin of Gothic through the application of Herder's evolutionary method to architecture. Thus architecture is the product of the 'customs, habits, climate, religion and character of a nation and of the type of materials available and of the way they are treated'.[1] He does not explain of course why this principle should not apply equally to other Gothic-producing countries.

This conviction leads Costenoble into the strangest travesties of the facts. Thus in his view German Gothic is the only pure style of Gothic, and this is one of the reasons why it had so much influence on its neighbours. It would be difficult to find a more topsy-turvy sentence than the following: 'The Old German style, as one finds it in English and in most French buildings, is too mixed with alien forms for us to reckon it as really pure architecture.'[2] Equally mad is the passage in which he attributes the French anti-Gothic prejudices in the eighteenth century to their dislike of everything German.

But Costenoble goes further still in his determination to vindicate the purity of the Old German style. Not only has it borrowed nothing from other nations; it has not even borrowed anything from nature. In this, of course, he is at odds with most German writers on Gothic from Goethe on. In Costenoble's view any resemblance that may exist between Gothic vaulting and arboreal forms is purely fortuitous. It is only in certain details of the decoration that we find a deliberate imitation of plant forms, and these occur just as, if not more, frequently in Greek and Roman architecture. He then turns to other explanations of the origins of Old German architecture, each of which he demolishes in turn. First, there is the theory that it arose through the imitation of debased Roman architecture by the Goths. This is true of Italy, but not of Germany, where there were no Goths anyway. Equally beside the mark are the suggestions that it derives from Byzantine architecture, or from a mixture of Oriental and Byzantine. No; Gothic architecture is a purely German invention, sprung spontaneously from the particular character and conditions of the German people.

(d) Stieglitz

By far the most important contributions to the study of Gothic architecture by a German Kunsthistoriker in the early decades of the nineteenth century are those of Christian Ludwig Stieglitz. Stieglitz, who lived and worked in Leipzig, was a man of many parts: jurist, architect, draughtsman, historian of architecture and amateur of landscape gardening. He even wrote some minor verse on medieval themes. Among his multifarious preoccupations he essayed the first

---

[1] Costenoble, op. cit. p. 2.   [2] Ibid. p. 66.

serious study of the Faust legend[1] and designed the first set of illustrations ever made for the First Part of Goethe's *Faust*—illustrations of which Goethe himself thought highly.[2]

But his main interest was the history of architecture from the earliest times to his own day, and this concern found expression in a long series of books on the subject extending over the whole of his working life. He appears to have been equally interested in ancient and medieval architecture, which was something almost unique at this date.

Stieglitz's interest in medieval architecture seems to have accompanied him throughout his career. The earliest evidence of this interest are the articles on 'Baukunst' (1792) and 'Kirche' (1796) in his *Enzyklopädie der bürgerlichen Baukunst* (5 vols. Leipzig, 1792–8), where he evinces an unexpectedly enlightened and informed attitude to the subject considering the comparatively early date of this work. In particular he is refreshingly free from prejudice on the matter of origins: 'The social history of the Middle Ages is the only true guide to the history of Gothic architecture, the only means of preserving us from the false notion that this architecture originated in Germany, which was in fact almost the last country to which it penetrated.'[3] In his view the style originated in Spain out of the cruder 'Old Gothic' architecture, which was itself a debased imitation of Greek and Roman architecture. Stieglitz then is the first architectural writer in Germany to make a distinction between Old Gothic (i.e. Romanesque) and New Gothic. And though he does not elaborate the point, he gives here in 1792 the hint which was first to be amplified by Friedrich Schlegel twelve years later.

From Spain the New Gothic style passed into France, England and Germany. Unlike other German critics of Gothic before and after him (with the solitary exception of Schelling) Stieglitz places the English contribution to the Gothic style above that of all other nations. Especially York Minster evokes his unbounded enthusiasm: 'It is not only the largest Gothic church, but indisputably the criterion according to which the beauties and failings of other Gothic churches can be measured . . . The visitor to this church is struck with awe and admiration by the astonishing sense of space and the height of the vaulting.'[4]

One of the distinguishing features of English Gothic is the size

[1] Cp. *Deutsches Museum* (Vienna, 1812), ii, 312–36, and *Historisches Taschenbuch*, ed. F. v. Raumer (Leipzig, 1834), v. 127–210.
[2] Cp. Benz, op. cit., pp. 172–3, and Goethe's letter to Stieglitz of 18 February 1810.
[3] Stieglitz, *Enzyklopädie*, i. vii–viii.   [4] Ibid. i. 203.

of the windows, especially those over the west door, 'which occupy almost the entire breadth of the building and give it a majestic appearance and which are to be found in few Gothic buildings in other lands'.[1] He even has a few brief remarks on Scottish and Irish Gothic. Modest in scope though it is, this is by many years the first account of British Gothic to appear in Germany.

Stieglitz at this stage has no high opinion of German Gothic, which he sums up as follows: 'In Germany one sees nothing like as many great and beautiful Gothic churches as in Spain, France or England; apart from Strasbourg Minster the only noteworthy examples are St. Stephen's in Vienna and the Sebaldskirche in Nuremberg.'[2] Cologne is not mentioned. In striking contrast to Goethe and his Romantic successors in the early decades of the nineteenth century, Stieglitz states categorically: 'New Gothic architecture indisputably came to Germany from France'[3]—a truly remarkable statement for the date at which it was written (1792). This truth was soon to be lost in the morasses of Romantic chauvinism, and fifty years were to elapse before a German critic of Gothic would dare to repeat this revolutionary assertion.

On the whole Stieglitz's attitude to Gothic in his *Enzyklopädie* is surprisingly positive, and much more space is devoted to it than to Renaissance architecture. It is, he says, a style 'which even now pleases all lovers and connoisseurs of art, because it gives food to the imagination, and through its richly decorated vaults, its stained glass windows, its great perspectives and subdued lighting fills the mind with pleasure and the soul with awe and reverence'.[4]

Stieglitz enlarges on the excellences of Gothic in his article 'Kirche' (1796). Like Laugier before him he finds the Gothic style more suitable than the classical for ecclesiastical purposes. It is true that the Gothic churches of the Middle Ages are frequently blamed for their total lack of classical beauty. But this type of architecture is so 'characteristic and original' that anyone entering such a building will be surprised and enchanted, so majestic and sublime is the impression it creates— an impression which is notably lacking in most of the modern churches built according to the rules of classical architecture. He does not go so far, however, as to recommend the building of new churches in the Gothic style, 'but one should imitate their good qualities, in order to reproduce the great effect which is characteristic of them'.[5]

It was nearly thirty years before Stieglitz published anything further on the subject of Gothic architecture—thirty years in which the

[1] Ibid. i. 202. [2] Ibid. i. 208. [3] Ibid. i. 207. [4] Ibid. i. 197. [5] Ibid. iii. 188.

whole approach to the Middle Ages and all its manifestations had been completely revolutionized. It is fascinating to trace this revolution in the development of his views between the *Enzyklopädie* of 1792–8 and his *Von altdeutscher Baukunst* of 1820.

Stieglitz's *Von altdeutscher Baukunst* is the first full-scale survey of German medieval architecture—for Costenoble's brief and tentative study scarcely deserves this title. Here at last is the comprehensive history for which Herder and Huth had called so many years before.

Stieglitz divides German medieval architecture into three main sections: (1) from the time of Charlemagne up till the tenth century. In this period the Germans had no distinctive style of their own, except in their castles; their ecclesiastical architecture was a development of the Byzantine style. (2) from the eleventh century to the first quarter of the thirteenth century. In this period a mixed art compounded of Byzantine, Arabic and German elements prevailed. (3) From the first quarter of the thirteenth century till the beginning of the sixteenth century. This was the period of German architecture proper, 'when the architects, inspired by the Romantic spirit which now pervaded everything, conjured forth a new kind of art, in which the masses disappeared and the buildings soared upwards in their marvellous lightness and delicacy of workmanship'.[1]

The greater part of Stieglitz's study consists of a wide survey of all the main monuments of medieval German architecture from the gatehouse at Lorsch down to the Late Gothic tower of Frankfurt Cathedral. Here for the first time the German reader had the chance to assess the architectural heritage of the German Middle Ages. From this heritage the author singles out for special commendation the cathedral churches of Strasbourg, Cologne, Vienna and Freiburg, with the first of which in particular he deals in considerable detail.

The contrast in spirit between this work and the articles on Gothic in his *Enzyclopädie* could scarcely be stronger. One could not wish for a clearer example of the influence of the Romantic movement on the approach to medieval architecture. In the first place the religious aspect of the style, which had played next to no part in the earlier articles, now assumes pride of place. In his Introduction Stieglitz writes of Gothic with the same reverence as Wackenroder had accorded to the painters of the Italian Renaissance. 'He who would recognize the peculiar spirit of this architecture must approach it with a childlike purity of mind, with a naive piety, and if he is lacking in this, let him pass by and not profane what is sacred. Wandering among the mighty

[1] Stieglitz, *Von altdeutscher Baukunst*, p. 10.

structures of the Middle Ages, thrilled by these marvellous forms, let us think with veneration of the power which undertook such mighty works and brought them to so splendid a conclusion.'[1]

Thus Gothic is the peculiarly appropriate style for the Christian church, and is therefore to be recommended for modern church building. For neo-classical churches remind one of heathen gods and so are a kind of desecration. However much we may admire the architects' skill, our hearts remain unmoved. Classical architecture is an affair of the head, Gothic of the soul.

But the most startling contract between Stieglitz's early and later utterances on the subject of Gothic architecture relates to the origins of the style. Here even more than in his views on its religious significance are we made aware of the impact of German Romanticism and more particularly of Romantic chauvinism. The man who in 1792 had roundly declared that Gothic came to Germany from France now asserts no less categorically that Gothic is a German invention and deserves the title 'German architecture'. 'German architecture', he says, 'reached France from Germany in the thirteenth century. Especially noteworthy examples are the cathedrals of Rheims, Bourges, Amiens and the churches of St. Ouen and Notre Dame in Rouen.'[2]

Stieglitz is quite specific about it: German architecture was invented at Strasbourg by Erwin von Steinbach, as Goethe had long ago recognized in his essay *Von Deutscher Baukunst*. From Strasbourg it spread to Italy, England, France and Spain.

This German priority was indeed inevitable, for the German Middle Ages, which produced Gothic architecture, were pre-eminent in all respects. Thus the Germans were in a position 'to create a truly indigenous art, an art which in view of their peculiarly religious cast of mind *could* only have been created by them'.[3] He does not believe that this new creation was due to a conscious imitation of the phenomena of nature, arboreal or otherwise, as Warburton and others had maintained. 'It was the spirit of the age alone which led to the employment of the pointed arch and vault.'[4]

He considers briefly the chief examples of 'German' architecture abroad—a survey which only serves to confirm the superiority as well as the priority of the German originals. The main difference between them lies in the superior lightness, boldness and variety of the German churches, and to judge from Strasbourg, Freiburg and Vienna they excel other countries no less in the beauty of their spires.

[1] Ibid. p. 5.　[2] Ibid. p. 164.　[3] Ibid. p. 110.　[4] Ibid. p. 13.

For Stieglitz, as for Hegel and the later Schlegel, Gothic is the specifically Romantic art, a part of the universal Romantic spirit of the Middle Ages which found expression also in medieval poetry and in the institutions of chivalry. Depth and boldness of imagination, the sense of the Infinite, religious awe, these are the qualities to be found in the great Gothic church:

The heavenward-soaring vaults, which lead the gaze into the Infinite, the manifold interplay of the transverse arches, the solemn twilight which suffuses the cathedral through the stained glass windows and which mingles so wonderfully with the bright shimmer of the glowing colours—all this fills the soul with awe and reverence. The richly decorated altars, chapels, pulpits, monuments, the great solemn perspectives, the subtle mixture of sublimity and delicacy—all this speaks to the emotions, to the imagination, from which it sprang.[1]

Stieglitz returned to the subject of medieval architecture in two further publications—*Geschichte der Baukunst vom früheren Alterthume bis in die neuern Zeiten* (1827) and *Beiträge zur Geschichte der Ausbildung der Baukunst* (1834)—in which Gothic is given its place, and a highly honourable place, within the total history of architecture, extending from primitive cave dwellings down to Stieglitz's own day. But these later works do not add anything very material to what he had already said in *Von altdeutscher Baukunst*.

It is unnecessary for our purposes to pursue the contributions of the art historians to the rehabilitation of Gothic beyond Stieglitz. He represents more completely than any other German art historian the Romantic approach to the style. He was followed in the next decades by men of a very different calibre: serious students of architecture, who brought to bear on the problems of Gothic new standards of historical scholarship and technical knowledge. In their hands the study of medieval architecture became a sober discipline, increasingly occupied with such matters as stylistic categories and dates, and with statics, mechanics and systems of construction. They belong to the history of architecture rather than the history of taste. They do not talk of the Infinite and the German Soul, but of lateral thrusts and stylistic epochs. Such were Johannes Wetter, who analysed the essentials of Gothic construction in his little guide to Mainz Cathedral[2], or Franz Mertens, who discovered St. Denis as the birthplace of the

---

[1] Ibid. p. 124.   [2] For Wetter see Paul, op. cit., pp. 525-9.

Gothic style.[1] These men were of much the same type and generation
as Arcisse de Caumont and Viollet-le-Duc in France and of William
Whewell and Robert Willis in England. They represent the turn
away from Romantic exuberance to archaeological exactitude and
technical analysis.

[1] For Mertens see Paul, op. cit., pp. 531–6.

4 · GERMANISTEN

(a) von der Hagen

The part played by the *Germanisten* in the Gothic Revival in Germany has no real parallel in England for the simple reason that professors of English language and literature did not exist at the time with which we are concerned, nor for that matter until many decades later. The nearest approach to a Gothicizing Anglist was, I suppose, Thomas Warton, but he belongs in any case to an earlier phase of the Revival.

The enthusiastic medievalism of the *Germanisten* in the early decades of the nineteenth century is closely bound up with the medievalizing tendencies of the Romantics. This is well illustrated by the case of the father of the *Germanisten*, Friedrich Heinrich von der Hagen, who attended A. W. Schlegel's Berlin lectures on the history of German poetry in 1803 and was inspired by them to undertake his edition of the *Nibelungenlied*. Hagen was primarily concerned with medieval literature, but he was interested in all manifestations of the German Middle Ages, including art and architecture.

The spirit of Romantic nationalism with which Hagen approached his medieval studies finds particularly clear expression in a passage from his book with the characteristic title, *Die Nibelungen: Ihre Bedeutung für Gegenwart und für immer:* 'I have devoted the best part of my life to this work and have done so, and still do so, gladly and joyfully . . . I have found therein a centre for my daily life, an unending task and my dearest avocation. In our fatherland's most shameful hour it was to me, and to many of my friends, a great consolation, a true inspiration, and an earnest of the resuscitation of German glory.'[1]

Hagen's views on medieval art and architecture are to be found in his *Briefe in die Heimat aus Deutschland, der Schweiz und Italien* (Breslau, 1818–21, 4 vols.). This account of his journey to Italy in the years 1816–17 forms a fascinating contrast to Goethe's *Italienische Reise*. No better example could be found of the revolution in taste which had taken place in the interval between the two journeys. Appropriately the author actually read the first volume of the *Italienische Reise* during his stay in Rome, and was quick to recognize the complete contrast between Goethe's experience of Italy and his own, especially in the cities of Verona and Vicenza. Hagen refuses to be particularly

[1] Breslau, 1819, p. 196.

impressed either by the Roman amphitheatre in the first or by the works of Palladio in the second.

He makes no bones about it. Even in Italy it is Gothic architecture that interests him primarily. Everything medieval, Gothic and Romanesque, is treated with respect and interest, the Renaissance and Baroque for the most part with indifference or contempt, ancient architecture itself without enthusiasm and often as a kind of foil to point the superiority of Gothic. This fundamental reversal of the attitude of Goethe and most eighteenth-century writers becomes especially clear in little details. For instance, when approaching Florence, Hagen regretfully sighs: 'This city has no real spires.' And, characteristically, the Duomo is blamed for not being Gothic enough. Of St. Peter's Hagen is highly critical. It lacks organic unity and all sense of the numinous. The proportions of the interior move him to the following comparison with Gothic: 'Ancient architecture, from which these proportions derive, seems fundamentally unsuited to express the sublime and the marvellous, or to excite those feelings of awe, reverence and humble adoration produced by an old Gothic cathedral.'[1] And he contrasts Michelangelo's dome to its great disadvantage with 'our glorious Gothic spires, which rise lightly and airily into the sky, as if they were alive and no longer subject to the laws of gravity'.[2]

This leads him on to a more general comparison between the character of classical and Gothic architecture. The superiority of the latter rests on its diversity and above all on its power of expressing the Christian faith. 'With all its symmetry classical architecture has something wearily monotonous about it, whereas Gothic blossoms in infinite variety.' Classical architecture lacks 'the transfigured vision into the Beyond, which Christian painting first revealed to us. In short, Gothic architecture is the true Christian architecture, and the Gothic church rises to heaven like a prayer, like a hymn with its accompaniment of organ and bells.'[3] By now then Gothic is firmly anchored for the rest of the nineteenth century and beyond as the specifically Christian style.

Once again, this time in connection with Paestum, Hagen is moved to a comparison between Classical and Gothic. His point of departure is the earthbound horizontality of classical architecture, compared with which Gothic rises into the sky like a living tree with all its leaves and branches. Everywhere the decorative foliage breaks into bud. All is light and transparent. Everything strives upwards to the topmost tip of the spire, hovering high in the blue of heaven. 'In short, the

[1] *Briefe in die Heimat*, ii. 284.   [2] Ibid. p. 289.   [3] loc. cit.

whole is like magic, like a phenomenon out of a transcendental world, like the wondrous Church of the Grail on Montsalvat, designed in one night by the hand of God . . . such a church is the freest, most sublime, indeed stupendous creation in the phenomenal world, and at the same time the most delicate, playful and charming of structures, cunningly and lovingly woven together out of infinite small details, pillars, arches, pinnacles and decorations.' It is true that to create such a building the poor stones must be tortured into shape (an allusion to Goethe's remarks on Milan Cathedral in his *Baukunst* essay), but all the more glorious will be their transformation: 'Like a liquid and as it were Christian crystal, forced upwards into a living fountain with its thousand rays, they shall form and dissolve in eternal flux.'[1]

This is indeed the apotheosis of Gothic. Further than this, one feels, it is scarcely possible to go. There are clear echoes of Forster and Friedrich Schlegel in the passage—even perhaps of *Von Deutscher Baukunst*—but Hagen goes far beyond them in the lyrical intensity of his appreciation. Under his gaze the Gothic church dissolves into a symbol of Romantic yearning itself. Two points are especially worth remarking: the stress on the other-worldliness of Gothic (a note first sounded in Forster's *Ansichten*); and the picturesque, unplastic quality of Hagen's vision, which evokes Wilhelm Schlegel's famous antithesis between Classical and Romantic art. His description reminds one indeed of some of Schinkel's Romantic designs or Caspar David Friedrich's Gothic visions.

(b) Büsching

Hagen is an amateur as far as architecture is concerned. His main interests lay elsewhere, but Gothic architecture was valuable to him as an important element of the German-Christian Middle Ages. A more significant part in the Revival was played by his friend and collaborator Johann Gustav Büsching.

Büsching, like Hagen, gave the best part of his life and energies to the study and propagation of the German Middle Ages. But whereas Hagen's interests were mainly concentrated on Middle High German and Old Norse texts, Büsching was also deeply concerned with Germanic archaeology, especially the archaeology and cultural history of Silesia. Moreover he was deeply interested in all aspects of German medieval art, and more particularly in German medieval architecture.

Büsching, who began his career as a lawyer, was appointed archivist

[1] Ibid., iii. 242–3.

in Breslau in 1811, with the task of collecting and cataloguing the works of historical and artistic interest which had been saved from the secularized monasteries. In 1817 he was created Professor of *Altertumswissenschaften* at the University of Breslau, where he lectured on every imaginable aspect of German medieval history and art. Many of his most important works in the sphere of Germanic philology were undertaken in collaboration with Hagen, e.g. *Sammlung Deutscher Volkslieder* (1807), *Deutsche Gedichte des Mittelalters* (1808), *Literarischer Grundriss der Geschichte der Deutschen Poesie von der ältesten Zeit bis in das 16. Jahrhundert* (1812), and their joint edition of Götz von Berlichingen's autobiography (1813).

Büsching's earliest utterance on the subject of German medieval architecture is to be found in the second and last volume of the periodical *Museum für Altdeutsche Literatur und Kunst* (1809–11), which he edited along with Hagen, B. J. Docen and (in volume two) B. Hundeshagen—a periodical which was otherwise devoted almost exclusively to medieval German literature. Büsching gives his views on Gothic in a review of Hundeshagen's book on the chapel at Frankenberg. He bases his theories expressly on Friedrich Schlegel's *Reisebriefe*, 'which contain splendid new insights and which, as we gladly confess, have served as our main guide in the evolution of our own ideas on the subject'.[1] Above all we owe to Friedrich Schlegel the clear distinction between the two types of 'Gothic' architecture: the 'hellenizing' and the 'German'. He also quotes Heinse's *Ardinghello*, whose description of the solemn Gothic cathedral with its stupendous spaces often occurred to him when contemplating a work of 'German' architecture.

The essay begins with an interesting testimony to the contemporary attitude towards medieval architecture. 'The time is past which looked upon "Gothic" and "tasteless" as almost synonymous. The feeling for the greatness and glory of the Middle Ages is growing increasingly and what until a few years age was confined to a few individuals now seems to be becoming common property.'[2] Much of the essay is concerned with the origins of the Gothic style, and Büsching's views on this problem are so remarkable that they deserve quoting at some length. Our author is the most thorough-going of all apostles of the 'vegetable' theory; he may be said to carry to its logical extreme Goethe's concept of Gothic as a living organism, partaking of the dynamic unity-in-multiplicity of nature. But upon this foundation Büsching has superimposed his bizarre theory that Gothic is the result of a

---

[1] *Museum für Altdeutsche Literatur und Kunst*, ii. 361.   [2] Ibid. p. 355.

marriage between Asia and the ancient Teutons. For it was from Asia, in his view, that the Goths brought the first seeds of the Gothic style to Europe:

The ancient Gothic buildings represent the union of the old sombre Germany and the merry laughter of Asia. The dense dark oak groves, inhabited by golden-locked Germans, found their counterpart in the stone vaults of the Gothic nave. The whole interior of the Gothic church is like a long avenue of thickly arching trees, and the very eeriness of the primeval forest is reproduced for us by the dimness of the lighting. Not so the exterior; there the flowers of merry India climb like creepers round the walls and turrets, their branches breaking into leaf and blossom ... and in the centre the main stalk of this flower shoots up, branch wound round branch until the lofty blossom touches the clouds, as in the spire of Strasbourg Cathedral ... And yet people dare to describe this pulsing mass as dull and lifeless. If it is still, then it has the still life of a plant. But it is not only still life, it is life itself in all its fullness. Ever and anon, in endless abundance, animal shapes peer from the branches; here a human head looks down, there some strange beast coils over a ledge.[1]

Büsching disagrees with Friedrich Schlegel's view that Gothic in the first place developed out of Greek and Roman architecture. On the contrary 'like all products of the Middle Ages it is something unique, new, and self-generated'.[2] Its basic principle, he is never tired of reiterating, is the imitation of the plant forms of nature; even the impression of dignity and serenity made by the Gothic church is borrowed from nature, and so is the tendency towards endless repetition of the same decorative motifs.

In 1816 Büsching began publishing his *Wöchentliche Nachrichten für Freunde der Geschichte, Kunst und Gelahrtheit des Mittelalters,* of which two volumes in weekly parts appeared in the first year. This was followed by two further volumes in monthly parts in 1817 and 1819 respectively. The periodical is dedicated to Goethe in words that clearly demonstrate the desperate desire of the Romantic generation to claim him as their own. They are also a measure of the encouragement which the Romantic medievalists had received from the recent indications of Goethe's renewed interest in the German Middle Ages, especially from the Rhine and Main essay in *Kunst und Alterthum.* This and the Erwin essay are enlisted by Büsching in the service of Romantic nationalism and Romantic medievalism alike:

For many a decade the Master of the Germans has absorbed into himself the many-sided impulses of our beloved fatherland in all its varying fortunes and has given expression to them in his works ... And the sublime creations of the German past, which had already moved his youthful soul to words

[1] Ibid. pp. 356–7.   [2] Ibid. p. 360.

which acted as an inspiration to all subsequent generations, now once again have been revealed to this man in his eternal youth and vigour; have been revealed to him in our liberated fatherland, which has at last found its soul and strives to find it ever more. And inspired by a similar vigour our fatherland and all its generations must follow again the magic strains which lead us to the well-spring of our people. For this a firm basis has now been won.[1]

The *Wöchentliche Nachrichten* was the first German weekly journal to be devoted solely to the Middle Ages and it is a remarkable testimony to the popularity of the subject at the time. As the title suggests, it deals with every aspect of the theme—poetry, legend, folklore, chronicles, fairy tales, art, architecture, sculpture, music, customs and costumes. It is concerned mainly but not exclusively with the German Middle Ages; Scandinavia and England also play some part. Middle High German literature takes pride of place. An ardent patriotism runs through the whole. Most of it was written by Büsching himself, but Hagen was also a fairly frequent contributor. The aim of the journal was to be both popular and scholarly at the same time.

Altogether this publication is a fascinating comment on Romantic medievalism and the impulses which inspired it: the love of the German past, the concept of the Middle Ages as the specifically German contribution to world history, and the reawakening of German national consciousness. Its most attractive aspect is the sense of discovery which informs it, the discovery of a long-lost heritage, whose endless riches had lain for so long dormant and forgotten through the blindness of the 'enlightened' generations.

In all this medieval architecture plays a considerable, though not a dominant part. Büsching supplies a detailed description in many instalments of Breslau Cathedral; there are many short notices of English works on medieval architecture (Britton's *Architectural Antiquities*, Scott's *Border Antiquities*, Dodsworth on Salisbury, Rev. W. Gunn on the origins of Gothic, &c.) Büsching's most ambitious contribution is an article on the octagonal shape of early medieval churches, which was issued separately in pamphlet form.[2]

In the autumn of 1817 Büsching made a tour through North Germany in search of Gothic monuments, the results of which he published two years later in his *Reise durch einige Münster und Kirchen des nördlichen Deutschlands im Spätjahr 1817* (Leipzig, 1819). This contains a series of very detailed descriptions of the churches and other medieval buildings which he visited in Brandenburg and Lower Saxony.

---

[1] *Wöchentliche Nachrichten*, i. i–ii.
[2] *Ueber die achteckige Gestalt der alten Kirchen mit besonderer Berücksichtigung von Breslau. Ein Versuch zur Aufhellung der Grundgestalt der Kirchen im Mittelalter* (Breslau, 1817).

One of the aims of the book, he says in his preface, is to serve as a complement to Fiorillo's *Geschichte der zeichnenden Künste in Deutschland und den Niederlanden*. He claims that he has described in detail what is excellent, and the less good he has at least assessed historically, while even what is bad he had designated as such, 'for though I extol the art of the Middle Ages with warmth and never faltering love and affection, one should not imagine that every botch and daub will find its admirer in me'.[1] This is in fact a first and very conscientious attempt at a regional guide to medieval art and architecture.

In 1823 appeared Büsching's book on *Das Schloss der deutschen Ritter zu Marienburg*. Goethe inserted a brief notice of it in *Kunst und Alterthum*, IV, 3, in the form of an introduction to a letter from Büsching describing the repairs and restorations which the building had undergone in the preceding decades. The book itself consists of a detailed description of the castle, whose architect was, in Büsching's view, 'one of the greatest architects of all time and a *German*'. In his conclusion the author looks back on the changing fortunes of this great monument of secular Gothic since the seventies of the preceding century, 'when we awoke from our slumber and the mists which had concealed from us the knowledge of our own glorious past began to lift'.[2]

Büsching is filled with admiration for the patriotic zeal of the East Prussians in supporting the project for the restoration of their great castle. King and people have united in this undertaking, which is a fair omen for all other territories of the kingdom. May it act as a beacon light for the banks of the Rhine, 'in order that the glory and splendour of Cologne Cathedral may equally be brought to completion, an undertaking which also can only be accomplished through an intimate union of sovereign and people'.[3] In an appendix he gives an account of the visit of the Crown Prince of Prussia on 20 June 1822. Eichendorff wrote a poem for the occasion which was duly recited by a minstrel to the accompaniment of a cither.[4] To the toast of the assembled guests the Crown Prince replied with the words: 'Alles Grosse und Würdige erstehe wie dieser Bau'. The whole scene is like an anticipation of the Kölner Domfeier in 1842.

But Büsching's most important contribution to the discussion on

---

[1] *Reise*, p. v. [2] *Das Schloss der deutschen Ritter zu Marienburg*, p. 76. [3] Ibid. p. 77.
[4] Many years later Eichendorff was to write a detailed account of the castle and its restoration, entitled *Die Wiederherstellung des Schlosses der deutschen Ordensritter zu Marienburg* (Berlin, 1844).

medieval architecture is his *Versuch einer Einleitung in die Geschichte der Altdeutschen Bauart* (Breslau, 1821), which consists of a series of lectures held in Breslau University in the summer of 1820—probably, incidentally, the first course of lectures ever held in Germany which were devoted exclusively to the subject of Gothic architecture.

We remember that Goethe consulted this work before writing his *Von Deutscher Baukunst 1823*, and that he refers to it appreciatively in the penultimate paragraph of the essay. Büsching for his part is our chief witness to the significance of Goethe's contribution to the Gothic Revival in Germany. He never lets slip an opportunity of acknowledging what the Romantic medievalists owe to the early eulogist of Strasbourg Minster. So here in his treatise on the 'Altdeutsche Bauart' Büsching takes the Erwin essay as his starting point. Goethe was the first, he says, to make two very important points: first, he showed that so-called Gothic architecture was in fact the invention of the Germans and something peculiar to the German race; and, secondly, he rescued 'German' architecture from the reproach of bad taste which had lain on it for so long. And even if, to Büsching's regret, the poet has not deemed 'this earliest effusion of a truly patriotic enthusiasm' to be worthy of inclusion in his collected works, nevertheless 'the seed that was sown by him has never ceased to bear the richest fruit, and especially at the present moment the prospect of a truly bounteous harvest is bright indeed'.[1] Here then we have the clearest possible assertion of the seminal value of Goethe's essay for the Gothic Revival in Germany.

Büsching is much concerned with the question of nomenclature. The problem is made more difficult by the necessity of distinguishing clearly between the two phases of medieval architecture—round-arched and pointed. Some writers have expressed this distinction by the terms 'altgotisch' and 'neugotisch'; some prefer the even more illogical pair 'vorgotisch' and 'gotisch'. He has no difficulty in showing how historically absurd all these designations are and demands categorically that the whole lot shall be banned in future from the discussion of medieval architecture.

Then there is the term 'Byzantine' or 'Neo-Greek', which was introduced by Friedrich Schlegel and adopted by the Boisserées to describe the older type of medieval architecture. This will not do at all, for it again has the effect of depriving the Germans of what is rightly theirs. Help comes, unexpectedly, from England, 'where we find *our* architecture again, which is hardly surprising in view of our

[1] *Versuch*, p. 3.

common Germanic origin'. Now the English call this early phase 'Saxon'; and this nomenclature strikes Büsching as most suitable, for, firstly, it shows that the oldest type of 'German' architecture is just as genuinely German an invention as the later *Schöne Altdeutsche Baukunst* (Beautiful Old-German Architecture); and, secondly, it indicates under which imperial dynasty this type of architecture specially flourished in Germany—'for it was the Ottonian or Saxon dynasty which was responsible for erecting the most important buildings of this type'.

'Saxon' architecture, then, began under Charlemagne and continued up to the end of the twelfth century, and its distinguishing characteristic is the rounded arch; 'Beautiful Old-German architecture' stretches from the beginning of the thirteenth century until well into the sixteenth century, and its distinguishing characteristic is the pointed arch.

To those who might object that examples of 'German' architecture are to be found in practically every country of Europe Büsching has the devastatingly simple answer that they were all built by German architects. For as the fame of the sublime 'German' minsters spread abroad, the people, and especially the clergy, of other lands came to view these miracles with their own eyes; and having marvelled, like Heinse's Ardinghello, at what they saw, they invited the German architects and German masons to come and erect similar edifices in their own countries.

Büsching then turns his attention to the question of the origin of the two types of German architecture. In this he recants somewhat the views he had put forward in the *Museum für Altdeutsche Literatur und Kunst*. Instead of finding the origins of 'German' architecture in blond Teutons and their dark dense oak groves, he now finds it unequivocally in Christianity. For 'German' architecture is at the same time 'Christian' architecture, and to reinforce his argument he quotes Friedrich Schlegel on the point.

Technically, Büsching sees the origin of 'Saxon' architecture to lie in the invention of the quadripartite vault, which profoundly affected every detail both of the interiors and exteriors of the buildings. 'It is these quadripartite vaults which distinguish Old-German architecture in both its phases from all other kinds of architecture; it is they which give it its uniqueness and which have sealed it with the stamp of an originality untainted by any kind of imitation.'[1] In Büsching's view the source of these vaults may well be traced to the castles built by the victorious Germans in their wars against the

[1] Ibid. p. 24.

Romans, an opinion for which he again finds support in Schlegel's *Reisebriefe*. At the same time he now accepts Schlegel's view that to some extent at least the earliest Christian architecture was based on late Roman originals.

Büsching distinguishes clearly between the two types of German medieval architecture. The 'Saxon' is characterized by its rounded arches, solid walls, usually without buttresses, narrow windows and above all quadripartite vaults. 'Beautiful Old-German architecture' should not be looked upon as something totally different from 'Saxon'; rather it is a sublimated form of the earlier phase. They have many points in common: cruciform plan, quadripartite vaults, deeply inset windows and thick walls [*sic*]. What chiefly distinguishes the later type from 'Saxon' is the introduction of the pointed arch, which transformed the clumsy bulk of 'Saxon' architecture into the soaring lightness and grace of an avenue of slender trees.

This last point gives Büsching the chance to reintroduce almost verbally the passage on plant forms already quoted from the *Museum für Altdeutsche Literatur und Kunst*. Nevertheless he now concludes that it would be a great mistake to derive the 'Beautiful Old-German architecture' solely from the imitation of natural forms, as an English writer, Sir James Hall, had done.[1] A much more likely explanation of the derivation of Old German architecture—or rather of its basic feature, the pointed arch—is to be found in the suggestion of the poet Gray, adopted by James Bentham in his history of Ely and referred to in Hall's book, that it originated in the intersected round arches of the wall arcadings to be found in many 'Old Saxon' churches. We have to imagine, says Büsching, a medieval architect who was so favourably impressed by the effect of pointed arches produced by these intersections that he said to himself: why should not a whole building be constructed in this bold and airy manner? He had only to persuade his masons of the idea, 'and there you have the origin of the Beautiful Old-German architecture'!

Despite his fantastic theories and crazy nomenclature Büsching is a figure of some significance in the history of the Gothic Revival in Germany. He is the Romantic Revivalist *par excellence*. In him Romantic medievalism and Romantic nationalism are one. He is the most passionate of all protagonists of the Gothic-is-German theory

[1] In his *Essay on the Origin, History and Principles of Gothic Architecture* (London, 1813). Büsching had already reviewed this work in the *Jahrbücher der Literatur* (Vienna, 1820), ix. 235 ff., arguing strongly against its main thesis that Gothic architecture originated in an imitation of wicker-work huts. Friedrich Schlegel, as we have already noted, was to return to the charge in the 1823 revision of his *Reisebriefe*.

and the most eloquent interpreter of Gothic as a living natural organism. In all his work he is deeply indebted to the Goethe of the Erwin essay and especially to Friedrich Schlegel, who is his main source and of whose *Reisebriefe* he makes lavish use. More clearly than any other Gothic enthusiast he demonstrates how deeply the origins of the Gothic Revival in Germany are rooted in the mental climate of the *Sturm und Drang* and *Romantik*.

(c) Carové

One of the most illuminating of the medievalizing publications of the second decade of the nineteenth century is the *Taschenbuch für Freunde altdeutscher Zeit und Kunst auf das Jahr* 1816 (Cologne, 1816). The editors were Eberhard von Groote and Friedrich Wilhelm Carové. Groote was a native of Cologne and a passionate lover of all things medieval. He edited Gottfried's *Tristan*, Gottfried Hagen's *Reimchronik der Stadt Köln*, and the poems of Muskatblüt; he was a friend of Boisserée, an enthusiastic supporter of the project for the restoration and completion of Cologne Cathedral and the founder of the *Dombauverein*. Carové was born in Coblenz and is chiefly notable for the ardour with which he espoused the cause of the *Burschenschaften*. He also wrote a fairy-tale, *Das Märchen ohne Ende*, which was translated into English by Sarah Austin and enjoyed an extraordinary popularity in this country.[1]

It was this *Taschenbuch*, it will be remembered, which published the article on Lochner's Adoration of the Kings by Wallraf that so roused Goethe's ire in his Rhine and Main essay. The 'enthusiastic mysticism, under the influence of which neither art nor knowledge can flourish' which Goethe discovered in Wallraf's article is characteristic of the whole publication. It exudes everything which Goethe found most repulsive in Romantic medievalism—the sentimental religiosity and the equally sentimental patriotism, in short the 'deutschtümelnde Frömmelei' which he had been doing his best to combat ever since the appearance of the *Herzensergiessungen*. And this despite the fact that the editors and contributors (who included Von der Hagen, Görres, Schenkendorf and the brothers Grimm as well as Wallraf) were thoroughly worthy and for the most part scholarly people. The two editors, who are responsible for the greater part of the contents, were both Catholic Rhinelanders, and this sets the tone. Much of the volume is concerned with Cologne and its cathedral, and above all with Lochner's *Dombild* and the cult of the

[1] *The Story without an End*, 1st ed. 1834.

Virgin. The foreword by the editors is a rhapsodic world history in miniature, suggested, it would seem, by Novalis's *Die Christenheit oder Europa*, both in respect of its style and content. The aim, as in Novalis's essay, is to point the contrast between the aridity of the godless present and the glowing ardour of the Age of Belief, where every aspect of life, in peace and war, the crusades no less than the cathedrals, were inspired by the same mystic faith. 'We opened again the long-closed portals of the dark cathedrals, but, alas, we were too accustomed to the dazzling light of day and could only with difficulty grow used to their soothing twilight. We no longer understood their mystical structure and wandered round like strangers in the holy places of our fathers.'[1]

The *Dom* and the *Dombild* serve as the central motifs of the *Taschenbuch*, both in verse and prose. In between is a miscellaneous collection of modernized versions of medieval songs and legends. From our point of view the most relevant contribution is an essay on German medieval art and architecture, 'Ansichten der Kunst des deutschen Mittelalters', by Carové.

This essay by an obscure author hidden away in a forgotten periodical is nevertheless an extraordinarily interesting document of Romantic medievalism at its most characteristic. The tone, the solemn rhapsodic note, is again set by Novalis. To put it in a nutshell, for Carové and his like the Middle Ages were quite simply fairyland, the Golden Age of childhood, the magic country where Goodness, Truth and Beauty reigned in a perpetual spring. Now the tables have been turned indeed: the dark obscure and worthless Middle Era between the glory of the ancient world and the splendour of the Renaissance has become the Central Age of history, to be valued above all others. As Carové succinctly puts it: 'The Middle Age is rightly so called, because like spring it lies between the harshness of winter and the parching heat of summer.'[2]

The essay shows all the symptoms of its kind in exemplary clarity. Romantic chauvinism runs riot. It is clear that for Carové the Middle Ages as such are a German achievement, the age in which the German spirit flourished most abundantly and brought forth its most glorious creations to the virtual exclusion of all other nations, in other words the *Middle* Ages were the *German* Ages. Even, for instance, the apparently regrettable fact that in the twelfth century the Germans borrowed their romances from the French in reality redounds to their credit and is a proof of the 'higher and more universal artistic

[1] *Taschenbuch*, p. xi.   [2] Ibid. p. 61.

and intellectural culture of the Germans as compared with their frivo-
lous neighbours, for the French in their arrogance did not bother to
translate any of Germany's national songs into *their* language'.[1]

After a highly coloured but somewhat vague survey of medieval
German literature, the author turns to the subject of medieval architecture. In this field, too, the Germans are no less pre-eminent and
original than in that of medieval poetry. Gothic architecture, in
Carové's view, is the specific creation and expression of the German
spirit, or at least of the German spirit in union with the spirit of
Christianity. 'From such a combination only the boldest and most
sublime creations could proceed. Beyond all ordinary proportions, as
lofty as human strength could raise them, the pillars, arches and
spires soared upwards . . . What stupendous, what almost foolhardy
ideas inspired these architects, and how high the unfettered yearning
of the spirit can raise the tardy stone is proved to us by those wondrous obelisks of Cologne and Strasbourg and by the cathedrals of
Vienna and Milan.'[2]

Carové sees Gothic in its context as part of the general spirit of
the German Middle Ages. 'Just as in those centuries the same spirit
gave birth to a deed of heroism and to a delicate *Minnelied*, so nothing
could exceed the elegance of decorative detail with which those mighty
builders embellished both the interiors and exteriors of their edifices.
And just as the *Minnesänger* borrowed their most charming images from
the spring, the forest and the flowery heath and rejoiced like children
in the blissful month of May,' so the medieval architects borrowed
the foliage of trees and flowers for their capitals and pinnacles.[3]

Never so far, not even in Friedrich Schlegel or Büsching, have
we met with such unqualified enthusiasm for the Gothic style as in
this essay of Carové. He leaves no doubt in the reader's mind that to
him at least Gothic is the supreme creation of German genius, the
summit and apotheosis of all architecture. He can only speak of it in
terms of religious rapture: 'When contemplating these structures one
can but marvel at the great and glorious heights which human art
is capable of reaching; and the sublime creations which the enchanted
gaze can scarcely compass raise the spirit irresistibly into those lofty
regions which their pillars and spires are striving to attain.'[4] It is
strange to think that less than forty years separate this effusion from
the remarks on Gothic in Sulzer's *Allgemeine Theorie der schönen
Künste*. There could be no better illustration of the complete revolution
of taste that had taken place in this comparatively short span of time.

[1] Ibid. p. 63.   [2] Ibid. p. 75.   [3] Ibid. pp. 75–76.   [4] Ibid. p. 78.

5. ARCHAEOLOGISTS AND ENGRAVERS

In his book on the Gothic Revival Sir Kenneth Clark has stressed the part played by the craze for archaeology at the end of the eighteenth and the beginning of the nineteenth centuries in the development of the English movement. From 1771—the date of Bentham's *History of Ely*—books and articles on Gothic architecture appeared in increasing numbers until by the opening years of the nineteenth century the flow had become a flood. Most of these publications were concerned either with the question of origins or of nomenclature.

From our point of view the most important result of this archaeological craze was the series of books of engravings which began appearing in the last decades of the eighteenth century, because it was these that most clearly influenced the Gothic movement in Germany. For these English publications soon found their way across the North Sea, where they were eagerly scrutinized by the Gothic enthusiasts and Romantic medievalists. Their popularity is attested by the number of reviews devoted to them in the journals of the time. Moreover they soon gave rise to similar undertakings in Germany, undertakings which in some cases surpassed in quality anything that had appeared in England. It cannot be doubted that these engravings of Gothic buildings—at a time when other forms of reproduction were not available—played a large part in the rehabilitation of medieval architecture in the first decades of the nineteenth century. The correspondence of Goethe is a good index of what they meant to the intelligent amateur.

The first collection of Gothic engravings of superior quality to appear in England was James Murphy's book on the Abbey of Batalha in Portugal. This was published in 1795 with an essay on the nature of Gothic architecture and was the first of such English publications to become well-known in Germany. Indeed, to judge from the number of references to it in journals and correspondence it seems to have enjoyed a greater popularity there than in its country of origin. (It is not mentioned either by Eastlake or Clark). Murphy advanced the theory that the origin of the pointed arch was to be found in the pyramids of Egypt, thus adding one more ingredient to the fantastic brew which befuddled the heads of earnest Gothic enquirers for so many years.

As we have seen, Herder knew the work and made it the basis of his own observations on Gothic in his freemason essays. All the leading German Gothicists—Boisserée, Moller, Costenoble, Büsching, Stieglitz—refer to it and had clearly studied it carefully. A German translation by J. D. E. W. Engelhard appeared in 1813.

Well-known, too, in Germany were the multifarious series of engravings by that indefatigable popularizer of Gothic antiquities John Britton. There was scarcely a cathedral or castle in the country that did not sooner or later become the object of his peculiar mixture of antiquarian zeal and business acumen. In Germany it was the series on York Minster that seems to have aroused most interest. Altogether, for some reason,[1] York Minster was usually taken as the prototype of English Gothic by Germans at this time.

(a) Gilly

Doubtless the example of the English engravers acted as a spur to the German Gothic enthusiasts to do likewise, though nothing so comprehensive as Britton's series was ever attempted in Germany. The first of the German productions was at the same time one of the finest, namely the book of aquatint engravings of the castle of Marienburg in East Prussia, issued by Friedrich Frick in 1799.[2] The best of the drawings had been made by the architect Friedrich Gilly on a journey to East Prussia in 1794. Gilly is one of the most interesting figures in the history of German architecture at the end of the eighteenth century, and his early death in 1800 at the age of twenty-eight was a tragic loss to European art. His designs, few of which were actually carried out, are a development of the Prussian neo-classicist tradition, a tradition of which his father, David Gilly, was a distinguished representative. But the best of them, such as the monument to Frederick the Great or the National Theatre in Berlin, have a stark monumental quality which is strikingly modern and original. His connection with the Gothic Revival is confined to these drawings of Marienburg and to the fact that he was the teacher and inspirer of Schinkel.

Gilly was responsible for six of the drawings; the rest are by Frick, who also engraved all the drawings, and Friedrich Rabe, who contributed the plans and architectural details. Frick's plates are inferior to Gilly's but they are nevertheless of a high standard. Altogether the

---

[1] Perhaps because of the passage from Stubbs's Chronicle referred to on p. 239.
[2] *Schloss Marienburg in Preussen. Nach seinen vorzüglichsten aeussern und innern Ansichten dargestellt* (Berlin, 1799).

whole production is greatly superior to anything of the kind that had appeared in England.

No wonder these drawings created a sensation when they were first exhibited at the Berlin Academy in 1795, though this sensation was probably due as much to their medieval subject matter as to their style. The latter is sufficiently remarkable in all conscience. For already in these early Gothic illustrations is to be descried the monumentality that distinguishes Gilly's great neo-classical designs. There is a Roman quality about his vision of Gothic, as shown in these sepia drawings; by his emphasis on broad surfaces and his handling of the masses he contrives to give the castle of Marienburg something of the weight and power of the Baths of Caracalla or of Piranesi's *Carceri*.

Apart from one or two sketch-book drawings there is no further evidence of Gilly's interest in Gothic. Nor is the cause far to seek. For the monumentality, which is already evident in the Marienburg series, found more appropriate expression in the manipulation of classical forms, especially of Doric forms. Of all architectural languages the Doric was the most congenial to Gilly, and most of his designs employ it.

Gilly also wrote an essay on the Marienburg which shows the same feeling for the picturesque and monumental qualities of the building as the drawings: 'The view of the castle chapel is particularly picturesque in its effect . . . The statue of the Virgin on the wall of the chapel is somewhat stiff in the manner of those times and brightly decorated. But through its very size the building as a whole makes a venerable impression.' And in writing of the palace of the Hochmeister he praises the 'truly admirable boldness' of the architect and the 'glorious vaults' of the refectory: 'The vaults rise from each pillar like a rocket . . . the total effect of this hall, as of all parts of the building, is both cheerful and impressive.' (Ibid., p. 205).[1]

(b) Hundeshagen

The productions of Bernhard Hundeshagen, an archaeologically minded advocate of Hanau, have none of the artistic qualities of Gilly's drawings and Frick's engravings. His first venture into the field of medieval architecture was a little book on the Gothic chapel

[1] Quoted from Hermann Schmitz, op. cit., pp. 203–5. Gilly has been rediscovered comparatively recently after a long period of total neglect. He is not even mentioned in the *Allgemeine Deutsche Biographie*, though there is a short article on his father David Gilly. For accounts of his life and work see Alste Oncken, *Friedrich Gilly, Forschungen zur deutschen Kunstgeschichte*, vol. v (Berlin, 1935) and Alfred Rietdorf, *Gilly Wiedergeburt der Architektur* (Berlin, 1940).

at Frankenberg in Hesse, published in 1808.[1] This consisted of ground plan, elevation and cross-section of the building together with a brief description, followed by some not very enlightening or enlightened 'thoughts' on Gothic architecture, which profess to give in miniature a history of Christian church building from the earliest times. Hundeshagen shares the usual belief in the essentially Germanic spirit of Gothic.

The author was encouraged by the reception accorded to this book to undertake a somewhat more ambitious work on Friedrich Barbarossa's palace at Gelnhausen.[2] This was first published in 1819, though it had been ready for publication in 1813, when war conditions intervened. The only interest of this very dryly written work is that it is one of the first, if not the first publication in German to be solely devoted to a Romanesque building.

(c) Benzenberg

The next in chronological order of these archaeological publications is of no more intrinsic value than Hundeshagen's books, but it derives a certain adventitious interest from being the first illustrated treatise to be devoted exclusively to Cologne cathedral. It thus anticipates, though on a very minor scale, the great work of Sulpiz Boisserée.[3]

The author of this brief work was Johann Friedrich Benzenberg, physicist and astronomer and for some years professor at the Lyceum in Düsseldorf. It consists of ten folio pages of introduction, followed by two engravings by Professor Thelott, one of the west front and one of the ground plan of the cathedral. The title page bears a quotation from the passage on Cologne in Georg Forster's *Ansichten*, constituting yet another tribute to the lasting influence of Forster's initiative in the field of Gothic appreciation.

In Benzenberg's view there is no question of completing the cathedral. He states categorically: 'This Colossus cannot be completed, for all-destroying time has already loosened much of the foundations on which further building would have to be based.'[4]

Moreover the stone of which the cathedral is built has weathered badly, especially through the action of frost. This last consideration moves him to pour scorn on the theory of the German origin of the Gothic style: 'Can you really imagine Gothic to have been invented in a clime where there is so much frost?' It is much more probable

[1] *Der alten gothischen Kapelle zu Frankenberg Grundriss, Aufriss und Durchschnitt, nebst Gedanken über die sogenannte gothische Kirchenbaukunst* (Frankfurt, 1808).
[2] *Kaiser Friedrichs I Barbarossa Palast in der Burg zu Gelnhausen* (Frankfurt, 1819).
[3] *Der Dom in Cöln* (Dortmund, 1810).   [4] Ibid. p. iii.

that Gothic, like the Goths themselves, came from the Far East. After all, the Gothic pillars with their spreading vaults bear much more resemblance to palm trees than to Nordic oak groves. And in any case the monuments of ancient India testify that 'this architecture was once native to the land of palms'.[1]

(d) Moller

The most important book on German Gothic architecture to appear in the first two decades of the nineteenth century is undoubtedly Georg Moller's *Denkmäler der deutschen Baukunst*.[2] This was the first attempt in Germany to provide a comprehensive illustrated survey of the outstanding monuments of German medieval architecture. The author is a leading figure in the early history of the Gothic Revival in Germany. Like Costenoble he had the advantage of being himself a practising architect. Indeed he was the foremost architect of the state of Hessen-Darmstadt in his day. His own buildings—which include the opera house and Ludwigskirche in Darmstadt and the state theatre in Mainz—are in the neo-classical style, but he was nevertheless one of the staunchest advocates of the study and preservation of medieval architecture, as enthusiastic as Büsching, but more discriminating and less fantastic in his theories.

The *Denkmäler* consist of three volumes of plates (the last not by Moller), which are as superior in scholarship as they are inferior in artistic merit to Frick's *Marienburg*, including examples from the eighth to the sixteenth centuries from all over Germany. The plates are prefaced by detailed explanations and by an introductory essay on the history and origin of medieval architecture. Cologne and Strasbourg are not included, since it is Moller's aim only to represent examples of German medieval architecture 'which are little known and not yet illustrated'. The fact that such outstanding examples as the cathedrals of Worms, Mainz and Ulm should be included under this rubric is interesting evidence of the ignorance of their medieval heritage which still prevailed among the Germans of this time. 'How can one explain the fact,' asks Moller in his introduction,

[1] Ibid. p. v.
[2] The precise dating of this publication presents some difficulty. The preface is dated August 1815, and on 10 November of that year Goethe wrote to thank Moller for the first two instalments of the *Denkmäler*, referring in his letter to the preface. On the other hand the notes of the introductory essay allude to publications of 1818 and 1819, and the anonymous English translator of 1824 gives the date of the *Denkmäler* as 1819–22. Finally there are two title pages, the first of which is dated 1815, and the second 1821. From all these indications it seems to follow that the introductory essay at least cannot have appeared before 1819, and perhaps not before 1821.

'that young architects go on measuring and delineating the ruins of Rome, which have already been drawn and engraved a hundred times, before they have gained even a superficial knowledge of the works of their forefathers which lie all about them'?[1]

But Moller acknowledges that this attitude is changing. The attention of the public has been stirred by the praise accorded to the medieval architecture of Germany by such men as Goethe, Herder and Georg Forster (the inclusion of Herder in this list is as strange as the omission of Friedrich Schlegel), and by the engravings and historical researches of Boisserée, Büsching, Costenoble, Fiorillo, Frick, Hundeshagen, Quaglio, Stieglitz and others.

On the matter of nomenclature Moller is more sensible than most of his fellows. He admits that the term 'Gothic' is unsatisfactory, but so for that matter are suggested alternatives like 'Byzantine', 'Saxon' and 'German'. He therefore proposes to designate the various styles of medieval architecture according to the century and country in which they flourished.

Moller's Herder-like definition of the *desiderata* of good architecture is also eminently sensible, in so far as it recognizes the influence of climate, building materials and national character on the architecture of different countries. Whatever architecture is the genuine product of these factors will be unique in its kind and self-consistent. All architecture, on the other hand, which contains undigested foreign elements will seem inappropriate and inconsistent until they have been properly assimilated to the national style. This criterion of a harmonious and characteristic national style can and should be applied to the architecture of all ages and all countries irrespectively.

Having extended this principle to the architecture of Egypt and Greece, which gets high marks on this score, and to Rome, which does not pass the test quite so well, Moller proceeds to apply it to the German architecture of the eighth to fifteenth centuries. He first divides the architecture of this period into two main styles. The first is foreign in origin and comes from the south; its distinguishing characteristics are Roman forms and decorations, flat or at least not very high roofs, semicircular arches and vaults, and great solidity of construction. He instances the gatehouse at Lorsch, the cathedrals of Speyer, Worms, Mainz and Aachen, and the abbeys of Paulinzella, Schwarzach and Ilbenstadt as examples of that he means. He makes no attempt to claim that there is anything specifically German about the style of such buildings.

[1] Ibid. p. 1.

The second style retains the semicircle at first, but employs higher roofs (which are more suitable for a northern climate). Then in order to harmonize with the shape of the roof, the spires become pyramidal, and the windows and vaults pointed, whilst all the minor ornaments still preserve the semicircular form. Later on even the details of the building follow suit and assume the shape of the pointed arch. 'To this latter type belong the grandest works of architecture which Germany possesses, works which will remain an object of admiration for all ages.'[1] This new style of building prevailed almost simultaneously in all countries of Europe. 'The great impression which these churches, particularly their interiors, make upon the mind of every unprejudiced person, on that of the simplest countryman no less than on the intelligent and well-informed, is truly wonderful; they combine the simplicity and majesty of the groves of the forest with the richness and beauty of its flowers and leaves—all is variety, greatness and sublimity.'[2] The heyday of this sublime architecture lasted from the middle of the thirteenth to the end of the fourteenth century; after which the style degenerated, exchanging its pristine austerity for arbitrary and fantastic ornamentation.

Moller now turns to the vexed question of the employment of the Gothic style in modern building. He is uncompromisingly opposed to this, on the good ground that the conditions which gave rise to Gothic architecture—political, commercial and above all religious—no longer exist, and that any attempt to imitate it is therefore necessarily doomed to failure. In a footnote he explains that the same considerations do not hold good for the neo-Greek style: 'In German architecture imagination and religion play the chief part, whereas Greek architecture is the fruit of enlightened understanding and correct aesthetic judgment. It limits itself strictly to the necessary, to which it strives to impart the most beautiful forms, and for this reason it will never cease to be capable of general application.'[3]

In his last chapter Moller discusses the problem of how the Gothic style originated. He enumerates five current theories:

(1) The sacred grove theory—which ultimately no doubt derives from Warburton, but which, as we have seen, was given fresh currency by the ingenious Büsching—according to which the slender pillars and bold vaults of the churches of the thirteenth century are supposed to be an imitation of the groves in which the ancient Teutons (or, according to Moller, Celts) worshipped their gods.

(2) The wicker-work theory, propagated by Sir James Hall, according

[1] Ibid. p. 12.   [2] Ibid. p. 17.   [3] Ibid. p. 17 n.

to which Gothic forms are derived from primitive huts constructed from withies.

(3) The theory that Gothic was originally an adaptation in stone of timber work structures, put forward by Thomas Pownall and Costenoble.

(4) Murphy's pyramidal theory, according to which the pointed arch is derived from the pyramids of Egypt.

(5) James Milner's theory—Moller refers explicitly to his *Treatise on the Ecclesiastical Architecture of England*—that the pointed arch arises from the intersecting semicircular arches of wall arcades in Norman churches.

(It is interesting to note that all of these theories derive from Englishmen.)

Moller has no difficulty in demonstrating the untenability of all these explanations. His own theory, as we know, is that the pointed arch derives from the pointed roof, and that its subsequent adoption in every part of the building was due to a desire for harmony of design.

He then addresses himself to the equally knotty problem of *who* was responsible for inventing the Gothic style. He considers the claimants in turn: Goths, Lombards, Arabs are easily eliminated; southern countries, such as Italy or Portugal, cannot stand up to investigation, since they do not pass the test of Moller's definition of national architecture, i.e. 'one which in its forms corresponds with the climate and building materials of the country, and which at the same time constitutes a consistent whole, excluding everything heterogeneous'.[1] In other words flat, not pointed roofs are indigenous to these countries, and flat roofs cannot have given rise to pointed arches. No, clearly the only countries which can fit Moller's definition are northern ones: Northern France, England or Germany. Now, you might think, the race is getting closer; but, on the contrary, the first two claimants are quickly disposed of. As to the first, you have only to look at the engraving of Notre Dame in d'Agincourt's *Histoire de l'art*. How horizontal the lines, how flat the towers, how lacking is everything in vertical aspiration! Nothing thirteenth century about this but the details.

And England: turn to the illustration of the west front of York Minster in Britton's *Cathedral Antiquities* and hear what Moller has to say about it:

Since the English lay such positive claims to the merit of having invented

[1] Ibid. p. 24.

and developed the pointed arch style of the thirteenth century, a closer examination of this church will not be deemed superfluous. Its main forms, the low
gable roof and the flat towers evidently belong to an originally southern style
of building. The whole system of decoration, on the other hand, is of northern
origin, and is obviously incompatible with those main forms. The pointed
gable, which crowns the middle window, and which is repeated in all the
details of the elevation, in no way harmonizes with the flat gable of the roof.
The flat roofs of the towers correspond as little with the other parts of the building; for they should have terminated in pyramids, since all the pinnacles of the
buttresses have this pyramidal form. All this shows the not very intelligent combination of two completely heterogeneous styles of building, and makes one
the less ready to accept the English claim to the originality of their ecclesiastical
architecture, as at the time York Minster was being built the German churches
already displayed the completest development of the art.[1]

Both France and England, then, are turned down on the strength
of one engraving each. Only Germany is left; the result is a foregone
conclusion. Moller has no difficulty in demonstrating from the cathedrals of Strasbourg and Freiburg and the Katharinenkirche at Oppenheim that German architecture alone triumphantly passes the test of
his definition. It alone possesses that perfect harmony between the
whole and the parts, in which the smallest detail repeats in miniature
the image of the entire structure. 'The scholar and the connoisseur',
he concludes, 'will now be able to judge which of the nations of
Europe displays the greatest degree of harmony and national character
in its buildings and which may therefore most confidently claim the
merit of having invented and developed the architecture of the
thirteenth century'.[2]

Despite this conclusion and despite his complaint of the lack of
verticality in French Gothic (which surely bids fair to be the most
absurd remark ever made in connection with the Gothic Revival)
Moller's Denkmäler is the most sensible and well-reasoned work on
medieval architecture which had yet appeared in Germany. It was at
least a step forward to admit that the Gothic style was not introduced
to the rest of Europe by German architects, but developed quasi-
independently and with its national idiosyncrasies in the various
countries of Europe. It was something to assert unequivocally that the
Germans were not the inventors of Romanesque architecture. Nor
can one cavil at Moller's definition of what constitutes a national
style. Finally, his common sense is well displayed in the way he demolishes the absurd theories of others as to the origins of Gothic.

The authoritative nature of the Denkmäler was recognized, and not

[1] Ibid. pp. 25–26.   [2] Ibid. p. 26.

only in Germany. As early as 1824 an anonymous translation appeared in London under the title *An Essay on the Origin and Progress of Gothic Architecture traced in and deduced from the Ancient Edifices of Germany, with references to those of England, etc. from the Eighth to the Sixteenth centuries.* This consisted of a translation of Moller's treatise together with his notes on the plates. The popularity of Moller's work in England is attested by the fact that a second edition of the translation with additional matter by W. H. Leeds was published in 1836. Leeds opens his preface with the following tribute to the author: 'On the merits of Moller's *Denkmäler* it is unnecessary here to expatiate; for such frequent and strong testimony has been borne in favour of the Work, as to render it superfluous to say more than that the buildings and details exhibited in it, are remarked by numerous peculiarities which distinguish them from those of contemporaneous date in this country . . . Although Moller's publication is exceeded in splendour by some of the costly architectural monographs by Sulpice Boisserée, &c., it has as yet no rival as a collection or series of various examples.'[1]

(e) Fischer

The success of Moller's *Denkmäler* naturally stimulated others to similar if less ambitious undertakings. There was, for instance, a work, whose title promises to do for Austria what Moller had done for Germany: *Denkmahle der Baukunst und Bildnerey des Mittelalters in dem Oestereichischen Kaiserthume*, with plates by Joseph Fischer and accompanying text in German and French by Prince Eduard Lichnowsky, published in Vienna in 1817. In fact, the title is misleading in the extreme, for the plates with three exceptions are devoted exclusively to the Viennese church of St. Maria am Gestade. Lichnowsky holds the usual views on the German origin of Gothic, and shares Moller's belief that its main characteristics are derived from the steep roofs of northern buildings, though they are also due in part to the German national character, 'which is distinguished by its capacity for bold and ambitious undertakings and by the dogged persistence with which it carries them out'.[2] He acknowledges the pre-eminence of the English in the field of architectural engravings, which is all the more remarkable, 'since the monuments of medieval architecture to be found in England cannot compare either in number or splendour, let alone in their state of preservation, with those in Germany'.[3]

---

[1] *Moller's Memorials of German-Gothic Architecture* (London, 1836), p. ix.
[2] Fischer, *Denkmahle*, p. i. [3] Ibid. p. iii.

(f) Quaglio

Of much greater consequence is the series of superb lithographs of German medieval buildings by Domenico Quaglio with text by Alois Schreiber, historian and topographer of Baden.[1] Domenico was the brother of Angelo Quaglio, who worked for Boisserée's *Domwerk*, and like him a master in his craft. The plates are outstanding examples of the lithographer's art in the service of Romantic sentiment. Though the architectural details are on the whole faithfully reproduced, the drawings are suffused by an atmosphere of picturesque medievalism. This shows itself, for instance, in incidental figures, which are frequently in historical costume, in the scenic settings, and in a Romantic exaggeration of scale reminiscent of Turner's exquisite etchings for the Waverley Novels. Gothic chapels nestle by rushing streams in mountain forests, and baronial castles, outlined against stormy skies, perch Valhalla-like on the crest of lofty crags.

The commentator, Alois Schreiber, is well aware and highly appreciative of this picturesque quality. In connection with Quaglio's illustration of the Ritterburg, Schloss Prunn im Altmühlthal, he writes: 'The light of the moon gives the wild region an Ossianic character, and the two knights, with whom the artist has so expressively embellished the landscape, lend it a Romantic element and transport the spectator into a mighty and inspiring past.'[2]

The reference to Ossian is not the only reminder of how closely the Romantic medievalist's vision of Gothic is bound up with literary associations. Of the courtyard of a Franconian convent we are told that the impression conveyed by Quaglio's drawing is that of 'a touching elegy or ballad'; and Schreiber appropriately ends his comment on a plate of Strasbourg Minster with a quotation from *Von Deutscher Baukunst*—an interesting proof, incidentally, that Goethe's essay was still remembered, even before its reprint in *Kunst und Alterthum*.

(g) F. H. Müller

A good example of an illustrated monograph confined to a single building is provided by Franz Hubert Müller's vast folio on St. Catherine's Church at Oppenheim.[3] The author, like Moller, came

---

[1] *Merkwürdige Gebäude des Teutschen Mittelalters nach der Natur und auf Stein gezeichnet von Domenicus Quaglio Königlich Baierischen Hofmaler. Historisch erläutert von Alois Schreiber grossherzoglich Badischen Hofrath und Historiographen.* (Carlsruhe, n.d.). There is no date on the title page, but the plates are dated from 1818 to 1823. [2] Ibid. p. 10.
[3] *Die St. Katharinen-Kirche zu Oppenheim. Ein Denkmal Teutscher Kirchenbaukunst aus dem 13ten Jahrhunderte* (Darmstadt, 1823).

from Darmstadt, where he was the director of the Grand Ducal picture
gallery. The fine plates are accompanied by a brief introductory text
on 'the German (teutsche) ecclesiastical style of architecture in the
Middle Ages', followed by special sections on the portals, stained
glass, foliage decoration, &c., of St. Catherine's.

Müller's introduction is inspired by the patriotic warmth which
had by now become a matter of course in the discussion of medieval
architecture. He is as convinced as Büsching that the Germans both
invented and perfected the style 'wrongly called Gothic'. At last his
countrymen are awakening to the 'sublime character of the monuments of German architecture, those witnesses to a great past, in
which is revealed the power and glory of our noble ancestors together with their gentleness and warmth of soul . . . In the German
style Christian church architecture reached the highest point of its
development.'[1]

As far as the church at Oppenheim is concerned Müller is of the
opinion that it was designed by the architect of Cologne cathedral,
so alike are they in the basic idea and in its execution down to the
smallest details. Unlike Moller he is in favour of a judicious use of
neo-Gothic forms in modern architecture, following in this the
example of the English 'who are so nearly related to the German
nation by their common descent from a Germanic race'.[2]

In the course of his introduction Müller pays high tribute to Sulpiz
Boisserée and his *Domwerk* and emphatically disclaims any intention
of rivalling this great undertaking, the first instalments of which
were eagerly awaited by all admirers of German art. Shortly after
writing these words the first instalments did in fact begin to appear.

(h) Boisserée

All other engravings of Gothic buildings pale beside the achievement
of Sulpiz Boisserée's *Domwerk*.[3] In every sense of the word it is a
monumental production. It is the crown of fifteen years of devoted
labour, worthy, one can say, not only of its author, but of the building
it commemorates.

As we know, Sulpiz began work on his great undertaking as far
back as 1808, and by the end of 1813 no less than twelve of the contemplated twenty drawings were ready; and yet ten further years
were to go by before the first instalment of the work appeared. What

[1] Ibid. p. 1.   [2] Ibid. p. 3.
[3] *Ansichten, Risse und einzelne Theile des Doms von Köln* (Stuttgart, 1821). Despite the
date 1821 on the title page the first instalment did not appear until September 1823.

were the reasons for this astonishing delay? In the first place, the difficulty of finding suitable engravers and publishers for so ambitious an enterprise, for Sulpiz was determined from the start that the work should be on a grandiose scale. As he explains in the preface to his *Domschrift*,[1] he began by himself undertaking the most meticulous measurements of the building; these in turn were repeated and checked by architects he employed for the purpose; then he sketched out the plans and elevations, adding the missing parts where necessary. For the actual drawings he enlisted the most distinguished architectural draughtsmen of the day—Angelo Quaglio, Maximilian Fuchs, Georg Moller, and others. These were then engraved under his supervision by the most competent craftsmen he could find for the purpose, including Darnstedt, Duttenhofer and Haldenwang. Cotta, who had at first fought shy of so bold a venture, later agreed to share the costs, and when it finally appeared the title page bore the rubric 'auf Kosten des Verfassers und der J. G. Cotta'schen Buchhandlung'.

In addition the troubled course of world events, the military and political tensions within and without Germany during these years, put every imaginable obstacle in the way of so ambitious a scheme. Even so—and remembering the (admittedly less ambitious) ventures of Hundeshagen, Moller, Quaglio, &c.—one cannot help feeling that the enormous delay must also have been due in part to some inherent dilatoriness or over-scrupulosity in Boisserée's make-up.

During the course of these years an event of considerable consequence for the prosecution of the *Domwerk* had occurred. Hitherto Sulpiz had only had the inadequate plates included in Crombach's book on the Three kings to help him in his reconstruction of the west front of the cathedral. Now his task was suddenly lightened by the rediscovery of the original medieval plans of the façade, in two sections: one of the north tower and one of the south. That of the north tower had been preserved in the cathedral archives until 1803, when the archives were removed to Darmstadt and there divided up by the representatives of the various authorities to whom the district of Cologne had been apportioned. In the general confusion the plan disappeared and despite all the efforts of Sulpiz was nowhere to be found. Then in 1814 it was rediscovered by a happy chance in a loft of the inn where the original distribution of the archives had taken

---

[1] The *Domschrift* was the convenient abbreviation used by Boisserée and his friends for the accompanying text to the *Domwerk: Geschichte und Beschreibung des Doms von Köln, nebst Untersuchungen über die alte Kirchenbaukunst, als Text zu den Ansichten, Rissen und einzelnen Theilen des Doms von Köln* (Stuttgart, 1823).

place. The parchment had been used in the drying of beans and for this purpose nails had been driven through it. Fortunately, apart from some nail holes and stains and one tear, no serious damage had been done. The finder had handed it over to Moller, who published a facsimile in 1818. Moller at once made his discovery available to Boisserée for the purposes of his *Domwerk*. The latter must have been gratified to find that it confirmed in almost every detail the accuracy of his own reconstructions.

Again by a happy chance, for which Moller was also in part responsible, the plan of the south tower was discovered by Boisserée in Paris in 1816. There is little doubt that these elevations were the actual plans used by the medieval builders for their work on the western towers, as far as it went. Sulpiz Boisserée's reconstruction of the west front (Plate V) was therefore an exact reproduction of the intentions of the medieval architect. But whether, as he believed, the original architect of the Cathedral, Meister Gerhard, was the author of these plans is another matter.[1]

Finally, it should be mentioned that for his reconstructions Sulpiz also had the use of two medieval plans lent to him by Wallraf, containing details of the choir and south tower.

The difficulties which Sulpiz encountered in arranging for the satisfactory reproduction of the plates in Germany eventually drove him, though with great reluctance, to entrust the work to craftsmen in Paris. He had in any case decided that there should be a French, as well as a German, edition of the *Domschrift*. And so in October 1820 we find him in Paris successfully concluding arrangements for the publication, but there were still to be many delays before the work actually appeared. He complains wearily to Goethe on 26 February 1822 of the birth-pangs which 'this elephantine monster' is causing him; and on 19 November of the same year, on sending Goethe some proof copies of the plates, he writes: 'You will no doubt be astonished at the magnificence of the production, but at the same time you will not be unmindful of the unending labour and sacrifices of every kind which it has cost your friend. In very truth I have had to pay dearly for having undertaken anything so great and perfect.'[2]

At long last, on 16 September 1823, Sulpiz is able to announce that all the hurdles have been surmounted and the first instalment has appeared. The work met with the reception which it deserved. The

---

[1] Cp. Helene Rosenau, op. cit., pp. 108-9.
[2] SB ii. 341.

Académie des Beaux-Arts greeted the splendid plates with enthusiasm, and in his own country the applause was universal.[1]

The *Domwerk* consists of 18 plates, which appeared in instalments between 1823 and 1831. They are on an enormous scale, and are extremely fine examples of their kind. The plates include views of the exterior and interior of the Cathedral, both as it was and as it would have been if completed. Of these the finest are Angelo Quaglio's view of the building from the South East, as it appeared in his day, and Moller's drawing of the vestibule, according to Sulpiz Boisserée's reconstruction— a superb vision of Gothic verticality. Apart from these general views there are cross-sections of parts of the building, ground plans, and details of stone carving and stained glass. Finally, for purposes of comparison, there are two plates with ground plans and side elevations of various other outstanding examples of Gothic architecture, including Salisbury and York.

Boisserée's reconstructions differ in only one important respect from the completed building as we have it today, and that is in his design for the central tower, a somewhat stocky octagonal structure, which would in fact have sorted ill with the slenderly tapering western spires.

The *Domschrift*, the accompanying text to the plates, which appeared at the same time as the first instalments of the *Domwerk*, is only a fragment of what Sulpiz had originally intended. For, as he explains in the preface, his aim was not only to investigate the origin and nature of Gothic architecture, but also to provide a history of medieval architecture from early Christian times to the beginning of the sixteenth century and to place it in the context of world architecture in general. Of this ambitious scheme only the first section—the history and description of Cologne Cathedral—was actually carried out, though even as late as 1842, the date of the second edition of the *Domschrift*, Sulpiz was still playing with the idea of completing the plan in a separate book.

The *Domschrift*, as we have it, is divided into three sections: a history of the cathedral, an explanation of the plates, and a description of the architecture. In the preface Sulpiz gives his reasons for choosing Cologne Cathedral as his grand exemplar for 'the Old Church Architecture mistakenly called Gothic'.[2] His first reason is that it is

---

[1] For a detailed account of Sulpiz Boisserée's visits to France and the production and reception of the *Domwerk* see Pierre Moisy, *Les Séjours en France de Sulpice Boisserée* (1820–5). (*Bibliothèque de la Société des Études Germaniques*, vol. x, Paris, 1956).

[2] Throughout the text of the *Domschrift* Boisserée uses the term 'Old Church Architecture' (alte Kirchenbaukunst) for Gothic, which at least has the merit of being

PLATE 6

Boisserée's Reconstruction of the Nave and Vestibule of Cologne Cathedral from
Ansichten, Risse und einzelne Theile des Doms von Köln.

one of the largest and most perfect buildings of its kind, even though it is incomplete; and the second, and more important, is that, unlike almost all other examples of Gothic architecture, which were built at different times and in varying styles, Cologne is the homogeneous expression of one master mind. 'Thus from what exists and from what was planned, a whole of the highest unity and perfection, as it proceeded from the mind of the architect, can be reconstructed.'[1]

We need not concern ourselves with Sulpiz's first section, a history of the cathedral, which is at the same time a scholarly and well-written history of the city of Cologne throughout the medieval period. But the last section, the description of the cathedral as a work of architecture, is very much our concern, for this constitutes one of the most important literary documents of the Gothic Revival in Germany, both on account of what it says and on account of the unique prestige of its author in this field. It is divided into a description of the interior (including stone carving, glass work, sculpture and painting), of the uncompleted parts of the building (crossing, nave, vestibule), and of the exterior. This is followed by a section on the main characteristics of Gothic architecture and by a final section on the problem of completing the structure.

Sulpiz opens his description of the exterior with a tribute to his literary forerunners:

Men of talent, like Georg Forster and others, have appropriately compared the interior of lofty churches built in the pointed style with the vaulted shades of the primeval forest . . . Friedrich Schlegel was reminded by the exterior of Cologne Cathedral of a gigantic piece of crystallisation, and Goethe, enraptured by the sight of the tower of Strasbourg Minster, compared it with a loftily sublime far-spread tree of God, which with its thousand branches, twigs and leaves proclaims to the world around the glory of the Lord its Master.[2]

Goethe, Forster, Schlegel, and now Boisserée, these are the landmarks in the literary background of the Gothic Revival in Germany.

Sulpiz then broaches a theme to which he recurs again and again in the course of his analysis of the architecture of the cathedral: the resemblance, indeed the indentity, between the underlying laws of Gothic architecture and those of organic nature. In this, as he himself

---

uncontroversial. Strangely enough, in the second edition, published in 1842, he reverts to the term so beloved of the Romantic medievalists, 'Old-German Architecture' (altdeutsche Architectur), whereas in his *Denkmale der Baukunst vom 7ten bis zum 13ten Jahrhundert am Nieder-Rhein* (1833) he speaks, like Goethe, simply of 'German Architecture' (deutsche Baukunst).

[1] *Domschrift*, p. i.   [2] Ibid. p. 33.

remarks, he is following in the footsteps of Schlegel's *Reisebriefe* and Goethe's morphological writings:

These comparisons are based not only on the similarity of the outward forms, but, as Goethe and Schlegel note, to an even greater extent on the correspondence with the organic processes of the above-mentioned natural phenomena. For the distinguishing feature of the Old Church Architecture is that rich complexity which arises from the infinite repetition and trans-mogrification of a few basic forms, that consistent and as it were autonomous articulation which as in the products of nature seems to multiply itself *ad infinitum*.[1]

When describing the towers and gables of the cathedral Sulpiz compares them to poplars and cypresses, whose branches with one accord strive upwards to the heavens. In this vertical emphasis of the whole and all the parts, together with the principle of the constant repetition of the whole in all the details, Sulpiz sees the essence of Gothic and the source of its inspiring effect upon the beholder. The basic form of the whole building, he explains, is an isosceles triangle or pyramid, and this form is repeated in a thousand different ways throughout the cathedral.

But of course the most obvious manifestation of the analogy between Gothic forms and natural phenomena is to be seen in the actual imitation of plant forms: in the roses, trefoils, vines and acorns, in the buds, leaves and tendrils, which trail over the capitals, windows, screens, pinnacles, gables and portals of the Gothic church. 'Through this abundance of foliage and flower-like ornaments, which we observe in all the great examples of this architecture in its heyday, an outward and visible form was given to the inward affinity with the processes of plant formation.'[2]

Though the imitation of natural forms has always been a favourite embellishment of art, in Gothic architecture this imitation is such an intimate part of the whole that it can no longer be called 'decoration' in the usual sense of the word, for it makes the impression not of something imposed from without, but of something which 'has sprouted forth from within'.[3] This, in Sulpiz's view, has misled some to see the origin of this style in the sacred groves of the ancient Teutons, a theory which cannot hold water for the simple reason that the early Christian (i.e. Romanesque) architecture of Germany and other Nordic countries shows not the faintest trace of such an imitation.

Sulpiz, like Schlegel and Büsching before him, finds the explanation

[1] Ibid. pp. 33–34.   [2] Ibid. p. 41.   [3] loc. cit.

of what he calls the 'vegetable' character of Gothic in 'the deep feeling for nature which has always distinguished the Germanic peoples, and which finds such vivid and charming expression in thirteenth century poetry in the form of a joyous, indeed ebullient veneration of spring, as well as in many still partly extant popular customs'.[1] Another expression of this same feeling is to be seen in the springlike landscapes of the German primitives.

The secret of Gothic lies in the union of this 'vegetable' character with the geometrical system of the basic pyramid and its polygonal derivations. It only needed the magic touch of an architect of genius to breathe life into these diverse elements in order to create such a harmonious whole as Cologne Cathedral.

Apart from the excellence of the plates, what is most to be admired in the *Domwerk* is the skill and accuracy of Sulpiz's reconstructions of the missing parts of the cathedral and the incisiveness of the accompanying text. His was by far the most thorough and scholarly study of a Gothic building that had yet appeared in Germany. A modern authority on the cathedral sums up his significance as follows: 'Thus Sulpiz is not only the champion of the project for completing the cathedral, but also the founder of the scholarly tradition of investigation as applied to the history of the building. Even if some of his conclusions were already outdated by his contemporaries, nevertheless his keen-sighted intuition was able to discern the true historical significance and aesthetic quality of the cathedral.'[2] And so accurate were his reconstructions that the actual completion of the edifice 'seemed to be little more than a question of finance and technical skill'.[3]

Simultaneously with the production of the *Domwerk* Sulpiz had begun to issue lithographic reproductions of his great collection of German and Netherlandish primitives. In 1819 the collection had been moved from Heidelberg to Stuttgart, where it enjoyed the benevolent patronage of the King of Württemberg. Under the devoted care of the brothers Boisserée and Bertram (the Three Kings of Cologne, as Goethe called them) the collection had been growing steadily in size and importance. In Stuttgart it could be housed in more favourable conditions and made more accessible to visitors.[4] For with the growth

[1] loc. cit.   [2] Rosenau, op. cit. p. 179.   [3] Ibid. p. 168.

[4] A letter of Bertram's to Sulpiz (13 July 1819; SB i. 366–7), soon after the move to Stuttgart, provides evidence of the growing popularity of German medieval art with the public at large. Some days as many as 100 or even 150 persons visted the collection, and the Stuttgart innkeepers rejoiced at the increase in the tourist trade which it occasioned.

of the collection had gone an increasing desire on the part of the owners to render this Newfoundland of art available to the German people, who were its rightful heirs. One important step in this direction was the decision to issue lithographed reproductions of a generous selection of the pictures.

Die Sammlung Alt- Nieder- und Ober-Deutschen Gemälde der Boisserée und Bertram is on as ambitious a scale as the *Domwerk*. For the reproductions Sulpiz employed one of the most accomplished lithographers of the day, Johann Nepomuk Strixner, a pupil of Senefelder, who had invented the lithographic process in 1796. Strixner had been responsible for the reproduction of the Dürer Prayer Book, which had so delighted Goethe, and he was at this time engaged on the immense task of lithographing the paintings from the Bavarian royal collections at Schleissheim and Munich, a task which he was nevertheless willing to interrupt in order to put himself at the disposal of the Boisserées. He had been in Stuttgart working on the collection since October 1820, and the first plates were ready in 1821. The undertaking proceeded much more expeditiously than the *Domwerk*, and by 1831 one hundred and fourteen plates had appeared. The lithographs are on a very large scale and of high quality. Through this work, for the first time, artloving Germans had the chance to become acquainted with the artistic heritage of their own medieval past. Through it the fame of the Boisserée Collection was spread far beyond the confines of Germany.

After the *Domwerk* Sulpiz Boisserée's most important contribution to the study of medieval architecture in Germany was his work on the Romanesque churches of the Rhineland, entitled *Denkmale der Baukunst vom 7ten bis zun 13ten Jahrhundert am Nieder-Rhein* (Munich, 1833). Like its predecessor this undertaking had occupied a large portion of its author's life span. Its beginnings went back almost as far as the origins of the *Domwerk*. At the time he started to make drawings and measurements of the most important Romanesque buildings doomed to destruction as a result of the secularization policy, and later he extended this to cover the most notable examples of those which survived.

This work is smaller in scale than the *Domwerk* (folio, but not large folio), and consists of seventy-two lithographed plates with descriptive text on each of the buildings illustrated. The greater part of the book deals with the Romanesque churches of Cologne, but it also includes such outstanding examples of Rhenish Romanesque as Maria Laach, Andernach, Bonn, and Sinzig, as well as dwelling houses in Cologne from the Romanesque period. The drawings are by Domenico Quaglio, Maximilian Fuchs and others.

Boisserée's *Denkmale* was the first large scale work that appeared in Germany to be devoted exclusively to the subject of Romanesque architecture. As we have seen, it was comparatively late in the history of the Gothic Revival before it was even realized that there were two widely differing styles of medieval architecture. Friedrich Schlegel in his *Reisebriefe* was the first to make the point clear and to attempt a characterization of the Romanesque style. There can be little doubt that Schlegel's insights in this matter were the result of joint explorations and discussions of the Romanesque churches of Cologne with the brothers Boisserée. Sulpiz's *Denkmale* is a measure of the distance covered since those days in understanding of the style.

According to the preface, his main aim is to trace the most important changes which took place in the Romanesque period and so to make intelligible the transition to 'German' architecture. But in fact there is no consideration of such general questions in the text, which consists of a detailed study, mainly historical, of the buildings illustrated. In this it differs fundamentally from the *Domschrift*.

In the course of the book Sulpiz pays tribute to the work of an Englishman, the Reverend William Whewell, at that time Professor of Mineralogy at Cambridge, later to become Professor of Moral Philosophy and Master of Trinity. Among Whewell's innumerable interests was that of German medieval architecture. He visited the country in pursuit of this hobby in 1829 and published the results in a slender volume entitled *Architectural Notes on German Churches, with Remarks on the Origin of Gothic Architecture* (Cambridge, 1830). This seems to have been the first book to appear in England on the subject of German medieval architecture, the first sign of reciprocity between the Gothic Revival in the two countries. The subject evidently aroused interest here, for by 1842 three editions of the work had appeared. The book is mainly concerned with German Romanesque and Transitional churches. (Incidentally, the *O.E.D.* lists it as one of the first books to use the work 'Romanesque' as an architectural term). Whewell finds the German churches specially useful to him in his search for the origin of the Gothic style. The answer is to be found, he believes, in the system of ribbed vaulting and the pointed arches to which it gives rise, which in their turn are reproduced throughout the rest of the building.

Sulpiz approves of Whewell's theory, and maintains that he has come to more or less the same conclusions by a different route. Other authorities with whom, he says, he agrees on the whole are Milner in England, de Caumont in Normandy, Rumohr in Italy and Moller in Germany, all of whom are at one in believing that the pointed arch style developed gradually and so to speak organically, and not through imitation of Arabian or any other foreign models.

Whewell, incidentally, is loud in praise of the achievement of the German engravers. Moller's *Denkmäler* 'contains excellent specimens of every style of German buildings, and offers additional interest and beauty in each new number: Mr. Müller's work on Oppenheim is of almost unequalled splendour of execution: Dr. Boisserée's magnificent engravings of the Cathedral at Cologne are already known and admired in this country.'[1]

It is not necessary to pursue this account of the pictorial revival of German medieval architecture beyond the achievements of Sulpiz Boisserée. Moller and Sulpiz between them had set a fashion which other Gothic enthusiasts were quick to follow. In the thirties and forties the craze reached ever greater dimensions, and by the middle of the century few Romanesque or Gothic buildings of any consequence remained unpictured. None of these ventures, however, attained in artistic excellence and historical importance to the level of the Boisserée productions.[2]

---

[1] Whewell, op. cit., p. xxix.
[2] For the sake of completeness there should be added to the list of Boisserée's works his paper on the description of the Temple of the Grail in the so-called *Younger Titurel*, in which he attempts to reconstruct the temple in the High Gothic forms of Freiburg and Cologne: 'Ueber die Beschreibung des Tempels des heiligen Grales in dem Heldengedicht: Titurel Kap. III.' *Abhandlungen der philosophisch-philologischen Classe der Königlich Bayerischen Akademie der Wissenschaften* (Munich, 1835), i. 307–92.

PART SIX

EPILOGUE

THE COMPLETION OF
COLOGNE CATHEDRAL

WITH the appearance of Sulpiz Boisserée's monumental works the long story of the rehabilitation of German medieval architecture is virtually completed. Gothic has now grown respectable, and more than respectable. It is fast becoming the object of an enthusiasm almost as uncritical as the indifference and contempt to which it had so long been subjected—an enthusiasm, moreover, which was coloured by elements both patriotic and religious that gave it a significance beyond the purely architectural.

The final seal may be said to have been set on this revolution of taste by the decision to complete the stupendous torso of Cologne Cathedral. It only remains for us to recount the main stages in this ultimate apotheosis of the Gothic Revival in Germany.

The leading figure in this story, it is hardly necessary to state, was Sulpiz Boisserée. Exactly when he first conceived the idea of translating his paper reconstructions into stone and mortar it is impossible to say. One can only assume that the thought had been at the back of his mind form the start, though he does not say so in his autobiographical fragment, and there are no references to the project in his letters and diaries until a comparatively late date. No doubt the idea developed gradually, and was reinforced by the warm reception accorded to his drawings of the Cathedral.

The project was sufficiently daunting in all conscience. There was no parallel in any country at that time for a Gothic undertaking on such a scale. Milan and Orleans are in a different category. In both these cases an original plan had been gradually modified throughout the centuries to suit the tastes and technical possibilities of the day. In Cologne, on the other hand, it was a question of realizing with as little modification as possible the original plan of the medieval architects. In the long interval since the final cessation of work on the building in the sixteenth century the secret of Gothic construction had been lost. Most important of all: where was to be found the army of skilled craftsmen necessary to carry out this delicate and complex task?

Although Sulpiz Boisserée claimed encouragingly that more than half of the cathedral was already in being, there still remained a vast task to be accomplished. Apart from the completion of the stupendously lofty western towers (one of which had only reached the second storey, while the other was hardly begun) there was the greater part of the space intervening between these towers and the choir— i.e. the vestibule, nave and transepts—still to be built.

Both Georg Forster and Friedrich Schlegel had lamented the unfinished state of the cathedral, but the first person to make a definite public appeal for its completion was Joseph Görres in his *Rheinischer Merkur* (20 November 1814). Görres's article was evoked by the agitation for the erection of national monuments to celebrate the liberation of the fatherland from the Napoleonic yoke. In his view the most appropriate monument to Germany's triumph would be the completion of Cologne Cathedral. For Görres the cathedral is primarily a peg on which to hang his patriotic phantasies. Thus the unfinished torso is a perpetual reproach to the nation which has lacked the faith and strength and unity to complete the work of the medieval master. He imagines the workmen as they dispersed for the last time, pronouncing a curse on the faithless generations: 'Long shall Germany live in shame and humiliation, a prey to inner conflict and alien arrogance, until her people return to the ideals from which they were seduced by selfish ambition, and until true religion and loyalty, unity of purpose and self-denial shall again render them capable of erecting such buildings as this, which in their degenerate state they now abandon.'[1] Let the intervening centuries vanish as if they had never been, and let us carry on where our medieval forebears left off. In its state of ruinous incompletion the cathedral is a fitting symbol of Germany since the Reformation; so let it now become a symbol of the new Reich which we are setting out to build.

It will be seen that architectural considerations play no part in Görres's appeal. He is not concerned with the cathedral as an example of the Gothic style, but as a symbol of German destiny. In this he set the tone for much of what was to be said and written on the subject in the ensuing decades.

Görres remained a faithful friend of the cathedral project. When Boisserée's *Domwerk* at last appeared he greeted it with the warmest eulogy in the *Heidelberger Jahrbücher* (No. 60, 1824), saluting it as a worthy memorial of the monument it celebrated: 'If Meister Gerhard, or whoever was the creator of this wondrous structure, were to see this admirable counterfeit, he would rejoice in his innermost soul and salute the author with the customary greeting of his craft as

---

[1] Görres, *Der Dom von Köln und das Münster von Strasburg* (Regensburg, 1842), pp. 2–3.

soulmate and friend. That is the highest praise we can bestow upon our friend and countryman for what he has achieved.'[1]

The *Domwerk* too, and its long history, is seen by Görres in relation to the spirit of the age. Begun in Germany's darkest hour it was completed under very different auspices. Though all is by no means well in the national sphere, at least a new spirit has begun to stir. Whereas only twenty years back the reproduction of so thoroughly teutonic a work ('eines so gründlich tüdesken Werkes') would have been met with doubt or at the most with condescending tolerance, now the renewed interest in the German past and the religious revival ensure it a warm welcome.

The appeal by Goethe in the *Kunst und Alterthum* essay, to which we have already referred, is of course quite without the patriotic note of Görres. Indeed it is not so much an appeal as a suggestion, and one couched in very qualified terms. In any case one cannot help having the impression that it was inserted mainly in order to please Sulpiz Boisserée, introduced as it is in immediate connection with Goethe's tribute to his work.

Sulpiz Boisserée's efforts on behalf of Cologne Cathedral were by no means confined to the *Domwerk*. It is, as we have said, not clear exactly when he decided to devote himself to the project for continuing and completing the construction of the building. In any case, as Goethe emphasized, the first and pressing task was not completion, but preservation, for if something were not done, and done quickly, there would be nothing left to complete. The cathedral had been deprived of virtually all its financial resources in consequence of the secularization decrees of 1803. Nor was the city council, which was itself in grave financial difficulties, in a position to make any contribution to the upkeep of the structure. Not even the most urgent repairs to roofs and gutters could be undertaken, and the noble torso was in serious danger of becoming a ruin. At last in 1807 the municipal authorities were persuaded to intervene on a small scale in order to stave off immediate collapse.

This state of affairs was naturally a source of the direst distress and concern to Sulpiz Boisserée, and he lost no opportunity of trying to win support for the cause of the cathedral. In August 1811 Napoleon's mother passed through Cologne on her way to visit her son King Jerome in Cassel, and Sulpiz was able to show her his portfolio in the Chapter House of the Cathedral. She expressed regret that the building had never been completed, to which Sulpiz tactfully replied, to her

[1] Ibid. p. 5.

great delight: 'Il ne faut qu'un ordre de sa Majesté, votre fils, pour l'achever.'[1] Two months later he is displaying his drawings to the Empress Marie Louise, who was accompanying Napoleon on a visit to the city, and who graciously accepted the dedication of the plates. On this occasion he persuaded the municipal authorities to petition the Emperor for an annual subsidy of 40,000 francs for the restoration of the cathedral fabric. But the suggestion was not accepted, and until the liberation of the city from French rule in 1814 nothing but the most urgent repairs to the roof could be taken in hand. Throughout these years, as is clear from his correspondence, Sulpiz became more and more the acknowledged authority on all matters pertaining to the cathedral, and was regularly consulted by those bodies, municipal or ecclesiastical, who were concerned with the structure.

When after the battle of Leipzig the sovereigns and statesmen of the Allies assembled in Frankfurt to decide on what to do next, Sulpiz promptly repaired thither with his portfolio, in order to lose no opportunity of pressing the cause of Cologne and its cathedral upon the mighty of the earth. Metternich, Stein, Gneisenau, Lord Aberdeen, the Emperor of Austria and the Crown Prince of Prussia all showed interest in his aims and ideals. In the following summer, now the Rhine provinces had been freed and their future was at stake, Sulpiz was again in Cologne, still busily displaying his drawings to all who might have the power or disposition to forward the cause.

Of these the most important was the Crown Prince of Prussia, who paid a visit to the city in July 1814. The later Frederick William IV, 'the Romantic on the throne of Prussia', was already at the age of nineteen susceptible to the lures of Romantic medievalism, and it was from this encounter between Sulpiz Boisserée and his future sovereign that the practical possibility—as distinct from the vague dream—of the completion of Cologne Cathedral may properly be dated. Sulpiz has given a vivid account of the occasion in a letter to his brother Melchior. He was deputed to conduct the Prince and his suite over the building. The young man was delighted with what he saw: 'He wanted to have the cathedral completed straightaway, and when we walked round the choir his enthusiasm knew no bounds. His companions freely confessed that nothing they had seen in France, the Netherlands or England came up to this.'[2] Sulpiz was assured that as soon as Prussia took over the Rhineland the cathedral would be thoroughly restored and all the surrounding houses would be removed. He also secured a promise that the military governor would immediately

<hr>

[1] SB i. 150.   [2] Ibid. p. 216.

put a stop to the destruction of all buildings of historical or artistic value in the city. Frederick William was to remain a true friend and supporter of Sulpiz's project to the end.

Despite this auspicious beginning nothing further seems to have been done in the matter for the next two years. The first decisive step was taken in 1816, when the King, Frederick William III, commissioned Schinkel to make a thorough enquiry into the state of the cathedral and to report back his findings to the Prussian government. Schinkel was frankly horrified at what he saw. The roof was in an appalling state of disrepair, the rainwater was choked in the gutters and seeping through to the interior, the buttresses were cracked and crumbling, the stone overgrown with moss. At any moment a major disaster might occur.

It would not have been surprising if Schinkel had decided that in these circumstances it would be a waste of time and money to attempt any further rescue operations with the venerable torso, but instead he advocated in the most definite terms that the building should not only be repaired and restored, but that it should be continued and completed—and this both for technical and patriotic reasons. On the same day as he finished his report to the Berlin authorities Schinkel wrote to Sulpiz Boisserée to invite his cooperation in the project, 'since no one else has penetrated so deeply into the inmost secrets of this artistic monument as yourself'.[1] Despite the frustration of Schinkel's hope that the responsible ministry in Berlin would appoint Sulpiz as official adviser on all matters relating to the cathedral, the latter was to remain behind the scenes the expert mentor not only of Schinkel, but of all those who were to be concerned in the preservation, restoration and completion of the structure in the next decades.

Schinkel's authoritative call for the completion of the cathedral was not to be answered for many years to come. Indeed it was several years before even the most necessary repairs to the existing fabric could be undertaken. The best that Schinkel could secure, with the help of the ever enthusiastic Crown Prince, was an order from the King that the torso should be preserved, though in the meantime no steps were taken towards this end. A new impulse was given to the whole matter by the restoration of the Archbishopric of Cologne in 1821 after the long interruption of the Napoleonic wars and their aftermath, and finally in 1823 the task of preservation was begun— slowly at first, but with gathering momentum as time went on.

The best part of twenty years was to go by before the work of

[1] Ibid. p. 317.

20

repairing the existing edifice was completed. Throughout this period the final direction of the whole enterprise was in the hands of Schinkel. For the first half of this period the architect in actual charge of the work was Friedrich Ahlert, an official of the Cologne administration who had little understanding of the spirit of the medieval builders. After Ahlert's death in 1833 Schinkel appointed one of his most gifted pupils, Ernest Friedrich Zwirner. From now on until his death in 1861 Zwirner was responsible for the progress of the work, and his name more than that of any other man is indissolubly linked with the completion of the building as we have it today. Zwirner cut loose from the neo-classicist spirit which underlay the Gothic work of his master Schinkel no less than of his predecessor Ahlert. He was in fact a Gothic purist—one of the first of a long line—whose aim it was to carry out the work of restoration as far as possible in the spirit and letter of the medieval builders.

In order to achieve this goal Zwirner expended endless energy and patience in training up a school of masons and other craftsmen in the conscientious imitation of medieval workmanship down to the smallest details of ornamentation. He naturally felt unwilling that all this expert skill should be disbanded and lost. The nearer the work of restoration approached completion, the more ardent grew Zwirner's desire to undertake, or at least to initiate, the stupendous task of continuing the work until the mighty fragment was completed. His first initiative in this direction was to enlist the aid of the Crown Prince, who had never forgotten the impression made on him by the cathedral on his first visit in 1814, and who promised to do all in his power to further the project.

The decisive moment had arrived. Either the carefully trained masons and other workmen must be dismissed and the scaffolding dismantled, or else the lapse of three centuries must be made good at last. Many factors combined to ensure that the latter alternative prevailed. In the first place there was a purely political factor: namely, the desire of the Prussian authorities to do something to appease the population of Cologne and the Rhineland, whose resentment at Prussian policy had been stirred to fever point by the arrest of the Archbishop of Cologne in November 1837. The proposal to complete the cathedral came as a welcome means of distracting the minds of the population from their grievances. The authorities in Berlin were therefore entirely prepared to give this laudable and harmless project their unqualified support, and on 12 January 1842 King Frederick William IV issued the order for the work to begin.

Secondly, and more important, there was the patriotic factor. Just as the medieval torso in its fragmentary condition had often been taken as a symbol of the parlous state of Germany in the Napoleonic era, so now the movement for the completion of the cathedral served in the manner of Görres's appeal as a symbol of the new spirit of German unity active since the War of Liberation—as a spiritual equivalent, so to speak, of the *Zollverein*. This aspect of the matter far outweighed all others. In the words of Leonard Ennen, the historian of Cologne Cathedral, the impetus behind the movement was less the desire to complete the mother church of the diocese than 'to erect a monument which should be the pride of the German nation, the symbol of German unity, strength and self-sacrifice . . . It was a question of completing the greatest and most inspired creation of German architecture, and in this way of affording a flattering gratification to German pride and of showing to the world what the German people are capable of, when they dedicate their strength and enthusiasm to a lofty ideal.'[1] Or, as a contemporary writer put it more aggressively: 'The Cathedral is the greatest of Germany's bulwarks, which she will either guard or perish, and which will only fall when the blood of the last Teuton has mingled with the waves of Father Rhine.'[2]

And thirdly there was the architectural or stylistic factor. By now the Gothic cause had completely triumphed. What up to the 1820's had been the hobby of a few antiquarians and other dedicated spirits had now found general acceptance. The success of the cathedral restoration had itself contributed not a little to this process. It was natural that Gothic enthusiasts should see the culmination of their ambitions in the scheme for completing the greatest of Germany's Gothic monuments. Moreover, since it was still accepted that Gothic was the specifically German style, this architectural factor was intimately bound up with the patriotic aspect of the campaign.

It was also bound up with the religious aspect. For Gothic was not only the specifically German style, it was also the specifically Christian style. What Heinse had boldly asserted in the 1780's had now become a commonplace. Despite a few dissidents like Gottfried Semper and Leo von Klenze, it was generally recognized that the appropriate style for the Christian church was Gothic and not Classical,

[1] Ennen, *Der Dom zu Köln von seinem Beginne bis zu seiner Vollendung* (Cologne, 1880), pp. 128–9.
[2] Anon., *Der Kölner Dom und Deutschlands Einheit* (Magdeburg, 1842). Quoted in Paul Clemen, *Der Dom zu Köln* (Düsseldorf, 1937), pp. 70–71.

unfortunately associated as the latter was with the heathen temple. The completion of Cologne Cathedral was among other things an impressive reminder of this fact.

Finally, there was the ecclesiastical factor. Naturally the prospect of completing what would become the greatest Catholic edifice in Germany was welcomed enthusiastically by the Catholic population, not only of the Rhineland, but of the whole country. It was a symbol, not only of German strength and German unity, but of the growing power and prestige of German Catholicism. Paradoxically, it also served in some quarters as a symbol of reconcilliation between the two creeds. It was this aspect of the matter which appealed especially to Frederick William. Catholics and Protestants contributed in equal measure to the cause, and the unstinted support of a Protestant King and a Protestant State alone made possible the gigantic enterprise.

Many were the currents, then, which united to create a wave of nation-wide enthusiasm for the project. This enthusiasm found practical expression in the formation of *Dombauvereine*, prototypes of the modern 'Friends of the Cathedrals' organizations, which were primarily concerned with collecting voluntary contributions for the scheme. The central *Dombauverein* in Cologne was constituted in February 1842, with Heinrich von Wittgenstein as President and August Reichensperger as Secretary. Honorary members included Sulpiz Boisserée and Franz Liszt. The former Crown Prince, who had succeeded his father as King Frederick William IV in 1840, gave it his warmest support and agreed to become its patron, at the same time promising generous financial aid. But the enthusiasm was not confined to Cologne; it transcended both political and confessional frontiers, and the central *Verein* was soon joined by subsidiary organizations all over the country and abroad.

The first important task of the *Dombauverein* was to organize the ceremony of the laying of the foundation stone to the cathedral extension. The propinquity of this event evoked three publications by old protagonists of the project—Zwirner, Boisserée and Görres. Zwirner's contribution—*Vergangenheit und Zukunft des Kölner Dombaues* (Cologne and Aachen, 1842)—consisted of engravings of the cathedral (very inferior in quality to Boisserée's) with an introduction, in which he gives a brief account of the architecture and history of the building, concluding with a review of the work of restoration up to the time of writing. He admits that the task of continuing and completing the work of the medieval builders is a colossal undertaking, from every point of view including the financial, but he sees ground for encouragement in three factors: first, the increased interest in artistic monuments among the population as a whole; secondly, the religious appeal; and, thirdly, the patriotic appeal.

Sulpiz Boisserée's contribution to the occasion took the form of an enlarged and revised edition of the *Domschrift*, dedicated appropriately to Frederick William IV. This second edition differs very considerably from its predecessor of 1823. In the first place it is reduced in size from giant folio to a handy quarto, in keeping with its more popular purpose. It also includes five engravings—four in reduced scale from the *Domwerk* and one new plate of the cathedral from the south east—for those who cannot afford the larger tome. The author has added two long sections on the work of restoration since 1823 and on the projected completion of the cathedral.

In his preface Sulpiz looks back on the long history and the many vicissitudes of his great project: on its modest beginnings thirty-four years before; on the constant help and encouragement of Melchior and Bertram, and of men like Wallraf, Reinhard, Goethe and Cotta; on the War of Liberation and the enthusiasm for all patriotic endeavours, to which it gave rise; on the discovery of the medieval plans; on the long-delayed publication and favourable reception of the *Domwerk;* and on the work of restoring the existing edifice. 'And now at last in my old age my youthful dream is being realized; the cathedral project is being supported with ardour and magnanimity by a wise and mighty sovereign, and throughout the country there is evident a desire to join actively in furthering a cause common to the whole German fatherland.'[1] After a passing tribute to those in Germany, England, France and Italy, who by their writings and engravings had helped towards an understanding of medieval architecture, he closes his preface with a vigorous protest against those who persist in calling Old-German Architecture 'Gothic', despite the fact that Germany possesses the greatest and most perfect examples of this architecture, and that it was given the name 'German' by both Italians and Spaniards in the past.

Sulpiz is optimistic about the future. Both financially and technically the project seems assured. Nor is there any doubt as to the manner in which the work should be carried out. The King in his wisdom has decreed that the Cathedral shall be completed in strict accordance with the medieval plan, and the *Dombauvereine* have adopted this principle in their statutes. Sulpiz is in full agreement with this purism: 'All objects in an alien style must be removed and replaced by others

[1] *Geschichte und Beschreibung des Doms von Köln* (2nd ed., Munich, 1842), p. vii.

in keeping with the character of the cathedral.'[1] In other words, all trace of Renaissance, Baroque or Neo-classical must be obliterated in favour of the purest Gothic. (Fortunately Sulpiz's advice in this respect was not rigidly followed.)

Finally, he puts forward the suggestion that the walls of the aisles and vestibule should be reserved for the monuments of those who have deserved well of their country. The completed cathedral would thus serve *inter alia* as a kind of national Valhalla, a symbol of the united fatherland.

A symbol of the united fatherland, not of the Catholic revival, nor of the revival of medieval architecture. A change has come over Sulpiz's attitude which is typical of the Gothic Revival in Germany altogether. More and more it has become identified with the patriotic movement for a united Germany, for a return to the real or imagined unity of the medieval Empire in Novalis's sense, including a unity of creeds. Again and again a parallel is drawn between the ancient torso and the divisions of Reformation Germany on the one hand, and between the cathedral project and the national and confessional unity of which it is a symbol on the other.

The third publication we have to consider came from that stout advocate of the cathedral project, Joseph Görres. On the eve of the foundation stone ceremony he issued a pamphlet entitled *Der Dom von Köln und das Münster von Strasburg*, the proceeds of which were to be devoted to the building fund. The pamphlet begins with reprints of Görres's original appeal in the *Rheinischer Merkur* and of his review of Boisserée's *Domwerk* in the *Heidelberger Jahrbücher*.

Primarily the pamphlet is an appeal for support, now the great project, so long mooted, so much discussed, so often postponed, is at last to be begun and the dream of centuries to be realized. The tone and theme remain the same as in the original appeal. Görres calls for support 'in order that the vows of our forefathers may truly be fulfilled and the cathedral become in very truth a monument of liberation: liberation not only from foreign oppression, but also from our own delusions, prejudices and contentions which alone have brought this oppression upon us'.[2]

Görres, as convinced and ardent Catholic, sees the surest hope for the successful conclusion of the work in the fact that it is being undertaken not as a monument to a dead faith, but to a living and revivified one. The congregation of the faithful awaits impatiently the completion of the task. To Görres, then, the cathedral project is in part at

---

[1] Ibid. p. 91.   [2] Görres, op. cit., p. 10.

least the visible symbol of a Catholic revival in Germany and his words are addressed primarily to his fellow Catholics.

Görres takes the two cathedrals as examples of two types of medieval architecture. On the one hand there is Cologne, the harmonious expression of one mind and one age; on the other, Strasbourg, built in many styles and in many ages. Here the harmony, if it does exist, consists not in the unity of one style, but in the succession of styles.

The first type, it must be admitted, is the highest: 'For every work of art of this kind is a self-sufficient entity, which contains within itself a deep seminal core, from which it must develop in all its members according to a pre-ordained, firmly established and immutable law, just as the human being develops from the seminal core of his personality.' Görres proceeds Goethe-wise to expand the comparison with the phenomena of nature: 'Throughout her realms nature takes the same paths. Every plant is produced from the seed according to its own law; stem, twigs and branches, number and form and position of the leaves, the flower itself—all are determined by the law which lies dormant in the seed and which develops in the process of growth.'[1]

Such is Cologne with its perfect unity of style, the product of one mind and of one age. And by a happy chance this age happens to be the best of all ages, the Middle Age, when nobility, dignity and sublimity reigned supreme. 'Therefore Boisserée was quite right in proclaiming Cologne Cathedral to be the criterion of "German" architecture altogether.'[2]

With Strasbourg[3] it is a different matter. Görres sees the minster as a repository of the changing phases of German history—Carolingian, Ottonian, Salian, Hohenstaufen, Habsburg. These glorious ages were succeeded by the sterile and destructive epoch of the Reformation and by the subsequent centuries of 'barbarian taste', 'tasteless ignorance' and the 'barbarisms of modern gallicisms', the pitiful traces in fact of an epoch blind to all that is noble and great. Here then the tables are turned indeed; the whirligig of taste has come full circle and the anti-Goths are hoist with their own petard. It is now not Gothic, but the prevailing modes of the seventeenth and eighteenth centuries, which are tasteless and trivial, and which pollute by their propinquity the noble dignity of Gothic.

Görres turns from the distinction between Cologne and Strasbourg

[1] Ibid. pp. 17–18. [2] Ibid., p. 59.
[3] The section on Strasbourg is a product of Görres's years of exile in that city and is reprinted from articles in the *Heidelberger Jahrbücher* for 1824.

to the origin and nature of the Gothic style itself. His views on these matters are strongly coloured by his own ardent German nationalism. He is indeed one of the most thorough-going of Gothic chauvinists. Thus he has no doubts whatever about the German nature and origin of the style, and adopts as a matter of course the term 'German' architecture. To him the Gothic cathedrals are the boundary stones of the Germanic spirit and its far-flung empire. Gothic is the logical outcome of the metaphysical yearnings of the German soul, which could not find satisfactory expression in the circumscribed language of Romanesque. In its self-contained perfection the circle (or rather semi-circle, for here it is a question of the rounded arch) may be all very well for harmonious (i.e. Latin) natures, but it imposes an intolerable restraint on the restless and aspiring genius of the German soul. Similarly the lack of inner logic, of organic unity, in Romanesque architecture is an offence to Germanic sensibility.

From all this the Germans were saved by the discovery and exploitation of the pointed arch. For the pointed arch and its combination with the clustered column opened the way to an architecture which possessed both the organic logic of a work of nature and the sublimity and profundity of a work of metaphysics—an architecture in fact which was calculated to satisfy the deepest yearnings of the German soul.

Görres has no difficulty in demonstrating that Gothic is an essentially German invention. It flourished chiefly in three districts: the Lower Rhine, North Western France and Southern England. In all these regions the original Celtic inhabitants were conquered by invading Germanic tribes, though it was only in the first that they were completely ousted by the invaders. To which of the three districts, then, belongs the honour of the invention of Gothic? The answer to this is supplied by the English, who themselves designated the new style as 'German'. This surprising statement is based on the quotation from Thomas Stubbs's *Chronicle of the Archbishops of York* to which we have already referred.

When Görres proceeds to examine more closely which part of Germany was responsible for this feat, he decides for that region 'where the Reich and its entire constitution first originated and developed in a purely Germanic style, and from where it then spread to the whole of the West'—namely, the territory of the Franks on the Middle and Lower Rhine. And of this region the central point, the cradle and focus of Gothic architecture, is Cologne—'the German Rome'. From this point, as from Byzantium and Rome of old, the new architecture radiated outwards in all directions. It found fertile soil awaiting it, for the ancient empire of the Germanic tribes had left its traces everywhere. Northern France, not unmindful of its Carolingian past, was the first to embrace the new German architecture; and of this region there excelled especially the province of Normandy, which doubly Teutonic through its Frankish and Norman admixtures had developed a race of inhabitants peculiarly gifted in the artistic sphere. They transported the new Germanic art to England, where it combined with the old Germanic spirit of the natives to produce the Gothic cathedrals which embellish the land.

It may well seem astonishing that anyone of Görres's reputation and intelligence should be capable at this late date of writing so much unmitigated twaddle. After all this was composed in 1842, a year after Franz Mertens[1] had established the fact that of all national claims to the invention of Gothic the French alone was valid, and almost twenty years after Sulpiz Boisserée had brought a more scholarly and reasonable note into the discussion of the subject.

Görres's book provides an appropriate coda to this study of the literary background of the Gothic Revival in Germany. It recapitulates themes which we have heard repeatedly in the course of our researches. Nor is this surprising, for it is mainly based on Sulpiz Boisserée's *Domschrift*, from which it sets out and to which it frequently returns; but there are also numerous echoes of Friedrich Schlegel and even of *Von Deutscher Baukunst*. In the first place, the concentration on the cathedrals of Cologne and Strasbourg to the exclusion of all other Gothic buildings and the exaltation of Cologne as the supreme example of its kind have, as we know, been characteristic of the Gothic Revival in Germany from the beginning.

Both in its good and in its bad qualities it may be said to summarize the main features of the Revival. The old fairy tales reappear: Gothic is a German invention, Gothic is the natural expression of the inborn qualities of the German race, Cologne is the greatest and most original of all Gothic buildings, the centre from which the new 'German' architecture radiated outwards to the rest of Europe. And so on and so forth.

At the same time it embodies some of the more reasonable convictions of the German Revivalists, especially the Goethean conception of Gothic as a living organism, and the equally Goethean conception of the Gothic building as the expression of an inner form and unity.

[1] Cp. Mertens, *Ueber den Dom zu Köln und die französische Bauschule in Deutschland. Programm zu den neuen Vorlesungen über Monumentalgeschichte* (Cologne, 1841).

The interpretation of Gothic as a kind of mystical mathematics, which we know from Friedrich Schlegel and others, is here elaborated in greatest detail. The old comparisons with the plant forms of nature, with crystallization and springing fountains, stir many echoes from past writers on the subject.

Finally, Görres gives unequivocal expression to a conviction which had been gradually gaining ground for many years: it was a conviction that involved a complete reversal of the aesthetic gospel of the preceding epoch—the conviction, namely, that it was Gothic which represented Good Taste and the architectural styles of the seventeenth and eighteenth centuries which represented Bad Taste.

The foundation stone of the cathedral extension was laid on 4 September 1842 by King Frederick William IV in the presence of a great company of distinguished guests, including the aged Metternich, Alexander von Humboldt, Prince George of Cambridge, the Earl of Westmorland, British Minister in Berlin, representatives of most of the Royal Houses of Germany, and a goodly array of generals, statesmen, and ecclesiastics. In his speech the King told his audience what the occasion signified for him: 'Gentlemen of Cologne, a great event is taking place among you. This is, as you are aware, no ordinary undertaking. It represents a common effort of all Germans and of all creeds. When I think of that fact, my eyes are filled with tears of joy and I thank God that I have lived to see this day . . . The spirit which builds these portals is the same which broke our fetters twenty-nine years ago, which brought to an end the humiliation of the Fatherland and the alien occupation of this province. It is the spirit of German unity and strength . . . I pray to God that the Cathedral of Cologne may soar over this city, may soar over Germany, over ages rich in peace until the end of time.'[1]

Of all the company who attended the ceremony none, we may be sure, was more deeply moved than Sulpiz Boisserée, the true author of the project. For him, too, it was indissolubly connected with the War of Liberation. 'I can only compare this great and significant occasion,' he writes to Melchior, 'with the days of 1813, 1814 and 1815, when all men were permeated by the same feelings of patriotic brotherhood. It is like the sunset of that great epoch, but it is at the same time the dawn of a new age, of a future, if we are not

---

[1] Quoted from *Das Buch deutscher Reden und Rufe*, ed. Friedrich von der Leyen (Wiesbaden, 1956), pp. 190–1.

mistaken, rich in hope and blessing.'[1] Nor were Sulpiz's services forgotten in this hour of his triumph. The King greeted him in the warmest terms, reminding him of their first meeting at Frankfurt twenty-nine years before, when the drawings of the completed cathedral moved him so deeply that he was unable, he says, to sleep for three nights. Sulpiz was decorated for his work in connection with the cathedral by both Frederick William of Prussia and Ludwig of Bavaria.

If one were to try and sum up the main differences between the Gothic Revival in Germany and England, the most striking surely would be the extent to which the German movement was bound up with the reawakening of the national spirit under the Napoleonic yoke. For this rebirth of German patriotism brought with it the yearning for the lost heritage of the German past, and of the greatest period of that past in the eyes of the Romantic generation—the Middle Ages, when Germany was for a time both politically and culturally the dominant power in Europe. The more painful the contrast with her present state of humiliation and impotence, the more alluring this vision of past greatness became. Now the most tangible and impressive witness to this greatest period of Germany's history was the heritage of Gothic architecture scattered throughout the land. And so in Germany the reawakened interest in the monuments of the Middle Ages was part and parcel of the nationalist reaction to Napoleon in a way for which there is no parallel in England. This nationalist element played a very small part, if indeed any part at all, in the English movement, which was primarily ecclesiological and aesthetico-ethical in inspiration. And though these elements were not absent from the German Revival they played a subordinate part in it.

The ceremony of September 1842 forms a fitting conclusion to the long story of the rehabilitation of Gothic in Germany. It is true that the whole cathedral project had acquired a highly political flavour, but at the same time it symbolized in the most striking way the supreme triumph of the Gothic Revival. For only a building erected in what was felt to be the specifically German style, in the greatest period of Germany's past, could act as a satisfactory symbol of her new-found unity and strength. The ceremony, then, set the seal upon the acceptance of Gothic as the greatest and most truly national of all architectural styles.

[1] SB i. 817.

APPENDIXES

1. HEINE AND THE GOTHIC REVIVAL

SINCE some of Heine's most important utterances on the Gothic Revival fall outside the time limits of this study, and since he is in any case too original and wayward a genius to fit neatly into any preconceived category, it is more convenient to deal with him in a separate appendix.

Heine's attitude towards medieval architecture was highly ambivalent, not to say contradictory.[1] In this it was only a reflection of his equivocal attitude towards Romanticism, and more especially towards Romantic medievalism, altogether.

In his youth Heine shared to the full the Romantic enthusiasm for Gothic, as for everything medieval. He compares Cologne Cathedral with the *Nibelungenlied* as two outstanding examples of medieval art, (*Über Polen*, 1822)[2], and in his sonnet to Heinrich Straube, co-editor of the medievalizing journal *Wünschelrute* (1818), he writes of the Cathedral in the most glowing terms of Romantic medievalism:

> Ich sehe wieder stolz gen Himmel ragen
> Den frommen Dom, den deutscher Glaube baute,
> Ich hör, der Glocken und der Orgel Laute,
> Dazwischen klingt's wie süsse Liebesklagen.[3]

Again in the well-known poem from the *Buch der Lieder* (*Lyrisches Intermezzo*, No. 11) he writes with lyrical fervour of the *Dom* and the *Dombild*, comparing the features of the Madonna in the latter with those of his beloved.[4]

But in the third part of the *Reisebilder—Reise von München nach Genua*—dating from 1828, Heine is already speaking of 'the dark rude spirit of the Middle Ages, which in clanking armour steps forth to meet us from the portals of Gothic churches' and referring to Munich's Frauenkirche as 'that barbaric cathedral, which still towers

---

[1] For Heine's attitude to the Middle Ages, including medieval architecture, see Georg Mücke, *Heinrich Heines Beziehungen zum deutschen Mittelalter. Forschungen zur neueren Literaturgeschichte*, no. 34 (Berlin, 1908).

[2] *Heinrich Heines Sämtliche Werke*, ed. Ernst Elster, 7 vols. (Leipzig, 1887–90), vii. 217. All references are to this edition.

[3] Elster, i. 57–58. [4] Elster, i. 69–70.

above the city in high-booted shape, hiding in its bosom the shadows
and spectres of the Middle Ages'.[1]

This negative attitude towards the Middle Ages and all its works
is confirmed and reinforced by Heine's conversion to Saint-Simonism
in the early thirties. Now, in Saint-Simonian parlance, the Middle
Ages have become the representative of spirit versus body, of
asceticism versus sensuality. Since the Saint-Simonian ideal was a
synthesis of the two, either of the poles in isolation is to be condemned.

For Heine the Middle Ages are essentially the era of Catholic
Christianity, of a religion, that is to say, which in his view is both
ascetic and masochistic. He compares the poetry of the period, using
the term to embrace all the manifestations of the medieval spirit,
including literature, art, and architecture, to 'a passion flower sprung
from the blood of Christ . . . a flower which is by no means ugly
but only spectral, the sight of which rouses a macabre pleasure in our
souls, like the convulsively sweet emotions which proceed from pain
itself. In this respect this flower would be the most appropriate symbol
for Christianity, whose most awful thrill consists precisely in the volup-
tuousness of pain.'[2]

It is a religion, he goes on to say, whose dogmas 'contain a condemnation of the flesh, and which not only assigns to the spirit
domination over the flesh, but which attempts to mortify the latter
in order to glorify the former'.[3] Now the artistic products of the
Middle Ages are a faithful echo of this religion 'and often their
whole task is to demonstrate this victory of spirit over matter'.[4]

It is in the light of this conception that Heine's most explicit utterance
on the subject of medieval architecture must be understood. It occurs
in Die Romantische Schule (written 1832–3), from which all these
quotations have been taken, and is couched in purely Saint-Simonian
terms. Heine has been saying that symbolism—or, as he prefers to
call it, parabolism—is characteristic of all medieval art in its attempt
to express the Infinite:

In architecture we find the same parabolic tendency as in poetry. When we
enter an ancient cathedral in these days, we are scarcely aware any more of the
esoteric meaning of its stone symbolism. It is only the total impression which
makes an immediate impact on our hearts. Here we feel the exaltation of the
spirit and the degradation of the flesh. The interior of the cathedral is itself
a hollow cross, and we move about within the very instrument of martyrdom;
the red and green lights which the many-coloured windows cast upon us are
like drops of blood or pus; hymns for the dead fill our ears with wailing;

---

[1] Elster, iii. 217.   [2] Elster, v. 226.   [3] loc. cit.   [4] Elster, v. 219.

beneath our feet are gravestones and decay; and together with the colossal
piers the spirit soars aloft, painfully tearing itself from the body, which sinks
to the ground like a cast-off garment. When we observe them from without,
these Gothic cathedrals, these stupendous structures, which are so airy, so
delicate, so transparent in their workmanship that one might take them for
fretwork or Brabant lace in marble, then indeed we are truly conscious of
the power of that epoch which was able to master stone itself, in such a way
that it appears to be almost ethereal, so that even this hardest of materials is
able to express Christian spirituality.[1]

Such a Saint-Simonian interpretation of the Gothic cathedral is
of course by no means purely negative. Heine may be repelled by the
aesthetic masochism of which it is for him a symbol, but at the same
time he is impressed by that very spiritualization of matter which in
other contexts he condemns. In his letters *Über die französische Bühne*
(1837) we find a surprisingly warm reference to Amiens Cathedral
as a 'monument of gigantic towering strength and indefatigable
dwarf-like patience'. And when he is asked how it comes that the
secret of such building has been lost, he replies: 'In the old days people
had convictions, we moderns have only got opinions, and something
more than opinions are necessary in order to erect a Gothic cathedral
like that.'[2]

Nevertheless this hardly prepares us for the fact that five years
later Heine actually consented to become vice-president of the Paris
branch of the *Dombauverein* for the completion of Cologne Cathedral,
which was founded on 6 March 1842.[3] It is true that its activities
appear to have been very limited and to have ceased altogether by the
end of the year, but it is sufficiently surprising that he should have
lent his name to the project at all. The explanation was probably that
despite everything Heine still retained a certain affection for the
building which had roused his sentimental attachment in his early
years; and secondly that the appeal to German unity, a unity trans-
cending all political and social barriers, which played so emphatic
a part in the propaganda of the *Dombauvereine*, was interpreted by
some of the liberal exiles in Paris as a possible step towards the united
democratic and republican Germany of which they dreamed.[4]

In any case his interest in the project was not of long duration.
By the time he had embarked on his visit to Germany in the late
autumn and winter of 1843 any desire he had felt for the completion

[1] Elster, v. 226.   [2] Elster, iv. 548.
[3] Cp. Eberhard Galley, 'Heine und der Kölner Dom', *Deutsche Vierteljahrsschrift
für Literaturwissenschaft und Geistesgeschichte* (Stuttgart, 1958), xxxiii. 99–110.
[4] Ibid. 103–4.

of the cathedral had turned into its opposite. He gives expression to this attitude in his *Deutschland, ein Wintermärchen*. This, one of the wittiest poems even Heine ever wrote, is an account of the reflections stirred in him by his brief return to German soil after a twelve years' absence. As he passes through Cologne he contemplates the cathedral which he had once sung with such Romantic nostalgia. Now it and the city of which it is the centre have become the symbol of medieval intolerance and superstition:

> Der Cancan des Mittelalters ward hier
> Getanzt von Nonnen und Mönchen . . .
>
> Die Flamme des Scheiterhaufens hat hier
> Bücher und Menschen verschlungen;
> Die Glocken wurden geläutet dabei
> Und Kyrie Eleison gesungen.
>
> Dummheit und Bosheit buhlten hier
> Gleich Hunden auf freier Gasse;
> Die Enkelbrut erkennt man noch heut'
> An ihrem Glaubenshasse.

The Cathedral, he declares, was intended to be a Bastille of the German spirit, in which reason and intelligence would pine away:

> Er sollte des Geistes Bastille sein,
> Und die listigen Römlinge dachten:
> 'In diesem Riesenkerker wird
> Die deutsche Vernunft verschmachten!'

But then came Luther and cried halt to the work, and from that day on the building has remained incomplete. And a good thing too, says Heine, for it is precisely its incompleteness which makes it a monument of Germany's strength and of her Protestant mission:

> Er ward nicht vollendet — und das ist gut.
> Denn eben die Nichtvollendung
> Macht ihn zum Denkmal von Deutschlands Kraft
> Und protestantischer Sendung.

And vain and foolish are the efforts of the *Domverein* (this was written in January 1844) to continue the interrupted task and complete the ancient symbol of spiritual tyranny; vain the rattling of the money bags even in the faces of Jews and heretics; vain even the charity matinées of Franz Liszt and the declamations of the Prussian monarch. Despite all this and much else it will never be completed, and indeed the time will come when, far from being completed, it will be degraded to the position of a stable:

> Ja, kommen wird die Zeit sogar,
> Wo man, statt ihn zu vollenden,
> Die inneren Räume zu einem Stall
> Für Pferde wird verwenden.[1]

From now on—to judge from his scanty references to the subject, e.g. *Kobes I*[2]—Heine seems to have retained this negative attitude to the cathedral project to the end of his life.

[1] Elster, ii. 438–9.   [2] Elster, ii. 214.

2. TRANSLATIONS OF POEMS
QUOTED IN GERMAN

p. 54.

> Beneath yon ruin'd Abbey's moss-grown piles
> Oft let me sit, at twilight hour of Eve,
> Where thro' some western window the pale moon
> Pours her long-levell'd rule of streaming light;
> While sullen sacred silence reigns around,
> Save the lone Screech-owl's note, whose bow'r is built
> Amid the mould'ring caverns dark and damp,
> And the calm breeze, that rustles in the leaves
> Of flaunting Ivy, that with mantle green
> Invests some sacred tow'r.

> (*The Pleasures of Melancholy*, London, 1747, pp. 5–6).

p. 59.

They, whose descendants now dwell on Scotland's mountains, the Cale-donians, who were never subjected to the Roman yoke, are of German race. Therefore to us too belongs the bard and warrior Ossian, more indeed than to the English.

p. 61.

> Where am I? Amid hermitages
> I find, I feel myself!
> Ghosts flitted away like shadows—abysses of thought
> Surge down and come to rest!—
>
> There where in the midnight grove
> fairies wandered on parting ways—
> And the dew from the cypresses rustled down
> on my bared head,
>
> Around me lie the graves of my brothers; spirit voices
> from the urn's womb—
> hark! how hollow they sound—hst! the mouldering dust
> whispers an answer and is still—
>
> And on dying tops of eternal elms
> wanders, O hark! the storm,
> which from crumbling feudal ruins
> mounts to my temple,

where before the altar ghosts initiate
the newcomer to the world of shades.
Through ancient windows Hecate herself
can scarcely spy her votaries,

and from the horned Gothic tower owls
utter a half sigh!—
and my father stands before me—I shudder, shuddering
I awake, and around me is night!

p. 347.

Before our eyes appears through sorcery
An ancient temple, massive as can be.
Like Atlas shouldering heaven long ago
Here stands its many columns, row on row;
And well they might suffice that weight of rock,
Two of them could support a city block.

You call that classical! I couldn't praise it;
Heavy and burdensome is how I'd phrase it.
The coarse and clumsy they call great and solemn,
I love the boundless urge of the slender column;
The pointed arch raises the soul on high;
Such edifices most can edify.

(*Faust*, translated by Louis Macniece, p. 185 [Faber and Faber, London, 1951.])

BIBLIOGRAPHY

GENERAL

Allgemeine Deutsche Biographie, 56 vols. (Leipzig, 1875–1912).
THIEME-BECKER: *Allgemeines Lexikon der bildenden Künstler von der Antike bis zur Gegenwart*, 36 vols. (Leipzig, 1907–47).

ADDISON, A.: *Romanticism and the Gothic Revival* (New York, 1938).
ALLEN, B. Sprague: *Tides in English Taste (1619–1800). A background for the study of literature*, 2 vols. (Cambridge, Mass., 1937).
Architectural Review, Gothic number (vol. xcviii, December 1945).
BANDMANN, G.: *Mittelalterliche Architektur als Bedeutungsträger* (Berlin, 1951).
BENZ, R.: *Die deutsche Romantik* (Leipzig, 1937).
BEERS, H. A.: *A History of English Romanticism in the Eighteenth Century* (London, 1899).
CLARK, Sir K.: *The Gothic Revival* (London, 1928; revised and enlarged edition, 1950).
EASTLAKE, Sir C. L.: *A History of the Gothic Revival* (London, 1872).
Essays in Gothic Architecture by the Rev. T. Warton, Rev. J. Bentham, Captain Grose, and the Rev. J. Milner (London, 1800).
FRANKL, P.: *The Gothic. Literary Sources and Interpretations through Eight Centuries* (Princeton, 1960).
KAMPHAUSEN, A.: *Gotik ohne Gott. Ein Beitrag zur Deutung der Neugotik und des 19. Jahrhunderts* (Tübingen, 1952).
KORFF, H. A.: *Geist der Goethezeit*, 5 vols. (Leipzig, 1923–57).
LEHMANN, E. H.: *Die Anfänge der Kunstzeitschrift in Deutschland* (Leipzig, 1932).
LOVEJOY, A. O.: *Essays in the History of Ideas* (Baltimore, 1948).
LÜDTKE, G.: ' "Gotisch" im 18. und 19. Jahrhundert' (*Zeitschrift für deutsche Wortforschung*, vol. iv, Strasbourg, 1903).
LÜTZELER, H.: 'Der Kölner Dom in der deutschen geistesgeschichte' (*Der Kölner Dom. Festschrift zur 700. Jahrfeier*, Cologne, 1948).
PEVSNER, N.: *An Outline of European Architecture* (7th ed. Harmondsworth, 1963).
PRICE, L. M.: *English Literature in Germany* (*University of California Publications in Modern Philology*, vol. xxxvii, Berkeley, 1953).
RAUMER, R. VON.: *Geschichte der germanischen Philologie* (Munich, 1870).
ROSENAU, H.: *Der Kölner Dom. Seine Baugeschichte und historische Stellung* (Cologne, 1931).
SCHEFFLER, K.: *Der Geist der Gotik* (Leipzig, 1917).
SCHMITZ, H.: *Die Gotik im deutschen Kunst- und Geistesleben* (Berlin, 1921).
STÖCKER, H.: *Zur Kunstanschauung des 18. Jahrhunderts von Winckelmann bis zu Wackenroder* (*Palaestra*, vol. xxvi, Berlin, 1904).
WAETZOLDT, W.: *Deutsche Kunsthistoriker*, 2 vols. (Leipzig, 1921).
WORRINGER, W.: *Formprobleme der Gotik* (Munich, 1912).

PART ONE—INTRODUCTORY

(i) The Eclipse of Gothic

BEER, E. S. DE.: 'Gothic: origin and diffusion of the term; the idea of style in architecture' (*Journal of the Warburg and Courtauld Institutes*, vol. xi, 1948).

—— 'Gothic and some other architectural terms' (*The Diary of John Evelyn*, vol. vi, introduction, Oxford, 1955).

CROMBACH, H.: *Primitiae Gentium seu Historia SS. Trium Regum Magorum* (Cologne, 1654).

EGGERS, J. VON.: *Neues Kriegs- Ingenieur- Artillerie- See- und Ritter- Lexicon* (Dresden/Leipzig, 1757).

FRISCH, J. L.: *Teutsch-Lateinisches Wörter-Buch* (Berlin, 1747).

GÖLNITZ, A.: *Ulysses Belgico-Gallicus* (Leyden, 1631).

KANT, I.: *Beobachtungen über das Gefühl des Schönen und Erhabenen* (Königsberg, 1764).

KÖNIG, J. U.: *Untersuchung von dem Guten Geschmack in der Dicht- und Rede-Kunst* (appended to Freiherr von Canitz's *Gedichte*, Leipzig/Berlin, 1727).

PANOFSKY, E.: 'Das erste Blatt aus dem "Libro" Giorgio Vasaris. Eine Studie über die Beurteilung der Gotik in der italienischen Renaissance' (*Städel-Jahrbuch*, vol. vi, 1930).

PFLAUMERN, J. H. VON.: *Mercurius Italicus* (Augsburg, 1625).

ROBSON-SCOTT, W. D.: *German Travellers in England 1400–1800* (Oxford, 1953).

RUBENS, P. P.: *Palazzi di Genova* (Antwerp, 1622).

SANDRART, J. VON.: *L'Academia Todesca della Architectura, Scultura e Pittura: oder Teutsche Academie der Edlen Bau- Bild- und Mahlerey-Künste*, 2 vols. (Nürnberg, 1675–9).

—— *Teutsche Academie der Bau- Bildhauer- und Maler-Kunst*, enlarged and revised by J. J. Volkmann, 8 vols. (Nürnberg, 1768–75).

SCHLOSSER, J.: *Präludien. Vorträge und Aufsätze.* (Berlin, 1927).

SCHREIBER, A.: *Frühklassizistische Kritik an der Gotik 1759–1789* (Diss: Leipzig, 1938).

SCRIBANIUS, C.: *Antverpia* (Antwerp, 1610).

SPONSEL, J. L.: *Sandrarts Teutsche Academie* (Diss: Dresden, 1899).

SULZER, J. G.: *Allgemeine Theorie der schönen Künste*, 2 vols. (Leipzig/Berlin, 1771–4).

VASARI, G.: *Le Vite de' piu eccellenti Architetti, Pittori ed Scultori Italiani* (Florence, 1550).

—— *Vasari on Technique*, translated by Louisa Maclehose, ed. by G. Baldwin Brown (London, 1907).

WEBER, C. J.: *Deutschland oder Briefe eines in Deutschland reisenden Deutschen*, 2 vols. (Stuttgart, 1827).

WOTTON, SIR H.: *The Elements of Architecture, Collected by Henry Wotton Knight, from the best Authors and Examples* (London, 1624).

ZEDLER, J. H.: *Universal-Lexicon*, vol. 25 (Leipzig/Halle, 1741).

(ii) The Survival of Gothic

BEHR, G. H.: *Strassburger Münster- und Thurn- Büchlein* (Strasbourg, 1732; new and enlarged ed. 1744).

BRAUN, G. and HOGENBERG, F.: *Beschreibung und Contrafactur der vornembster Strätt der Welt* (Cologne, 1574).

BRAUN, J.: *Die Kirchenbauten der deutschen Jesuiten.* (*Stimmen aus Maria-Laach*, Ergänzungsbände xxv, xxvi, Freiburg i/B., 1908–10).

CLEMEN, P.: *Der Dom zu Köln* (Düsseldorf, 1937).

CROMBACH, H.: *Primitiae Gentium seu Historia SS. Trium Regum Magorum* (Cologne, 1654).

FRICK, E.: *Templum Parochiale Ulmensium* (Ulm, 1718).

JABLONSKI, J. T.: *Allgemeines Lexicon der Künste und Wissenschaften* (Leipzig, 1721).

JANTZEN, H.: *Das niederländische Architekturbild* (Leipzig, 1910).

KIRSCHBAUM, E.: *Deutsche Nachgotik. Ein Beitrag zur Geschichte der kirchlichen Architektur von 1550–1800* (Diss: Maastricht, 1930).

MÜNSTER, S.: *Cosmographia* (Basle, 1544).

QUAD, M.: *Teutscher Nation Herligkeit* (Cologne, 1609).

RANISCH, B.: *Beschreibung aller Kirchen-Gebäude der Stadt Dantzig* (Danzig, 1695).

SCHADAEUS, O.: *Summum Argentoratensium Templum: Das ist: Auszführliche und Eigendtliche Beschreibung dess viel Kostbaren, und in aller Welt berühmten Münsters zu Strassburg* (Strasbourg, 1617).

WIMPHELING, J.: *Rerum Germanicarum Epitome* (Hanau, 1594).

WINHEIM, E.: *Sacrarium Agrippinae* (Cologne, 1607).

ZINCGREF, J. W.: See appendix to Opitz's *Teutsche Poemata* (Strasbourg, 1624).

(iii) *English Influences*

(a) *Rococo Gothic*

ALLEN, B. SPRAGUE: *Tides in English Taste (1690–1800). A background for the study of literature,* 2 vols. (Cambridge, Mass., 1937).

BACHMANN, E.: 'Anfänge des Landschaftgartens in Deutschland' (*Zeitschrift für Kunstwissenschaft*, vol. v, Berlin, 1951).

CHIPPENDALE, T.: *The Gentleman and Cabinet-Maker's Director* (London, 1754).

CLARK, SIR K.: *The Gothic Revival* (London, 1928; revised and enlarged edition, 1950).

CLEMEN, P.: 'Strawberry-Hill und Wörlitz' (*Neue Beiträge deutscher Forschung, Wilhelm Worringer zum 60. Geburtstag*, ed. Erich Fidder, Königsberg, 1943).

DECKER, P.: *Gothic Architecture Decorated* (London, 1759).

An Eighteenth-Century Correspondence, ed. Lilian Dickins and Mary Stanton (London, 1910).

GOETHE: *Das Luisenfest* (WA I. 36).

—— *Schema zu einem Aufsatze die Pflanzencultur im Grossherzogthum Weimar darzustellen* (WA II. 6).

GOTHEIN, M. L.: *Geschichte der Gartenkunst,* 2 vols. (Jena, 1914).

GROTE, L.: *Das Land Anhalt* (Berlin, 1929).

HALFPENNY, W. and J.: *Chinese and Gothic Architecture properly ornamented* (London, 1759).

HALLBAUM, F.: *Der Landschaftgarten* (Munich, 1927).

HEIDELBACH, P.: *Die Geschichte der Wilhelmshöhe* (Leipzig, 1909).

Hosäus, W.: *Grossherzog Carl August von Sachsen-Weimar-Eisenach und Goethe in ihren Beziehungen zu Herzog Leopold Friedrich Franz von Anhalt-Dessau* (Dessau, 1877).

Hussey, C.: *The Picturesque* (London, 1927).

Kamphausen, A.: *Gotik ohne Gott. Ein Beitrag zur Deutung der Neugotik und des 19. Jahrhunderts* (Tübingen, 1952).

Langley, B.: *New Principles of Gardening* (London, 1728).

Langley, B. and T.: *Ancient Architecture restored and improved* (London, 1742).

—— *Gothic Architecture improved, by rules and proportions* (London, 1747).

Lovejoy, A. O.: 'The Chinese Origin of a Romanticism' (in *Essays in the History of Ideas*, Baltimore, 1948).

—— 'The First Gothic Revival and the Return to Nature' (in *Essays in the History of Ideas*, Baltimore, 1948).

Manwaring, E.: *Italian Landscape in Eighteenth Century England* (New York, 1925).

Möser, J.: *Patriotische Phantasien*, vol. 2 (Berlin, 1778).

Neumeyer, A.: 'Die Erweckung der Gotik in der deutschen Kunst des späten 18. Jahrhunderts' (*Repertorium für Kunstwissenschaft*, vol. xlix, Berlin/Leipzig, 1928).

Over, C.: *Ornamental Architecture in the Gothic, Chinese and Modern Taste* (London, 1758).

Paetow, K.: *Klassizismus und Romantik auf Wilhelmshöhe* (Cassel, 1929).

Pevsner, N.: "The Genesis of the Picturesque" (*Architectural Review*, vol. xcvi, November 1944).

Pope, A.: *The Works of Alexander Pope*, ed. William Warburton, vol. 3 (London, 1751).

Rave, P. O.: *Gärten der Goethezeit* (Leipzig, 1941).

Reil, F.: *Leopold Friedrich Franz, Herzog und Fürst von Anhalt-Dessau* (Dessau, 1845).

Rode, A.: *Beschreibung des Fürstlichen Anhalt-Dessauischen Landhauses und Englischen Gartens zu Wörlitz* (Dessau, 1788).

Schlegel, R.: *Woerlitz, ein Landschaftsidyll und ein Kunstkreis in Anhalt* (Berlin, 1926).

Schiller, F.: Review of Cotta's *Gartenkalender auf das Jahr 1795* (*Säkular-Ausgabe*, vol. xvi).

Schmitz, H.: *Die Gotik im deutschen Kunst- und Geistesleben* (Berlin, 1921).

Stukeley, W.: *Itinerarium Curiosum* (London, 1724).

Temple, Sir W.: *The Works of Sir William Temple*, Bart. (London, 1720).

(iii) *English Influences, cont.*

(b) *The Gothic Mood*

Barnstorff, J.: *Youngs Nachtgedanken und ihr Einfluss auf die deutsche Literatur* (Bamberg, 1895).

Creuz, F. C. C. von.: *Die Gräber, ein philosophisches Gedicht in sechs Gesängen* (Frankfurt/Mainz, 1760).

Cronegk, J. F. von.: *Schriften*, 2 vols. (Leipzig, 1765–6).

Gerstenberg, H. W. von.: *Vermischte Schriften*, 3 vols. (Altona, 1815).

BIBLIOGRAPHY 315

HAFERKORN, R.: *Gotik und Ruine in der englischen Dichtung des achtzehnten Jahrhunderts* (*Leipziger Beiträge zur englischen Philologie*, Heft 4, Leipzig, 1924).

HARTMANN, C.: *Friedrich Carl Casimir Freiherr von Creuz und seine Dichtungen* (Heidelberg, 1891).

HERDER, J. G.: *Sämmtliche Werke*, ed. B. Suphan, 33 vols. (Berlin, 1877–1913).

KANDER, L.: *Die deutsche Ruinenpoesie des 18. Jahrhunderts bis in die Anfänge des 19. Jahrhunderts* (Diss: Heidelberg, 1933).

KIND, J. L.: *Edward Young in Germany* (*Columbia University Germanic Studies*, vol. 2, New York, 1906).

KLOPSTOCK, F. G.: *Sämmtliche Werke*, 10 vols. (Leipzig, 1854–5).

MALLET, D.: *The Excursion* (London, 1728).

MALLET, P. H.: *Introduction à l'Histoire de Dannemarc*, 2 vols. (Copenhagen, 1755–6).

MUNCKER, F.: *Friedrich Gottlieb Klopstock* (Stuttgart, 1888).

PRICE, L. M.: *English Literature in Germany* (*University of California Publications in Modern Philology*, vol. xxxvii, Berkeley, 1953).

TIEGHEM, P. VAN.: *Le Préromantisme. Études d'histoire littéraire européenne*, 3 vols. (Paris, 1924–47).

TOMBO, R.: *Ossian in Germany* (*Columbia University Germanic Studies*, vol. i, New York, 1901).

WARTON, T.: *The Pleasures of Melancholy* (London, 1747).

YOUNG, E.: *The Complaint, or Night Thoughts on Life, Death and Immortality* (London, 1742–5).

—— *Dr. Edward Young's Klagen, oder Nachtgedanken über Leben, Tod und Unsterblichkeit. Aus dem Englischen ins Deutsche übersetzt von J. A. Ebert*, 2 vols. (Brunswick, 1760–3).

ZACHARIÄ, F. W.: *Poetische Schriften*, 9 vols. (Brunswick, 1763–4).

(iv) *French Influences*

BLONDEL, F.: *Cours d'architecture* (2nd ed. Paris, 1698).

CORBLET, J.: 'L'Architecture du moyen-âge jugée par les ecrivains des deux derniers siècles' (*Revue de l'art chrètien*, vol. iii, 1859).

DUCHESNE, A.: *Les Antiquitez et recherches des villes, chasteaux, et places plus remarquables de toute la France* (Paris, 1609).

FÉLIBIEN DES AVAUX, J. F.: *Recueil historique de la vie et des ouvrages des plus célèbres architectes* (Paris, 1687).

—— *Dissertation touchant l'architecture antique et l'architecture gothique* (appended to *Les plans et les descriptions de deux des plus belles maisons de campagne de Pline le Consul*, Paris, 1699).

FÉNELON, F.: *Lettre sur l'éloquence* (appended to *Dialogue sur l'éloquence* 1st ed. Paris, 1716).

HERRMANN, W.: *Laugier and 18th century French theory* (London, 1962).

KLOPFER, P.: *Christian Traugott Weinlig und die Anfänge des Klassizismus in Sachsen* (*Dresdner Baumeister. Beiträge zur Bauwissenschaft*, vol. v, Berlin, 1905).

LANSON, R.: *Le goût du moyen âge en France au xviii siècle* (Paris/Brussels, 1926).

LAUGIER, M. A.: *Essai sur l'architecture* (Paris, 1753).
Observations sur l'architecture (The Hague, 1765).
MIDDLETON, R. D.: 'The Abbé de Cordemoy and the Graeco-Gothic Ideal:
a prelude to romantic classicism' (*Journal of the Warburg and Courtauld
Institutes*, vol. xxv, 1962).
MONVAL, J.: *Soufflot* (Paris, 1918).
MORLIÈRE, A. DE LA: *Antiquitez, histoires et choses les plus remarquables de la
ville d'Amiens* (Paris, 1627).
SABLON, V.: *Histoire de l'auguste et vénérable église de Chartres* (Chartres, 1671).
SCHMITZ, H.: *Die Gotik im deutschen Kunst- und Geistesleben* (Berlin, 1921).
WEINLIG, C. T.: *Briefe über Rom*, 3 vols. (Dresden, 1782–7).

PART TWO—STURM UND DRANG

  (i) *Herder*

GAERTNER, J.: *Johann Gottfried Herders Anschauungen über eine christliche Kunst*
(Diss: Berlin, 1938).
HAMANN, J.: *Sämmtliche Werke*, ed. J. Nadler, 6 vols. (Vienna, 1949–57).
HAYM, R.: *Herder in seinem Leben und seinen Werken*, 2 vols. (Berlin, 1877–85).
HERDER, J. G.: *Sämmtliche Werke*, ed. B. Suphan, 33 vols. (Berlin, 1877–1913).
—— *Aus Herders Nachlass*, ed. H. Düntzer and F. G. v. Herder, 3 vols. (Frank-
furt, 1856–7).
—— *Von und an Herder. Ungedruckte Briefe aus Herders Nachlass*, ed. H. Düntzer
and F. G. v. Herder, 3 vols. (Leipzig, 1861–2).
—— *Herders Briefwechsel mit Nicolai*, ed. O. Hoffmann (Berlin, 1887).
—— *Herders Briefe an J. G. Hamann*, ed. O. Hoffmann (Berlin, 1889).
LÜDTKE, G.: ' "Gotisch" im 18. und 19. Jahrhundert' (*Zeitschrift für deutsche
Wortforschung*, vol. iv, Strasbourg, 1903).
MAY, K.: *Lessings und Herders kunsttheoretische Gedanken in ihrem Zusammenhang*
(*Germanische Studien*, Heft 25, Berlin, 1923).
MEINECKE, F.: *Die Entstehung des Historismus*, 2 vols. (Munich/Berlin, 1936).
MURPHY, J.: *Plans, Elevations, Sections and Views of the Church of Batalha . . .
To which is prefaced an Introductory Discourse on the Principles of Gothic Archi-
tecture* (London, 1795).
ROBSON-SCOTT, W. D.: 'The Legend of Herder's Medievalism' (*Publications
of the English Goethe Society*, New Series, vol. xxxiii, 1963).
ROUCHÉ, M.: *La philosophie de l'histoire de Herder* (*Publications de la faculté
des lettres de l'Université de Strasbourg*. Fascicule 93, Paris, 1940).
SALMONY, H. A.: *Die Philosophie des jungen Herder* (Diss: Zürich, 1949).
SALOMON, G.: *Das Mittelalter als Ideal in der Romantik* (Munich, 1922).
SHAFTESBURY, ANTHONY ASHLEY COOPER, 3RD EARL OF: *Characteristicks of
Men, Manners, Opinions, Times*, 3 vols. (London, 1711).
STEINKE, M. W.: *Edward Young's 'Conjectures on Original Composition' in
England and Germany* (*Americana Germanica*, no. 28, New York, 1917).
STOLPE, H.: *Die Auffassung des jungen Herder vom Mittelalter. Ein Beitrag zur
Geschichte der Aufklärung* (*Beiträge zur deutschen Klassik*, vol. i, Weimar,
1955).
UNGER, R.: *Hamann und die Aufklärung*, 2 vols. (Jena, 1911).

WALZEL, O.: *Das Prometheussymbol von Shaftesbury zu Goethe* (2nd ed. Munich, 1933).

WEISER, G. A.: *Shaftesbury und das deutsche Geistesleben* (Leipzig/Berlin, 1916).

WELLS, G. A.: *Herder and After. A Study in the Development of Sociology (Anglica Germanica*, vol. i, The Hague, 1959).

WREN, C.: *Parentalia* (London, 1750).

YOUNG, E.: *Conjectures on Original Composition*, ed. E. J. Morley (*Modern Language Texts*, Manchester, 1918).

(ii) The Young Goethe

Architectural Review, Gothic Number (vol. xcviii, December 1945).

BAGGESEN, J.: *Baggesen oder Das Labyrinth*, translated and edited by C. F. Cramer (Altona/Leipzig, 1795).

BENYOVSKY, K.: *Adam Friedrich Oeser, der Zeichenlehrer Goethes* (Leipzig/ Bratislava, 1930).

BEUTLER, E.: *Von Deutscher Baukunst. Goethes Hymnus auf Erwin von Steinbach. Seine Entstehung und Wirkung (Freies Deutsches Hochstift, Reihe der Vorträge und Schriften*, vol. iv, Munich, 1943).

—— *Bilder aus dem Frankfurter Goethemuseum*, ed. Ernst Beutler und Josefine Rumpf (Frankfurt, 1949).

FEULNER, A.: *Der junge Goethe und die Frankfurter Kunst* (in *Freies Deutsches Hochstift, Festgabe zum Goethejahr 1932*, Halle, 1932).

Frankfurter Gelehrte Anzeigen vom Jahr 1772 (Deutsche Litteraturdenkmale des 18. und 19. Jahrhunderts, vols. vii, viii, Stuttgart, 1882).

GOETHE: *VonDeutscher Baukunst* (1773); also ed. G. Witkowski (Kürschner's *Deutsche National-Literatur*, vol. cvii, Stuttgart, 1892).

HERDER, J. G.: *Von deutscher Art und Kunst* (Hamburg, 1773); also ed. H. Lambel (*Deutsche Litteraturdenkmale des 18. und 19. Jahrhunderts*, vols. xl, xli, Stuttgart, 1892) and E. Purdie (Oxford, 1924).

—— *Briefe an Johann Heinrich Merck*, ed. Karl Wagner (Darmstadt, 1835).

HERING, R.: 'Das Elternhaus Goethes und das Leben in der Familie' (in *Die Stadt Goethes. Frankfurt am Main im xviii. Jahrhundert*, ed. H. Voelcker, Frankfurt, 1932).

HUTH, G.: *Allgemeines Magazin für die bürgerliche Baukunst*, 4 vols. (Weimar, 1789–96).

JAHN, J.: 'Das künstlerische Leipzig und Goethe' (*Goethe*, vol. xii, 1950).

JUSTI, C.: *Winckelmann und seine Zeitgenossen* (5th ed. Cologne, 1956).

LANDSBERGER, F.: *Die Kunst der Goethezeit* (Leipzig, 1931).

LEHMANN, E. H.: *Die Anfänge der Kunstzeitschrift in Deutschland* (Leipzig, 1932).

MORRIS, M.: *Der junge Goethe*, 6 vols. (Leipzig, 1909–12).

PEVSNER, N.: 'Goethe e l'Architettura' (*Palladio*, vol, iv, 1951).

ROBSON-SCOTT, W. D.: 'Goethe and the Gothic Revival' (*Publications of the English Goethe Society*, New Series, vol. xxv, 1956).

—— 'On the Composition of Goethe's "Von Deutscher Baukunst" ' (*Modern Language Review*, vol. liv, 1959).

SCHERER, W.: *Aus Goethes Frühzeit* (Strasbourg, 1879).

SCHULZE, F.: *Adam Friedrich Oeser, Der Vorläufer des Klassizismus* (Leipzig, n.d.).

SCHOENBERGER, G.: 'Kunst und Kunstleben in Frankfurt am Main' (in *Die Stadt Goethes, Frankfurt am Main im xviii. Jahrhundert*, ed. H. Voelcker, Frankfurt, 1932).

SUDHEIMER, H.: *Der Geniebegriff des jungen Goethe* (*Germanische Studien*, Heft 167, Berlin, 1935).

TREVELYAN, H.: *Goethe and the Greeks* (Cambridge, 1941).

ZIMMERMANN, R. C.: 'Zur Datierung von Goethes Aufsatz "Von deutscher Baukunst" ' (*Euphorion*, vol. li, 1957).

(iii) Heinse—Forster—Nicolai

BURNEY, C.: *The Present State of Music in Germany, the Netherlands, and the United Provinces*, 2 vols. (London, 1773).

FORSTER, G.: *Ansichten vom Niederrhein, von Brabant, Flandern, Holland, England und Frankreich, im April, Mai und Junius 1790*, 3 vols. (Berlin, 1791–4).

—— *Georg Forsters Werke*, ed. Deutsche Akademie der Wissenschaften zu Berlin: vol. ix. *Ansichten vom Niederrhein*, bearbeitet von Gerhard Steiner (Berlin, 1958).

—— *Briefe und Tagebücher Georg Forsters von seiner Reise am Niederrhein, in England und Frankreich im Frühjahr 1790*, ed. A. Leitzmann (Halle, 1893).

—— *Georg Forsters Tagebücher*, ed. Paul Zincke and Albert Leitzmann (*Deutsche Litteraturdenkmale des 18. und 19. Jahrhunderts*, No. 149, Berlin, 1914).

—— *Sämmtliche Schriften*, 9 vols. (Leipzig, 1843).

GOOCH, G. P.: *Germany and the French Revolution* (London, 1920).

HEINSE, W.: *Sämmtliche Schriften*, ed. Carl Schüddekopf, 10 vols. (Leipzig, 1902–25).

JESSEN, K. D.: *Heinses Stellung zur bildenden Kunst und ihrer Aesthetik* (*Palaestra*, vol. xxi, Berlin, 1901).

KERSTEN, K.: *Der Weltumsegler. Johann Georg Adam Forster 1754–94* (Berne, 1957).

KLENZE, C. VON.: 'The Growth of Interest in the early Italian masters from Tischbein to Ruskin' (*Modern Philology*, vol. iv, Chicago, 1907).

LEITZMANN, A.: *Georg und Therese Forster und die Brüder Humboldt* (Bonn, 1936).

NICOLAI, C. F.: *Beschreibung einer Reise durch Deutschland und die Schweiz im Jahre 1781*, 12 vols. (Berlin/Stettin, 1783–96).

ROBSON-SCOTT, W. D.: 'Georg Forster and the Gothic Revival' (*Modern Language Review*, vol. li, 1956).

SCHLEGEL, A. W. and F.: *Charakteristiken und Kritiken*, 2 vols. (Königsberg, 1801).

PART THREE—THE ROMANTIC MOVEMENT

ANDREWS, K.: *The Nazarenes* (Oxford, 1964).

BOISSERÉE, M.: *Sulpiz Boisserée*, 2 vols. (Stuttgart, 1862).

BENZ, R.: *Die deutsche Romantik* (Leipzig, 1937).

BRENTANO, C.: *Werke*, ed. M. Preitz, 3 vols. (Meyers Klassiker-Ausgaben, Leipzig/Vienna, 1914).

ENNEN, L.: *Zeitbilder aus der neueren Geschichte der Stadt Köln, mit besonderer Rücksicht auf Ferdinand Franz Wallraf* (Cologne, 1857).

GILLIES, A.: 'Wackenroder's Apprenticeship to Literature: his Teachers and their Influence' (*German Studies presented to H. G. Fiedler*, Oxford, 1938).

HALL, SIR J.: *Essay on the Origin, History and Principles of Gothic Architecture* (London, 1813).

KLENZE, C. VON.: 'The Growth of Interest in the early Italian masters. From Tischbein to Ruskin' (*Modern Philology*, vol. iv, Chicago, 1907).

KÖPKE, R.: *Ludwig Tieck. Erinnerungen aus dem Leben des Dichters nach dessen mündlichen und schriftlichen Mittheilungen* (Leipzig, 1855).

KOLDEWEY, P.: *Wackenroder und sein Einfluss auf Tieck. Ein Beitrag zur Quellengeschichte der Romantik* (Leipzig, 1904).

LÜTZELER, H.: 'Die Deutung der Gotik bei den Romantikern' (*Wallraf-Richartz Jahrbuch*, vol. 2, Leipzig, 1925).

MINDER, R.: *Ludwig Tieck* (*Publications de la faculté des lettres de l'Université de Strasbourg*. Fascicule 72. Paris, 1936).

RITTER, C.: 'Die Ruinen am Rhein' (*Rheinisches Archiv für Geschichte und Litteratur*, vol. i, 1810).

ROBSON-SCOTT, W. D.: 'Wackenroder and the Middle Ages' (*Modern Language Review*, vol. 1, April 1955).

SCHELLING, F. W. J.: *Sämmtliche Werke*, ed. K. F. A. Schelling (Stuttgart/ Augsburg, 1859).

SCHLEGEL, A. W.: *Über schöne Litteratur und Kunst*, ed. J. Minor (*Deutsche Litteraturdenkmale des 18. und 19. Jahrhunderts*, vols. xvii–xix, Stuttgart, 1884).

—— *Über dramatische Kunst und Literatur*, 3 vols. (Heidelberg, 1809–11).

—— *A Course of Lectures in Dramatic Art and Literature*, translated by J. Black, revised by A. J. W. Morrison. *Bohn's Standard Library* (London, 1846).

—— *Poetische Werke* (Heidelberg, 1811).

—— *Briefe von und an August Wilhelm Schlegel*, ed. J. Körner, 2 vols. (Vienna, 1930).

SCHLEGEL, F.: *Kritische Friedrich-Schlegel-Ausgabe*, ed. E. Behler (Munich, &c., 1959, &c.).

Abt. I. vol. iv: *Ansichten und Ideen von der christlichen Kunst*, ed. H. Eichner.

Abt. I. vol. vi: *Geschichte der alten und neuen Literatur*, ed. H. Eichner.

—— *Briefe auf einer Reise durch die Niederlande, Rheingegenden, die Schweiz, und einen Theil von Frankreich* (in *Poetisches Taschenbuch auf das Jahr* 1806).

—— *Grundzüge der gothischen Baukunst* (*Sämmtliche Werke*, vol. vi, Vienna, 1823).

—— 'Über die deutsche Kunstausstellung zu Rom, im Frühjahr 1819, und über den gegenwärtigen Stand der deutschen Kunst in Rom.' (*Jahrbücher der Literatur*, vol. vii, Vienna, 1819).

—— *Europa*, ed. F. Schlegel, 2 vols. (Frankfurt, 1803).

—— *Deutsches Museum*, ed. F. Schlegel, 4 vols. (Vienna, 1812–13).

—— *Briefe von und an Friedrich und Dorothea Schlegel*, ed. J. Körner (Berlin, 1926).

22

SCHMIDT, E.: 'Die Entdeckung Nürnbergs' (in *Charakteristiken*, 1st Series, Berlin, 1886).

STANGE, A.: *Deutsche Malerei der Gotik*, 11 vols. (Berlin, 1934–61).

STEINEN, W. VON DEN: 'Mittelalter und Goethezeit' (*Historische Zeitschrift*, vol. clxxxiii, 1957).

SULGER-GEBING, E.: *Die Brüder A. W. und F. Schlegel in ihrem Verhältnisse zur bildenden Kunst* (Munich, 1897).

TECCHI, B.: *Wackenroder* (Florence, 1927).

TIECK, L.: *Schriften*, 28 vols. (Berlin, 1828–54).

—— *Phantasus*, 3 vols. (Berlin, 1812–16).

—— *Franz Sternbalds Wanderungen*, ed. J. Minor (*Deutsche National-Litteratur*, vol. cxlv, Berlin/Stuttgart, 1885).

—— *Briefe an Ludwig Tieck*, ed. Karl von Holtei, 4 vols. (Breslau, 1864).

—— *Letters of Ludwig Tieck*, hitherto unpublished, 1792–1853, ed. E. H. Zeydel (New York, 1937).

—— *Ludwig Tieck und die Brüder Schlegel. Briefe mit Einleitung und Anmerkungen*, ed. H. Lüdeke (Frankfurt, 1930).

—— *Tieck and Solger. The complete correspondence*, ed. P. Matenko (New York, 1933).

VENTURI, L.: *Il Gusto dei Primitivi* (Bologna, 1926).

WACKENRODER, W. H.: *Werke und Briefe*, ed. H. Höhn (Berlin, 1938).

—— *Reisebriefe*, ed. H. Höhn (Berlin, 1938).

—— *Herzensergiessungen eines kunstliebenden Klosterbruders*, ed. A. Gillies (Oxford, 1948).

WAETZOLDT, W.: *Deutsche Kunstwerke beschrieben von deutschen Dichtern* (Leipzig, 1940).

WÖLFFLIN, H.: 'Die Herzensergiessungen' (*Kleine Schriften*, Basle, 1946).

ZEYDEL, E. H.: *Ludwig Tieck, the German Romanticist* (Princeton, 1935).

PART FOUR—GOETHE AND BOISSERÉE

ARNDT, E. M.: *Meine Wanderungen und Wandelungen mit dem Reichsfreiherrn Heinrich Karl Friedrich von Stein* (Berlin, 1858).

BAYER, J.: *Köln um die Wende des 18. und 19. Jahrhunderts* (Cologne, 1912).

—— *Die Franzosen in Köln. Bilder aus den Jahren 1794–1814* (Cologne, 1925).

BENZ, R.: *Die deutsche Romantik* (Leipzig, 1937).

—— *Goethe und die romantische Kunst* (Munich, 1940).

—— 'Goethes Anteil am Wiederaufbau des Kölner Doms' (*Goethe*, vol. vii, 1942).

BEUTLER, E.: 'Die Boisserée-Gespräche von 1815 und die Entstehung des Gingo-biloba-Gedichts.' (*Essays um Goethe*, vol. i, 3rd ed. Wiesbaden, 1946).

BOISSERÉE, M.: *Sulpiz Boisserée*, 2 vols. (Stuttgart, 1862).

CATEL, L. F.: *Grundzüge einer Theorie der Bauart protestantischer Kirchen* (Berlin, 1815).

CHÉZY, H. VON.: *Unvergessenes* (Leipzig, 1858).

DOCEN, B. J.: 'Neudeutsche, religiös- patriotische Kunst. Gegen die Weimarischen Kunstfreunde.' (*Jahrbücher der Literatur*, vol. viii, Vienna, 1819).

EINEM, H. VON.: *Beiträge zu Goethes Kunstauffassung* (Hamburg, 1956).

ENNEN, L.: *Der Dom zu Köln von seinem Beginne bis zu seiner Vollendung* (Cologne, 1880).

FIRMENICH-RICHARTZ, E.: *Die Brüder Boisserée.* Vol. i. *Sulpiz und Melchior Boisserée als Kunstsammler. Ein Beitrag zur Geschichte der Romantik* (Jena, 1916). This volume deals only with the activities of the Brothers Boisserée as collectors of German and Flemish Primitives; the second volume, which would have dealt with their activities on behalf of medieval architecture, has never appeared.

FISCHER, T.: *Goethes Verhältnis zur Baukunst* (Munich, 1949).

GOETHE: *Goethes Werke. Weimarer Ausgabe,* 143 vols. (Weimar, 1887–1919).

—— *Goethes Werke. Hamburger Ausgabe,* 14 vols. (Hamburg, 1948–60). vol. xi: *Italienische Reise,* ed. H. v. Einem. vol. xii: *Schriften zur Kunst,* ed. H. v. Einem.

—— *Goethes Werke. Artemis Ausgabe,* 24 vols. (Zürich, 1948–54). vol. xiii: *Schriften zur Kunst,* ed. C. Beutler. vols. xviii–xx: *Briefe,* ed. E. Beutler, &c. vols. xxii–xxiii: *Gespräche,* ed. W. Pfeiffer-Belli.

—— *Propyläen,* 3 vols. (Tübingen, 1798–1800).

—— *Ueber Kunst und Alterthum,* 6 vols. (Stuttgart, 1816–32).

—— *Tagebücher und Briefe Goethes aus Italien an Frau von Stein und Herder,* ed. E. Schmidt (*Schriften der Goethe-Gesellschaft,* vol. ii, Weimar, 1886).

—— *Zur Nachgeschichte der Italienischen Reise. Goethes Briefwechsel mit Freunden und Kunstgenossen in Italien* 1788–90, ed. O. Harnack (*Schriften der Goethe-Gesellschaft,* vol. v, Weimar, 1890).

—— *Goethe und die Romantik,* ed. C. Schüddekopf and O. Walzel (*Schriften der Goethe-Gesellschaft,* vols. xiii–xiv, Weimar, 1898).

—— *Goethes Briefwechsel mit Heinrich Meyer,* ed. M. Hecker (*Schriften der Goethe-Gesellschaft,* vols. xxxii, xxxiv, xxxv, Weimar, 1917–33).

—— *Briefwechsel zwischen Goethe und Reinhard in den Jahren* 1807 *bis* 1832 (Stuttgart, 1850).

GRISEBACH, A.: 'Goethe in Heidelberg und der Kölner Dom' (*Goethe und Heidelberg,* Heidelberg, 1949).

HAGEN, E. VON DER: *Goethe als Herausgeber von 'Kunst und Alterthum' und seine Mitarbeiter* (Berlin, 1912).

HARNACK, O.: *Deutsches Kunstleben in Rom im Zeitalter der Klassik* (Weimar, 1896).

HÜBNER, A.: 'Goethe und das deutsche Mittelalter' (*Kleine Schriften zur deutschen Philologie,* Berlin, 1940).

JAHN, K.: *Goethes Dichtung und Wahrheit* (Halle, 1908).

KOETSCHAU, K.: 'Goethe und die Gotik' (*Festschrift zum 60. Geburtstag von Paul Clemen,* Bonn, 1926).

KORFF, H. A.: 'Goethe und die bildende Kunst' (*Zeitschrift für Deutschkunde,* Leipzig, 1927).

MEYER, J. H.: *Kleine Schriften zur Kunst,* ed. P. Weizsäcker (*Deutsche Litteraturdenkmale des 18. und 19. Jahrhunderts,* vol. xxv, Stuttgart, 1886).

PEVSNER, N.: 'Goethe e l'Architettura' (*Palladio,* vol. iv, 1951).

POENSGEN, G.: 'Die Begegnung mit der Sammlung Boisserée in Heidelberg' (*Goethe in Heidelberg,* Heidelberg, 1949).

PYRITZ, H.: *Goethe und Marianne von Willemer* (Stuttgart, 1943).

ROSENAU, H.: *Der Kölner Dom. Seine Baugeschichte und historische Stellung* (Cologne, 1931).

SCHEIDIG, W.: *Goethes Preisaufgaben für bildende Künstler 1799–1805 (Schriften der Goethe-Gesellschaft*, vol. lvii, Weimar, 1958).

TICHY, W.: '*Ueber Kunst und Alterthum in den Rhein- und Mayn-Gegenden.' Goethes Schrift, ihre Entstehung und ihre Bedeutung* (Diss: Marburg, 1953).

VOLBEHR, T.: *Goethe und die bildende Kunst* (Leipzig, 1895).

WEICKERT, C.: *Die Baukunst in Goethes Werk* (*Vorträge und Schriften der deutschen Akademie der Wissenschaften*, Heft 28, Berlin, 1950).

WOLFF, E.: 'Dürer und Goethe' (*Deutsche Vierteljahrsschrift für Literaturwissenschaft und Geistesgeschichte*, vol. vi, Halle, 1928).

PART FIVE—THE TRIUMPH OF GOTHIC

BENZENBERG, J. F.: *Der Dom in Cöln* (Dortmund, 1810).

BOISSERÉE, S.: *Ansichten, Risse und einzelne Theile des Doms von Köln* (Stuttgart, 1821).

—— *Geschichte und Beschreibung des Doms von Köln, nebst Untersuchungen über die alte Kirchenbaukunst, als Text zu den Ansichten, Rissen und einzelnen Theilen des Doms von Köln* (Stuttgart, 1823). 2nd revised and enlarged edition, with 5 plates (Munich, 1842).

—— *Die Sammlung Alt- Nieder- und Ober- Deutscher Gemälde der Brüder Boisserée und Bertram, lithographirt von J. N. Strixner* (Munich, 1822–36).

—— *Denkmale der Baukunst vom 7ten bis zum 13ten Jahrhundert am Nieder-Rhein* (Munich, 1833).

—— 'Ueber die Beschreibung des Tempels des heiligen Grales in dem Heldengedicht: Titurel, Kap. iii.' (*Abhandlungen der philosophisch-philologischen Classe der Königlich Bayerischen Akademie der Wissenschaften*, vol. i, Munich, 1835).

BÜSCHING, J. G.: *Museum für Altdeutsche Literatur und Kunst*, ed. J. G. Büsching, F. H. v. d. Hagen, B. J. Docen and B. Hundeshagen, 2 vols.

—— *Wöchentliche Nachrichten für Freunde der Geschichte, Kunst und Gelahrtheit des Mittelalters*, 4 vols. (Breslau, 1816–19).

—— *Ueber die achteckige Gestalt der alten Kirchen mit besonderer Berücksichtigung von Breslau. Ein Versuch zur Aufhellung der Grundgestalt der Kirchen im Mittelalter* (Breslau, 1817).

—— *Reise durch einige Münster und Kirchen des nördlichen Deutschlands im Spätjahr 1817* (Leipzig, 1819).

—— *Versuch einer Einleitung in die Geschichte der Altdeutschen Bauart* (Breslau, 1821).

—— *Das Schloss der deutschen Ritter zu Marienburg* (Berlin, 1823).

CAROVÉ, F. W.: 'Ansichten der Kunst des deutschen Mittelalters' (*Taschenbuch für Freunde altdeutscher Zeit und Kunst auf das Jahr 1816*, Cologne, 1816).

CLEMEN, P.: *Der Dom zu Köln* (Düsseldorf, 1937).

COSTENOBLE, J. C.: *Ueber altdeutsche Architektur und deren Ursprung* (Halle, 1812). *Deutsches Museum*, ed. F. Schlegel, 4 vols. (Vienna, 1812–13).

EICHENDORFF, J. VON.: *Die Wiederherstellung des Schlosses der deutschen Ordensritter zu Marienburg* (Berlin, 1844).

FIORILLO, J. D.: *Geschichte der zeichnenden Künste von ihrer Wiederauflebung bis auf die neuesten Zeiten,* 5 vols. (Göttingen, 1798–1808).

—— *Geschichte der zeichnenden Künste in Deutschland und den Vereinigten Niederlanden,* 4 vols. (Hanover, 1815–20).

—— *Kleine Schriften artistischen Inhalts,* 2 vols. (Göttingen, 1803–6).

FRICK, F.: *Schloss Marienburg in Preussen. Nach seinen vorzüglichsten aeussern und inneren Ansichten dargestellt* (Berlin, 1799). Text in German and French: Berlin, 1803.

GRISEBACH, A.: *Carl Friedrich Schinkel* (Leipzig, 1924).

HAGEN, F. VON DER: *Briefe in die Heimat aus Deutschland, der Schweiz und Italien,* 4 vols. (Breslau, 1818–21).

HALL, SIR J.: *Essay on the Origin, History and Principles of Gothic Architecture* (London, 1813).

HEGEL, G. W. F.: *Vorlesungen über die Aesthetik (Werke,* Abt. II, vol. ii, ed. H. G. Hotho, Berlin, 1837).

HUNDESHAGEN, B.: *Der alten gothischen Kapelle zu Frankenberg Grundriss, Aufriss und Durchschnitt, nebst Gedanken über die sogenannte gothische Kirchenbaukunst* (Frankfurt, 1808).

—— *Kaiser Friedrichs I Barbarossa Palast in der Burg zu Gelnhausen* (Frankfurt, 1819).

KERN, G. J.: *Karl Blechen. Sein Leben und seine Werke* (Berlin, 1911).

LICHNOWSKY, E.: *Denkmahle der Baukunst und Bildnerey des Mittelalters in dem Oesterreichischen Kaiserthume. Gezeichnet von Joseph Fischer. Deutsch und Französisch beschrieben durch Fürst Eduard Lichnowsky* (Vienna, 1817).

MERTENS, F.: *Ueber den Dom zu Köln und die französische Bauschule in Deutschland. Programm zu den neuen Vorlesungen über Monumentalgeschichte* (Cologne, 1841).

MILNER, J.: *A Treatise on the Ecclesiastical Architecture of England during the Middle Ages* (London, 1811).

MOISY, P.: *Les Séjours en France de Sulpice Boisserée (1820–5). (Bibliothèque de la Société des Etudes Germaniques,* vol. x, Paris, 1956).

MOLLER, G.: *Bemerkungen über die aufgefundene Originalzeichnung des Domes zu Köln* (Darmstadt, 1818. 2nd ed. Leipzig/Darmstadt, 1837).

—— *Denkmaehler der deutschen Baukunst,* 3 vols. (Darmstadt, 1815–51).

—— *An Essay on the Origin and Progress of Gothic Architecture, traced and deduced from the Ancient Edifices of Germany, with reference to those of England, &c. from the Eighth to the Sixteenth Centuries* (London, 1824).

—— *Moller's Memorials of German-Gothic Architecture; with additional notes, and illustrations from Stieglitz, etc.; by W. H. Leeds* (London, 1836).

MUELLER, F. H.: *Die St. Katharinen-Kirche zu Oppenheim. Ein Denkmal teutscher Kirchenbaukunst aus dem 13ten Jahrhunderte* (Darmstadt, 1823).

MURPHY, J.: *Plans, Elevations, Sections and Views of the Church of Batalha . . . To which is prefaced an Introductory Discourse on the Principles of Gothic Architecture* (London, 1795).

ONCKEN, A.: *Friedrich Gilly (Forschungen zur deutschen Kunstgeschichte,* vol. v, Berlin, 1915).

RAVE, P. O.: *Schinkel in der Mark (Brandenburgische Jahrbücher,* vol. vii, Potsdam/Berlin, 1937).

—— *Karl Friedrich Schinkel. Sein Lebenswerk,* ed. P. O. Rave (Berlin, 1939, &c.).

RIETDORF, A.: *Gilly. Wiedergeburt der Architektur* (Berlin, 1940).

RUMOHR, C. F. v.: 'Fragmente einer Geschichte der Baukunst im Mittelalter' (*Deutsches Museum*, ed. F. Schlegel, vol. iii, Vienna, 1813).

—— 'Vom Ursprung der gotischen Baukunst' (Ibid.).

—— 'Einige Nachrichten von Alterthümern des transalbingischen Sachsens' (*Deutsches Museum*, vol. iv, Vienna, 1813).

—— *Italienische Forschungen*, 3 vols. (Berlin/Stettin, 1827–31).

SCHINKEL, K. F.: *Aus Schinkel's Nachlass. Reisetagebücher, Briefe und Aphorismen*, ed. Alfred Freiherr von Wolzogen, 4 vols. (Berlin, 1862–4).

SCHREIBER, A.: *Merkwürdige Gebäude des Teutschen Mittelalters nach der Natur und auf Stein gezeichnet von Domenico Quaglio Königlich Baierischen Hofmaler. Historisch erläutert von Alois Schreiber grossherzoglich Badischen Hofrath und Historiographen.* (Carlsruhe, n.d.).

STEIG, R.: *Clemens Brentano und die Brüder Grimm* (Stuttgart/Berlin, 1914).

STIEGLITZ, C. L.: *Encyklopädie der bürgerlichen Baukunst*, 5 vols. (Leipzig, 1792–8).

—— *Von altdeutscher Baukunst* (Leipzig, 1820).

—— *Geschichte der Baukunst vom früheren Alterthume bis in die neuern Zeiten* (Nürnberg, 1827).

—— *Beiträge zur Geschichte der Ausbildung der Baukunst*, 2 vols. (Leipzig, 1834).

Taschenbuch für Freunde altdeutscher Zeit und Kunst auf das Jahr 1816, ed. E. v. Groote and F. W. Carové (Cologne, 1816).

WAETZOLDT, W.: *Deutsche Kunsthistoriker*, 2 vols. (Leipzig, 1821).

WETTER, J.: *Geschichte und Beschreibung des Doms zu Mainz* (Mainz, 1835).

WHEWELL, W.: *Architectural Notes on German Churches* (Cambridge, 1830).

PART SIX—EPILOGUE

BOISSERÉE, S.: *Geschichte und Beschreibung des Doms von Köln.* 2nd revised and enlarged edition (Munich, 1842).

Das Buch deutscher Reden und Rufe, new and enlarged edition, ed. Friedrich von der Leyen (Wiesbaden, 1956).

CLEMEN, P.: *Der Dom zu Köln* (Düsseldorf, 1937).

ENNEN, L.: *Der Dom zu Köln von seinem Beginne bis zu seiner Vollendung* (Cologne, 1880).

GOERRES, J.: *Der Dom von Köln und das Münster von Strasburg* (Regensburg, 1842).

LÜTZELER, H.: 'Der Kölner Dom in der deutschen Geistesgeschichte' (*Der Kölner Dom. Festschrift zur 700. Jahrfeier*, Cologne, 1948).

ROSENAU, H.: *Der Kölner Dom. Seine Baugeschichte und historische Stellung* (Cologne, 1931).

SEPP, J. N.: *Görres und seine Zeitgenossen 1776–1848* (Nördlingen, 1877).

ZWIRNER, E.: *Vergangenheit und Zukunft des Kölner Dombaues* (Cologne/Aachen, 1842).

APPENDIX—HEINE AND THE GOTHIC REVIVAL

BUTLER, E. M.: *The Saint-Simonian Religion in Germany. A Study of the Young German Movement* (Cambridge, 1926).

BUTLER, E. M.: *Heinrich Heine. A Biography* (London, 1956).

GALLEY, E.: 'Heine und der Kölner Dom' (*Deutsche Vierteljahrsschrift für Literaturwissenschaft und Geistesgeschichte*, vol. xxxii, Stuttgart, 1958).

HEINE, H.; *Sämmtliche Werke*, ed. Ernst Elster, 7 vols. (Leipzig/Vienna, 1887–90).

MÜCKE, G.: *Heinrich Heines Beziehungen zum deutschen Mittelalter* (*Forschungen zur neueren Literaturgeschichte*, no. 34, Berlin, 1908).

INDEX

A. PERSONS

# INDEX

331

Schuckmann, Kaspar Friedrich von, 202, 203
Schütz, Christian Georg, 76
Scorel, Jan van, 204
Scott, Sir George Gilbert, 84
Scott, Sir Walter, 256
Scribanius, Carolus, 7
Seidler, Louise, 207
Semper, Gottfried, 293
Shaftesbury, Anthony Ashley Cooper, 3rd Earl of, 26, 57-8, 59, 60, 62, 83, 85, 86
Shakespeare, 58, 59, 60, 61, 62, 86, 87, 92
Soufflot, Jacques-Germain, 48-49, 88
Stein, Charlotte von, 32, 163, 164
Stein, Heinrich Friedrich Karl, Freiherr vom und zum, 196-7, 199, 202, 203, 216, 290
Steinbach, Erwin von, 44, 80-91, 103, 107, 248
Stieglitz, Christian Ludwig, 94, 137, 189, 244-9, 265, 269
Strixner, Johann Nepomuk, 169, 218, 282
Stubbs, Thomas, 239, 265 n, 298
Stukeley, William, 27, 28
Sulzer, Johann Georg, 12-14, 15, 16, 18, 58, 84, 85, 91 n, 263
Süvern, Johann Wilhelm, 202

Tacitus, 39, 40
Temple, Sir William, 25
Tieck, Johann Ludwig, 9, 111, 113, 122-4, 139, 149 n, 208, 211, 233, 238, 240, 241
Tieghem, Paul van, 35 n, 36 n, 37
Trautmann, Johann Georg, 76

Vasari, Giorgio, 5-6, 8, 9, 13, 14, 18
Veit, Dorothea, 156
Villani, Filippo, 4
Viollet-le-Duc, Eugène Emanuel, 250
Volkmann, Johann Jacob, 9, 10, 52

Wackendroder, Wilhelm Heinrich, 9, 68, 114-21, 123, 136, 247; *Herzensergiessungen eines kunstliebenden Klosterbruders*, 113, 115, 117, 118, 121, 124,

156, 211; and medieval painting, 114, 115-9; on medieval architecture, 115; *Phantasien über die Kunst*, 115, 156; and the Nazarenes, 118-9; and the Urban Picturesque, 119-21; Goethe's attacks on, 166, 208, 209; and Fiorillo, 238, 240
Wallraf, Ferdinand Franz, 132, 172, 197, 205, 261, 295
Walpole, Horace, 29, 34, 36, 87, 88
Warburton, William, 27, 28, 45, 248, 270
Warton, Thomas, 36, 41, 251
Weinlig, Christian Traugott, 52-53, 88, 94
Wetter, Johannes, 249
Weyden, Rogier van der, 191, 200
Whewell, William, 250, 283-4
Wieland, Christoph Martin, 37, 91, 165, 179
Willemer, Marianne von, 190, 192, 199, 200, 201
William IX, Landgrave of Hesse, 33
Willis, Robert, 250
Wimpheling, Jakob, 19, 20, 21
Winckelmann, Johann Joachim, 16, 63, 67, 77, 104, 128, 238
Winheim, Eberhard, 20
Wittgenstein, Heinrich von, 294
Wotton, Sir Henry, 8
Wren, Sir Christopher, 67, 73
Wurmsser von Vendenheym, Hans Jakob, 7
Württemberg, Charlotte Augusta Matilda, Queen of, 161
Württemberg, Ludwig Friedrich, Prince of, 7

Young, Edward, 37-38, 41, 58-60, 86

Zachariä, Friedrich Wilhelm, 36, 36 n, 37
Zedler, Johann Heinrich, 10
Zelter, Karl Friedrich, 202, 206, 211
Zincgref, Julius Wilhelm, 21
Zwirner, Ernest Friedrich, 292, 294-5

B. PLACES AND SUBJECTS